Law and the Modern Mind

LAW AND THE MODERN MIND

Consciousness and Responsibility in American Legal Culture

SUSANNA L. BLUMENTHAL

Harvard University Press

Cambridge, Massachusetts, and London, England 2016

Printed in the United States of America

First printing

Library of Congress Cataloging-in-Publication Data
Blumenthal, Susanna L., 1967– author.
Law and the modern mind : consciousness and responsibility in American legal culture / Susanna L. Blumenthal.
pages cm
Includes bibliographical references and index.
ISBN 978-0-674-04893-5
1. Insanity (Law)—United States. 2. Mental health laws—United States. 3. Liability (Law)—United States. 4. Common law—United States. 5. Common sense. I. Title.
KF9242.B58 2016
346.7301'38—dc23
2015012785

For my parents,
Marsha and Malcolm Blumenthal

Contents

Law and the Modern Mind

Introduction

"IN A PROPER SENSE," Oliver Wendell Holmes wrote in 1894, "the state of a man's consciousness always is material to his liability." This was a rather curious statement, coming as it did from the author of *The Common Law*, an 1881 work that famously chronicled (and generally lauded) the evolution of Anglo-American law from subjective standards, rooted in vengeance, toward more objective norms of conduct. On this account, "modern" judges made no attempt to "see men as God sees them." Instead, they determined civil and criminal responsibility by reference to what was blameworthy in the "average man," taking no account of "the infinite varieties of temperament, intellect, and education which make the internal character of a given act so different in different men." Indeed, "the man of ordinary intelligence and reasonable prudence" was arguably the hero of Holmes's story, signifying the movement of American legal culture "from barbarism to civilization."[1]

Yet, even the Holmes of 1881 would admit that there were certain exceptions to this rule, epitomized by the blind man, the infant, and the madman. The first was "not required to see at his peril." Nor was the second obliged to exercise the discretion of an adult; the child could only be expected to "get as near as he can to the best conduct possible for him." When it came to the subject of madness, however, the jurist equivocated, finding it difficult to state any general rule, because many insane persons remained "perfectly capable" of exercising ordinary prudence in their daily affairs. Holmes nonetheless seemed to contemplate the existence of a threshold of mental ability, implying that those who clearly fell below it were not legally bound to act the part of the reasonable man. But there the matter was left in *The Common Law*, which remained centrally concerned with reasonableness as an external standard rather than a psychological condition.[2]

In the everyday legal culture lying just outside the jurist's imagination, these exceptional persons were not so marginal. For, at the very time Holmes was writing, American courts were plagued with capacity litigation, with suits that placed the mind "in issue," calling into question whether a given individual could be held responsible for his or her actions. It is worth recalling that 1881 was the year of the sensational insanity trial of the assassin Charles Guiteau—an event that divided legal, scientific, and public opinion regarding the basis of criminal responsibility.[3] But no less remarkable were the capacity suits initiated by civil litigants. These litigants were, in fact, often all too eager to assert their own incompetence in order to escape liability for their extravagant, imprudent, and careless conduct. And many more asserted the incapacity of others—typically grantors and testators—who had made "unnatural" dispositions of their wealth, at least from the perspective of those who stood to gain if the will were set aside. The ensuing contests often rivaled criminal insanity trials in their length and notoriety, generating voluminous transcripts and commanding front-page coverage, particularly when a large estate was involved. Even in the common run of civil cases, it was not unusual for each party to enter the courtroom flanked by medical experts and an army of lay witnesses who offered diametrically opposed portraits of the alleged incompetent. In thus proceeding, they demonstrated how easy it was to disagree about what counted as sufficient mental capacity to be deemed legally responsible.

Law and the Modern Mind explores the problematic relationship between consciousness and liability in the history of American law, focusing on the formative era from the nation's founding to the turn of the twentieth century. In the everyday practice of the law, members of the bench and bar were beset with what they regarded as "embarrassing" questions about the constitution of the human mind. Their attempts to address them—sometimes explicit, sometimes implicit—raised profound dilemmas at the time, and leave intriguing puzzles for historians today. Was consciousness rightly understood as an immaterial and immortal aspect of the soul, constituting the locus of individual identity and freedom? Or was mental life solely the result of physical processes, rendering human beings nothing more than "conscious automata"? Were all individuals innately endowed with the same basic capacity for rational and moral action, or was this attribute unequally distributed among human beings? Was the mind a reliable instrument, generating accurate impressions of the self, the external world, and other minds, or were there reasons for doubting the "testimony of consciousness"? What were judges to do if they could not trust even their own minds, let alone the recollections of those who were called to the witness stand?

These questions lurked, sometimes disturbingly, in the background of American law reports and treatises, becoming more prominent as leading jurists worked to bring inherited common law rules in line with developments in the human sciences. Aspiring lawyers were schooled in Enlightenment mental philosophy, which traced out the physical, intellectual, and moral powers of mankind, a word they commonly used in a generic sense but was nonetheless freighted with assumptions about sexual and racial difference. This body of learning was deemed to be foundational knowledge in the law books that circulated most widely in the early republic. Only with an understanding of "our nature," they provided, would it be possible to "make laws fit for it, and calculated to improve it."[4] Some members of the profession pursued the subject further, taking an interest in the burgeoning religious and scientific literature on mesmerism, spiritualism, phrenology, and hypnotism. However, the works that excited the greatest interest (and controversy) among lawyers were produced by an emergent group of medical specialists claiming expertise in the diagnosis and treatment of "mental alienation." This term of art denoted a loss of reason that might be partial or total, entailing an estrangement or dispossession of the self, such that the sufferer was no longer in his or her right mind. Drawing upon their experiences within the insane asylums that increasingly dotted the antebellum landscape, these self-styled "alienists" took aim at the traditional common law of *non compos mentis,* complaining that legal proceedings were riddled with inconsistencies and perpetuated unscientific ways of seeing the insane that effectively authorized "judicial murder." Their critiques came to form a distinct field of medical jurisprudence, which was soon mined by enterprising lawyers in their briefs to the court. In the ensuing trials, the varieties of mental unsoundness were dramatically described by lay and expert witnesses, often in lurid detail, prompting judges to reconsider the limits of human knowledge, freedom, and responsibility, subtly but significantly altering the ways they understood both consciousness and the law.

Law and the Modern Mind begins in the revolutionary era, as Americans struggled to make sense of the liberty they had wrested from the English crown. In this era, Calvinist doctrines of divine determinism and innate depravity gradually gave way to more liberal forms of Protestantism, which affirmed the benevolence of God, the innate goodness of man, and the freedom of his will. Of the many expositors of this optimistic perspective, Americans were especially drawn to the writings of the Common Sense philosophers of the Scottish Enlightenment. These philosophers provided scientific confirmation that human beings were divinely endowed with rational faculties of intellect, volition, and moral sense, enabling them to shape their own destiny, in this world and the next. The rapid expansion of the market in this period operated to intensify perceptions of the future as open-ended and individuals as capable of mastering their own fate. By the early 1800s, these various religious, philosophical, social, and economic forces had coalesced into what Jackson Lears has described as a "culture of control"—one that melded Enlightenment ideals of rationality and autonomy with Protestant moralism, placing the freely choosing, self-made man at the center of the universe, and promoting an ethic of self-mastery through disciplined efforts to "'*use* all that is called fortune.'"[5]

Members of the nascent American legal profession were among the most prominent exponents of the liberal humanist outlook, though their discourse and practices served at once to fortify and to problematize this scheme of self-rule. Animated by the revolutionary principle of popular sovereignty, early republican jurists marked a profound shift in ideas about legitimate authority, rejecting inherited forms of government, particularly those justified on grounds of birth and status rather than free and knowing consent. Yet their invocations of the concept of self-government were ambiguous, carrying with them the older, more conservative meaning of "corporate independence—that of a right of a people to organise into a body free of external interference"—as well as a newer, more radical sense of autonomous selfhood—that of a right of individuals to determine their own fate, free from all coercive outside authorities, "whether Gods, Kings, or Parents." The privileging of consent focused attention on the choosing subject, forcing members of the bench and bar to confront the individualistic implications of their moral and political philosophies in the concrete circumstances of the new republic. Yet they were not united in the belief that "men may be trusted to govern themselves without a master." The question of who was capable of exercising the sovereign prerogative of choice divided them along partisan lines. On the whole, Democratic-Republicans tended to display more confidence in human nature those of the Federalist persuasion. "In what sense is it true that any people, however free, are self-governed?" the Boston lawyer Fisher Ames anxiously asked in an 1805 essay on "The Dangers of American Liberty." Gloomily forecasting the inevitable failure of the nation's political experiment, he worried that "If they have in fact no government but such as comports with their ever-varying and often inordinate desires, then it is anarchy." "The individual who is left to act according to his own humor is not governed at all." Although few of his colleagues across the political spectrum harbored such deep pessimism, most would have agreed that the passions had to be contained and regulated by reason within the psyche as well as the polity if the newly established constitutional order were to survive.[6]

This was the problem of the self in postrevolutionary America, where the legitimacy as well as the viability of the institutions of government rested upon the mental competence of citizens, on their ability to exercise a "rational liberty." Assuming the role of republican spokesmen, legal elites were centrally involved in the task of stabilizing sovereign individual who was supposed to stand at the foundation of this new nation. They cast themselves as agents of the people, as "*ex- officio* natural guardians of the laws" who stood as "sentinels over the constitutions and liberties of the country," modeling virtuous self-command in their professional lives and inculcating and strengthening "the love of liberty and the love of law" in the citizenry. The legal order as they envisioned it would integrate free individuals into a wider web of obligations, channeling the creative energies of this democratizing, market-oriented society in directions that benefitted the whole without compromising the ideal of personal sovereignty. Properly administered, the laws of the land would help to make individuals self-governing by holding them responsible for the consequences of their freely chosen actions and working to secure their possession of the only liberty worth having, that of voluntarily conforming to the dictates of reason. In speaking in these terms in both professional and popular writings, these lawyers illustrated the extent to which they had incorporated liberal Protestant conceptions of moral agency and accountability into their ways of thinking about "the *subjects* of the law," many joining in common cause with ministers and secular moralists in a character-building campaign, one that promoted the ideal of self-reliance. Expressing faith in the educative power of the law, they aimed to do more than simply bring its precepts into greater alignment with the facts of human nature and the realities of social life; they believed the law could be used to promote improvement, at the level of the individual as well as society at large.[7]

The shifting fortunes of this cultural project can be traced through the legal discourse of the nineteenth century. Registering an anxious awareness that "'the world is all before us where to choose,'" American jurists alternately exulted in and agonized about the unprecedented nature of their undertaking. They defined their task in comprehensive terms, projecting confidence that the law could serve as a source of intellectual coherence and national cohesion. The bounds of legal science were boldly drawn to encompass most other forms of human knowledge in the courses of study prescribed for aspiring lawyers, the recommended reading lists amounting to "virtual bibliographies of the Enlightenment." The cultural standing of law as a learned profession was further reinforced with the publication of ponderous tomes, the scope and length of which was justified by the fact that the law extended to "every tie which is endearing to the affections, and has a concern on every action which takes place in the extensive circles of public and private life."[8]

Yet the jurists stressed that it was no part of their design "to create a monopoly of their acquisitions." They emphasized the importance of simplifying the language of the law "so as to make it level to the comprehension of all" with the spread of "the doctrine of universal suffrage" in the 1820s, which conferred upon white male citizens the "high prerogative . . . to have a direct and personal participation in all public affairs." Elementary law texts "designed as a first book for students" were also "adapted to popular instruction" and marketed as indispensable guides, supplying knowledge that was "essential to the proper discharge of the various duties of a citizen" and further suggesting that "self-interest should induce every man to understand his own rights and obligations." Although finding a model in William Blackstone's *Commentaries on the Laws of England*, which remained the primary source of legal education for the common run of American lawyers well into the first half of the century, text writers were eclectic in their approaches, promising to improve upon their English ancestors and boasting of their freedom to do so because "none of our laws are so deeply radicated by time, as to claim the veneration due to antiquity, or the indulgence accorded to natural prejudices arising from long use." Starting from the "first principles" of a "universal jurisprudence" that was rooted in "the nature and moral character of Man" as a "social being," they elaborated a scheme of legal ordering fitted to the unnervingly fluid circumstances of the new nation, effectively supplying the ground rules of everyday life, ones that would contain the atomistic, self-seeking tendencies that Alexis de Tocqueville famously termed "individualism" and associated with the spread of "the equality of condition."[9]

The distinctive outlines of this American jurisprudence emerged most clearly in the treatment of "the rights of persons" as distinct from "the rights of things." While the headings they used to categorize those who stood in different relations to the law than the fully autonomous individual, such as minors, married women, slaves, and persons *non compos mentis*, were borrowed from Blackstone, jurists emphasized that legal classifications of persons were greatly simplified in the United States "in consequence of our entire abolition of privileged orders." Indeed, it is possible to trace through these texts the gradual dismantlement of a "law of persons" with roots in feudal society and its replacement with a construct that I call the "default legal person," modeled in accordance with the Enlightenment "science of man." Under the traditional law of persons as they figured it, status was assigned, not chosen; the legal order ratified and sustained a system of social, economic, and political relations, defining the people as subjects of the king and determining their placement in hierarchical relationships, many of which were hereditary in nature. This was a society "governed by fictions" that violated "the rights of man" and inverted "the order of nature, through the hereditary assumption of dynastic perpetuity, by which childhood governs age, profligacy virtue, folly wisdom, and a wife her husband." Happily, they affirmed, these status-based distinctions had—at least rhetorically—been cast off as "artificial" constraints on human liberty in the American republic, making way for the institution of a more rational system of government that was structured in accordance with what were regarded as natural differences in people's mental and physical attributes.[10]

Within this new order, the "free and independent man" was recognized as the only legitimate sovereign, and legal rights and duties were supposed to be allocated on the basis of individual choice, virtue, and talent rather than social rank or condition. The ubiquitous references to "man" were meant in a gendered and implicitly racialized sense, as these jurists—all of whom were themselves white men—generally took men like themselves as the standard of humanity. Few contemplated, let alone supported, the extension of political rights to women, and most considered "our doctrine of equality" as fully applicable only to white men. The serious discrepancies between the Revolution's universalistic ideals and the particularistic rules of law implemented in the several states have long been recognized by scholars. Despite some legal reforms, new hierarchies and ever more rigid categories of identity were erected during the early nineteenth century. As Nancy Isenberg has aptly summarized the situation, "white men were still born to their station as citizens, for descent implied one's race, caste, and gender classification." Inequalities based on race and gender, which functioned as intersecting and often mutually reinforcing categories, rationalized the subordination of some persons to others and even tended to legitimize the legal reduction of persons to things that the institution of slavery required.[11]

Early nineteenth-century treatises are littered with declarations that American liberty is compatible with the maintenance of patriarchal, status-based hierarchies. Legal writers assumed that those who count as citizens are white, male heads-of-household, while defining their wives and children as these men's dependants rather than as autonomous and accountable persons. The existence of slavery and the civil incapacities of free blacks proved considerably more difficult for these jurists to square with their principles, moving many to rely on arguments from necessity and others to hope for the gradual emancipation of those held in bondage. But few could see how, once liberated, "this unhappy class of people" was to be incorporated into the nation. "The early impressions of obedience and submission, which slaves have received among us, and the no less habitual arrogance and assumption of superiority, among the whites, contribute equally to unfit the former for *freedom*, and the latter for *equality*," observed the Virginia jurist St. George Tucker in his 1803 notes to Blackstone's *Commentaries*. Invoking the Exodus story as a metaphor for the American Revolution with a pessimistic twist, he remarked: "'We have in history but one picture of a similar enterprize, and there we see it was necessary not only to open the sea by a miracle, for them to pass, but more necessary to close it again to prevent their return.'"[12]

The telling elision between the generic and the gendered and racialized meanings of "man" expresses deeper tensions within Enlightenment thought, which shaped understandings of whiteness and masculinity in relation to marginalized and excluded others. Following the convention of Common Sense philosophers like Reid, most American thinkers took for granted the existence of sexual differences, treating the feminine side of this binary as particular and problematic; they tended to accord women special treatment "as a designated *branch* of humanity," though they varied considerably as to whether "the fairer sex" was naturally endowed with the same intellectual faculties as her male counterpart and the extent to which her observed capacity to cultivate morals and manners was inborn or the product of social conventions. Whiteness also operated as a presumptive norm from which deviations were measured and found wanting, with doubts increasingly registered as to the capacity for "civilization" and self-rule among Native Americans and persons of African descent. Here, too, there were conflicting views as to whether these deficiencies were innate or the result of environmental causes. For answers, many drew upon a new transatlantic discourse of racial science produced by a growing number of naturalists, physicians, and anthropologists who undertook to systematically compare the skull sizes and other physical features of various subgroups within the "human family" in order to test assumptions about the mental and moral attributes of non-white racial groups as well as women, children, and idiots. Their findings did more to inflame than resolve debates about the sources and significance of human difference and inequality, intensifying controversies as to whether humankind was a single "unit of creation," as the Bible indicated, or instead composed of biologically distinct species that naturally fell into a graded sequence, with Caucasians enjoying pride of place, especially but not only on account of their intelligence, and "Ethiopians" relegated to the lowest rung, just a step above the orangutan.[13]

Yet race and gender did not simply supersede titles of nobility as the determinative characteristics of legal personhood, for American jurists articulated the rules of legal capacity and responsibility in psychological terms, setting up additional criteria for regarding individuals as qualified to act independently which they proceeded to apply to white men as well as to others. They presumed a mental baseline in the form of the default legal person who possessed a set of intellectual, moral, and volitional faculties that enabled him to follow the precepts of reason and natural justice, as well as those of the positive law. Although many relational categories of the common law, such as husband and wife, master and servant, and parent and child, survived or acquired new significance in American jurisprudence, the vocabulary of the self that jurists used to justify their existence was turned to a multiplicity of purposes by practicing lawyers and their clients over the course of the nineteenth century, posing a continual threat to the integrity and stability of those asymmetrical relationships and the social inequality they enshrined. The subordinate positions of women, children, and slaves within this scheme of things were subject to contestation and even the white propertied male who set the standard for legal personhood was dogged by fears of impotent effeminacy and of enslavement to his own appetites or delusions, showing the influence of these excluded categories on the dominant definition of the autonomous individual.[14]

The American law of persons was thus built upon shaky conceptual foundations. The jurists posited a certain relationship between mental capacity and legal responsibility: an individual's capacity for self-determination implied his responsibility for the consequences of his acts. There was, however, a fundamental problem with this legal formulation, for it rendered irrational, immoral, and impulsive behavior almost by definition unaccountable, in both senses of the word. After all, if rational and moral faculties were innate and universal, what explained the great differences of opinion among individuals upon matters of right and wrong, such as slavery? Why were some led to commit acts that were, to others, patently irrational or downright evil? And to the extent there *was* a common sense about the dictates of reason and moral sense, why did some people act in defiance of it? Alienists and moralists of the day were quick to supply answers, attributing deviant behavior to mental defects that were rooted in the person's physical constitution and surrounding environment. Pointing to these determinative causes of mental alienation, however, only exacerbated lawyers' difficulties, implying that all forms of human perversity were indicators of "mental unsoundness," and virtually erasing the distinction between sin and disease. For better or worse, these metaphysical quandaries soon became the subject of litigation. By midcentury, capacity suits of varying sorts were a common occurrence, confronting judges with daunting evidentiary issues, and a deeper paradox as well. Their working model of the mind encouraged them to identify freedom with rationality and morality. This, in turn, pointed toward the uncomfortable and unworkable conclusion that the only *fully* responsible agents were those who would never depart from the law's behavioral norms—those who would never commit a crime or tort, execute an eccentric contract, or write an unnatural will.

So it was that in an age when confidence in human ability soared to unprecedented heights, courts were ironically confronted with claims of incapacity across civil and criminal fields of law. The strategic uses of the new medical psychology by criminal defendants have been well documented in a range of scholarly works, which collectively illustrate the extent to which nineteenth-century courts were pressed to recognize mental debilities short of the "total deprivation of reason" required under traditional common law rules. The medical experts called to the stand provided grounds for thinking that the moral freedom of the accused had been compromised by partial forms of insanity, called "delusions" or "monomanias," which operated to impair the rational faculties. Lay witnesses were also presented to bolster the defendants' case, introducing other factors mitigating guilt, such as improper socialization, arrested development, hereditary defects, intoxication, and duress. But remarkably little attention has been paid to the civil litigants who made representations of these sorts, either about themselves or others they putatively aimed to protect. Surveying this side of the docket, it appears that judges were regularly asked to determine whether a given individual was a "fit subject" for guardianship or commitment to an insane asylum. In many other cases, parties contested the validity of "inofficious" testaments and "improvident" contracts, requiring courts to decide whether the disputed document was an authentic expression of the maker's will or instead the "offspring" of a delusion. And even in the field of tort law, the issue of incapacity was sometimes raised, as defendants sought to prove that their harmful acts and omissions were unintended, involuntary, or otherwise beyond their control. The very facts revealed through these trial processes slowly chipped away at the intellectual foundations of the antebellum "culture of control." All the while, destabilizing developments beyond the courthouse walls—the disorienting effects of a boom and bust economy, the "shock of Darwin," the trauma of the Civil War and its aftermath, and the disruptions occasioned by rapid industrialization and successive waves of immigration—also engendered doubts about whether human beings were as morally free and as mentally capable as Enlightenment philosophers had made them out to be.

As intellectuals, scientists, and popular writers wrung their hands about the human condition, projecting nightmarish visions of "the degeneration of the race," common law judges continued to be called upon to make determinations of legal responsibility. This they did, mindful of all the disintegrative forces around them operating to undermine Enlightenment faith in the benevolence of God, the autonomy of the will, and the basic intelligibility of the universe. The Gilded Age courtroom was, in fact, a place where epistemological and metaphysical worries were more likely to be allayed than confirmed. For experience taught judges the perils of following the logic of Common Sense and deferring to the alienists' expertise. Such lines of thought led in deterministic directions, pointing toward outcomes that were not only impracticable, undermining moral and legal order, but also self-contradictory. Judges had also come to see that "what is rational to one man is highly irrational to another," accepting that there was much that could not be known about another mind. These realizations did not, however, move judges toward a radical subjectivism, allowing every person to make the law for himself. Nor did they embrace the opposite extreme of objectivism, prescribing and enforcing standards of conduct regardless of individual mental ability. Instead, judges in this era eschewed abstract speculation, scientific jargon, and high-toned moralizing, recasting the default legal person along more pragmatic lines. They developed an autonomously "legal sense" of what it was to be sane or insane, free or coerced, capable or incapable—distinct from their meanings in "metaphysical or medical science." In the closing decades of the century, judges worked to strengthen the common law presumption of sanity through a variety of procedural means, and they grew only more resolute in rejecting insanity pleas that were based upon what they saw as "mere eccentricity of conduct, harshness of temper, revengefulness of heart, or a depraved, cruel, and malicious disposition." As they admitted an ever-widening array of perverse behavior within the bounds of the "normal," the default legal person underwent a change of character. Once held out as a realistic ideal, it increasingly came to be viewed as a sort of legal fiction, practically necessary in a world without absolutes. Indeed, this "standard man" embodied a rather ingenious way of contending with the existential dilemmas that daily confronted those who presided over nineteenth-century insanity trials.

As *Law and the Modern Mind* reverses the emphasis of *The Common Law*, shining the spotlight on the default legal person standing behind Holmes's reasonable man, a few words about their distinguishing features are in order here. While both figures constituted legal norms, they were operationalized by judges in distinct and yet interrelated ways in everyday adjudication. Four points of distinction are worth highlighting.

First, the default legal person was not primarily intended to regulate conduct, as was the reasonable man. Instead, he stood at the borderline of legal capacity, identifying those who were properly exempted from the rules of law that were applicable to everyone else. Second, judges tended to treat deviations from each of these two norms in nearly opposite ways. The failure to behave like the reasonable man usually supplied grounds for imposing liability, while the inability to function like the default legal person tended to result in a suspension or mitigation of liability. Still, there was a division of labor between these two norms, which points toward the third distinction to be drawn. The default legal person worked primarily at the descriptive level, defining the preconditions of liability. In doing so, he effectively delimited the universe of capable individuals who could be made subject to the prescriptive authority of the reasonable man. The rules that were formulated and applied by the *reasonable* man were derived by thinking from the objective standpoint he provided—by contemplating what this man of ordinary intelligence and prudence would have done had he been in the situation of the actor whose liability was in question. Herein lies the final and most subtle sense in which the reasonable man differed from the default legal person, for this latter character had no particular point of view of his own. He was, in the end, but a bare-bones sketch of almost anyone, which enabled him to move in a chameleon-like fashion from case to case, assuming the perspective, personal characteristics, and circumstances of the party whose competence was in question.

Given their contrasting roles, it becomes easier to see why the reasonable man has tended to overshadow his competent cousin. By design, the default legal person was supposed to remain at the margins of the common law, standing for the presumption of sanity that, jurists expected, would be warranted in most cases. The strength of this presumption was severely tested across the nineteenth century, in civil as well as criminal trials. Although the historical scholarship on the plea of insanity has been mainly concerned with homicide cases, they do not begin to represent the nature and extent of nineteenth-century capacity litigation. Concededly, most civil suits involving questions of competency did not present the same sorts of problems of radical human evil commonly confronted in the trials of murderous men and women who pled insanity. Nor were the civil contests treated as occasions for addressing major questions of public policy, as the participants remained focused on the equities of the private parties. But their effects were more subtle and far-reaching than the sensational trials of homicidal maniacs. For in these civil matters, courts routinely engaged in consequential acts of social sorting; in identifying, disciplining, and punishing individuals who fell below the threshold of competency as well as those who neglected and exploited them, they were also expressing and reinforcing conceptions of social welfare and distributive justice. The fact that these judgments were considered matters of private law should not be allowed to obscure the cultural work they performed, for the categorical designation itself sheds considerable light on the problem of dependency as Americans grappled with it in a variety of relationships.[15]

Looking at what transpired in the courtrooms where the mind was placed in issue, quite often without much fanfare by petitioners in the most ordinary of circumstances, enables us to see how remarkably common capacity challenges were in a country that placed so much stock in the ideal of the autonomous individual. Because people chose this public forum with such regularity, we are able to scrutinize some of their most intimate and private affairs, becoming privy to the family secrets and hidden infirmities that were revealed in open court in order to gain financial advantage, avoid further harm, or simply settle a score. Filled with drama, intrigue, and pathos of the most quotidian sorts, some of these trials dragged on for months or even years, presenting stark and disquieting images of mental dysfunction and degeneration—of deluded minds, overborne wills, and moral insensibility. No doubt these maladies were often strategically exaggerated by those who argued and testified for one or the other side in these trials. But this only complicated the problem before the court: who were "the really insane," whose deviant acts were rightly attributed to "disqualifying diseases" rendering them legally irresponsible?

The litigants who placed the mind in issue were thus not only asking members of the bench to pass judgment on a wide variety of domestic and commercial transactions and altercations. They were also raising the touchy subject of competency in ways that tested the basic presumptions of liberal democracy in America. These lawsuits provided occasions for airing doubts about the capacity of citizens to be self-governing and they display the difficulties that participants encountered in attempting to set the threshold of legal competence. Though the litigation was about abnormality, the alleged maniacs unwittingly dramatized the vulnerability of the freestanding individual. Presiding judges tried and failed to definitively delimit insanity, as it proved "no respecter of the theoretical boundaries with which jurists have sought to circumscribe it." Precisely because the matter of mental soundness was so problematic and yet pivotal, it was perpetually turned into a judicial question. While this was widely lamented in popular and professional literature, there was a certain cultural logic to this process.

In a society shorn of aristocratic marks of distinction, as Tocqueville observed during his travels in America, the legal profession formed "a sort of privileged body in the scale of intellect," constituting "the most powerful, if not the only, counterpoise to the democratic element." Judges and lawyers contained and directed "the unreflecting passions of the multitude" most visibly (though not solely) through "the courts of justice," where they were accorded the greatest deference in "matters of civil law." Tocqueville found the legal establishment remarkably unaffected by political change and popular opinion, despite the fact that many aspects of civil law were "repugnant" to Americans' "social condition," as well as antithetical to their declared ideals. The association between intellect and authority was embedded in "the language of the law," which became "a vulgar tongue" in this democratic republic. It shaped how Americans thought about themselves and their relationships with one another, providing a meritocratic measure of human difference and thus a powerful way of explaining and justifying inequality. As mental and moral attributes, generally combined under the heading of "character," assumed the form of capital in "the increasingly competitive and chaotic public worlds of politics and the market economy," it became apparent that, like money, they could be acquired and lost much too readily. Asylum superintendents tallied the mental casualties of capitalism; their "statistics of insanity" confirmed that "speculative mania" was a leading cause of psychological as well as financial troubles, frequently resulting in a state of mental and moral bankruptcy. It is thus no wonder that Americans resorted to court to contend about mental soundness in much the same ways they did with respect to other valuable assets.[16]

Seen in this light, the capacity contests at the heart of this book and the jurisprudence of insanity that was elaborated to resolve them can be understood as part and parcel of the problem of self-rule in nineteenth-century America. Taken together, these cases and commentaries revealingly illustrate the dilemmas of democratic governance, providing a vantage point from which to view the struggles of courts to reconcile the era's dual tendencies toward individuation and standardization. They also exhibit the curious persistence of the Common Sense conception of the self and the judicial inclination to fortify it—to validate it as common sense—in spite of its manifest inadequacies. Although each case revolved around an eccentric individual, they were representative in a certain sense, exemplifying the perils of too much freedom. Indeed, because these disabling diseases were so often described as episodic departures from or exaggerations of the sufferer's normal ways of being, arrayed along a continuum from a perfect sanity to a total deprivation of reason, they presented the haunting prospect that the insane might be taken to represent all persons, at least potentially.[17] This sense of insecurity was further reinforced by a steady stream of popular and professional writings associating insanity with advanced societies that placed a high premium on individual liberty, suggesting it was "part of the price we pay for civilization," doctors and lay reformers finding an odd sort of consolation in statistical studies purporting to show that Native Americans, blacks, and other "primitive" and "barbarous" peoples rarely suffered from this form of mental disorder. Those most susceptible seemed instead to be the self-determining individuals directly and regularly exposed to the psychic strains and emotional tumults of modern American, even and perhaps especially the white men taken by jurists to constitute the default legal person. Insanity was thus recast in democratic terms, bearing a haunting resemblance to the open and fluid society it shadowed. A condition long thought to be "the exclusive province of the raving lunatic and the total incompetent," permanently deprived of their reason, was now reconceived as "a state of mind in which anyone could find themselves, and from which they could return."[18]

Judges accordingly tread carefully in the all too common run of capacity contests, proceeding with a marked ambivalence as they attempted to give "our doctrine of equality" practical effect. In doing so, they evinced awareness of the growing gap between subjective experience and objective reality. For they readily recognized it was impossible to "dive into the mind of another" and were forced to rely, by and large, on behavioral signs, which were susceptible to multiple, sometimes contradictory, readings. Quite apart from this basic difficulty, the judges' discomfort was compounded as they contemplated the broader implications of a decision in either direction. To enter a judgment of incapacity, they feared, might well set a dangerous precedent, opening the door to baseless lawsuits, threatening the stability of economic transactions, and forcing individuals to conform to conventional behavioral norms. The slippery slope these judges nervously imagined terminated with half the nation consigned to "straight waistcoats." And yet, to dismiss the plea could be just as uncomfortable a decision. For judges were often moved by the equities of the individual case and clearly invested in an underlying vision of what it was to be a "rational and moral civil agent," which could be quite difficult to square with the evidentiary record. In observing the judges' tendency to vacillate between these two positions, it becomes clear that their opinions concerned more than the discrete issue of legal capacity; they also involved broader questions about the nature of personal identity, the bounds of individual freedom, and the very basis of moral desert.

In recounting these trials, *Law and the Modern Mind* seeks to contribute to current understandings of law and society in several key respects. Working at the intersection of legal, intellectual, and cultural history, it revises conventional stories about the path of the law in nineteenth-century America that have been told largely in socioeconomic terms. It attends, in particular, to the religious and scientific influences informing the work of lawyers and judges, contending that the oft-noted "concern for objectivity" in this period had deeper spiritual roots and higher ideological stakes than previous scholars have recognized. As this book demonstrates, the capacity contests of the nineteenth century were expressions of widespread uncertainty and confusion about an array of interconnected economic, social, political, and metaphysical matters. Drawing on the insights of historians and theorists of selfhood, I attend to "the double meanings of terms like 'agency,' 'identity,' and 'subjectivity,' which connote at once autonomy and dependence" as they operate in legal discourse, regarding the courtroom as an ideal setting within which to trace the changing legal significance and broader cultural implications of what might be called responsibility talk within American culture. These trials register the fluidity of social relations, indicating a general lack of clarity about the operative norms of behavior in the household and the market. The testimony about alleged incompetents provided running commentaries on capitalism as a lived experience of psychological fracture as well as social upheaval. And the dynamics of these disputes were in many respects at odds with capitalist ways "of being, of seeing, and of believing," casting serious doubt on the notion that everything could be made comparable. To litigate the issue of mental capacity was also, almost unavoidably, to raise a host of questions about generational equity, social justice, and the meaning of freedom. These questions were, in turn, intimately bound up with deeper perplexities about the nature of the self and the processes of identity formation. The final judgments rendered in these trials provided a certain sort of closure to these matters, though most did not admit of complete resolution. Accordingly, the judges' opinions may best be read as anxious meditations on the meaning of mental health and the bounds of human potential in the United States. Just as importantly, however, this study emphasizes that the legal system did not simply reflect contemporary concerns about sanity and selfhood. Case by case, nineteenth-century American judges performed important cultural work, elaborating a conception of consciousness that worked to dispel the specters of solipsism and determinism that haunted the philosophical and literary discourse of the era. This conception proved remarkably resilient within American legal culture, exerting a powerful hold on lawyers and judges even as the twentieth century brought new insights from such fields as psychoanalysis, behavioral psychology, and neuroscience.[19]

Law and the Modern Mind concludes by underscoring the double-edged nature of the law's pragmatic turn. As judges worked to strengthen the presumption of sanity in the last quarter of the century, disparities in mental ability were rendered less salient as a matter of law. The protective role of the courts was correspondingly diminished, leaving individuals freer, in a certain sense, to act on their own ideas and impulses, however eccentric, perverse, or just plain foolish. This judicial tendency might be interpreted as part of the general movement toward abstraction and generalization in the jurisprudence of the period, which historians have long seen as essentially anti-redistributive in spirit. But when the trial transcripts and opinions of the court in everyday capacity contests are read alongside the treatise literature, it becomes apparent that there was no straightforward path from subjective to objective principles of liability. Though fin de siècle jurists attempted to standardize the rules of law applicable to "normal" as opposed to "abnormal persons," their contemporaries on the bench never fully embraced this style of categorical thinking. To the contrary, most judges seemed to adopt the medical approach to mental unsoundness, insofar as they treated it as a matter of degree, with each case to be considered "on its own special and peculiar circumstances." In so doing, these judges expressed their abiding concern with comprehending subjective and objective points of view in their everyday determinations of responsibility. Thus it would seem that long before Holmes changed his mind on the matter, other members of the bench had already come to see that it was neither possible nor desirable to "think away consciousness."[20]

PART ONE

The Testimony of Consciousness

WITH MOUNTING DESPAIR about the state of the union, Benjamin Rush penned a letter to John Adams in November 1812 about a recent dream of his, which was occasioned by the hapless manner in which his fractious countrymen were prosecuting a second war for independence from England. In the dream, Rush fancied he stood "elevated upon a bench in our Hospital yard surrounded by between 60 and 70 of my lunatic patients" whom he proceeded to lecture on matters of national security. "While I was speaking," Rush recounted, "one man came up to me and said, 'I am Solon,' a second said he was Wm. Penn, a third said he was Numa Popillius, and all of them asked me how I dared to attempt to instruct them upon the means of defending our country." Without awaiting an answer, the crowd of patients unceremoniously turned on their keeper: "A 4th spat in my face, a 5th hissed me, a 6th called me a fool, a 7th said I was crazy, an 8th took up a stone and threw it at me." The imminence of this assault jolted Rush back into consciousness, with certitude "that such would have been my treatment in the House of Representatives in Washington, had I addressed them upon the same subject and had they not been restrained by the habits of civilized life."[1]

Though he spoke of dreams as "nothing but incoherent ideas" and attributed them to morbid action in the blood vessels of the brain, Rush nonetheless found meaning in their contents, routinely drawing insights and intimations from them about himself as well as his patients, his fate as well as that of the American republic. Nor was it only while sleeping that he saw inhabitants of this new polity as insane persons. In the fall of 1787, as the delegates to the Philadelphia Convention were finalizing the framework of the new government, he was preparing a medical essay entitled "An Account of the Influence of the Military and Political Events of the American Revolution upon the Human Body," which documented the novel mental diseases contracted by those who lived through this violent upheaval. Those on the losing side were prone to a type of melancholy Rush termed "*Revolutiana*," brought on by the loss of power, status, property, and friends, and the accompanying "neglect, insults, and oppression" they experienced during the course of the military conflict and its aftermath. The contrastingly healthy effects of the war on the friends of the Revolution were exemplified by "hysterical women," who were cured by devoting themselves to "the successful issue of the contest." Yet the "uncommon cheerfulness" exhibited by many victors was also a worrying sign, especially as their "passion for liberty" was now redirected into trade and speculation. "It unhinged the judgment, deposed the moral faculty, and filled the imagination, in many people, with airy and impracticable schemes of wealth and grandeur" that "could not be removed by reason or restrained by government," effectively constituting "a species of insanity which I shall take the liberty of distinguishing by the name of *Anarchia*." This medical diagnosis was intended to make a political point that Rush pressed with ever more urgency in the 1780s. "The minds of the citizens of the United States were wholly unprepared for their new situation," he observed, emphasizing time and again that the Peace of 1783 "did not terminate the American revolution"—that "it remains yet to establish and perfect our new forms of government, and to prepare the principles, morals, and manners of our citizens for those forms of government after they are established and brought to perfection."[2]

The apprehensions about mental disorder that this physician-statesman channeled into his life's work mark him as a transitional figure who vividly illustrates the sorts of challenges faced by revolutionary Americans as they struggled to make sense of the liberty they had wrested from the English crown. Patriots who had fought a war to secure the "right of self-government" betrayed a pronounced uneasiness about its exercise, commonly registering concern that "the people may come to forget that part of self-government which relates to being governed, and only remember that part which consists in governing." Indeed, the specter of a will out of control and of a people mad with freedom haunted the cultural landscape of the early republic as Americans grappled anew with age-old questions about the moral agency and accountability of humankind. Having declared independence from England in ambiguous language, this severing of ties rendered "necessary" by "the course of human events," the former colonists soon fell to arguing about the significance of the words they had used to justify their actions. Though the sovereign individual was commonly cast as the source of all legitimate authority and the essence of American identity, this expansive conception of the autonomous self was as problematic as it was pervasive in the discourse of the era. Freedom of the will stood at once as a self-evident truth, a point of theological and philosophical controversy, and an ever-present threat to the visions of ordered liberty projected by the nation's founders. Self-consciously aware of the novelty of their undertaking, they reached for a new word with which to express the perplexities of their situation and talked about self-government as both a psychological and a political project. That word was *responsibility*.[3]

Coming into currency in the aftermath of the Revolution, the abstract noun responsibility made some of its earliest recorded appearances in the debates between Federalists and anti-Federalists over the ratification of the Constitution. It was used in this political context in two main senses, which were given their most prominent expressions in *The Federalist* by Alexander Hamilton and James Madison. In the course of demonstrating that "an energetic executive" was not only consistent with "the genius of republican government" but necessary to its proper maintenance in *Federalist* 70, Hamilton contended that this end was best achieved by vesting power in "a single hand" to ensure "a due dependence on the people, and a due responsibility." A plurality in the executive was likely to yield the opposite result, for it would be all but "impossible, amidst the mutual accusations, to determine on whom the blame or punishment of a pernicious measure . . . ought really to fall," thus leaving the public "in suspense about the real author." Aiming to show that the Senate was likewise accountable to the people, Madison's *Federalist* 63 defended the somewhat paradoxical proposition that it was the relative *in*frequency of elections of its members, as compared with the House of Representatives, that "produces this responsibility." Yet the word took on a different meaning as Madison elaborated his argument: "Responsibility, in order to be reasonable, must be limited to objects within the power of the responsible party, and in order to be effectual, must relate to the operations of that party, of which a ready and proper judgment can be formed by the constituents." On this rendering, responsibility meant more than simply being answerable to the electorate. It also carried with it the notion of being able to respond, of having the ability to understand and act upon a considered sense of the public good, which Madison thought might well entail protecting the people themselves from "their own temporary errors and delusions."[4]

This positive sense of what it was to be a responsible agent of the people was widely assailed as a veiled form of aristocracy by anti-Federalist writers, many of whom cast the Constitution's "scheme of power and office-making" as a mortal threat to republican liberty. In view of what was known about human nature, and the limitations of reason even in the "best" of men, greater restraints had to be imposed upon those given the "reins of authority" in order to contain their "lust of domination" and prevent those they were supposed to represent from being reduced to "a servile and depraved creatures." The "responsibility" of which the anti-Federalists spoke was almost always that of the elected to their electors, which could only be ensured by keeping the government close to "the common people," by enabling them to choose as their representatives "men from among themselves" who "think as they think, feel as they feel," who were "genuinely like themselves."[5]

The divergent conceptions of responsibility and republicanism articulated in the ratification debates were clearly animated by concerns about bounding and safeguarding liberty in a political sense. But the metaphysics of liberty were hardly cordoned off from consideration as postrevolutionary Americans contended about "the degree of freedom and self-government in which a society may venture to leave its individual members." To the contrary, politics were inextricably bound up with theology and psychology in the statesmen's elaborations of what it meant to institute "free and responsible government" upon the principle of "popular sovereignty," their disputations about constitutional design reflecting varying estimations of human potential once released from the artificial constraints of traditional authorities, belief systems, and social structures. The unifying rhetoric of the patriots all too quickly became a source of conflict and division in the aftermath of the Revolution, with controversy about the very meaning of freedom only intensifying after the ratification of the Constitution. Indeed, this discourse about political liberty became ever more entangled with and complicated by the writings of warring theologians and philosophers who were endeavoring to reconcile the Enlightenment "science of man" with the orthodox Calvinist doctrines of innate depravity and divine determinism. These abstruse and often vituperative exchanges about the metaphysics of moral government conveyed the hopes and fears of a founding generation acutely conscious of its unprecedented situation at the beginning of an entirely new chapter in "the history of man." The forces of liberal humanism would ultimately prevail in nineteenth-century America, as clerics across denominational lines joined with other learned professions in forging a new consensus about the mind of the moral agent that was grounded in the Common Sense realism of the Scottish Enlightenment. Yet paradoxically, the strongest defenders of free will as a metaphysical matter shaped up to be among the most "anxious controllers" in this democratizing society, remaining as worried as Benjamin Rush about how unprepared American minds were for the challenges of their new situation.[6]

The two chapters that comprise this first part of the book, "The Testimony of Consciousness," chronicle the efforts on the part of lawyers, moralists, educators, and doctors in the early republic to contain the problem of the "untrammeled self" through various intellectual and institutional means. As they cast about for solutions, Chapter 1 shows, many were drawn to the writings of the Scottish Common Sense philosophers, whose psychological models offered assurances that the capacity for self-government lay within the mind of every individual. Proceeding by way of introspection, the Common Sense philosophers identified three distinct sets of mental faculties: the "rational" powers of intellect, will, and moral sense; the "animal" passions, desires, and appetites; and the "mechanical" habits and instincts. While typically arranging them in hierarchical order so as to suggest that reason ought to rule over the other faculties, the Common Sense philosophers emphasized that this "balanced character" could be attained only through concerted effort; it was imperative that the faculties be properly cultivated in childhood by parents and teachers and further developed by means of "self-culture" over the course of adult life. At once descriptive and prescriptive, the Common Sense model of the mind projected an ideal of "balanced character" that individuals were capable of and therefore accountable for achieving. This mental model was inculcated by various means in antebellum America, ranging from college textbooks to conduct manuals, which collectively promoted an ethic of self-improvement, fostering the fixity of moral character by teaching the individual to become "a law unto himself." As its leading exponent, the religious liberal William Ellery Channing, famously put it in a widely reprinted 1838 lecture on the subject, "Self-culture is possible, not only because we can enter into and search ourselves. We have a still nobler power, that of acting on, determining, and forming ourselves. This is a fearful as well as a glorious endowment, for it is the ground of human responsibility."[7]

Although advice writers presented a fairly uniform front, theirs was "a fragile fortress," for their ways of talking about the powers and potentialities of the individual "rested upon introspection," as Henry May has observed, "and introspection is difficult to control." Having explained and justified these changes by reference to the commonplaces of Common Sense, they increasingly found themselves on the defensive, as the vocabularies of the self they put into circulation were infused with new meanings and turned to a variety of ends that were not easily harmonized with one another. To be sure, the advice writers who peddled their wares in this expanding market society continued to promote self-*discipline* among aspirants to the middling classes, projecting a gendered ideal of propertied independence, a well-ordered society composed of male-headed households, enjoying "a competency" in the economic sense: the material means to make a living "without superfluity" or the need to work for others. This message was reinforced by politicians of both Jacksonian and Whig persuasions, for in the very act of trading the insults of "aristocrat" and "leveler" they converged a common precept of equal opportunity, which entailed a relative but not absolute equality of condition, so that success in life was determined by talent and industry rather than birth or patronage. Yet this egalitarian ethos contained the seeds of its own destruction, as Tocqueville trenchantly observed, for it paradoxically awakened towering ambitions and insatiable desires as it "opened the door to universal competition," which explained "this strange unrest of so many unhappy men, restless in the midst of abundance," apparently unable to "enjoy their independence without anxiety and without impatience." Nor was he first to notice the problem. By the time his travelogue was published, it had become almost proverbial among Americans themselves that "the very freedom of our institutions, by creating universal strife, and increasing the mental activity of all classes, causes much insanity." In other words, Rush's nightmare vision of anarchia seemed on the verge of becoming a lived reality in antebellum America, calling into question the moralists' teachings about individual freedom and responsibility and prompting reconsideration of the jurists' ways of modeling legal personhood as well as the philosophical premises upon which they were built.[8]

As the attribution of responsibility was made to turn more directly upon the moral ability of humankind, an increasing degree of scrutiny was trained upon those whose powers of reason and self-government appeared deficient. The philosophers' arsenal of explanations for departures from moral and legal norms, citing failures in mental cultivation and self-discipline, or pointing to corrupting influences in the surrounding environment, seemed insufficient, especially in extreme cases. Alternative explanations were soon supplied by a new band of medical men, specializing in the diagnosis and treatment of "mental alienation."[9] As Chapter 2 illustrates, their psychological models supplied reasons for thinking human deviance was often—but certainly not always—the product of mental disease that rendered its victim less than fully responsible for his or her behavior. These medical doctrines were presented and debated in the new literature of medical jurisprudence, through which it is possible to trace the convergence of doctors and lawyers upon a problematic yet surprisingly serviceable way of defining insanity as a matter of law: a radical and unaccountable change in character. While this formulation served to clarify the nature and extent of responsibility, the doctrinal case studies that comprise Part Two of this book demonstrate that these limits remained eminently contestable, owing in no small part to the fact that the law's definition of insanity essentially begged the question of why an individual ought to be held accountable for his or her character in the first place.

CHAPTER 1

Common Sense and Common Law

> The art of government is the medicine of the mind, and the most useful part is that which prevents crimes and bad habits, and trains men to virtue and good habits by proper education and discipline.
>
> Thomas Reid, 1768

RISING TO ADDRESS an illustrious audience that included President Washington and the First Lady, the newly appointed professor and Supreme Court justice James Wilson contemplated America's destiny in his inaugural law lecture at the College of Philadelphia in December 1790. "We have passed the Red Sea in safety: we have survived a tedious and dangerous journey through the wilderness: we are now in the full and peaceable possession of the promised land." As one of the architects of the 1787 Constitution, he was sanguine about the prospects of new government and yet exceedingly wary about returning to such "fleshpots of Egypt" as William Blackstone's *Commentaries,* riddled as it was with fatal errors about the fundamentals of law. He likened the enlightened jurists of his generation to the intrepid explorers who had lately discovered the source of the mighty Nile in "a collection of springs small, indeed, but pure," rather than "a superior orb," as poets had worshipfully imagined. Intellectual inquiry into the true basis of all legitimate authority similarly pointed to a natural and singular point of origin: "The dread and redoubtable sovereign, when traced to his ultimate and genuine source, has been found, as he ought to have been found, in the free and independent man."[1]

In declaring the sovereignty of the individual "the first and fundamental principle in the science of government," Wilson did not mean to suggest that man was a law unto himself, as he fully recognized the supreme authority of God. But divine rule amounted to "one paternal command— Let man pursue his own perfection and happiness." To illuminate the way, this benevolent God endowed human beings with "reason and conscience, the divine monitors within us," and he provided further direction "by the sacred oracles, the divine monitors without us." Yet within the realm of human government, "the all-wise Author of our existence" expected "that we should also do much for ourselves." The starting point of this endeavor was the study of the laws of our own nature, which was "the most curious and the most important" field of human knowledge. In the investigation of this subject, it would be treacherous to rely on the accumulated wisdom of philosophers from Plato and Aristotle to Locke, Berkeley, Hume, Hartley, and Priestly, all of whom worked from the faulty premise that the mind "takes no direct cognizance of external things" and that the world around us can only be known through the medium "of certain shadows or images of them," which the ancients called *"forms"* and the moderns renamed *"ideas."* Voicing a common Enlightenment critique, Wilson remarked that, reasoning as they did by means of "hypothesis and analogy" rather than "observation and experience," their writings were "destructive of all knowledge and virtue" because they sowed the seeds of skepticism and materialism. Deliverance from these dark labyrinths of thought had been provided by "the enlightened and candid Dr. Reid," a well-known Scottish philosopher, whose appeals to the authority of "our common sense" supplied the surest way of attaining the self-understanding that was essential to the project of self-government.[2]

Wilson insisted that lawyers would "scarce deserve to be ranked among the learned professions" if they were not required to climb to "the vantage ground" afforded by "metaphysical knowledge," which he understood to mean "the philosophy of the human mind." With this prelude, he launched into a set of prolix lectures concerning "man, as an individual, as a member of a society, as a member of a confederation, and as a part of the great commonwealth of nations." He spoke in gendered terms, designating "publick government and publick law" as masculine domains and insisting that women were "made for something better," by which he meant "domestick society."[3]

Much of what he said about the human mind was paraphrased or drawn verbatim from the Common Sense philosophy of Thomas Reid, a Presbyterian clergyman associated with the moderate faction of the Scottish Enlightenment.[4] Historians have often treated Wilson's pronouncements on "the moral government of the universe" as telling illustrations of the idiosyncratic, even quixotic faith that distinguished him from the other, more worldly-wise framers and fueled a self-destructive pattern of speculation that finally cost him both his reputation and his sanity. While other delegates to the Federal Convention of 1787 endeavored to construct constitutional mechanisms to contain selfish passions and counterbalance competing interests, ultimately regarding the protection of property as the primary aim of government, Wilson contended that its greatest object was "the cultivation and improvement of the human mind." But while he was more fixated on this point than most other framers, he was hardly unusual among lawyer-statesmen in the new nation in his appreciation of Scottish Enlightenment philosophy as a means of bringing order to their bewildering circumstances and fulfilling the professional role they had assumed as the natural guardians of republican liberty. As exhilaration about beginning the world over again was mixed with anxiety about the excesses and abuses of freedom that appeared to be the undoing of the French Revolution, the Common Sense school provided a reassuring way of thinking about the self that was exceptionally well suited to the practical challenges that confronted governing elites in the half century after independence as they worked out the concrete implications of their political ideals.[5]

The Moral and Mental Constitution of the "Free and Independent Man"

This conception of the self was deployed to stabilize postrevolutionary American society. This chapter situates Wilson's "free and independent man" within the wider cultural ferment over the meaning of moral freedom and the locus of authority in the early republic. The unifying rhetoric of the Revolution quickly gave way to conflict as disputations about the metaphysics and politics of liberty were reconstituted in the changed circumstances wrought by war, prompting Americans to think anew about the relationship between human nature and moral government. In this era, orthodox Calvinist doctrines of humans' innate depravity and divine determination of their salvation or damnation gradually gave way to liberal forms of Protestantism, which recast God as a loving father who had endowed his creatures with the capacity for self-determination. Perceptions of human agency were intensified by the growth of capitalism, which encouraged individuals to see the future, not as inevitable, but as something they were daily bringing into being. Liberating though this prospect was, it also rendered vulnerable existing social hierarchies and norms, generating an undercurrent of anxiety about the autonomous individual.[6]

In the midst of this tumult, the Common Sense philosophy of Reid and his followers seemed to provide an effective anodyne, psychologically and politically, because it offered scientific assurance that the obligatory rules of good governance lay within the human mind. Invoking the epistemic authority of "common sense" against "dogmatical theories" and "metaphysical absurdities," they insisted upon the self-evidence of a unitary "I" that was more than a bundle of perceptions and irreducible to mere matter. Treating man as a subject for systematic study, they deployed a method of induction that started with the philosopher's own consciousness, delineating "an anatomy of the mind" with the ultimate aim of revealing its "powers and principles of action." The faculties of the mind were of three distinct sorts: the "rational" powers of intellect, will, and moral sense; the "animal" appetites, desires, and affections; and the "mechanical" instincts and habits. While arranging them in a hierarchy which implied that the rational powers were supposed to reign supreme over the animal and mechanical ones, the Common Sense philosophers emphasized that this mental model could be maintained only through concerted effort; the mind required proper cultivation by parents and teachers in childhood and then vigilant self-discipline. The fact that individuals were so endowed was what rendered them "moral and accountable beings," answerable to "our Maker" and "our fellow-men in society."' Justice dictated "a perfect correspondence between *power*, on the one hand, and *moral obligation* and *accountableness*, on the other." While moral agency was a divine gift conferred upon all of humankind, the extent of moral accountability depended upon a person's "power over the determinations of his will," though little was said about how this crucial factor was to be gauged as a practical matter. In sum, responsibility was part and parcel of a process of self-making that was as consequential as it was humanly difficult to assess.[7]

Despite or perhaps because of its glossing over of such perplexities, the Common Sense philosophy was a remarkably serviceable mode of ethical reasoning that was readily turned to sociopolitical purposes. Colleges institutionalized it by placing these "eminently safe and sane" works at the center of a capstone course in moral philosophy designed to elevate the character of their young male students and fit them for positions of leadership. Some educators wrote their own versions adapted to American conditions and concerns, often incorporating the writings of thinkers outside the Common Sense school while presenting the same basic notions about the powers of the human mind and the imperative duties to self, family, society, state, and God that flowed from the possession of these faculties. In the early nineteenth century, this "moral science" and the closely related project of character building were increasingly directed to a popular audience of women as well as men, chiefly in the form of sermons, instructional treatises, lyceum lectures, reform pamphlets, and magazine articles composed by a broad array of ministers and secular moralists. Through their concerted efforts, they elaborated an ideal of "balanced character" as well as a set of techniques to develop it.[8]

The proliferating vocabularies of the self in antebellum America testify to the influence of the moral philosophers' models of character formation and their preachments about responsibility. But as self-talk enjoyed widening appeal in this democratizing, increasingly market-oriented society, it became ever more ambiguous in its meaning and implications. Despite their sweeping language of the philosophers' pronouncements, their universalistic prescriptions were not meant to apply to everyone in the same fashion. American expositors of Common Sense tended to use the philosophy to differentiate the populace along republican lines; they encouraged individuals to develop their unique "gifts of mind" and advocated social policies that opened careers to "talents," with the aim of forging a polity at once egalitarian and meritocratic. None went so far as to advocate equality of condition, which they knew full well would fatally undermine the institutions of slavery and marriage, as well as jeopardizing private property. All agreed that mental faculties were differentially distributed among persons who occupied different social positions. While some believed these mental attributes varied by age, race, and sex, others leaned more heavily on religious and social rationales for maintaining or renovating existing hierarchies within and beyond the household.[9]

Speaking in terms that obscured more than they revealed about the sources of human difference and inequality, those who translated Common Sense into common sense in the decades before the Civil War were inclined to accentuate the positive: they affirmed the limitlessness of individual capacity and, therefore, responsibility for self-improvement, even as they acknowledged the unequal distribution of natural endowments and social resources across the population.[10] This way of thinking about human potential inspired a range of interventions into the lives of those who suffered from mental disorders and debilities. Yet because the reformers' underlying philosophies of mind were built upon introspection and substantiated by appeals to consciousness, the effects of their character-building campaigns were not easily controlled. Though clearly formative in the constitution of middle-class morality and the forging of an industrial capitalist order, the Common Sense revelations of individual willpower also inspired critiques of these social norms and structures in the name of the autonomous self.

The law's relationship to this Enlightenment project and the disciplinary institutions and practices it generated is a matter of considerable complexity. One of the most durable narratives in the history and historiography of nineteenth-century America has cast the law in the role of providing "the conditions of freedom." According to this line of interpretation, members of the legal profession in the new nation elaborated and operationalized a "will theory of law" designed to facilitate "the release of creative human energy," chiefly toward the end of economic development. The law is viewed as responsive to and reflective of the needs of an entrepreneurial class, whose interests were furthered by the construction of a legal distinction between public and private that worked to maximize the bounds of individual initiative and insulate commercial enterprises from "the dangers of state interference and redistribution."[11]

This instrumentalist account has been called into question by social and cultural historians, who have pointed to the forms and degrees of unfreedom upon which the will theory was premised. Tracing the deep connections among legal, scientific, and popular conceptions of selfhood, these scholars underscore the persistence of status hierarchies throughout the nineteenth century, showing how the subordination of women, children, racial-ethnic minority groups, and wage laborers was both rationalized and contested within a liberal worldview.[12] The simultaneous emergence of liberalism and new disciplinary mechanisms is taken as a point of departure in many narratives, which document their operations not only within the confines of penitentiaries, insane asylums, and poorhouses but also in factories, schools, and families. The dueling impulses to liberate and to constrain human willpower found at the heart of these endeavors express "deep-seated apprehensions about the maintenance of public order once individuals were freed from tradition, community, and social hierarchy."[13] Yet their conceptions of the relation between law and discipline have varied substantially. Some have positioned law as anterior to disciplinary power, with the capacity to enable or constrain it, while others have figured law as displaced or overwhelmed by disciplinary institutions and practices that were better equipped "to regularize moral life and create citizens and workers for the new liberal capitalist societies of the nineteenth century."[14]

"The philosophy of the human mind" that James Wilson commended to his law students might be viewed as one of the "technologies of the self" that was deployed for such purposes.[15] Yet it has not been mined by the historians of American law, despite their focus on processes of identity formation and constructions of legal personhood. The mental philosophers and their disciplinary techniques are placed front and center here. The pages that follow examine the cultural significance and sociopolitical implications of their teachings about moral freedom and personal responsibility as they were absorbed and put to use by postrevolutionary American educators and reformers as well as jurists, most of whom displayed considerable concern about limiting the individual will. Attending to the dialogue between law and other realms of social practice, religious and scientific inquiry, economic activity, and cultural expression, this chapter shows how Common Sense philosophy provided aspiring lawyers with tools of self-knowledge and self-mastery and shaped their thinking about responsible agency and human potential. More broadly, the philosophers' representations of the free-standing individual came to operate as the presumptive subject of the law, what I call the "default legal person." While it did not simply replace the English common law of persons, this model of responsible selfhood both informed and stimulated the efforts of antebellum legal scientists to align the rules governing personal relations with "our doctrine of equality" as they elaborated a distinctly American jurisprudence.

The treatises, tracts, and addresses composed by the sons of founding fathers like James Wilson drew upon Common Sense philosophy in order to bring order and fixity to an unnervingly fluid society. The cultural imperative "to preserve their inheritance of liberty and transmit it to future generations" weighed heavily upon this generation, generating considerable anxiety about anarchic energies and corrupting influences and prompting them to promote the internalization of social norms of rationality and self-reliance. While profoundly ambivalent about the social implications of this ideal, they valorized the individual who became "a law unto himself."[16] Despite its apparent contradictions, this notion made sense to jurists who believed in a universal moral faculty, though even the most optimistic among them did not think that the moralists' disciplinary efforts were sufficient to contain the centrifugal forces that threatened the republic. The rule of law they conceived to be necessary for its survival stood over and above the other improving institutions and practices that mushroomed in the decades before the Civil War, its supremacy justified by the fact that it was authorized by "the people themselves."

The deeper the doubts about the ruling capacities of the people, the more abstract the people appeared in the law books, a discursive move that begged the question of what was to be done with those who failed to measure up to the law's expectations. How was a court to determine with certitude that a given actor had the capacity to rule himself, that his moral freedom was not fatally compromised by a faulty education, congenital defect, or other factor beyond his control? Was not a deviant action itself evidence of mental unsoundness, rendering the person less than fully accountable for his conduct? For all the assurance Common Sense provided about the moral ability of humankind, it generated at least as many problems as it solved for the legal system when it came to the subject of responsibility.

The Metaphysics of Moral Government

The life of James Wilson (1742–1798) epitomizes the shift from Calvinist theology to Common Sense philosophy and the passage of the Scottish Enlightenment to America. His education began in his native Scotland, where his father, a lowlands farmer and Presbyterian elder, sought to prepare his eldest son for the ministry. Troubled by the growing prevalence of a deistical "religion of nature" that instilled a perilous "self-confidence," the elder Wilson took to preaching beyond his family circle. By his lights, Scripture made it abundantly clear that God was not obliged to pardon penitent wrongdoers, even those who sincerely endeavored to make amends and obtain his forgiveness. He tellingly reinforced this point by analogy to earthly polities: "It would not be reckoned a sufficient security for any government among men, if rebels and criminals in every case should have a title to pardon upon their repentance. Such a principle as this would unhinge government, and open a door for the greatest disorders amongst men."[17] James initially followed the route his father prescribed for him: grammar school, St. Andrews, and the university's divinity school. But by 1766 he was in Philadelphia aspiring to enter the legal profession. He brought to the law a firm grounding in the work of Enlightenment thinkers. Equipped with training in the classics as well as the disciplines of logic, metaphysics, moral philosophy, and natural philosophy, Wilson rapidly rose to prominence in his adopted country. His checkered career of constitutional politics and land speculation was animated by a peculiar sort of optimism that left him faithful to the last, despite his bankruptcy. Just days before his death, he assured his long-suffering wife that he would soon have a way to satisfy his creditors: "The Time is opening, in which, I think, Something very effectual may be done."[18]

Although there was a distinct pathos to Wilson's fall from grace, his experiences were emblematic of the momentous spiritual, political, and economic transformations that marked the passage from the Revolution to the new republic. By the time Wilson arrived in America, liberal humanism was prompting a thoroughgoing reconsideration of the metaphysics of moral government not only by ministers and theologians but also among politicians, lawyers, physicians, and other "men of affairs." Despite their other differences, religious and secular leaders tended to converge upon the conceptions of human nature and divine judgment elaborated by the new moral philosophers of the eighteenth century, particularly those associated with the Scottish Enlightenment. Reflecting a more general historical movement from a God-centered to a human-centered universe, these philosophers endeavored to render the transcendent creator of orthodox Protestant theology "understandable in human terms." They presumed that divine "expectations of human beings as moral creatures could be discovered independently of the traditional sources of religious authority, through a close investigation of human nature" that would reveal "certain Rules of life." In this respect, they followed the inductive approach set out by Francis Bacon and developed by Isaac Newton, believing that matters of divinity, ethics, and epistemology could and should be scientifically pursued by means of the same empirical methods of inquiry that were used to comprehend the physical world. Defined against "metaphysical," "theoretical," and "speculative" ways of knowing, Baconian philosophy was built upon "generalized facts" accumulated by means of careful observation, whether of nature, the mind, social life, or scriptural passages, which were then organized into taxonomies that delineated the powers and potentialities of humankind.[19]

At the core of this Enlightenment discourse about human nature was a certain ambiguity about the meaning of "*nature*." While the term was often used to denote a "human essence, understood by and in relation to the divine," in many contexts it also carried the implication that human beings were powerfully connected with the natural world and embedded within groups and societies that displayed their own lawlike regularities. Indeed, one of the distinguishing features of the "science of man" as it developed over the course of the eighteenth century was its sense that individual identity was most immediately shaped by history, geography, society, and experience, with divine influence figuring only in the remote background. "Man" was commonly used in the generic sense to refer to humankind, with most writers taking the existence of sexual difference for granted without attending systematically to the nature of "woman." To the extent that comparisons were drawn between the sexes, the feminine side of this binary was rendered "as a designated branch of humanity" that presented complexities requiring special treatment. Moreover, as the diversity of races was increasingly subject to the gaze and classificatory zeal of naturalists, scientists arranged various "types of mankind" hierarchically by reference to their physical, mental, and moral traits, with the Caucasian enjoying pride of place and the African occupying the lowest rank. This continuum encouraged reconsideration of the relations between men and brutes, with some investigators finding evidence of animal intelligence that challenged long-standing beliefs in the unity of the human species and the uniqueness of human reason.[20]

Even as, and likely because, they were confronted with expanding bodies of knowledge about natural differences, Enlightenment philosophers tended to abstract away from them in their writings on epistemology and ethics. In search of generally applicable laws, their investigations were premised upon a universal human nature that was consonant with their shared conviction "that understanding should start from and return to common experience as a basis for civil society." Nonetheless, their estimations of man's natural condition and his capacity for knowledge and virtue varied widely. Most stood arrayed against the famously disparaging account of Thomas Hobbes, which defined man as inherently selfish and saw his will as a natural mechanism responding to pleasure and pain. Some gravitated toward the neutral position staked out by John Locke, who imagined the human mind as devoid of innate ideas and without any natural tendency toward good or evil. But others were drawn to the more flattering portraits of ethical rationalists or sentimentalists, who posited the existence of an innate moral sense that rendered morality not only natural but pleasurable and pointed to what they regarded as irrefutable evidence of man's natural sociability and inborn and irresistible compassion for others, with the implication that anyone who remained untouched by this fellow feeling was "a sort of monster or anomalous production." In many respects, these philosophical reflections on the human condition operated to perpetuate rather than resolve long-standing religious debates as to whether God's grace or man's free will was "the fundamental moral agent." Yet over the eighteenth century, this contentious matter was increasingly recast in terms of "moral" and "physical" causes, a gradual but momentous shift marked by a heightened awareness of and concomitant anxiety about "the malleability of man."[21]

Enlightenment estimates of human ability that were more consistent with republicanism tended to replace the varieties of Protestantism that had predominated among the colonial elite. Jonathan Edwards, who sought to reconcile the doctrine of divine determination of individuals' eternal fate with a concept of free will through the subjective experience of spiritual salvation that endowed people with new "affections" and a disposition toward virtue, ardently appealed to "the 'common sense' of 'the common people'" in his effort to hold people responsible for their actions.[22] But a Calvinist view of "the *parent* of the universe" hardly comported with "every man's natural sense." "Let a man look into his own breast, and he cannot but perceive Inward freedom," averred Congregational minister James Dana in 1770. Published five years before he committed himself to the Patriot cause and took to sermonizing on republicanism, Dana's declaration of independence indicates the extent to which the sovereignty of God was subtly but significantly diminished as Americans expanded the bounds of man's "moral liberty" on the eve of the Revolution.[23]

The distinctive synthesis of republican and Christian conceptions of liberty forged by religious and secular leaders to justify their independence from the British crown, which had previously been imagined as representing the divine sovereign in earthly affairs, supplied postrevolutionary Americans with a powerful new vocabulary for questioning entrenched power and inherited authority. It simultaneously registered and contributed to the social tension and dislocation that marked the last decades of the eighteenth century. Faced with the mixed blessing of forging a nation in an era when clerics no longer enjoyed uncontested cultural power, orthodox and liberal ministers alike joined with other learned professions in forging a new consensus about the constitution of the human mind and moral government that was grounded in the Common Sense realism of the Scottish Enlightenment.[24]

Consciousness of Freedom

The Scottish philosophers built an elaborate intellectual system upon the epistemic authority of common sense, conceiving of it as both a mental science and a moral cause.[25] Thomas Reid was a key exponent of this intellectual movement, producing a trilogy of works that won him fame in the United States as well.[26] Most significantly, his version of Common Sense was strikingly well suited to legal purposes. Not only were American lawyers schooled in his epistemology, but they found it particularly useful in thinking about the legal responsibility of those whose actions were called into question in court.

Proceeding in a distinctly forensic mode, Reid presented himself as an expert concerning "the common sense of mankind," making liberal use of legal terms, notions, principles, procedures, and standards of proof as well as those drawn from natural theology and the natural sciences. Indeed, his inductive-introspective mode of philosophizing and its reformist bent exemplified the debt the Enlightenment science of man owed to the field of law. His method was crucially shaped by philosopher-jurists such as such as Bacon and Lord Kames (Henry Home) and bore the imprints of natural law jurisprudence, especially early modern legal discourse concerned with establishing protocols of fact-finding in jury trials with both expert and lay witnesses. In eliciting the "testimony" of consciousness and other faculties of the mind and recognizing common sense as the "tribunal of final appeal" whose dictates he proceeded to codify, Reid used law as more than a rhetorical resource. The legal system was a critical site of experimentation and reflection concerning the nature and limits of the human capacity for virtue and knowledge. It also provided a powerful set of conceptual tools and practical techniques for grappling with the fallibility of human judgment, many of which had been gradually absorbed, consciously incorporated, or creatively appropriated within other realms of Anglo-American culture. Empirical philosophers who followed Locke played an instrumental role in generalizing the legal concept of fact and giving it currency well beyond the trial setting, and their works were, in turn, summoned up by jurists in specialized treatises on the law of evidence. The symbiosis between law and epistemology is especially clear in Reid's work, which operates on the premise that "what is absurd at the bar, is so in the Philosopher's chair. What would be ridiculous, if delivered to a jury of honest, sensible citizens, is no less so when delivered gravely in a philosophical dissertation." Legal modes of reasoning and knowing were part and parcel of the philosophical case he made against skepticism, which might also be read to provide scientific validation of the norms and procedures of common law adjudication.[27]

Reid described common sense as a set of innate faculties or "first principles" that "irresistibly govern the belief and the conduct of all mankind in the common concerns of life"—or at least those who were of sound mind. In his view, common sense was a rational power that rendered objective judgments that were widely shared rather than subjective feelings that might be idiosyncratic. He defined the functional relationship between common sense and reason in a passage that pointed to the legal significance of these terms:

> We ascribe to reason two offices, or two degrees. The first is to judge of things self-evident; the second to draw conclusions that are not self-evident from those that are. The first of these is the province, and the sole province of common sense; and therefore it coincides with reason in its whole extent, and is only another name for one branch or one degree of reason. . . . [I]n the greatest part of mankind no other degree of reason is to be found. It is this degree that entitles them to the denomination of reasonable creatures. It is this degree of reason, and this only, that makes a man capable of managing his own affairs, and answerable for his conduct toward others.

Possession of the first degree of reason, which was inherent in human nature but could be obscured by bodily and mental ills, was an indispensable precondition for the acquisition of the second degree, which was "learned by practice and rules." Moreover, common sense provided the foundation of all "just reasoning" and retained "jurisdiction" over all thinking processes; any conclusion that contradicted "any decision of common sense" was by definition false.[28]

This judgment was generally rendered with respect to the skeptical philosophers, who had presumptuously erected "a tribunal of inquisition" and ruled out of existence everything in the universe that was "neither an impression, nor an idea copied from some impression." Dogmatically imposing their hypothetical view of the mind without allowing for a fair hearing of all the evidence, "the votaries of this Philosophy . . . have endeavoured to call to her bar the dictates of Common Sense. But these decline this jurisdiction; they disdain the trial of reasoning, and disown its authority." The ridiculousness of these proceedings was underscored by the inquisitors' implicit "assent" to the "sovereign authority" of common sense. For in prosecuting the case they could not help but rely upon the veracity of the very mental faculties they placed in question, and even the most zealous skeptic among them would surely sidestep perceived dangers in all avenues of his life despite his stated disbelief in the testimony of his senses. Indeed, Reid contended, these philosophers' inconsistency only confirmed the old adage that "too much learning is apt to make men mad." Such was the fate of all doubters of common sense: sooner or later they would be revealed to be hypocrites, self-deceived, or afflicted with "metaphysical lunacy," a condition that was usually cured by coaxing the patient out of the closet of speculation, though if it persisted he might be "clapt into a mad-house." In view of these facts, it was best for philosophers "to make a virtue of necessity," "to reconcile our reason" to the orders of this "inward tribunal," "for if Reason should stomach and fret ever so much at this yoke, she cannot throw it off; if she will not be the servant of Common Sense, she must be her slave."[29]

One of the most useful and pressing tasks a properly chastened philosophy could perform was to codify the decisions of common sense, enumerating the self-evident principles "in which all reasonable men shall acquiesce." Reid seems to have meant not only the "first principles" or basic "axioms" of human thought upon which all reasoning was based but also a wider and rather amorphous array of things that people take for granted in their everyday lives. The fact that they were not susceptible to direct proof, however, made them difficult to reduce to a list and distinguish from "vulgar errors or prejudices." A philosopher could usefully provide criteria for identifying genuine first principles, or at least those with a "good claim" to be considered as such. To this end, Reid supplied a set of "rational means" by which beliefs could be tested.[30] It was in this matter-of-fact fashion that Reid arrived at a resolution of the vexing problem of free will that worked to solidify the foundations of virtue as well as knowledge. Invoking the authority of common sense, he simultaneously assumed the roles of scientist, advocate, judge, juror, and codifier and attributed greater active agency to the mind than other philosophers had done.[31] Consulting his own consciousness and attending to the behavior of other men, Reid pronounced the conviction that "we have some degree of power over our actions, and the determinations of our will" to be among the first principles of common sense. This conviction was "so general, and so interwoven with the whole of human conduct, that it must be the natural effect of our constitution, and intended by the Author of our being to guide our actions."[32]

The case for the freedom of the will was made most fully in Reid's pair of essays on the "intellectual" and "active" powers of the human mind.[33] He tended to use these words interchangeably with the traditional faculty psychology terminology of "understanding" and "will" and regarded them as analytically distinguishable, yet intrinsically interconnected. Reid declared that in mental operations "we are both intellective and active."[34] The active powers constituting the will were relatively autonomous from the other mental faculties, including the intellectual powers, though it was the person in possession of all these powers rather than the will itself that exercised control over both thought and action. Although motives were influential, Reid imagined them as analogous to "advocates pleading the opposite sides of a cause at the bar": they provided instruction and reasons for action but did not compel any particular outcome. Accordingly, he renamed them "principles of action" and presented them in hierarchical order, reflecting their authority within the internal "commonwealth" that was the mind. Placed at the top were the rational faculties, including the moral sense or conscience. Beneath them were the animal appetites, desires, and affections, which exerted varying degrees of force without being irresistible in the mind of a sane and healthy adult. At the bottom were the mechanical instincts and habits, which operated without judgment or will, though habit formation was to some degree a matter of choice. This model was meant to be both descriptive and prescriptive, establishing that man was a reasonable creature with the liberty to choose whether he would act the "manly" or the "brute" part in the "theatre of life." The fact that he had this capacity for self-government rendered him a responsible agent, answerable to God and man for the use of this mental power.[35]

In thus casting the relationship between divine and human agency, Reid understood the individual as endowed with "some degree of active power, and of reason, to direct him to the right use of his power," which rendered him a servant rather than a tool in his master's hands. The individual who faithfully discharged his duty was worthy of praise, and his credit was only enhanced by the effort he had to expend in struggling against his depraved instincts and bad habits to accomplish this end.[36] This conclusion presumed that God observed human norms of justice, which reveals the contradictory implications of his common sense way of reasoning about moral liberty. Even as he affirmed self-determination, Reid implied that the grounds of individual responsibility were much narrower than was conventionally believed. In contrast to many theologians and members of the bench and bar, who restricted the provision of excuses to those who labored under profound cognitive impairments or external physical constraints, Reid contemplated a considerably wider array of mitigating and exonerating factors.

This stance is clearest in his renderings of our ways of thinking about civil and criminal liability, which he presented as matters of fact in support of his claims that we are endowed with active power, though they reflect his own ideals rather than standards of legal practice. In the course of arguing for our moral liberty, for example, he utilized legal terms: "When I plight my faith in any promise or contract, I must believe that I shall have the power to perform what I promise. Without this persuasion, a promise would be downright fraud." Although "there is a condition implied in every promise, *if we live*, and *if God continue with us the power which he hath given us*," this social act was not commonly understood to carry with it the added proviso "*if we shall be willing*," as the "system of necessity" would have required, nor would this give rise to any obligation to be willing, for "the will not being in our power, we cannot engage for it." But if it were "a dictate of common sense, that we can be under no obligation to do what is impossible for us to do," Reid would have had to concede that the common law was rather more equivocal on this score, especially with respect to insanity. Contemporary jurists disagreed about whether and to what extent mental incapacity constituted an excuse from contractual liability.[37]

The divergence of Reid's Common Sense philosophy from the opinions and practices of contemporary religious and legal authorities appears in even sharper relief in his consideration of the ordinary language and everyday actions of blaming and punishing, which were likewise summoned up in support of the case for moral liberty. He observed that "blame supposes a wrong use of power," that condemnation of oneself or another implies "our power to have done better." The same was true of the wrongdoer's feelings of remorse and any resolutions made and exhortations received "to do better" in the future. Reid submitted that this power necessarily implied more than the bare capacity to do as one willed, which he took to be descriptively true of animals, infants, madmen, and idiots, none of whom were considered blameworthy or punishable for their harmful acts in criminal proceedings.[38]

In his treatment of the subject of madness, too, he claimed to be summoning up facts about the legal system which did not align with contemporary thought and practice. Conceiving of the essence of insanity to lie in an excess of passion rather than a defect of understanding, as it had long been defined at common law, Reid understood those afflicted to be voluntary actors who were nonetheless "absolutely deprived of the power of self-government"; their wills were "driven as by a tempest, which, in lucid intervals, they resolve to oppose with all their might, but are overcome when the fit of madness returns." Because madmen were impelled by "irresistible" passions, moral responsibility for their actions could not be imputed to them. By extension, Reid reasoned, "violent passions, and violent motives alleviate what is done through their influence, in the same proportion as they diminish the power of resistance."[39] Though he represented these as mitigating factors routinely taken into account "in criminal courts, as well as private judgment," he exaggerated significantly on both counts. Indeed, he verged upon making sin its own excuse in suggesting that the moral faculty could be degraded or destroyed by "inveterate habits" in ways that courts were bound to recognize, charged as they were with approximating the norms of divine justice, which dictated "a perfect correspondence between power, on the one hand, and moral obligation and accountableness, on the other."[40]

Taking for granted that this conception of moral agency prevailed in everyday life, Reid did not develop the full implications of the Common Sense way of thinking about the limits of personal responsibility, for his animating philosophical purpose was to illuminate the full extent of man's ability to determine his own character and destiny. Although the animal principles of action that constituted his "natural temper" might be good or bad, they could be tamed and properly directed by his rational and moral faculties, which were "capable of a high degree of culture . . . by means of good education, of proper instruction, of persuasion, of good example, and by the discipline of laws and government." Declining to speculate about why God had put man in such a predicament, he sought to channel the mental energies of his readers toward the noble ends that lay before them, marveling at "what a divine employment of human power is here assigned us" and aiming "to rouse the ambition of parents, of instructors, of lawgivers, of magistrates, of every man in his station, to contribute his part towards the accomplishment of so glorious an end." Reid was confident that through such concerted efforts, "human nature, in individuals and in societies, may be exalted to a high degree of dignity and felicity, and the earth become a paradise."[41]

It fell to the popularizers of Reid's Common Sense philosophy to dispense "the medicine of mind" that would most effectively stabilize and govern self and society while also staving off dangerously disabling forms of doubt. By the late eighteenth century, it had been simplified and presented in a manner designed to persuade a broad audience, and commentators had outlined its practical applications in the arts and sciences, law, economics, politics, and education. These conceptions of man's moral agency and his capacity for self-improvement found an especially receptive audience in postrevolutionary America. Common Sense served as a crucial intellectual resource that was readily appropriated by educators and governing elites as they endeavored to forge a new paradigm of causality and an accompanying ethic of personal responsibility in a republic that was unsettled by its own independence and ever more disoriented and atomized by the forces of democratization and capitalism.[42]

Making Responsible Citizens

In a society that had cast aside the traditional pillars upholding moral order, even the most orthodox of Calvinists ultimately came to see the appeal of the Scottish Common Sense philosophy. Bracketing ultimate questions about the sources of evil and all but banishing paradox from the domain of rational thought, its expositors focused on the part man was created to play in "the theatre of life." The ground for the favorable reception of this philosophy in revolutionary America was prepared by a wave of Scottish immigrants who, as tutors and instructors in colonial seminaries and colleges, disseminated many of the key texts of the Scottish Enlightenment, which treated not only the philosophy of mind but also rhetoric (as the art of logical argument was then called), politics, economics, history, and jurisprudence. The rising generation of American men imbibed a characteristic sense of moral certitude from these sources. Although the complex strains of thought that comprised the Scottish Enlightenment have led scholars to differ sharply in their assessments of its effects, all agree that Common Sense philosophy had attained a position of cultural dominance in the United States by the turn of the nineteenth century, winning adherents across occupational, political, regional, and denominational lines.[43]

Indeed, Common Sense became hegemonic in American thought to a greater degree than it did in Great Britain. Historians have emphasized how well it functioned as an intellectual means of managing the crises of authority that threatened to undermine the United States' democratic experiment, as its citizens became ever more embroiled in controversies about the practical implications of their political ideals. The stakes were raised by the excesses of the French Revolution, which dramatized the potency of radical Enlightenment ideas of liberty and equality. Apprehending the fragility of their newly established constitutional order, American clerics and statesmen recognized the need for "moral and political guidelines that were available equally and reliably to all." Common Sense philosophy proved "immensely useful as an intellectually respectable way for political leaders to reestablish virtue and for religious leaders to defend Christian truth on the basis of a science unencumbered by tradition." It occupied "a critical place in the chain of connections whereby American Protestants struggled to co-opt the Enlightenment" by showing morality to be a science that "led to Christian rather than mechanistic conclusions." But what ensured the widespread acceptance of this philosophy was its flexibility: it could be turned to a variety of ends that were not entirely compatible with one another. Indeed, in the American context it was not so much a theoretical system as an "attitude" or "mood," providing "broader habits of mind or reassuring conventions of thought."[44]

It was precisely because Common Sense philosophy was so reassuring to so many that its problematic recasting of the grounds of human responsibility was only slowly grasped by its adherents. In their efforts to reconcile Enlightenment science with traditional religious doctrines concerning divine sovereignty and human freedom, Reid and his followers had unwittingly introduced a new element of complexity into the discourse about human nature. In asserting that the moral liberty of humankind was simply a fact of consciousness, they rendered the existence and persistence of human perversity newly puzzling. Whereas the orthodox Calvinists of the colonial era had comprehended such transgressions as manifestations of an innate and total human depravity, those who adopted Common Sense views in the early republic were prompted to regard sin as an unnatural deformity that was often attributable to environmental causes that might be minimized or eradicated. Both evangelicals and liberals increasingly came to hold, "almost in spite of themselves," that human beings were born with the mental ability and therefore the duty to actively pursue a virtuous life.[45] At the same time, their optimism was tinged by an acute awareness of the mind's susceptibility to corruption by society; they feared that the exercise of voluntary choice in religion, politics, the market, and countless other arenas of American life was fraught with as much peril as promise. For the freedom that came with independence could be easily lost through negligence, and without proper cultivation it might not be realized at all.[46]

In this exhilarating yet disorienting environment, religious, medical, and lay educators and reformers took it as their self-appointed role to provide moral guidance. Believing that the fate of the democratic experiment hinged on the "virtue and intelligence" of its citizenry, they drew upon Common Sense in their prescriptions for the proper development and discipline of the mind. The most systematic self-help theorists were the academic moralists who occupied chairs in mental and moral philosophy at the Protestant denominational colleges that educated clerics, physicians, lawyers, and businessmen.[47] Displaying a clear debt to Reid's philosophical system, they articulated a "science of duty" based on a broad consensus about the "facts of human consciousness." The preeminence of moral philosophy was conveyed by its position as the capstone of the college curriculum, a course taught by the college president with the aim of providing "education, inspiration, and exhortation" and developing "the analytical mind," "the committed intellect, the pious heart, and the dedicated will."[48]

The manner in which these students were trained to think about themselves can be reconstructed from one of the earliest and most influential set of textbooks on mental philosophy, which were produced by Thomas Cogswell Upham, professor of mental and moral philosophy at Bowdoin College.[49] Seeking to present a "just and impartial," though "eclectic," account of the subject, Upham declared that he would search out "the truth wherever it may be found," but he deliberately excluded debatable points and differences of opinion, which he feared would only perplex his young readers until they became "distrustful of everything."Upham's textbooks were relatively faithful restatements of the key tenets of Common Sense philosophy. Although he presented his "threefold division of the mind" as a significant intellectual advance beyond the works of Locke, Edwards, Stewart, and Reid, the separate treatment he accorded to the will was more remarkable for its length than its originality. The differences were mostly matters of emphasis, as he seemed more concerned with distinguishing the common sense notion of self-determination from the "entire contingency" of the will.[50]

Yet in insisting that the will had its own law, Upham heightened without resolving the fundamental tension between liberty and law in the conception of human nature as free and yet governed by rational principles. He asserted that "perfect freedom in the will" resulted from "perfect harmony in other parts of the mind," which entailed the subordination of the passions and appetites to the higher faculties of reason and moral sense. Those who fell short of this ideal were less than fully free, for "every diminution of harmony will be attended with a corresponding diminution of liberty." In illustrating the truth of this proposition, he enumerated myriad forms of mental "disorder and alienation" that were "abundantly confirmed by painful experience and observation," including but not limited to those that were commonly known as "insanity or madness" and thought to "infringe upon moral accountability." Collected and published as *Outlines of Imperfect and Disordered Mental Action* under the auspices of Harper's Family Library series in 1840, the fruits of Upham's investigations were offered to a popular audience so that they might come to understand "the facts and causes" of mental derangement and "the principles on which a restoration may be possible!"[51]

In pursuing this line of inquiry, Upham was something of an innovator. Unlike most mental and moral philosophers of his time, who summoned up idiots and madmen mainly as exceptions proving the rule of rationality, he conceived of insanity as encompassing any and all deviations from mental soundness, most of which were rooted in or connected with some sort of physical disorder. He described "the Philosophy of Insanity" as running "parallel with that of Sanity," the two occupying "the same wide field" and being "mutually correspondent in their subordinate divisions." Working from "the Statistics of Insanity" supplied by a pioneering cadre of medical writers, who had shown that the moral as well as the intellectual faculties of the mind were prone to derangement, he sought "to impress order and philosophic symmetry" upon this "mass of valuable but chaotic materials" so as to clarify "the relations they sustain to the immutable principles of Mental Philosophy." He aimed to enable the public to guard against or at least "rightly estimate" this dreaded affliction, which was now so common that "no individual, whatever may be his present soundness of mind, is at liberty to consider himself as permanently exempt." While this statement underscored a common vulnerability, it also suggested that insanity was subject to human control, that it might be prevented or treated by means of proper mental cultivation and self-discipline. But that begged the question of whether an individual was as much to blame for falling ill as he was for succumbing to sin.[52]

Upham attempted to address this conundrum by distinguishing "natural" from "voluntary" mental defects, classing the former as misfortunes for which an individual could not be held morally accountable and the latter as abuses of liberty that were truly sinful. But to provide this definition was not to say how the one was to be distinguished from the other. Perhaps perceiving this problem but not knowing how to solve it, he applied the Common Sense dictate that responsibility should extend no further than power rather more stringently than did Reid, particularly if a man had allowed his unruly propensities to harden into unalterably vicious habits and thus brought the resulting "enthrallment of the will" upon himself. "If we permit the undue and unholy exercise of any appetite or passion, we are indeed ENSLAVED," Upham observed, "but we are not, therefore, removed beyond the reach of accountability and guilt; but, on the contrary, are both accountable and highly criminal, *so long as there remain in our minds, either in the Will or anywhere else, any powers of right judgment and resistance.*"[53]

This ethic of responsibility was propounded even more bluntly in the textbooks devoted to moral science, which were designed to instruct readers in how to live a virtuous life. Francis Wayland's *The Elements of Moral Science*, published in 1835 when he was professor of moral philosophy and president of Brown University, was the best-selling and most influential. The book was suffused by a sense of urgency, reminding readers of the probationary nature of human existence and the cosmic importance of the habits they were daily forming; their lives from moment to moment presented them with "the apparent paradox of a state of incessant moral change, in which every individual change has a *tendency* to produce a state that is unchangeable." He supplied a five-page list of "plain rules" for moral conduct, as well as a more elaborate compendium of man's duties to God, society, and self, which emphasized people's obligations as moral and social beings, the rights and duties existing between parents and children, husbands and wives, buyers and sellers, citizen and state, and man and God.[54] Much of it restated the obvious and rationalized the status quo, as Wayland studiously avoided ambiguity and points of controversy, most notably the contentious subjects of slavery and women's rights.[55] Although he was criticized for his evasions and compromises, his platitudinous approach to moral science inspired a host of imitators who appeared equally certain as to what morality entailed and equally committed to ensuring that it was everywhere observed as "the common law of the country."[56]

A burgeoning cottage industry in self-help literature promoted both individual improvement and reform movements. Lamenting the partisan politics, social divisions, and reckless speculation that ran rampant in society, authors warned against the "spirit of anarchy" that threatened to upend "our experiment of self-government." Ever more convinced that the constitutional machinery set in motion in 1789 could not contain the atomizing forces of democratization and commercialization, reformers across religious, social, and political divides recognized citizens' moral character as vital to the health of the republic. Indeed, the first half of the nineteenth century was marked by "a growing interest in the shaping of individual and collective identities, not through the kind of institutional engineering that had concerned the framers of the Constitution, but through such cultural means as manners, literature, education, and voluntary benevolence." Reformers focused almost obsessively on child rearing and exhibited a notable fixation on the figure of "the raw country youth entering the city to seek his fortune," who was "coming to symbolize the American-on-the-make." While manuals such as William Alcott's *Young Man's Guide* (1838) provided instruction on matters of mental discipline, diet, and deportment as well as the sorts of pastimes and companions to be avoided, they were not of much use if the reader's parents and teachers had not already instilled in him a fixity of moral purpose.[57]

Mothers, who were generally regarded as superior to fathers in moral purity and psychological influence, were particularly tasked with guiding the young. Catharine Beecher's best-selling *Treatise on Domestic Economy for the Use of Young Ladies at Home and at School* (1841) was built upon the universalistic premises of Common Sense, which she had previously laid out in a textbook on *The Elements of Mental and Moral Philosophy.* These works manifest a basic tension that ran through her career as an educator: she insisted that men and women were born with the same intellectual capabilities, yet she promoted gender differentiation, maintaining that female selflessness and subordination to male authority were "heaven-appointed" measures that shielded women from the corruption to which men were liable. Without them, the morality on which democratic order was based would collapse.[58]

But one woman's domestic economy was another's domestic slavery, as advocates for women's rights such as Sarah Grimké and Margaret Fuller made abundantly clear. They were equally well schooled in Common Sense philosophy, which demonstrates that the rights and responsibilities to be drawn from this shared conception of human nature were eminently contestable. The model of self-improvement put forward by textbooks on mental and moral philosophy inspired critiques as well as defenses of middle-class norms and the sharp divisions they implied between femininity and masculinity, household and market, private and public. As historians have long recognized, the very notion of self-improvement was multivalent, comprehending the behavioral ideals of self-culture and self-expression as well as self-control and self-denial. These ideals were freighted with varying significance as they were directed toward and interpreted by differing segments of the population.[59]

Indeed, the discourse about character formation encouraged thoroughgoing reconsideration of traditional distinctions based not only upon gender but also upon class, race, ethnicity, and age and the social structures and practices that had been grounded on them. While drawing on a common discourse and voicing a shared commitment to equality of opportunity, participants in this wide-ranging and increasingly anxious conversation about the relationship between material and moral progress split into factions along multiple lines of fission. In partisan politics, those in the Federalist-Whig camp promoted a more activist state than did the Jeffersonian-Jacksonians. In the course of this debate, the democratizing potential of this vocabulary of the self was repeatedly tested, as the disputants could not agree on who was capable of improvement and how it might be accomplished. The authority that moral philosophers conferred upon individual conscience with the aim of promoting social cohesion proved ever more difficult to contain, paradoxically inspiring radical acts of nonconformity ranging from the civil disobedience of Henry David Thoreau to the cataclysmic violence of John Brown. The philosophers' belief in the self-evidence of a transcendent moral law was severely tried in the literature of the American Renaissance, which disturbingly mirrored the moral conflict that culminated in civil war.[60]

All the while, dissenting philosophers voiced an abiding skepticism. The utilitarian lawyer-polemicist Richard Hildreth provided an especially trenchant takedown of Common Sense moralism in his 1844 *Theory of Morals*:

> So long and so far as there is a perfect coincidence between what is called the reason, conscience, moral sense, or moral sentiment of all men, like that which exists in the perception of forms, colors, and sounds, this theory answers sufficiently well. But it is precisely because there are great differences among men upon questions of morals, that the nature or law of moral distinctions becomes an object of such anxious inquiry. What we want is, some test by which to distinguish, in cases of dispute, what is Right, and what is Wrong. But so long as each man appeals to his own particular reason, his own particular conscience, his own particular moral sentiment, as the ultimate and infallible tribunal, just as he appeals to his eye in matters of color . . . no such test does, or can exist. All consciences do not agree, like all ears and all eyes.[61]

Such doubts hardly diminished the ardor of moralizing improvers; most held fast to the belief that men and women could be made to see rightly if they adhered to the prescriptions of Common Sense. But mounting evidence to the contrary challenged even the most confident among them. By positing a human nature born free and good and pointing to sources of deviance outside of the conscious self, such as adverse social circumstances, faulty education, bodily diseases, and constitutional defects, they introduced "a disturbing ambiguity about the relativity of sin and the degree of individual responsibility."[62] Who was to decide when all consciences did not agree? To the extent that immorality and crime were understood as psychological, physiological, and social problems, were all individuals equally responsible for their actions? Rather than confronting these questions directly, academic moralists and social reformers tended to treat most forms of mental disorder as products of the sinful neglect of education and self-culture, but their use of organic, animalistic, and mechanical imagery to illustrate what happened to untended minds obscured the nature and extent of individual agency in the degenerative process. While they recognized that bad habits could harden into uncontrollable propensities and reduce the individual to a condition of "mental slavery," such "voluntary" disabilities were distinguishable from the "natural" deprivations of the idiot and the madman. There might well be borderline cases in which it would be difficult to judge whether and to what extent an individual was culpable for his condition, but still, sin was supposed to be one thing and disease another. The insane were to be regarded as "memorials of human weakness" and "useful commentaries on the pride of the intellect."[63]

The Common Sense philosophers who emphasized the justice and benevolence of their Maker rendered the perversities of human nature more unaccountable than they had been before. In affirming that the divine "law of rectitude" was "inscribed on every heart," they made the source of moral knowledge and obligation essentially subjective and incapable of direct proof. The problems of human judgment were compounded by the fact that the moral sense required cultivation, which meant that no one could be completely sure that their perceptions of what was just and true were entirely reliable. Moreover, it was not at all clear that a criminal was any more to blame for his wrongdoing than were his neglectful parents, social environment, or physical constitution. Indeed, in so closely identifying freedom with rationality and morality and casting the defiance of common sense as the liberty of a madman, the Common Sense philosophy came uncomfortably close to equating sin with irresponsible error.[64]

This logic led to the paradoxical conclusion that the only fully responsible agents were those who never deviated from the laws of God and man. Moralists such as Upham took a significant step in this direction by recognizing that there was such a thing as *moral* derangement, a notion that was implicit in the way Reid had conceived of madness and responsibility. To think of mental disorder in this way was to conjure up unsettling notions of materialism, which threatened to eliminate the metaphysical basis for holding individuals accountable for their actions.

This prospect proved especially troubling to American jurists who were steeped in the Common Sense philosophy and yet daily forced to reckon with the fact that depravity was not easily distinguished from disease within this Enlightenment worldview.

Toward an American Law of Persons

The image of the human subject projected by lawyers, judges, and jurists in the early republic bore the unmistakable imprint of the culture they inhabited. The expansive view of human agency that was the hallmark of postrevolutionary American thought brought a new conception of the basis of individual accountability. Liberal Protestantism explicitly premised responsibility upon "moral ability," specifically the human power of self-determination. Within American legal culture, questions of capacity and liability were increasingly thought to turn on states of mind rather than on status distinctions regarded as remnants of "feudal" social order. This "enlightened" revision of the determinants of legal personhood was set out most explicitly in elementary law books designed for students, though its shaping effects can also be discerned in the treatises devoted to elaborating a distinctly American jurisprudence. The works were aimed at building an indigenous legal tradition on the universalistic premises of Enlightenment mental and moral philosophy.

One of the earliest and most learned contributors to this endeavor was James Wilson.[65] In his *Law Lectures*, posthumously published in 1804 he elaborated the distinctive features of American jurisprudence, associating the laws and government of the United States with the venerable common law tradition, which he deemed to be based in consent, while correcting the errors of the English commentators, particularly Blackstone. By Wilson's lights, the "learned Author of the Commentaries" had wrongly supposed that human laws implied the existence of a superior and inferiors and failed to trace the source of sovereignty back to its ultimate origin in the "free and independent man." This figure stood at the center of Wilson's educational enterprise. In characterizing the legal subject, he favored the "enlightened and candid Dr. Reid" over "Mr. Locke," warning that the "artful use of 'ideas' in metaphysicks" was no less "destructive of liberty" than the "artful use of 'superiority' in politicks."[66]

Common Sense provided the rationale for Wilson's approach to legal education as well as the content of many of his lectures. His inaugural address emphasized law students' duty to qualify themselves "to be great and good citizens" by means of "proper culture" and diligent pursuit of the first principles of law. He also acknowledged on that occasion that the success of his enterprise hinged upon "the female part of my audience," as early education was the province of the fairer sex. His course was designed to convey "just conceptions of man in two most important characters, as an author, and as a subject of law; as accountable for his own conduct, [and] as capable of directing the conduct both of himself and of others." Comprehending the study of the law as an Enlightenment project, he pointed toward its ultimate aim: "The laws, which God has given to us, are strictly agreeable to our nature; they are adjusted with infallible correctness to our perfection and happiness. On those, which we make for ourselves, the same characters, as deeply and as permanently as possible, ought to be impressed. But how, unless we study and know our nature, shall we make laws fit for it, and calculated to improve it?"[67]

Wilson's lectures "on the law of nature," as well as those considering "man as an individual" and "man as a member of a society," emphasized that human beings are born free and equal and bound together by sympathies and affections more sacred and durable than mere selfishness. These lectures drew heavily on Reid's mental philosophy, often word for word though without explicit attribution. Wilson was more inclined to speak of "Nature" than God or Scripture, but he was as sure as Reid that the universe was governed by an "all-gracious Creator, Preserver, and Ruler," whose "wisdom and skill" were most impressively displayed in the architecture of the human mind. Proceeding in accordance with the philosopher's intuitive realism, Wilson grounded his analysis on the first principles of common sense, confident that the faculties of the mind were trustworthy instruments and that man did not reside in an "enchanted castle, imposed upon by spectres and apparitions." He pursued the same line of attack against "the sceptical system," submitting that it was surely not Nature's "pastime . . . to put such tricks upon a silly creature and then take off the mask, and show him how he has been befooled." Here he invoked Reid's authority directly, adding that skepticism is as destructive in law and politics as in theology. Moreover, he underscored the absurdity of such theories when applied in a legal context.[68]

Wilson's model of the mind of a moral agent essentially reproduced the Common Sense philosophers' hierarchy of intellectual and active powers, confirming that human beings were endowed with the ability to gain accurate knowledge of the external world and coexist harmoniously. In line with Reid, he insisted that reason was not "the sole directress of human conduct" and placed the moral sense in a commanding position; while reason conveyed "knowledge of truth and falsehood" and could speak to what was prudent, it was conscience that enabled us to perceive what was "just and unjust, proper and improper, right and wrong." Without this moral faculty, "we should appear a fabrick destitute of order: but possessed of it, all our powers may be harmonious and consistent." The possession of this faculty was required to render us "moral and accountable beings," a designation that Wilson appeared willing to extend to "any of the human species above the condition of an idiot."[69]

Aside from this passing reference, Wilson had little to say about mental disorder, tending to view differences in intellectual and moral ability as positive rather than problematic aspects of the human condition. He integrated inequality into his vision of democracy by echoing an idea that had been expressed by John Winthrop in 1630. "When we say, that all men are equal," Wilson explained, "we mean not to apply this equality to their virtues, their talents, their dispositions, or their acquirements. In all these respects, there is, and it is fit for the great purposes of society that there should be, great inequality among men." This diversity tended to produce "social happiness," for it encouraged "the friendly intercourse of good offices" that "could not be enjoyed, unless men were so framed and so disposed, as mutually to afford and to stand in need of service and assistance." It also induced "different persons to choose different professions and employments in life," which rendered them "mutually beneficial to each other" and limited "violent oppositions of interest in the same pursuit." The only sense in which all men were equal was in their rights and obligations under "the laws of God and nature." "The weak and artless" were as entitled to "their small acquisitions" as "the strong and artful" to their "great possessions." These laws also imposed limits on "the wisest and the most powerful," restraining them from "inflicting misery on the meanest and most ignorant." It was to secure the just acquisitions of individuals and the collective benefits of social life that the constitutional government of the United States had been instituted, marking in Wilson's estimation a notable landmark in the advance of "the principles and the practice of liberty."[70]

The aim of bringing the science of man and the common law into greater alignment was advanced by the rising generation of American lawyers who formed Wilson's primary audience, though the results were decidedly mixed. Many clung tenaciously to the certainty and universality of Enlightenment thought as they sought to establish their cultural authority as the expounders and custodians of republican liberty who could stave off the twin bogeymen of "despotism and anarchy."[71] Emphasizing the importance of self-culture in a flood of treatises, tracts, and lyceum addresses about the nature of their profession, elite members of the bench and bar made common cause with academic moralists.[72] They regarded mental and moral philosophy as part and parcel of the liberal learning that legal educators should seek to impart, treating it not only as foundational knowledge but also as an indispensable means of mental discipline and moral inoculation that would enable new practitioners to steer clear of such occupational hazards as excessive technicality, selfish acquisitiveness, and overzealous advocacy of the cause of any particular client. Indeed, some asserted that law was the highest moral science. Inaugural law lectures often began by repeating the famed instructions of Lord Bolingbroke: "Students of the law must pry into the secret recesses of the human heart, and become well acquainted with the whole moral world, that he may discover the abstract reason of all laws."[73]

The extent to which these admonitions were translated into action is questionable, not least because university legal education did not become the dominant mode of training lawyers until the last quarter of the nineteenth century. Nonetheless, the study of philosophy figured importantly in the formative years of many members of the bench and bar, both because the moralists' texts were central to the curricula of the seminaries and colleges most had attended and because the works of Common Sense philosophers and law lectures based on them were frequently included in courses of study designed for students who "read law" with an established practitioner rather than attending law school.[74]

Members of the legal profession, like other educated Americans, found room for substantial disagreement within the framework supplied by the Common Sense philosophers, particularly with respect to the role of the government in the process of character formation. While the higher echelons of the profession tended to lean in the Federalist-Whig direction, emphasizing the educative power of the law, a vocal minority aligned with Jeffersonian-Jacksonian forces regarded such exercises of state power as invasions of individual liberty. But this was ultimately more a matter of emphasis within a broader consensus about the importance of mental culture and self-discipline. Each faction "put primary emphasis on one half of the idea of self-improvement": the Jeffersonian-Jacksonians emphasized self, while the Federalist-Whigs emphasized improvement. Ultimately, those on both sides agreed that the essence of freedom lay in the capacity for self-government, which was now understood as a state of mind which might be proved or disproved in court.[75]

The Default Legal Subject

The influence of this liberal Enlightenment view of the self is apparent in legal literature, through which it is possible to trace the gradual replacement of the traditional common law of persons with a generic model of the legal subject whose civil capacity and criminal responsibility rested upon his possession of a certain set of mental attributes. The most elaborate discussions of this model were presented in treatises and tracts that addressed the subject of jurisprudence. These works typically began with consideration of man "as a single individual," offering a detailed examination of his "physical, moral and intellectual constitution." Most were resolutely dualistic, portraying man as "a being composed of a *growing, vital,* and *sentient* substance, denominated body, and of a subtile or immaterial *something,* called soul" or "mind." Following the introspective method of the Common Sense philosophers, they identified four key attributes of the presumptive subject of the law, which I have termed the default legal person. First, he was said to have the capacity for self-knowledge and knowledge of others. His second attribute was the power of self-determination, enabling him to control and direct his thoughts, feelings, and actions, effectively forming his own character. In other words, he had the power to *choose* the motives that would determine his behavior. Third, he was possessed of and actuated by an innate moral sense, which allowed him to distinguish right from wrong and, at the very least, to regret his own wrongdoing. Finally, the faculties of his mind were thought to be organized in a hierarchical order, with the rational powers reigning over the animal and mechanical ones. In the healthy human mind, as they defined it, the intellect provided motives to the will, encouraging action in conformity with the moral sense.[76]

In outlining this model, American jurists did not deny the existence of individual differences in physical and mental capacities or the possibility of disease, but they tended to minimize their significance and strained to show that they did not compromise the "unity of the moral law." The prominent jurist and legal educator David Hoffman was especially thorough in his treatment of the subject, going on at considerable length about "the origins and nature of man" in his *Legal Outlines* (1829). Hoffman asserted that man was a single "unit in the creation," forming "a class by himself, in which, though there are varieties, there are neither different orders nor genera, nor species." As far as he could see, the variations within the "human family" appeared to be merely physical, owing to hereditary and environmental factors, and there was no reason to believe that they implied any fundamental differences in "moral constitution." Therefore, Hoffman concluded, "we cannot but regard all minds as essentially the same," from which it followed that all men were rightly regarded as "moral and responsible beings" equally subject to divine and human laws. "God may have given to one man a greater talent than to another," but it was *every* man's preeminent duty to "cultivate with assiduity all the functions of his mind, and to preserve in health and vigour all the powers of the body, since it is by their united action that man becomes useful in every condition of life."[77] Like most jurists, Hoffman tended to emphasize the inalienability of the moral sense in order to insulate the bar against the threat of moral relativism.

The default legal person stood as the embodiment of widely shared assumptions about human agency and accountability, constituting a part of the common sense of the American legal profession in the nineteenth century. This figure often hovered in the background of legal discourse after being introduced and anatomized in elementary law lectures and treatises. Moreover, this legal model never entirely displaced the traditional English law of persons. American jurists continued to speak in terms of status relations, though many attempted to rationalize them on new grounds and suggested their retention was compatible with the founding principles of the republic.

The most prominent illustration of this point is Timothy Walker's *Introduction to American Law*, first published in 1837, which earned him accolades as "the American Blackstone." His discussion of the law of persons began by calling readers' attention to "the fundamental difference there is between personal relations in this country and in England, in consequence of our entire abolition of privileged orders." A simpler scheme prevailed in the United States: "With us, in theory at least, all men start equally; they are born with equal rights; and their distinctions in after-life, are mainly made by themselves." Thus, it was possible to describe the primary divisions of persons "in half the space" required in Blackstone's *Commentaries*. Walker illustrated his point by reducing the matter to a single paragraph:

> 1. Persons are either natural or artificial. 2. They are either public or private. 3. They are either citizens or aliens. 4. They are either males or females. 5. They are either infants or adults. 6. They are either sane or insane. 7. They are either freemen or slaves, masters or servants, principals or agents. 8. Indians sustain relations different from any other persons. 9. The death of persons creates the relations of ancestors and heirs, devisors and devisees, and executors or administrators.[78]

Seeking to bring theory and practice closer together, Walker's treatise, ardently but with some perplexity, pointed toward reforms, particularly those concerning married women and slaves. While the denial of political rights to women was rooted in an inveterate custom and "the most refined and enlightened" among them "would be the last to desire a change, which would involve them in the turmoil of politics," the law on the books governing the marital relation degraded wives—at least in theory—"almost to the level of slaves." He insisted that there was "no foundation in reason or expediency, for the absolute and slavish subjection of the wife to the husband"; were she "the abject thing the law in theory considers her to be when married," he submitted, "she would not be worthy of the companionship of man." When women organized to seek equal rights, however, Walker demurred. By mid-century, he had become convinced that the "reform spirit of the day" was animated by a dangerously distorted understanding of the constitutional principles of liberty and equality, typified by Amazonian women's rights advocates who were no longer satisfied with the influence they wielded at home and now organizing conventions to secure political rights so that they could be "voters, legislators, governors, judges, and, for aught I know, generals and commodores." He urged audiences North and South to be wary of demagogues who propounded leveling principles and projected illusory visions of a future earthly state where "the human condition could be perfectly equalized, so that there should be no high or low, no rich or poor, no master or servant."[79]

Walker's apprehension about the contradiction posed by slavery was still greater than his concern about the subjection of women, and his sense of dread about its possible consequences were even more pronounced. In 1837, he expressed deep distress regarding the condition of the slaves in the southern states who suffered a complete deprivation of their natural right of liberty, which could be "justified upon no principle but that of uncontrollable necessity." Presented with a "choice of evils," the framers had reluctantly and ambiguously written slavery into the Constitution, a compromising compact "without which the Union could not have been formed, and cannot now be preserved." All but ruling out the hopeful notion that slavery would gradually wither away with the advance of American civilization, Walker acknowledged that "its extinction baffles all calculation," anxiously observing that "shadows, clouds and darkness rest upon the prospect." Whether the nation could withstand the intensifying strife between slaveholders and their foes, "which threatens to be carried on with increasing violence," he deemed a "fearful question, which only time can answer."[80]

Similar distinctions between the independent men who constituted the citizens of the republic and the women and slaves who were marginalized or excluded from the privileges of equality were drawn by other American jurists, more or less apologetically, depending upon the extent to which they perceived these status relations as contradicting republican principles. But one common law division remained unquestioned: the distinction between the sane and the insane. American jurists seemed to regard mental soundness as a perfectly legitimate means of discriminating between theoretically equal individuals for all sorts of legal purposes.[81]

So unexceptionable was this division that it received relatively little attention in discussions "of persons" in the treatises published in the first half of the nineteenth century. To the extent that the matter was considered in any detail, jurists tended to recite long-standing definitions and rules drawn from such old English authorities as Edward Coke, Matthew Hale, and Blackstone, most of whom reserved the designation of insanity for those suffering from "a total deprivation of reason." There was something of a gap between the jurists' positive renderings of the accountable agent and their negative characterizations of what it was to be of unsound mind, but they did not take much notice of this problem in their formal writings. Although this might be read as mere inadvertence on the jurists' part, it is perhaps better understood as an expression of their faith in the liberal Enlightenment vision of human ability. They shared the Common Sense philosophers' belief in the innate capacity of most, if not all, human beings to master their passions and act in accordance with higher dictates of reason. Though individual efforts to realize this ideal might be frustrated by defects in education and environment, such unfortunate circumstances would not, as a rule, be accepted as excusing conditions as a matter of law. Indeed, the Federalist-Whig-leaning jurists tended to view the law as a socializing agent in its own right, expecting that the imposition of liability would play a character-building function and teach wayward individuals how to become responsible subjects.[82]

As they stood amidst the remains of the English law of persons, American jurists constructed a scheme in which mental ability rather than social status constituted the primary determinant of legal capacity and responsibility. Yet, as the imposition of liability was now more squarely premised upon the intellectual and moral powers of humankind, an increasing degree of scrutiny was trained upon individuals whose capacity for self-government seemed deficient. The default legal person embodied many of the ambiguities and tensions latent in the Common Sense philosophy. The philosophers' arsenal of explanations for departures from the law's norms—citing failures in mental cultivation and self-discipline or pointing to corrupting influences in the surrounding environment—seemed worryingly insufficient, especially in extreme cases. What were judges and lawyers to make of the individual with a proper religious and moral upbringing who committed murder without any apparent motive, or could not be reasoned out of believing "I am the Christ"? Were their thoughts and actions to be regarded as instances of self-determination, however eccentric, perverse, or deluded, or as signs of disease that rendered them unaccountable under the law?

Answers to these questions were eagerly supplied by the new profession of medical men who claimed expertise in the diagnosis and treatment of mental alienation and suggested that the common law rules of capacity and responsibility expected rather too much of human nature. Their critiques formed a new field of study: the "medical jurisprudence of insanity." It remained to be seen whether the default legal person was capable of withstanding the critical scrutiny of the alienist's gaze.

CHAPTER 2

The Medical Jurisprudence of Insanity

> The analogy of disease and evil you see is very *striking.*
>
> Benjamin Rush

SPEAKING BEFORE HIS MEDICAL STUDENTS in 1810, the Philadelphia physician Benjamin Rush recounted a recent call he had made, in consultation with a Dr. Physick,[1] on "a lady in this city, equally admired for her amiable virtues and elegant accomplishments." Appearances proved deceiving, however, as she related her medical complaint. "I am blessed with one of the best of husbands, and a family of promising children, whom I love most affectionately," she began, "and yet, in the paroxysms of my disease, and with the perfect exercise of my reason, I wish for an ax, that I might split open their heads, and lay them all dead at my feet." Upon hearing this terrible confession, Rush was convinced he was faced with a case of "moral derangement," "that state of mind in which the passions act involuntarily through the instrumentality of the will," which he linked to an underlying physical disorder. Since this form of insanity commonly revealed itself in "acts of barbarity and bloodshed," often with some consciousness of their wrongfulness, it was easily—and tragically—mistaken for ordinary depravity in courts of law. Were his patient ever to succumb to her morbid impulses, nothing would save her "from expiating her disease by an ignominious death." The injustice inherent in holding people who were ill responsible for their own condition extended to civil matters as well. The "morally deranged" were left free to make wholly unnatural dispositions of their estates, to the great injury of their unoffending families. In light of this troubling state of affairs, he told his students that it was a physician's civic obligation to extend the benefits of his science "to the protection of property and life" through the cultivation of a distinctly "medical jurisprudence."[2]

Rush published *Medical Inquiries and Observations upon the Diseases of the Mind* in 1812, the first such study produced by an American physician. Written to educate the public as well as aspiring medical and legal professionals, the treatise provided a systematic analysis of the "cause, forms, and symptoms" of mental disorders, by means of which the author sought "to rescue persons affected with them from the arm of the law, and to render them subjects of the kind and lenient hand of medicine." The work provided a concrete demonstration of the utility of "the science of the mind" in a manner that was clearly intended to privilege the expert authority of physicians over and above that of philosophers. Expansively defining "the empire of a physician" to encompass the mental and moral welfare of the nation, he identified his work with the cause of Christian republicanism. Although Rush's vision of social medicine proved controversial, his *Diseases of the Mind* enjoyed wide circulation and encouraged lawyers as well as other doctors to build upon this foundation. This chapter examines medico-legal tracts and treatises addressing the central problem Rush identified: the attribution of responsibility to those whose minds are deranged.[3]

Historians have tended to portray the medical and legal participants in this discussion as engaged in a debate that could never be resolved because of their fundamentally incompatible ways of conceptualizing the human subject. As the story is conventionally told, nineteenth-century lawyers remained beholden to traditional notions of free will and individual responsibility, while their colleagues in medicine subscribed to a deterministic discourse that explained human behavior in physiological terms and left little space for moral agency.[4] In casting doctors and lawyers in two warring camps, historians have captured important tensions in their interprofessional dialogue, but this approach has tended to obscure their common philosophical concerns and religious commitments. In addition, it has left us with the false impression that American jurists were only superficially influenced by medical writers and tended to discount or dismiss their opinions. A closer examination of the jurisprudence of insanity as it had coalesced by the mid-nineteenth century reveals a far more complex process of interaction among doctors, lawyers, and the public. The default legal person did not emerge unscathed from these spirited exchanges, and it was largely in response to physicians' pointed critiques that members of the bench and bar were forced to rethink the conceptions of responsible agency they deployed in everyday adjudication.

This chapter begins with Enlightenment mental science, which forged new understandings of madness that were less supernatural in orientation and more concerned with the natural causes of disease. It then examines the moral and legal implications of this scientific framework by exploring various attempts of medical men to address the attributive dilemma left unresolved by the Common Sense philosophers: the question of whether and when mental disorders were to be recognized as excusing individuals from responsibility for their actions. The analysis focuses on a group of American physicians who specialized in the diagnosis and treatment of "mental alienation." These self-styled alienists served as superintendents of the growing number of insane asylums that were built on the outskirts of booming cities or in the countryside far beyond them, standing as indicators of both the ill effects of unbounded liberty and an abiding faith in the human capacity for self-renovation.[5] Working from Enlightenment premises, these physicians tended to conceive of mental disease in far broader terms than doctors in previous centuries. Deviant behavior that had traditionally been attributed to the innate and universal depravity of humankind was reinterpreted as the result of mental illness. The alienists worried that the conditions of life in the new republic were especially conducive to the incidence of insanity, suggesting that there was a direct correlation between the freedoms enjoyed by their countrymen and the maladies they suffered if they overindulged in them. Aiming to redress this public-health problem and enhance their own professional stature, they publicized their findings in works of medical jurisprudence, which were unabashedly intended to advertise the curative effects of their scientific approach and to promote legal reform. First, they called for the modernization of the traditional legal category of *non compos mentis*, urging judges to recognize the existence of a host of partial forms of insanity called "monomanias," including nonintellectual disorders of the moral sense, will, and emotions, loosely referred to as "moral insanity." Second, they exposed lamentable inconsistencies between the civil and criminal rules of responsibility, regarding it as especially problematic that an individual might be declared a lunatic and deprived of his property in one proceeding, only to be found criminally liable and punished in another.

The chapter then considers legal responses to medical jurisprudence, concentrating on American jurists who sought to incorporate the alienists' clinical findings into the common law of insanity. Although many legal writers expressed frustration and ambivalence as they undertook this task, they were not primarily engaged in fending off the incursions of medical science. The concept of moral insanity may have seemed overly materialistic, and its signs were difficult to distinguish from mere criminality. But jurists found other ways to make allowances for those who had lost command of their will. Many made "insane delusion" a ground for excuse from criminal and civil liability, recognizing that the will or moral sense might be completely overwhelmed by uncontrollable thoughts. Some proposed schemes of graduated responsibility, contemplating the involvement of court-appointed medical experts in order to take greater account of the "myriad phases of mental unsoundness." The advocates of these reforms aimed to calibrate punishment to reflect each defendant's "distinct degree of moral culpability" for his unlawful acts. Their proposals met with objections from lawyers who remained committed to an adversarial model of justice and skeptical of the "mad-doctors'" claims of expertise. Moreover, it was not at all obvious how or whether the reformers' conception of diminished capacity could be applied on the civil side of the docket, particularly in cases involving disputed wills, deeds, and contracts.

What was clear as medical jurisprudence came into its own as a field of knowledge was that the default legal person was eminently contestable. The new medical psychology pushed jurists to rethink the determinants of legal capacity and reconsider how courts were to ascertain whether an individual measured up to this standard. In the process, they confronted more fundamental questions about what human judges could know about other minds, which prompted them to ponder anew the grounds of human responsibility. Meanwhile, litigants and their lawyers crowded through the door medico-legal writers had opened, making the most of the unruly jurisprudence of insanity. Their elaborate treatises scripted and almost invited capacity contests that grew ever more unwieldy and embarrassing to those who sat in judgment.

The Madness of Mankind

Among the sermons Benjamin Rush heard as a child, he was especially impressed by one delivered in 1754 by his maternal uncle, the evangelical Presbyterian minister Samuel Finley, on "The Madness of Mankind." Taking a passage from Ecclesiastes—"And Madness is in their Heart while they live, and after that they go to the Dead"—as his text, Finley compared "this World to a great Bedlam, filled with Persons strangely and variously distracted," heedlessly and perilously disregarding "divine Revelation, and the Reason of Things." These words returned to Rush's mind in the last years of his life, as he ruefully contemplated a still-unfinished revolution in letters to John Adams. Lamenting the "unchristian spirit" animating party politics, Rush confessed that he felt a kinship with the poet and inmate of England's Bedlam Hospital, Nathaniel Lee, who had thought "the world was mad, but . . . the world had said the same thing of him, and . . . he had been *outvoted.*" With an air of resignation, Rush lamented to Adams that "we shall I fear always be *outvoted* by the fools and knaves and madmen of our country."[6]

While the madness Finley found in the hearts of men was a symbol and manifestation of the terrible consequences of sin, Rush brought new meaning to the word over the course of his long and storied career as a patriot physician. After losing his father at an early age, he had been raised in the evangelical Presbyterian faith of his mother, Susanna, and spent his formative years under the tutelage of revivalist preachers. These experiences infused Rush with a warm piety, public spiritedness, and millennial hope that animated his later endeavors. Yet the very intensity of his religious upbringing led him to doubt his spiritual capacity for the ministry. He had initially ruled out medicine, owing to "an uncommon aversion from seeing such sights as are connected with its practice," and decided upon the law, expecting that his literary and oratorical talents well fit him to practice this "babblative art." But Finley persuaded his nephew to choose "physic" over law, which was "full of temptations." After an apprenticeship in Philadelphia, he studied medicine in Edinburgh, London, and Paris, where he was exposed to various strains of Enlightenment thought, introduced to leading Whigs and *philosophes,* steeped in republicanism, and schooled in the new medical psychology.[7]

Rush's career path traces out a broader set of intellectual and cultural transformations, for he came of age at a time marked by profound reconsideration of the relationships among mind, body, and behavior and the proper roles of clerics, lawyers, and doctors in treating mental illness. In colonial America, medical historian Mary Ann Jimenez has shown, "religious, biological, and moral explanations were woven into a unified model of madness in which God, devil, and human actors all played various roles." Although this affliction was generally understood as a manifestation of sin, colonists drew on an expanding body of philosophical and medical knowledge concerning the causes and cures of "Trouble of mind." The identification of the biological sources of mental disturbances did little to clarify the moral implications to be drawn from individual cases: what one cleric regarded as a "Diabolical possession" invited by the sinner, another might see as a divinely induced madness designed to test the faith of the saint or call the community of believers to repentance. Over the course of the eighteenth century, demonic forces receded in the face of the Enlightenment's confidence that madness could be managed if not eradicated by scientific means.[8]

The anatomists of abnormality were medical men well-versed in the philosophical systems of the previous century, particularly those of

Bacon, Descartes, and Locke. The first generation of British doctors who addressed mental illness offered "a secularized alternative to the religious discipline of the mind," treating mental troubles as manifestations of bodily dysfunction and assigning what ministers had understood as "normal spiritual-emotional experiences to an aberrant pathological category." Although this renegotiation of the meaning of madness has long been cast in terms of secularization and medicalization, recent scholarship has underscored the complexity and ambivalence of the historical interaction among medicine, religion, and society. In this view, medical science has been mobilized both to challenge and to reinforce existing belief structures and social hierarchies. These accounts demonstrate that the responses to unreason in Enlightenment Britain were far too heterogeneous and irresolute to fit Foucault's description of a "great confinement." What emerged was not a centralized effort to police madness but rather a "trade in lunacy" that was more responsive to market forces than the dictates of the state. Moreover, the marking out of a professional domain of mental medicine, concerned with a distinctive set of maladies that lay outside the province of traditional divines and general physicians, proceeded gradually and haltingly. The emerging discipline is best seen as a reconception of the realms of the supernatural and the natural and relations between mind and body, rather than a reduction of spirit to matter. These physicians advanced visions of the relations among God, spirit, and matter designed not only to expand the empire of medicine but also to bring a measure of order and stability to British society after the civil war.[9]

The physiologies of mental disturbance elaborated by medical writers reflect an abiding concern with both avoiding any taint of atheistic materialism and containing the disruptive effects of religious enthusiasm.[10] The new medical psychology was popularized in advice books written for an upper-class and upwardly mobile clientele, effectively recasting the social geography of mental disturbance. George Cheyne's *The English Malady* (1733) exemplifies this cultural-transmission process, as he was an entrepreneurial doctor with fashionable practices in London and Bath. Intimately acquainted with the vanities and anxieties of those who thought of themselves as genteel, Cheyne elaborated a theory of nervous disease as an exclusive affliction that struck the cultured classes on account of their refined organs of thought and feeling and their sedentary and luxurious ways. Shifting the focus from what were generally understood as more serious mental pathologies, such as mania and melancholy, he concentrated on hypochondria and hysteria, which had been gendered male and female by previous generations of medical writers who located the former disorder in the spleen and the latter in the womb. By the early eighteenth century, these theories had been displaced by etiologies centered on the nervous system and the brain, leading physicians to conceive of hysteria and hypochondria as "but one and the same Disorder." It might be more common in women owing to their comparatively weaker constitutions, but in both sexes it resulted from "a surfeit of success and civilization." Cheyne dramatized the perils of excess consumption, compiling case studies that treated the nerves as sensitive communication networks linking body and mind as well as self and society. This double-edged medical discourse imagined the nerves as both means of personal integration and social cohesion and conduits of contagion threatening to infect nations as well as individuals.[11]

Edinburgh was an important center of medical psychology by the time Rush arrived there and came under the tutelage of William Cullen. Typifying the Scottish Enlightenment concern with studying man in society and uncovering the natural history of the human mind, Cullen provided a systematic account of the "vital principle" that animated the nervous system. He conceived of the brain as an active and reactive organ that determined the health of the body even as cerebral actions were themselves shaped and regulated by custom and habit. In his view, too much or too little excitement of the brain issued in mania or melancholy. His effort to comprehend the mental states that constituted disease helped to incorporate Enlightenment philosophies of the mind into medical discourses about madness. With respect to insanity, after conceding that "no one can be supposed to know it except those who are or have been in the state themselves," he proceeded from the standpoint of "a sensible man." He equated sanity with consistent thought and action in conformity with "the common sense of mankind." Indeed, Cullen came perilously close to defining insanity as a breach of propriety:

> If a man comes into a company, there are certain observances which custom has established, and his behavior is suited according to the company he comes into;—if it is a company of his usual merry companions, presently all their thoughts are of merriment, the laugh arises and the joke goes round; but if it is a company for business that he is to take a part in, he sits down seriously, speaks of the business in hand, and attends to what the other persons are engaged in; but if he were to treat the last company as he does the first, he would pass for a madman; thus too in the first company I supposed, he may speak of his amours or of his mistress; but if he finds the same men among the number of ladies of honour and virtue, and he renews his discourse there, he would be thought a madman.

Yet, as "men differ greatly from one another without any of them being reckoned delirious," distinctions were commonly drawn between error, whim, or folly and outright madness. Cullen suggested that mental health be determined by reference to an individual's "ordinary judgment, and . . . usual train of thinking"; insanity constituted a marked deviation from his habitual state of mind.[12]

In "physiologizing" the psychology of Locke and Hume and "psychologizing" the medical discourse about madness, Cullen participated in a momentous renegotiation of the relationship between philosophers and physicians as well as the normal and the abnormal. Human nature, the basis of personal responsibility, the locus of expertise and authority to treat, and the ethics of care were all subject to reconsideration. While maintaining that insanity was a physical disease, the doctors who took charge of madhouses saw their clinical work as providing evidence of the mind's active role in precipitating it. Striking case studies detailed the "individual and personal" circumstances that attended mental disorder and illustrated its protean character and devious operations. Appearing in innumerable guises, sometimes mimicking other diseases and always playing on the variability of human nature, insanity often eluded detection by even the most intimate and well-informed observers and seemed almost to mock experts' efforts to contain it within their classification schemes. Faced with such challenging patients, nerve doctors had to be as artful and versatile as the disease they aimed to cure, or so they attempted to convince each other and the broader public as they worked to solidify their economic and professional standing. Close encounters with institutionalized patients inclined them to see insanity as a matter of degree rather than a difference in kind, for remnants of reason were to be found in all but the most furious of maniacs. These medical men summoned up their day-to-day experiences among the mad in testimonials publicizing the virtues of a "moral treatment," which appealed to the patient's latent rationality and desire for esteem, as distinct from the physical restraints and cures traditionally dispensed at London's infamous Bedlam by successive generations of the Munro family.[13]

The Mind and the Body Politic

Radicalized by his exposure to Enlightenment ideas, especially "that by management the human species may be moulded into any conceivable shape," Rush returned to his native Philadelphia in 1769 a confirmed believer in the regenerative powers of medical science. Indeed, he summoned up his experiences abroad as vivid illustrations of the formative powers of social environment in the autobiography he penned in 1800. The innovative thinkers he encountered aroused skepticism toward traditional systems of thought and established authorities, providing an intellectual basis for rejecting the divine authority of kings and accepting the social compact theory of government. While Rush had already registered his opposition to the Stamp Act before he journeyed across the Atlantic, it was in Edinburgh that he was converted to "the republican principles of our ancestors," a deliberative process through which he became convinced that no form of government can be rational, but "that which is derived from the Suffrages of the people who are the subjects of it" and therefore fully committed to the revolutionary cause.[14]

When Rush was called upon to lecture at the University of Pennsylvania in 1791, he found it necessary "to try the foundations of my opinions," now suspecting "error in everything I had been taught or believed." Even as an ardent revolutionary, Rush had worried about the dangerous potentialities inhering in "the republican ferment," for the "commotions" it generated could be psychically and politically damaging if they were not properly managed by men of faith and learning. Enlightened but far from egalitarian in his vision of social order, Rush sought to establish new schemes of government that were congruent with the principles of the natural and human sciences as well as the precepts of Christianity. Reasoning by analogy across fields of knowledge, he articulated a modality of rule grounded upon scientific expertise, modeled after the practice of medicine, and intended to promote an internalization of social discipline that would "guard against our own ignorance and licentiousness" and prepare the way "for that world where justice and benevolence eternally prevail."[15]

Seeking a far more perfect union than most of his fellow founders, Rush cut a distinctive figure in the constitutional politics of the early republic. Although he had collaborated with Thomas Paine on the production of *Common Sense,* he was a vocal opponent of the radical Pennsylvania Constitution of 1776, which he saw as the institution of "mobocracy," resulting from the unbridled passions, factionalism, and self-seeking that plagued postrevolutionary politics. The principle of popular sovereignty, as he understood it, required that "all power is derived *from* the people," not that "all power is seated *in* the people." He emphasized that "the wills of the people" had to be "fitted to each other by means of education before they can be made to produce regularity and unison in government." Rush sought no less than a complete renovation of the psychological and social dimensions of American life: as he famously put it, "to convert men into republican machines" so they could "perform their parts properly in the great machine of the government of the state."[16]

With a sense of sacred mission, the patriot physician committed himself first and foremost to "disseminating the seeds of virtue and knowledge," which he believed to be the only method "of rendering a republican form of government durable." Addressing both professional and lay audiences, Rush systematically articulated the principles of physiology and psychology. He represented the "natural history" of the mind's faculties and operations as "the most *certain* of all kinds of knowledge" because it consisted "of facts only"; questions about whether the mind was material or immaterial and what became of it after death were matters of opinion that had no direct bearing on the work of the physician. His medical lectures presupposed only "that we believe that we have a mind, that it is acted upon by the body, that the body is acted upon by the mind, and that in its present connection with the body it cannot acquire a single idea, nor perform a single act, without the intervention of bodily impressions." Though indebted to the Common Sense philosophers in many respects, Rush took issue with their division between the active and passive powers of the mind; he presented them as innate capacities that all needed to be "awakened" by external physical stimuli. Just as important, he dismissed the Scottish philosophers' "common sense" as nothing more than the "feelings and opinions" of "the majority of mankind" at a given time and place.[17]

Rush also diverged from Reid in his treatment of the will, which he did not regard as self-evidently and entirely free. Recognizing that this question "has divided the philosophers and divines of all ages and countries," he suggested that the doctrines of necessity and free agency were "alike true." The convoluted train of thought that led Rush to this ambivalent opinion was fundamentally rooted in our consciousness of both volition and constraint. "While we are compelled by our reason to believe that we act from necessity, we are compelled by our feelings to believe that we act freely." Even the consciences of the wickedest men "bear a constant and universal testimony in favor of our acting freely." "Were it otherwise," he added pragmatically, "we should destroy all responsibility for immoral actions."[18]

Yet all this was true only of "the healthy state of mind," which was especially difficult to sustain in the precarious circumstances of postrevolutionary America. Indeed, man's susceptibility to diseases that could derange the faculties and operations of the mind was the theme and variation of all of Rush's teachings, which did more to confuse than clarify what distinguished illness from depravity. Consider, in this regard, the doctor's most influential pronouncement, *An Inquiry into the Influence of Physical Causes upon the Moral Faculty*, delivered before the American Philosophical Society in 1786. After calling attention to the shaping effects of such environmental factors as climate, diet, and air quality, as well as education, worship, labor, amusement, and punishment, he outlined a "physics of moral reform." Asserting that doctors had it within their power "to prevent or cure vice," he claimed an expansive province for medicine. Disorders of the mind and body were responsive to the same sorts of physical remedies that physicians were best equipped to administer, though he was careful to present them as supplementing rather than replacing "religious, moral, or rational instruction."[19]

Rush cast his inquiry as opening the way for more extensive medical exploration of the proper care and treatment of "the moral faculty," a term he borrowed from the Common Sense philosopher James Beattie. The doctor described it as "a power in the human mind of distinguishing and chusing between good and evil," which was a "native principle" "capable of improvement by experience and reflection." Seated in the will, it was personified as "a law-giver," yet it operated quickly and without reflection, while the conscience, which was situated in the understanding, performed the deliberative duties of "a judge." This constitutional scheme of checks and balances, divinely designed to prevent "the fatal consequences of immoral actions," was no longer fail-safe in humanity's fallen state, but Rush held out the prospect of moral regeneration through the instrumentalities of medical science. He suggested that "shattered and crooked" or vicious thoughts were as amenable to physical correction as broken limbs. Summoning up illustrations from Scripture, travelogues, biographies, memoirs, and imaginative literature, as well as medical texts and his own clinical experiences, Rush showed that the moral development of individuals and nations was profoundly dependent upon the quotidian routines of everyday life.[20]

Rush's moral science was thus built upon Enlightenment philosophy, bearing no small resemblance to "the medicine of mind" dispensed by Reid and his followers. Yet they tended to use such language metaphorically, anxiously avoiding any implication of materialism. Because Rush saw no necessary connection between the immateriality and the immortality of the soul, by contrast, he readily analogized the workings of mind and matter in ways that were intended to be taken literally. He introduced his listeners to the idea of moral derangement by posing a series of rhetorical questions, ingeniously arranged to lead them to the inexorable conclusion that the faculties of the intellect were shaped by physical influences. Drawing his examples from commonplace experiences and popular notions of maturation, the inheritance of talents and virtues as well as disabilities and vices, and the similarities between the delirium produced by a high fever and chronic dementia, he contended that both moral and intellectual character were attributable to physical causes. Since bodily ills accounted for the impairment of memory or judgment, he submitted, was there not as strong a basis for concluding the same was true of moral deficiencies, even when other mental faculties remained sharp?[21]

The audience was not so easily persuaded. Though the oration enjoyed wide circulation, it excited considerable criticism and a fair amount of derision. The patriot lawyer Francis Hopkinson satirized it in "Some Thoughts on the Diseases of the Mind; with a Scheme for Purging the Moral Faculties of the Good People of Pennsylvania; Quite New and Very Philosophical." The main lesson he derived from the doctor's oration was that physicians and metaphysicians were and ought to remain distinct professions, the one prescribing "corporeal physic" for bodily diseases and the other "mental remedies" for disorders of the mind. "This scheme of whipping the mind over the body's shoulders, will not, I apprehend, answer any permanent purpose," Hopkinson cautioned. He went on to pose a rhetorical question of his own: "Has government ever cured a propensity to theft by the administration of the whipping-post or wheel-barrow?"[22]

As a send-up of Rush this struck a false note, for he had fought vociferously against the public imposition of corporeal punishment, taking particular aim (as Hopkinson did) at a law inflicting humiliation as well as hard labor on convicts that was passed by the Pennsylvania legislature in 1786. Casting aside the "barbarous" disciplinary techniques of the Old World, Rush advocated a combination of physical and moral remedies that were aimed both to liberate and to constrain, to release vicious men from the thrall of bad habits and educate them to virtuous citizenship. At once democratic and hierarchical, his reform project reinforced the perceived differences in the natural aptitudes and proper social positions of men and women, as well as perpetuating racial and class distinctions. The implementation of this social vision was to be directed by scientific experts. Elite reformers would close the gap between common sense and reason as they worked to abolish slavery and capital punishment, promote temperance, and build public schools, penitentiaries, and hospitals for the insane. All these initiatives and institutions were designed to teach "the lesson of obedient freedom."[23]

What was most problematic about Rush's moral science was his evasion of the questions of agency and accountability it raised. Conceiving of the individual as a complex product of his environment, the locus of physical forces that animated but might also derange his intellectual and moral faculties, the doctor blurred conventional categories of sin, vice, and disease. Although his enlargement of the definition of mental disease to include moral as well as intellectual impairments seemed to mitigate afflicted individuals' responsibility for wrongdoing, Rush stopped short of suggesting that all criminals were innocent victims of their circumstances or that they ought to be treated like madmen. But he believed that serious misdiagnoses were woefully common in court proceedings because the principles of pathology had not been adequately incorporated into the nation's civil and criminal laws.

It was to redress this unjust state of affairs that Rush took up medical jurisprudence in the 1790s, redirecting his energies to this nascent field as he grew ever more dispirited about republican politics both at home and abroad. His comprehensive treatise, *Medical Inquiries and Observations upon the Diseases of the Mind,* published less than a year before his death in April 1813, and going through five editions by 1835, was the culmination of his career. Alarmed by what (despite the lack of data)[24] he perceived as the rising incidence of madness, Rush asserted that "this must be ascribed to an increase in the number and magnitude of objects of ambition and avarice, and to the greater joy or distress, which is produced by gratification or disappointments in the pursuit of them." Believing that "the cause of madness" was "seated in the blood vessels of the brain," his treatise was designed to promote legal reforms that would "relieve judges and jurors of the painful necessity of acting in a discretionary manner." His treatise was designed to "relieve judges and jurors from the painful necessity of acting in a discretionary manner." Yet the distinction between the responsible moral agent and the person who was diseased and therefore blameless remained sketchy at best; Rush suggested, by turns, that it was self-evident, or not for him as a physician to draw.[25]

Even as he wrote despairingly of the madness of mankind in private letters, a feeling no doubt amplified by the mental illness of his son and his own inability to cure him, Rush labored to complete *Diseases of the Mind.* Intended to make the case for placing those afflicted under "the dominion of medicine," the work comprehended moral deviations that neither the ministers nor the lawyers of his youth would have recognized as grounds for any sort of excuse from responsibility. This delineation of "the states of mind which should incapacitate a man to dispose of his property, to bear witness in a court of justice, and exempt him from punishment for commission of what are called crimes by the laws of our country" reverses the emphasis of most works of mental philosophy, concentrating upon those who had lost or never acquired the capacity for self-command. Detailing the "undescribable, even incomprehensible" torments patients endured, Rush found himself periodically overwhelmed by the task of documenting them. "How slender the tenure by which we hold our intellectual and moral existence! and how humiliating our situation from its loss!" he reflected in pained wonderment. "I should lay down my pen, and bedew my paper with tears, did I not know that the science of medicine has furnished a remedy for it." Then his tone brightened into exaltation: "Blessed science! which thus extends its friendly empire, not only over the evils of the bodies, but over those of the minds, of the children of men!"[26]

The schema that Rush devised to capture all the various ways each faculty of the mind might be deranged—partially or totally, separately or in concert with others—betrays a similar inconsistency. His arduous attempts to trace the devious course and constantly shifting forms of mental disease finally convinced him that the nomenclature he had carefully elaborated was useless. "From this view of the successive and alternate changes of the different forms of madness into each other," he derived "fresh proofs of the unity of its cause, and the necessity of renouncing all prescriptions for its names, and of constantly and closely watching the disease, in order to vary our remedies with its varying forms." Most remarkable of all was the manner in which Rush ultimately shrugged off the very question *Diseases of the Mind* had been written to address. "How far the person whose diseases have been mentioned, should be considered as responsible to human or divine laws for their actions, and where the line should be drawn that divides free agency from necessity, and vice from disease, I am unable to determine."[27]

"To Give Rules to Folly"

The emergence of psychological medicine marked the growing interest in comparing "normal" and "disordered" mental operations. American alienists who carried forward Rush's project recognized the importance of becoming "acquainted with the human mind in its sane state." Most would affirm that every individual was "endowed by the Deity with an equal gift of mind" and that the "exactness" of its operations essentially depended upon "physical organization," mental cultivation, and self-discipline. Yet the very fact of this original equality spurred mental pathologists to explore the "diversity of different natures," confident that their inquiries would yield new insights into disease processes and methods of cure. As they traversed the expansive and largely unexplored territory between "perfect mental health" and "total insanity," alienists took pains to distinguish their scientific approach from that of the "metaphysician," who was "directed in his course solely by his own self-consciousness." If the powers and limitations of the human mind were to be fully comprehended, it was necessary to quit the "narrow circle" of one's own reflections and become "conversant" with the subject of mental disorder, ideally through clinical observation and treatment of afflicted individuals.[28]

American alienists shared Rush's concern with the treatment of insanity in the courtroom. They aimed to enlighten legislators, lawyers, and judges, as well as potential medical witnesses, so that "the scale of justice" might weigh "the facts of nature." A profusion of tracts, manuals, and multivolume treatises began to circulate at the turn of the nineteenth century under the broad banner of medical jurisprudence. Many were penned by practicing "alienists," physicians who specialized in diagnosing and treating "mental alienation," a clinical term for people who were out of their mind. These medical men assumed an even more deferential posture toward the legal profession than Rush had, assuring readers that they did not presume to "dictate to that constituted authority denominated law." They aimed only to provide the pathological, physiological, and behavioral information needed to determine the questions of legal capacity and responsibility that seemed to be arising with ever greater frequency along with mental disorder itself. Along the way, medical writers offered some cautionary words about the ease with which insanity could be both feigned and concealed. They deepened the perplexity by describing a variety of mental disorders and debilities that fell short of insanity, including epilepsy, old age, and nostalgia.[29]

The legal implications of these conditions were typically left ambiguous, though the tendency of these maladies to "terminate" in full-blown insanity if left untreated was often noted. Most writers simply concluded that mental capacity had to be assessed on a case-by-case basis, conveying the impression that medical specialists were instrumental, or even indispensable, to the proper administration of the legal system. In refusing to provide determinate answers, they created a new market for their services. To try cases without expert medical advice was to run the risk that a lunatic would "receive his cure at the gallows," that the insanity plea might be used as a "cloak for crime," or that a mere eccentric might be condemned to live indefinitely "among the idiotic and the mad." This horrific image recurred throughout the early nineteenth century, as medical writers warned that "no man can confidently reckon on the continuance of his perfect reason."[30]

In taking up the task of reform, physicians were immediately beset with the nettlesome questions of definition that Rush had left unresolved. "Who can mark precisely the frontiers, which separate insanity from sanity? Who can number the degrees by which reason declines and falls into annihilation?" asked lawyers, judges, and jurists. Even making such an attempt was, in effect, "to prescribe limits to that which is illimitable, to give rules to folly, to be bewildered with order, to be lost with wisdom." For this reason, the common law had always defined insanity in the narrowest possible terms, recognizing only those cases where the individual had wholly and indisputably lost "the use of his reason."[31] Medical writers did not deny the difficulties inherent in their project. Although no "infallible definition" could be formulated, alienists might offer more accurate illustrations of the various "species" of insanity, drawn from asylums and hospital wards, than the "crude" portraits of the afflicted found in common law commentaries and those "caricatures of disease which the stage represents or romances propagate." Yet they were well aware of the perils of requiring a "perfect sanity," apprehending that "too nice an investigation of eccentricities and imperfections may lead to oppression and injustice."[32]

Medical critiques of the common law generally focused on the need for modernization of the traditional rules of capacity and responsibility. They took issue with the most commonly cited sources: Lord Coke's categories of persons *non compos mentis* were said to be underinclusive in focusing exclusively on cognitive disorders, and Sir Matthew Hale's "total deprivation of reason" test of insanity set a standard that even the most seriously afflicted asylum inmates could not easily meet. Complaints were also made about the "looseness" and "inconsistency" with which the law was administered. It was difficult to fathom why a "glimmering of reason" was routinely deemed sufficient to establish the guilt of an accused criminal, while a single note "sounding to folly" might invalidate a testator's will. More fundamentally, their works collectively challenged the "philosophy of the intellect" that animated the Anglo-American legal system as a whole. In the alienists' estimation, this philosophy was built upon the "groundless and gratuitous" premise that "reason is the directress of human actions" "and that he who reasons must be rational." Expert observers had come to see that the "occasional gleams" of the "reasoning faculty" were seldom reliable signs of the mind's integrity.[33]

In presenting these criticisms, medical writers brought to the surface the gap between common law and Common Sense notions of responsibility that Reid seemed almost willfully to ignore. Physicians accorded a powerful role to the emotional faculties in both normal and abnormal mental processes, which served to underscore reason's precarious hold over thought and action.[34] Most divided mental disease into four basic categories: mania, monomania, dementia, and idiotism. The most innovative aspect of this scheme was the concept of monomania, which most commonly referred to a circumscribed intellectual derangement consisting of a "delusion" concerning a single idea or topic, such as religion or politics. The behavioral signs of this disorder could vary dramatically, but afflicted individuals exhibited two distinctive characteristics. First, their delusions were discrete enough to leave them capable of reasoning properly on all other subjects; second, they showed "a high level of excitation" when laboring under the influence of their delusion. As one medical writer vividly put it, "Sufferers are pursued day and night by the same ideas and affections, and they give themselves up to these with profound ardour and devotion. They often appear reasonable, when conversing on subjects beyond the sphere of their delirium, until some external impression suddenly arouses the diseased train." In those moments, alienists explained, the delusion impelled the individual to perform unintended acts for which he or she could not justly be held accountable, as a matter of either civil or criminal law.[35]

The concept of monomania sometimes also designated various forms of mental derangement principally affecting the nonintellectual faculties, which were rather indiscriminately lumped together as "moral insanity." English alienist James Cowles Prichard, who was responsible for coining the term, depicted the disorder as "a morbid perversion of the natural feelings, affections, inclinations, temper, habits and moral dispositions, without any notable lesion of the intellect, or knowing and reasoning faculties, and particularly without any maniacal hallucination."[36] Medical writers conceded that its symptoms could easily be confused with signs of moral depravity or mere eccentricity and admitted that vice was among the causes of the disease, yet they attempted to provide a way of distinguishing illness from immorality. In one breath, moral insanity was said to be marked by an abrupt and inexplicable change in affections, conduct, and physical appearance, yet in the next it was allowed that gradual alterations of character and ingrained behavioral oddities might constitute indicia of disease. Moreover, many of its supposed symptoms were indistinguishable from crime; the first and only indicator that a patient was afflicted with *monomanie homicide* was often the act of murder itself. With these ambiguities in view, most legal tribunals stopped short of recognizing nonintellectual forms of mental disease. Many medical writers betrayed doubts of their own, suspecting that those diagnosed with moral insanity also suffered from some intellectual disturbance. Even those who did not share this skepticism might be persuaded that the "safety of civil society" required that the offenses committed by the morally insane be punished as crimes. But a vocal minority claimed to represent "the cause of truth and justice" as they ardently pled the case for moral insanity before other medical and legal professionals and the public at large.[37]

Perhaps the most outspoken advocate of this view was the American physician Isaac Ray, whose influential 1838 treatise, *The Medical Jurisprudence of Insanity*, criticized the prevailing common law rules of capacity and responsibility from the viewpoint of medicine. He offered a systematic overview of the "various forms and degrees of mental derangement" and considered them "in reference to their effect on the rights and duties of man." Indulging in a bit of exaggeration, he cast judges, lawyers, and jurists as benighted traditionalists who obstinately adhered to the "metaphysical dogmas" inscribed in the common law even when they obviously clashed with the "dictates of true science." The targets of his critiques countered that the doctor's doctrines, especially the notion of moral insanity, verged upon an atheistic materialism. This line of attack was, however, far from the mark.[38] Not only was the doctor a confirmed dualist, but his medical psychology flowed from Common Sense assumptions about the constitution of the healthy mind. "Man, being destined for the social condition, has received from the author of his being the faculties necessary for . . . understanding his relations to his fellow-men, and possesses the liberty, to a certain extent, of regulating his conduct agreeably or directly opposed to their suggestions." Endowed with these intellectual and moral powers, we are "accountable for the manner in which they are used . . . to our fellow-men, when the institutions of society are injured." So it stood to reason that an impairment of either kind of power might diminish or eliminate an individual's liability for his acts. Where an individual was shown to be incapable of "feeling the influence of those hopes and fears and of all those sentiments and affections that man naturally possesses," Ray held that "an essential element of legal responsibility is wanting, and he is not fully accountable for his actions."[39]

Accordingly, it was with considerable dismay that Ray surveyed the "legal relations of the insane," cataloging the infirmities of the legal system and suggesting specific remedies. He examined scores of judicial decisions so the reader could "see for himself" how many insane defendants were unfairly placed "on the same footing with men of the soundest and strongest minds" and sent to the gallows, though they displayed but the "the slightest vestige of rationality." The treatment of insanity was no less problematic on the civil side of the docket, where the slightest signs of mental disorder might be grounds for stripping an individual of control over his property and person. Ray could find no "physiological or psychological ground" for this civil-criminal distinction. Indeed, it appeared to him that the common law had gotten the matter exactly backwards. The disposal of property was often a rather routine affair, having "nothing in it, to deprive the mind of all the calmness and rationality of which it is capable." The same could not generally be said of criminal acts. While "abstractly wrong," they might be "right and meritorious" under certain circumstances, and "if strongest and acutest minds have sometimes been perplexed on this point, what shall we say of the crazy and distorted perceptions of him, whose reason shares a divided empire with the propensities and passions?" The ease with which criminal liability was found in such cases compelled the conclusion that the common law took "more account of property than life."[40]

Ray's program for legal reform was transparently and unapologetically self-serving: he proposed that both substantive and procedural rules be revamped so as to maximize the influence of medical specialists. In place of all the "fallacious" tests and "fancied" standards of mental soundness promulgated by common law judges, he proffered the single alternative most often recommended by practicing alienists. Their clinical researches demonstrated that the surest sign of insanity was "a well-marked change of character, or departure from the ordinary habits of thinking, feeling, and acting, without any adequate external cause." There were no objective criteria for determining states of mind; each individual subject had to be "compared with himself, not with others." What was lunacy in one might "speak relatively to health" in another, though the doctor hastened to add that "striking peculiarities of character, such as amount to *eccentricity*, furnish strong ground of suspicion of predisposition to madness." In order to implement this reform properly, Ray insisted, courts would have to liberalize their rules of evidence, admitting "proof drawn from the nature of the act in question" as well as more general testimony regarding the actor's "natural character" as exhibited over the course of his lifetime. Only then would it be possible to ascertain whether the act was, in fact, attributable to him. Ray claimed that questions of civil and criminal responsibility could be properly resolved only by consulting doctors who possessed "a well-earned reputation in the knowledge and management of mental derangement."[41]

Ray was soon joined by a chorus of asylum superintendents, who formed the core of the emergent profession of psychiatry in nineteenth-century America. They compared notes through the *American Journal of Insanity* (which began publication in 1844), collectively elaborating a scientific framework within which to understand and treat mental disease, one that confirmed many of the conceptual changes that had been wrought in the preceding decades. While in the eighteenth century insanity was described in terms of "intellectual incoherence," these professional men tended to speak in terms of "will out of control." In their view, it was also a more "democratic" ailment, no longer conceived as a state of being outside the bounds of humanity but instead as a state of mind into which anyone might fall and from which they might recover.[42] The implications of this new conceptualization were profound, especially for the legal system. In the 1840s and 1850s, alienists were increasingly called to testify as expert witnesses. Appearing in all sorts of civil and criminal proceedings, their testimony unsettled the presumption of sanity that had long structured these legal contests.

Medical experts' psychological models were at odds with the "philosophy of intellect" upon which Anglo-American jurisprudence was based. While it was at least conceivable that the law's cognitive tests of insanity could be widened to encompass delusional states of mind, they could not easily accommodate moral monomania. This diagnosis implied that an intact intellect was no sure indicator of moral agency, that thought and volition were not invariably connected as was supposed at common law. Their diagnoses of moral insanity threatened to throw many a legal proceeding into utter disarray, while raising the far more disturbing possibility that moral freedom was itself a delusion. As they contemplated the prospect of such chaotic courtroom scenes, American lawyers were prompted to reconsider the Common Sense premises and common law practices of their profession and to compose treatises of their own on the jurisprudence of insanity.

"Illusive Liberty"

The first work of this kind published in the United States, Thomas Cooper's *Tracts on Medical Jurisprudence* (1819), offered readers reprints of the "most approved" treatises on the subject by British physicians, along with some medical notes of his own and a digest of the common law relating to insanity. From his marginal comments, it appears that Cooper had been convinced by medical specialists that all mental ills ultimately arose from physical causes. Yet the lawyer had remarkably little to say about the legal implications of that viewpoint.[43] Several other English treatises written by practicing barristers were quickly exported to the United States.[44] Three deserve extended consideration, as they enjoyed wide circulation and clearly display the gradual process by which the new medical psychology was assimilated into legal analysis: George Dale Collinson's *Treatise on the Law Concerning Idiots, Lunatics, and Other Persons Non Compos Mentis* (1812); Leonard Shelford's *Practical Treatise on the Law Concerning Lunatics, Idiots, and Persons of Unsound Mind* (1832); and

Joseph Chitty's *A Practical Treatise on Medical Jurisprudence* (1834). Collinson's citations of medical authorities were substantially outnumbered by allusions to mental philosophers, as well as an array of literary figures; Shelford struck a fairly even balance between medical and nonmedical writers; and Chitty looked almost exclusively to physicians for insights into the workings of the diseased mind. Nonetheless, all three jurists acknowledged that the scientific norms of their own profession dictated greater incorporation of the concepts and classification schemes newly promulgated by medical men.[45]

Collinson's *Treatise* was organized around the traditional common law categories of persons *non compos mentis* but included two "philosophical" chapters on "the nature of lunacy" and "the justice and expediency" of the laws governing those of unsound mind. Collinson located the seat of lunacy in the faculty of the imagination and observed that it was most often a "hereditary complaint, or the offspring of some violent passion." Allowing that insanity might be brought about by the misconduct of the sufferer, Collinson underscored the extent to which this scientific conception of mental disease created new problems for the legal system. If insanity was ultimately a bodily disorder, then courts could sensibly repeat the ancient common law maxim that the madman was "sufficiently punished by his madness alone."[46] But if the onset of disease could be tied to the person's conduct, should he not be held accountable for the actions he performed under its influence? Sensing that he had only begged the question of responsibility in his discussion of the nature of lunacy, Collinson endeavored to provide an answer, but his effort collapsed into incoherence. Although perfectly willing to accept evidence of irrational conduct as sufficient grounds for the imposition of civil restraints, he insisted upon more substantial proof of involuntariness before that person could be excused from liability for his crimes. Indeed, the jurist bluntly acknowledged that insanity was more narrowly conceived in the criminal context so as to exclude "sudden gusts of passion, and the insensibility of intoxication, which are obviously and immediately referrable to ourselves." He intimated that this exclusion could be defended on grounds of expediency, if not justice, for it was practically necessary to draw such lines in order to deter harmful conduct. In the end, however, Collinson was not clear in his own mind about the constitution of the moral agent or the basis of legal responsibility.[47]

The perplexity about human agency and accountability only deepened as medical authorities were more fully integrated into discussions about legal responsibility, a process that can be traced in the works of Shelford and Chitty. Though these jurists also drew upon Enlightenment philosophers in constructing their view of "what constitutes mind in its healthy state," this mental model was destabilized as they drew out the legal implications of recent advances in psychological medicine. The chief lesson that Shelford and Chitty learned from the medical writers was that rational conduct was at best an equivocal sign of sanity and an uncertain basis for determining legal responsibility. The jurists' task was rendered all the more challenging in view of the "want of entire coincidence respecting the precise standard of mental health," even among medical men. Without a common measure, it was hard to determine what constituted a deviation severe enough to be deemed a legally disabling disease.[48]

In conformity with the alienists' schemes, Shelford characterized insanity as a bodily disease that could affect any or all of the mind's faculties and had "moral" as well as "physical" causes, listing a variety of contributing factors without distinguishing between those that were and those that were not a product of human will. All the while, he emphasized that only "serious and complicated" mental aberrations indicated disease. As he surveyed the alienists' attempts to clarify what it was that distinguished insanity from depravity and eccentricity, Shelford found them all wanting. In the end, his ambivalence about scientific definitions of defining insanity led him to reaffirm the traditional common law rules of responsibility. Indeed, he strenuously urged that civil incompetence not be found on proof of "extravagant" conduct alone, and he was no more inclined to authorize a legal inference of insanity from the fact of a criminal offense. As a practical matter, he remained convinced that it was "dangerous in judicature" to excuse proven offenders from punishment so long as they retained the capacity to distinguish right from wrong.[49]

While a more enthusiastic consumer of medical science, Chitty was even less willing to countenance reforms of existing common law rules and procedures. Though his volume was suffused with the language of anatomy, physiology, and pathology, his engagement with these disciplines had little apparent effect on the way he thought about the "law of insanity." Chitty appeared at first to support the physician's bid to speak to matters that were often thought to be the province of "the *moralist* or the *metaphysician.*" He firmly declared that the brain was the "seat" of the mind and that mental disorder was essentially a disease of the body. He then considered the current state of the field of mental pathology and the latest judicial decisions rendered on the question of mental unsoundness, which "unhappily are of frequent occurrence." His medico-legal analysis illustrates the convergences and divergences in the treatment of mental disease by the two professions. Unfortunately, the systems of law and medical science were not aligned. On the side of medicine, Chitty noted, physiologists had irrefutably demonstrated the powerful influence of the emotions on mental and physical health, singling out the *"evil passions"* as common causes of mental disease and a host of other bodily disorders. Moreover, alienists suggested there might be a distinctly moral form of monomania, in which the *"intellectual faculties* continue perfect, and even struggle against . . . the effects of this disorder . . . of the *natural feelings."* Yet as far as the common law was concerned, this condition did not fit the description of insanity. English judges continued to require evidence of delusion or some other intellectual disturbance before they would make such a finding. Chitty concurred in this result. Despite the pathogenic potential of the emotions, the jurist ultimately held that the intellect was "so superior" to the rest of the mind and body that it "can, and in *legal consideration* ought" to control and regulate all of the other elements in the human frame.[50]

Though stating this judgment in unqualified terms, Chitty seemed to remain caught on the horns of the medico-legal dilemma he had presented so clearly. For example, he suggested that persons exhibiting deviant temperaments might not be fully responsible for the selfish and malevolent acts prompted by the worst parts of their nature. "It is true that we ought to struggle and endeavor to counteract and control such a predisposition, but sometimes the greatest anxiety to prevent its effects will not succeed, and as the predisposition may be inherent, allowance should be made in certain circumstances." He observed that a killer acting under strong provocation might find his offense mitigated from murder to manslaughter under common law. And it seemed to him that the criminal acts of a drunkard were distinguishable from those of a person of "choleric disposition," since the latter was not guilty of a *"voluntary* deviation" from the law. As he added these qualifications, Chitty only succeeded in obscuring the basis for distinguishing among wrongdoers who had failed to keep their perverse tendencies in check.[51]

Judging Moral Alienation

The problem of responsibility lay at the center of a number of American treatises on medical jurisprudence published by lawyers in the mid-nineteenth century. By their estimates, insanity was on the rise and so too were claims of incapacity in both civil and criminal cases. Although litigation rates cannot be accurately determined from the surviving records, the ensuing trials were often protracted and remarkably acrimonious, exposing the extent to which medical and legal professionals were divided among themselves as well as from each other with respect to the basic rules and standards that ought to operate in these cases. The issue that generated the greatest heat and the least light concerned the medical and legal status of "moral insanity," which stood for everything that was new and unsettling about these doctors' perspectives on deviance.

The shaping effects of this controversy upon the legal discourse about responsibility appear with particular clarity in three of the most prominent and widely cited treatises: Amos Dean's *Principles of Medical Jurisprudence* (1850); Francis Wharton's *Treatise on Medical Jurisprudence* (1855), coauthored with Dr. Moreton Stillé;[52] and John Elwell's *A Medico-Legal Treatise on Malpractice and Medical Evidence* (1860). These authors shared a common preoccupation with the doctrine of moral insanity, though they held different opinions on the matter. While Dean was a sincere believer, Wharton proved to be more of a skeptic, and Elwell repudiated it altogether, insisting that moral insanity covered "a *multitude* of sins." The progression of thought from one jurist to the next is representative of the general tendencies within the legal profession as the nation was convulsed by the moral crisis that culminated in the Civil War. During this tumultuous period, lawyers, judges, and jurists came to perceive psychological medicine as a significant threat to the legitimacy of their own profession, prompting many to consider anew what constituted the mind of a moral agent as a matter of law.

Dean's *Principles of Medical Jurisprudence* displays his preoccupation with mental discipline as a legal educator. Never much inclined to practice law, he spent most of his career in the academy teaching and writing about medico-legal issues. Though conversant with a range of medical authorities, he adopted the perspective of Isaac Ray on the law of insanity. Filled with illustrative cases of moral and intellectual derangements, Dean's book was intended to convince readers that it was "manifestly absurd and irrational to punish either one of these classes for disobedience, as it would be to punish a mere machine, either because it would not go at all, or because when it did go, it went all wrong." Like Ray, Dean complained that the decisions of Anglo-American judges were riddled with vacillations and contradictions; an "irrational act, irrationally done" might supply the basis for stripping the actor of his civil rights while leaving him responsible for his crimes. Though crediting judges with moving beyond the "total deprivation of reason" standard of the traditional common law, he found little to praise in the alternatives they adopted. Whether formulated in terms of the incapacity to distinguish right from wrong, the presence of a delusion, or the absence of premeditation, these tests attended only to cognitive impairments and failed to comprehend the possibility of an emotional or volitional disorder. In order address this lacuna, Dean suggested that "we might find in *irresistibility* a principle upon which all might agree," as it seemed to him beyond dispute that an actor could not be held accountable for the results of an action over which he had no control. The obvious difficulty with this test, which Dean himself recognized, lay in identifying what indicated irresistibility. Certainly it would not do for courts to simply take a murderer's own word for it when he testified to feeling *"destined to do it"* or credit an inebriate's self-assessment that he *"could no longer resist temptation."* But were there any more reliable signs of a truly uncontrollable act? After struggling for several pages with this dilemma, Dean finally made recourse to Ray's concept of a change in character. He felt compelled to add, however, that self-consistency might also be a sign of insanity, for the habitual indulgence of a vicious propensity might slowly add to its original strength until it was at last rendered "irresistible."[53]

The challenge of modernizing the law of insanity was presented in sharpest relief in Wharton and Stillé's *Treatise on Medical Jurisprudence*, which aimed to incorporate the latest French and German medico-legal learning and unite "the medical and legal standpoints" so that the "information required by each profession might be collected and viewed at the same time and within the same compass." But separate chapters treated mental unsoundness "legally" and "psychologically," the first elaborating "the tests of unsoundness" applied by courts in civil and criminal cases, and the second addressing "the general theories of mental unsoundness" and the means of detecting and distinguishing it from unrestrained passion or mere drunkenness. While intended to promote synthesis, this organizational move accentuated professional differences, with subsequent editions leaving the impression that they did not admit of complete alignment. Surveying the legal landscape, Wharton found that the American common law of insanity was keeping pace with the advances of medical science, as courts were beginning to take monomania into account. With respect to the medical doctrine of moral insanity, however, the judicial record was more conflicted, as was Wharton's own opinion. He approvingly noted that some of the nation's most "eminent" judges had recognized the disorder as an excusing condition. But, though he committed twice as many pages to moral as to intellectual disorders, he made inconsistent statements about the legal responsibility of the morally insane. Indeed, a deep strain of moralism ran through his analysis that was difficult to square with the idea of moral insanity; he attributed many cases of madness to the indulgence of vicious habits. At bottom, Wharton believed "that our state of health, mental as well as bodily, principally depends upon ourselves!" In later editions of his *Treatise*, he repudiated moral insanity as a matter of psychology and law, advocating a system of graduated punishment that imposed penal discipline on insane as well as sane offenders to "promote the joint ends of personal reformation and the preservation of the well-being of the community at large."[54]

Following Wharton, a rising generation of American alienists rebelled against the field's founding fathers in the late 1850s, making opposition to the "dangerous" and "materialistic" or "metaphysical" doctrine of moral insanity their clarion call. This new group of medical men advanced two main lines of argument, one primarily scientific and the other more pragmatic. Empirically, they found no clinical evidence in support of the existence of moral insanity. In all purported cases, they insisted, some intellectual disturbance was detectable; if it was not, the problem was simply moral depravity. The tenacity with which they maintained this position left the unmistakable impression that their attacks on the concept of moral insanity were primarily motivated by concerns about the "practical effects" of this diagnosis. As they repeatedly observed, the "logic of moral insanity" dictated that "the more depraved an act, the greater the indications of the disease," fatally undermining the basis for legal responsibility. Shuddering at the thought, the alienist John P. Gray rendered a strongly worded verdict against the doctrine in 1858, holding in no uncertain terms that moral insanity was "the usual condition of those, who, in plain speaking times, were called *bad men*."[55]

Members of the bench and bar were inclined to share Gray's perspective on moral insanity. He won an especially zealous adherent in John Elwell, who trained for the medical profession before taking up the study of law and then worked at the intersection of the two fields. His *Medico-Legal Treatise* was expressly designed to "promote the great ends of Science and Justice," promising to reduce the two perspectives to a single "practical system" in order to promote a better working relationship between the professions. Moral insanity, he declared, was a "specious and dangerous" diagnosis that threatened the legal system's ability to maintain social order. "If this theory is to be followed in this department of Criminal law, the courts launch at once upon an unexplored and unknown sea, without chart or magnet." Though Elwell mainly repeated Gray's words as he attacked the idea, his critical commentary exposed more basic shortcomings in psychological medicine as a whole. "After a protracted, learned and almost profitless discussion between the two schools of psychologists," "materialist or pathological" and "the spiritualist," Elwell pronounced the mind-body relationship "as far from being settled as when the question was first propounded." He, like Wharton, suspected that "both the mind and body are at fault" in most cases of mental unsoundness and "*their relation*" was most likely diseased. Yet he confessed a sneaking suspicion that the truth of the matter lay outside "*the boundaries of human knowledge*," reprising the old common law refrains about the unruliness of the subject and suggesting that the line separating sanity from insanity was no more perceptible than that between daylight and darkness, infancy and maturity, frugality and avarice, or virtue and vice.[56] In the end, the jurist could only conclude that "'we are in a great measure left to our own unaided mental sense—to the uncertain guidance of our deceptive experience, and alas! often fallible judgment.'"[57]

Proceeding as best he could upon this unreliable basis, Elwell turned his attention to the "prime question of responsibility." He cast this issue as a distinctly legal inquiry that had little to do with the finer points of medical diagnosis. A judge should start with the presumption of sanity, although the courts should be willing to entertain the alienist's hypothesis of insanity provided it had a direct bearing on the civil or criminal act in issue. Medical witnesses were regularly subject to searching cross-examinations and sharp rebukes from the bench, but Elwell maintained this was all part of the truth-gathering process. In fact, these supposed experts quite often brought the abuse upon themselves, for they routinely disagreed among themselves and proved to be of precious little assistance to courts "*in determining who are really insane.*" Although the concept of a change in character regarded by many alienists as a sign of mental disease proved useful in many proceedings, lay witnesses were usually better equipped to provide enlightenment on this score. In any event, the legal issue to be decided was not the presence of insanity per se but "what extent of deviation from the standard of a well-balanced mind there may be, before the responsibility of the party is lost." For Elwell, such a ruling would not be warranted unless and until the person in question was shown to be "absolutely without the power of self-restraint."[58]

Although this test of legal responsibility bore a superficial resemblance to the version famously enunciated by Lord Hale, it was essentially concerned with volition rather than cognition, stemming more directly from Common Sense than the common law. Indeed, Elwell spoke in a liberal humanist vein, conceiving of individuals as having the capacity for self-formation and reformation and presuming that they were endowed with moral liberty. His universalism was tempered by an acute awareness of individual differences in bodily organization and environmental circumstances, which might make it more difficult for some persons to maintain the self-command necessary to regulate their own conduct. Yet none of this dampened Elwell's conviction that "we have all our duties to perform, and one of the most important of these is, that we should strive against whatever evil tendency there may be in us," whether arising from physical or moral causes. Even if these impulses and ideas were truly irresistible at the time deviant acts were perpetrated, which Elwell tended to doubt, it was almost always possible to find an earlier moment when they might have been checked and placed under the actor's control. Elwell maintained that "negligence" or "the want of resolution" lay at the root of most criminal insanity. Leaving aside metaphysical concerns about the ultimate causes of human depravity, the jurist submitted that for all intents and purposes the law had to treat each individual as if "the evil ends with himself."[59]

While this practical way of thinking about sin, disease, and the basis of human responsibility held a certain appeal for midcentury jurists, even Elwell did not go so far as to advocate a return to the traditional common law categories of *non compos mentis*. Yet as jurists moved, however haltingly, toward a more scientific jurisprudence of insanity, they found it difficult to contain the effects of the new medical psychology, which seemed to underwrite capacity contests of every imaginable variety. Although the alienists who wrote and testified on the subject of mental disease never denied the distinction between insanity and mere depravity, eccentricity, or mental weakness, their theories tended to occlude rather than illuminate this vexed question, going to show that "giving rules to folly" was truly a contradiction in terms. The collective efforts of doctors and lawyers to produce a medical jurisprudence of insanity advertised the manipulability of the various forms of insanity, attracting enterprising lawyers who found in these volumes ready-made scripts for courtroom use.

PART TWO

The Mind in Issue

IN THE 1855 PREFACE to the treatise on medical jurisprudence he coauthored with the recently deceased Moreton Stillé, Francis Wharton promised to bring "the Legal and Medical points of vision" together "stereoscopically—if the metaphor can be permitted." Here he was referring to the stereoscope, a mechanical device that at once simulated and enhanced the power of binocular vision, enabling viewers to see the world in sharper relief than was possible with their eyes alone. Invented in 1838 by a British physicist to investigate the mental aspect of depth perception—how it was that "the mind perceives an object of three dimensions by means of the two dissimilar pictures projected by it on the two retinae"—the stereoscope focused attention on the subjectivity of vision and its vagaries, which were found to be entangled with physiological processes. The device was put to use by a transatlantic community of researchers, whose experiments indicated that our sense of the solidity of objects resulted from actions of the body and could be artificially induced, challenging the assumption of a one-to-one correspondence between external reality and its visual realization. The findings of this new field of physiological optics destabilized long-standing models of vision that had figured the eye—in the singular—as a passive instrument, perfectly reflecting and transmitting images of the outside world to the brain and thus constituting the best evidence for the argument from design. Laboratory experiments suggested otherwise, bringing to light the illusionistic aspects of binocularity, with the implication that "the revelations of vision" were not necessarily trustworthy; indeed, some researchers went so far as to conclude that "the objects of vision are but a mere phantasmagoria of the organs of sight," and many others evinced new doubts about the testimony of consciousness.[1]

The "wonders" of the stereoscope were soon communicated to a broader audience, including readers of the *Christian Recorder, American Journal of Science*, and *Godey's Lady's Book*, the last of which indicated that "nothing can be more subject to deception than vision." Yet this new scientific dispensation seemed, on balance, to engender more light-hearted bemusement than serious concern on the part of the general public. As the device was retooled for mass consumption as a form of "rational amusement" by commercial photographers in the 1850s, "presenting optical illusion as a commodity," the problematics of perspective were almost entirely obscured. In the hands of its popularizers, the stereoscope was said "to represent *two eyes* in *one head*," a characterization that not only naturalized its workings but also was taken to prove that "our double vision is but perfect vision." For a modest price, Americans could see for themselves, as portable, hand-held devices, attractively ornamented for use in middle-class parlors, were made widely available along with double-imaged stereographs of foreign and domestic landscapes and monuments, fine and decorative arts, battles and other current events, scientific specimens, celestial bodies, family portraits, and depictions of human curiosities, all of which would appear in three dimensions, as if they were directly before the viewer's eyes. Virtually identifying illusion with reality and implying that images were to be preferred to their originals, promoters and satisfied customers insisted that the visual features of most objects were "seen more vividly and naturally in this than in any other manner," enhancing the power of the naked eye and obviating the need for "the toil of travel" as "we can visit, with our sight, all the memorable places on the globe" without leaving the confines of the drawing room.[2]

No one sold the stereoscope as means of escaping the boredom of bourgeois existence (without giving up any of its prerogatives or comforts) more eloquently and arrestingly than the physician-author Oliver Wendell Holmes, Sr., who was also the creator of the best-selling American device. "Of all artificial contrivances for the gratification of human taste," only dress, architecture, and music contributed more "to the enjoyment of the civilized races" than this "self-picturing" device, he enthused in one of a series of essays published anonymously in the *Atlantic Monthly*, crediting this new visual technology with liberating form from matter, as it captured the essence of everything. Lest he be charged with extravagance or overstatement, Holmes took readers on a "stereographic trip" of the places they could go in their minds. Waxing nationalistic about the edification to be found in this virtual tour of notable sites and scenery, he concluded: "You may learn more, young America, of the difference between your civilization and that of the Old World by one look at this than from an average lyceum-lecture an hour long." Like P. T. Barnum, Holmes equated seeing not only with knowing but also with possessing. Yet, unlike the great showman, Holmes never tried to hide the illusory nature of stereoscopic vision. He openly admitted that the stereoscope produced "an appearance of reality which cheats the senses with its seeming truth," noting that this was but to mimic a trick the mind played on itself. Eliding the questions that laboratory scientists had raised about the relationship between objects and observers, Holmes projected an unabashed confidence in the veracity of the stereoscope, suggesting it could achieve virtual omniscience with its "celestial eyes," perfectly transcribing "the book of God's recording angel." He accordingly submitted that "the stereoscopic twins" would be the most reliable of witnesses in a court of law, as they could not only see and record more reality than any one set of human eyes but also were incapable of perjuring themselves, as the images themselves would reveal traces of any efforts to touch them up.[3]

Readers who looked through Wharton's metaphorical stereoscope expressed far more skepticism about what they saw in his treatise. Indeed, his use of this optical analogy seemed to have a boomerang effect, engendering doubts about whether the medical and legal professions could reason together about the subject of insanity and whether it could be scientifically apprehended in any objective sense. Isaac Ray voiced a common criticism in an 1856 review of the work published in the *American Journal of Insanity*, complaining that Wharton was too indiscriminate in his rendering of "the mingled science of medical jurisprudence," at least as it pertained to mental unsoundness. "In his desire to flood his subject with light from every source" he had neglected to give "due prominence" to his own opinion, "abstaining from the judicial function of the author," so that "the reader often fails of obtaining a clew to what is really the truth." Unfortunately for Ray, who continued to espouse the notion of moral insanity, among the few decisive opinions Wharton ventured was his unequivocal condemnation of the idea in the preface to the 1873 edition, attributing it to a "psychological romanticism which sober-minded men have learned to feel is as repugnant to science as it is hostile to society." He expectantly hailed "this advance of science, towards a common reconciliatory stand-point . . . now met by a corresponding advance of law."[4]

Anyone paging beyond this preface would have seen that Wharton was overstating the case for convergence. Indeed, his monumental opus reproduced rather than resolved the problems plaguing medical jurisprudence. The 1873 edition listed over 800 appellate decisions, which went mostly to show that the law of insanity remained unsettled and filled with contradictions. The same was true of his wide-ranging treatment of the state of medical theory, as it exposed deepening fault lines within the field of mental science regarding the existence of volitional and emotional disorders. Wharton chronicled the troubles frequently presented by these rival schools in Anglo-American courtrooms, where disputing parties were permitted to call their own expert witnesses to the stand to offer medical opinions on the issue of insanity. He recognized how easily and often their lawyers secured the services of "theorists" who were all too willing to testify to "extravagant," "whimsical," or patently "absurd" psychological doctrines that were tailor-made to sway the jury and benefit their clients. As he followed the twists and turns of the decisional law, he depicted judges visibly struggling to ascertain who was professionally qualified to testify concerning "states of mind" and who was a "quack." Given the range of disagreements among self-styled experts, it was hard for the courts to reliably determine the existence of insanity in any given case, particularly given the absence of a judicial consensus as to whether this was a question of fact, law, or medical science. Despite his authorial designs, what Wharton really brought into focus by means of this sprawling work was a full-blown crisis of credibility, conveying to readers a sense of perceptual instability that was kaleidoscopic in its effects. Inadvertently, this effort at synthesis demonstrated the jurist's inability to assimilate the multiple and incompatible perspectives brought into the courtroom, suggesting as well the profound disarray regarding insanity that pervaded the culture he inhabited.[5]

By the 1870s, mental unsoundness had become an "embarrassing" problem in American courtrooms, producing obvious tensions between and among medical experts and legal authorities that rose to the notice of the general public. While precise numbers are impossible to recover, insanity trials were widely perceived to be increasing at alarming rates, appearing as unmanageable as the disease itself, not least because doctors so often disagreed among themselves when called to testify. Homicide trials in which the defendant attempted to escape punishment by using "the insanity dodge," as the plea was disparagingly called in the popular press, made for arresting headlines, but they were just the tip of the iceberg. Lawsuits placing an individual's competency and responsibility in issue were, in fact, more commonly found on the civil than the criminal side of the docket in this period. Drawing strategically on the authorities handily collected in works of medical jurisprudence produced by leading writers like Wharton, contending lawyers dramatized the perplexities of reading minds in the most ordinary of circumstances and intimate of spaces in American life. The ensuing trials were also forms of popular entertainment, filled with theatrical gestures (including allusions to Shakespeare and popular novels), which made them saleable newspaper copy. In case after case, the lay and expert witnesses called to the stand testified at great length about the life and times of the putative author of the act in question, from which lawyers fashioned competing biographies designed to support the dueling hypotheses of of depravity or disease. The predictable ways these stories were told about the alleged incompetent inspired more than a few editorials lampooning the whole enterprise of juridical medicine, fueling popular suspicions that forensic psychologists would say anything for a price. Their expertise was also contested by the diagnosed lunatics themselves, who found both formal and informal ways to contest their placement in this class, the loudest and most insistent complaints unsurprisingly coming from those confined to asylums. Some filed petitions for *habeas corpus* and also, or alternatively, sued their keepers for wrongful confinement or malpractice, while others managed to escape and write lurid exposés of life inside the madhouse, and still others gained notoriety by visiting violence on themselves or others after being released as cured. Although their prominence in the popular press was likely out of proportion to their numbers, such actions raised the stakes of capacity litigation, conjuring up harrowing images of "enchained reason" and "lunatics at large."[6]

Closing ranks, leaders in the field of medical jurisprudence redoubled their efforts to secure control of and authority over "the divided empire of insanity," forming new professional associations and placing the reform of the system of expert testimony at the top of their agenda. As was true of the Victorian scientific community more broadly, members of these medico-legal societies applied a similar logic of investigation to the mental as they did to the physical sciences, presuming as well that the finding of facts in law and medicine "rest on the same great assumptions—the general uniformity of nature and the general trustworthiness of the senses." Yet they were far from agreed as to the significance of the conflicts of opinion within the field of psychological medicine. While those trained as lawyers tended to see these "collisions" as "the fruit of a mercenary and partisan spirit," many physicians countered that disputation was vital to the progress of their "experimental science," taking issue with "the double standard of the legal community, which prided itself on its adversarial ideology, but interpreted scientific disagreements as signs of moral corruption." There was nonetheless a general consensus that the adversarial nature of the jury trial operated to distort the presentation of scientific testimony about mental states, tarnishing the reputations of the most reputable of experts, especially but not only when they were subject to the "mortification" of cross-examination. Particular concerns were raised about the "arbitrary" tests of insanity formulated from the bench and attorneys' use of long and shamelessly slanted hypothetical questions, which were supposed to keep experts from speaking to "the ultimate issue" and thereby invading the province of jurors, whose competence was at best questionable in the eyes of many medical jurists. The institutional reform that won the most favor was the lunacy commission, composed of officially designated experts who would serve as "semi-judicial assessors" of mental soundness, limiting if not eliminating the role of lay jurors and reliably guiding the judge toward the right result. Although some questioned whether this scheme was compatible with the common law tradition and the constitutionally protected right to a jury trial, the idea was appealing enough to prompt a number of state legislatures to experiment with their use. But more often than not commissioners became embroiled in partisan politics and stained with charges of corruption, only adding to the problems already evident in courtrooms and amplifying unresolved "tensions between democracy and the elitism inherent in experts' professionalism."[7]

The dilemmas posed by these medico-legal reformers are encapsulated in the story of John Ordronaux's rise and fall from the position of lunacy commissioner in the State of New York. Ordronaux had unimpeachable credentials: he was a well-regarded professor of medical jurisprudence at the Law School of Columbia College, holding degrees in both law and medicine, and he had considerable administrative experience as well, having served as a medical adviser to the United States Sanity Commission during the Civil War. Once installed in 1874, he worked to codify the statutes pertaining to insane persons and to centralize the oversight of asylums and poorhouses at the state and county level. Perhaps because he was trained to see stereoscopically, Ordronaux was well aware of the limits of human vision, clearly appreciating that there was no way to completely reconcile the divergent perspectives of differently positioned observers so as to produce a full convergence of opinion regarding sanity and madness. He nonetheless labored to dispel popular misconceptions and minimize misunderstandings between doctors and lawyers by articulating a clearer division of labor between law and medicine. Although the two professions did not always attach the same significance to the word insanity, Ordronaux insisted that "these differences are not contradictory. They simply represent the mental parallax of an individual as computed under the different latitudes of the two sciences." What insanity meant in medicine was "an established and prolonged departure of an individual from his natural mental condition, arising from bodily disease and not the immediate consequence of self-production." In law, the word was used more narrowly in the process of determining whether the conduct in dispute was that of "a rational, free moral agent, or simply an event in his life in which he was automatically and therefore involuntarily implicated through the agency of disease." Owing to the existence of "the physical law that empowers bodily diseases to fetter moral freedom, as well as to obscure mental lucidity, a law which courts of justice must recognize as operating upon all mankind, it follows that in all issues of insanity the legal problem must resolve itself into the inquiry whether there was mental capacity and moral freedom to do, or to abstain from doing the particular act."[8]

Physical laws impinged upon the judgment process itself, Ordronaux was careful to add, underscoring what doctors and lawyers were up against as they confronted "that inscrutable principle which we call MIND" and its mysterious but nonetheless "indissoluble" connection to the body. He displayed a keen appreciation of the perpetual and yet futile human striving "to transcend the inexorable limits of finite intelligence" even as he undertook to assess the mental infirmities of others in all manner of civil and criminal cases. Aligning himself with "the more enlightened Positivism of modern times," he disclaimed any professional interest in divining "what mind *is*, or where it is located," leaving such questions of ontology to metaphysicians, and "turning instead to study how it acts, and how it is acted upon," for this was the only basis upon which questions of legal competence and responsibility could be justly decided. Yet precisely because "our senses permit us only to see the *phenomena* of things, we are, through the deceitful character of these physical interpreters constantly exposed to the error of commuting the subjective for the objective, of seeing as we *feel* rather than as we can intellectually prove we should see." Understanding this problem to be built into the discipline of medical jurisprudence, which was infinitely complicated by the fact that "no two minds are alike, either in health or in disease," Ordronaux came perilously close to suggesting that human judgments of mental unsoundness were projections of the subjective mind: "inasmuch as the angle of vision determines the parallax of the object viewed, it follows that a mental act may wear a very different aspect to two minds beholding it simultaneously, but from different standpoints."[9] His self-critical gaze was, however, overmatched by the challenges to his "fitness and efficiency" made by a host of detractors who dogged him from the moment of his appointment forward. Motivated by all sorts of personal, professional, and political grievances, they finally elicited a resignation from him in 1882 after the finance committee of the state senate voted to cut his salary to a pittance, "simply to express its judgment that the office was a useless one and ought to be abolished."[10]

Judging competence thus proved a profoundly contentious matter, as it became painfully obvious that there was no "common sense of science"—no agreed upon standard that could be used to distinguish the true from the false expert, let alone to decide who was actually insane. To place the mind in issue was to set in motion a self-reflexive process that implicated everyone, for even the most confident of professional men admitted that "no living man can entirely project himself into the consciousness of another," save "the Omniscient One, who alone reads the whole heart of man." To be sure, Ordronaux registered this realization more acutely than most as he undertook to investigate "the misty realm of mental alienation." But those who joined him in this endeavor likewise expressed a growing sense of subjectivity as a distinct problem, not only within the field of psychological medicine but also the administration of law.[11] In fixating on the eccentric and the exceptional, they were hardly idiosyncratic. Like many professional men in the last third of the nineteenth century, living in a nation still recovering from the Civil War and ever prone to new forms of fracture amidst the dizzying changes brought by unprecedented levels of immigration, industrialization, and urbanization, they evinced a flagging confidence in the Enlightenment project that grew out of nagging suspicions that it was built upon an illusory rationalism. Advances in the human sciences ironically raised new doubts about the capacity of the individual to know and control himself and the world around him. For as the province of the professional scientist was ever more strictly delimited to exclude amateurs and quacks, the standards of what constituted knowledge were defined to bracket out the "metaphysical," which many now associated with outmoded introspective methods. Adhering as closely as they could to a standard of objectivity, which served at once as a means of managing complexity and of disciplining their own minds, researchers in the physical and biological sciences worked to uncover the invariable, law-like mechanisms governing all natural phenomena, humans included, which inspired others to search for analogous regularities in "the social organism," emboldened by the findings of moral statisticians. The cumulative effect of these various strains of scientific naturalism, articulated most famously by Charles

Darwin and Herbert Spencer, was to diminish the power and significance of the individual will.[12]

In the face of these revised estimates of human nature and potential, the pioneering generation of asylum doctors who had worked to expand the legal definition of insanity ironically redoubled their efforts to spread the gospel of self-discipline as a preventative ethic. Nonetheless, their reconceptualization of madness as a physical disease prepared the way for physicalist explanations of human behavior in general, elaborated by a new cadre of neurologists and psychologists who were fast advancing toward "the mysterious citadel of the will." The reduction of mental phenomena to matter in motion suggested that human consciousness of freedom was a waking dream. Those who brought news of these scientific developments to popular audiences cashed out their consequences with equal parts bemusement and horror, often insinuating that their readers could not afford to take these truth claims too seriously. For if they were to be believed, then "at no moment are we our own masters, any more than we can decree as to the secretions of our kidneys," from which it further followed that there was no such thing as "the sinfulness of sin," leaving no solid foundation for moral and legal order. Americans accordingly received these scientific dispensations with a strange admixture of alarm, wonder, and bewilderment, and their sense of their place in the universe was daily rendered all the more uncertain as novel technologies seemed to invert the relationship between man and machine and corporate forms took on lives of their own, so much so that they were recognized as agents in their own right, attaining the status of legal persons, at least in the "artificial" sense.[13]

Situated betwixt and between the realm of positive science and that of practical affairs, medical jurists found themselves in an especially trying position as they confronted the sociopolitical consequences of new determinisms they had helped to disseminate. Disturbed by the disjunction between moral disarray and material progress and worried that the world seemed to moving much faster than their comprehension of it, most remained committed to the character-building project initiated in the early nineteenth century, though their reassertions of the advice writers' slogans and ideals did not carry with them the same conviction as they had earlier. Professionally preoccupied with the troublesome capacity contests that seemed to be not only crowding court dockets but also compromising the integrity of the discipline they had labored so long and hard to establish, medical jurists attached a heightened significance to the ideal of manly independence; they stridently insisted that character was capital and railed against those who espoused the notion of "irresistible impulse" that was lamentably advancing "from court to court, spreading like a moral contagion over the land," potentially supplying an excuse for every form of human failing. Here again Ordronaux vividly exemplifies the tortuous reasoning and contradictory doctrines espoused by postbellum exponents of the "dual science" of juridical medicine. Often sounding more anxious than convinced by what he was saying, he overcompensated by repeating himself as he moved from one forum to the next, conveying the same basic message to law and medical students, established members of the two professions, politicians, and the general public, speaking as if its reiteration would provide a sort of inoculation.[14]

In tones reminiscent of Emerson, Ordronaux preached self-reliance to a graduating class of medical students in an 1867 address, arguing that although no one is perfectly free, it is our duty to make the most of our natural attributes and to defy the pressures of our social environment. "The despotism of temperament, the insatiable appetite of the intellect, the promptings of inflated ambition all seek to subjugate our inner life; while customs and traditions, associations and professions—idols of the tribe or idols of the market-place—limit and circumscribe our external freedom." Conceding that "it is perhaps too late to cry out against that social tyranny which demands conformity as the price of success, and compels each man to fuse his nature into that of the community at the peril of ostracism," he defiantly maintained the man who was "of uncompromising individuality, of earnest convictions, of determined action" could carve out his own course. These qualities were especially necessary for those who would contribute to scientific knowledge and ascertain fundamental principles: "No man, in entering into a learned profession, is compelled to surrender his individual liberty of opinion. . . . He comes into it a freeman, and he alone can enslave himself. The choice is left to him—either to stand as a man and a high priest at the altar of science delivering the law as he interprets it for himself, and not as it was written by another, from a different stand-point of observation, and for application to a different occasion; or, surrendering this high prerogative, to follow rules blindly, oblivious of the fact that the principle underlying the rule is always broader than the rule itself, and therefore calculated for adaptation to variety of circumstance, while the rule only adapts itself to uniformity of circumstance. . . . In science, in philosophy, or government," he contended, "we must . . . explore for ourselves whether that be truly good which claims to be so, and that truly honest which is called so by the multitude." Using language filled with religious allusions and ethical mandates notwithstanding his skepticism of absolutes, Ordronaux concluded this peroration by juxtaposing his millennial hopes with the manifold moral perils facing individuals and society.[15]

Ordronaux was an equally impassioned critic of what he regarded as particularly dangerous theories in medical jurisprudence. In scholarly contributions to professional journals, he trained his rhetorical fire on the remarkably resilient doctrine of moral insanity, which constantly appeared in new and ever more ingenious guises, none of them constituting anything more than whimpering about fate and foreordination. In an 1874 article in the *American Journal of Insanity*, "Is Habitual Drunkenness a Disease?" he thundered against the proposition "that inflexible laws not only govern matter in its lower chemical affiliations, but even compel the mind to act in settled and irrefragable lines of conduct," connecting it with "the growing tendency to apologize for every sin" by pointing to an irresistible bodily condition. This way of thinking "converts a vice into a disease, and renders its author and its victim, (both combined in the same person,) irresponsible for his own suffering." After enumerating the various other culprits—environmental and constitutional—that were often blamed, he submitted: "Is there anything more demoralizing to a man than to convince him that he has lost his moral liberty, and is the slave of a blind physical necessity? Let him be taught that his redemption is in his own hands, and the noblest victory that which he accomplishes by his *will*. . . . He alone subjugates it actively, and if he will but avoid *doing* (that is drinking,) his willpower to abstain will both continue and strengthen with time. It is a mistake to do too much for weak, sinful men . . . and the truest charity is that which teaches men to win their own independence, by convincing them that they are never morally enslaved except by themselves." Unable to contain his contempt for physicians who propounded such doctrines, he declared: "The great center round which now revolves the dogma of human helplessness, fatalism, and irresponsibility, is that of disease. Every vice, every crime is disease, nothing short. And if the crime be so great that human endurance is provoked into an attempt to punish it, the criminal is at once surrounded by an army of sentimental protectors, whose prayers are not so much for his reform, as for scientific light whereby they may explain and extenuate his offense to the world. When insanity can not be invoked, it is something else, but always disease, or that can't-help-it justification which is supposed to admit of no answer."[16]

In pursuing this line of thought, Ordronaux assumed that it is impossible for us to be at once authors and victims of our own acts even as he cast those who those believe in moral or emotional insanity as simultaneously dupes and deceivers. But who was to say he was not playing a joke on himself, acting the part of the self-deluded trickster as he affirmed the reality of human freedom? What emerges most clearly from his professional writings is a deeply conflicted portrait of the sovereign self, poignantly figuring the conundrums of individuality in nineteenth-century America. To comprehend how he got so tangled up in his own reasoning and why he was not alone in this regard, it is necessary to return to the scene of the courtroom where the trials of insanity were regularly staged. Time and again, as will become apparent in the pages that follow, the medical jurists' classifications, codifications, and analyses proved inadequate to the tasks for which they were designed, seeking as they did to clarify "the reason of the laws governing the civil and criminal status of the insane"—a class of persons that defied definition. To a significant degree, this was a problem of their own making. For in elaborating a scheme of liability that hinged upon an invisible and irreducibly mysterious entity—in insisting so uncompromisingly "that where there is no mind, there is legally no man; and where there is no man, rational and reflective, there can no law of responsibility apply"—medical jurists like Ordronaux simply set the terms of capacity contests, effectively providing the playbook for litigation that was as vexing to those who sat in judgment as it was entertaining to the public.[17]

In reconstructing these trials, Part 2 concentrates on the testimony, arguments, and opinions rendered in the common run of civil contests rather than the notorious trials of madmen who committed wanton murder.[18] Accustomed as we are to thinking of the insanity plea as the last resort of the violent criminal, rarely successful even in cases involving sociopathic killers, the uses (and abuses) of this excuse by civil litigants have largely gone unnoticed by historians. In their petitions to the court, they chronicled the multifarious ways Americans were falling short of the ideal of the autonomous individual, suffering from a wide array of mental maladies robbing them of their capacity to govern themselves in their everyday dealings with strangers and intimates in the separating spheres of home and market. Some were said to be so far deprived of their reason as to be wholly incapable of managing their affairs, thus presenting threats to property and, more than occasionally, life as well. But many more were portrayed as victims of circumscribed delusions and prejudices that captivated their minds and moved them to perform unintended acts, whether in the form of a will, contract, deed, or tort. Claims of mental weakness short of insanity were also commonly made, usually in conjunction with allegations of fraud, undue influence, and duress that operated to compromise the autonomy of the actor. While these declarations of dependence were seldom as arresting as the insanity plea of the homicidal maniac, they nonetheless contained the potential to alarm because it was easy for judges, jurors, spectators, and the broader reading public to imagine losing their mind or the control of their will in more or less the same fashion. For this very reason, they have more subtle and far-reaching implications for common conceptions of mind, law, and personhood, shedding a broader and more diffuse light on the history of self-making and the language of responsibility that gave moral weight to this enterprise.

Litigating incapacity was a fact-intensive enterprise and "voluminous" transcripts were the norm. In the absence of some sort of "moral photography" by means of which the workings of the mind could be "accurately registered," courts were forced to rely on behavioral signs as they appeared in the testimony of a wide array of witnesses, extending well beyond the family circle to encompass neighbors, friends, and casual acquaintances representing many different walks of life, as well as medical experts, "many of whom had never personally examined the individual whose capacity was in question. Defining insanity in terms of a marked and unaccountable change in character, judges found it difficult to determine the outer limits of relevance, tending to allow attorneys to range far and wide in their examinations and cross-examinations of witnesses because most any aspect of the alleged incompetent's biography—including the mental diseases of blood relatives—could conceivably bear on the matter of his mental soundness. It was almost as if the accumulation of details could make up for the fact that the key determinant of liability remained hidden from view. The representations made about diseased minds and overborne wills were no doubt stylized for strategic purposes. Nonetheless the forensic battles they touched off constitute telling indicators of the growing sense of a split between subjective experience and objective reality in a country that valorized the sovereign self. The diversity of perspectives in play within the courtroom mirrored and magnified those that were daily proliferating beyond its walls, epitomizing the difficulty of "generating commonality out of innumerable individualities" in this sprawling democratic society. Although mediated by lawyers, the witnesses' testimony expressed the strains, tensions, and anxieties middle-class Americans experienced as their lives became more subject to the vagaries of the market and they could less stably define themselves in relationship to others within this fluid social order. The trial stories crafted into arguments by the attorneys evidence the abiding force of "the self-making axioms of an age of free men and free labor," but they also reveal the ways this ideological structure was being undermined by the corrosive dynamics of industrial capitalism. As they contended about what it meant to be a responsible individual, the litigants and their lawyers manifested the mental stresses and psychic traumas occasioned by these transformations, giving voice to what cultural historians of the period have described as "an existential dread of failing not just in business but in life."[19]

It was the self-made *man* whose capacity was typically challenged in these proceedings. Across jurisdictions and over time, the mental fitness of propertied white men was litigated with the greatest frequency on the civil side of the docket. Since few white women and even fewer nonwhite women or men owned and controlled property, this bias stands to reason, even as it forces us to reckon with how many property holders perceived themselves or were perceived by others to be incapable of rationally managing their possessions. Because the laws that assigned white men these rights did so upon the basis of their presumed competence, implicitly or explicitly setting this mental baseline by negative reference to the women and children who were their dependents, and, before emancipation, to the slaves who were legally their property, any sign that they had been unmanned could serve as a basis for claiming incapacity. The new field of psychological medicine supplied a putatively scientific explanatory framework as well as an extensive arsenal of words and phrases for conveying how and why they fell below the threshold of the default legal person at the discrete moment when they were supposed to have executed the civil act or committed the civil wrong in question. The shadows of those groups against which full masculinity was defined—women, children, and racial others—loomed ever more threateningly over white men in the second half of the nineteenth century as many found themselves reduced to propertyless "hands" or relegated to sedentary jobs that engaged the trained mind but not the active body. Fears of effeminacy and of dependency on employers eroded the aggressively self-confident white manhood that had prevailed during the postrevolutionary period, lending a special intensity to the widespread apprehension that the supposedly autonomous individual was becoming a cog in a machine. This diminished sense of causal potency, in turn, may have heightened the perception of insanity as an ever present peril in modern society, looming over everyone, even or perhaps especially those who were propertied, white, and male.

Placing the mind in issue in the nineteenth-century courtroom concretized the threat insanity posed to ordinary Americans. In this legal forum—evocatively cast by one nineteenth-century judge as "life in little"—mental diseases were characterized as agents and fingered as the source of all sorts of human failings, both in business and in life.

Although the conduct typically involved in these cases was nowhere near as horrible as murder, the use of insanity as an excuse was nonetheless unsettling, chipping away at the cultural ideal of self-making. Each trial had its own peculiar mix of financial, reputational, and emotional stakes, but most were, at turns, tragic, comic, and incredibly tedious, sometimes leaving the parties poorer than when they started, the litigation costs exceeding the amount in dispute. Public interest unsurprisingly centered on cases concerning large estates, famous people, and virtuoso lawyers, who knew how to turn courtroom narratives into front-page news. Playing so obviously to the press, especially but not only in will contests, their arguments were at times so cynically crafted and melodramatically delivered as to provoke sharp rebukes from the bench, though sarcastic interjections were more commonly used to discipline this sort of behavior, the darkly funny mood marked with a parenthetical [laughter] in trial transcripts.[20]

This reminds us that the nineteenth-century courtroom was a peculiar performance space where so much was scripted for strategic purposes, where there was a debatable middle ground between truth and falsity that seemed, at times, to be at least as wide as that between the perfectly sane and the raving lunatic. The drama of the trial, like the illusion of the stereoscope, "flowed in an easy confluence with the Victorian regard for transparency." Yet even the most theatrical trials were not pure theater and they diverged most sharply from dramatic plays in their indeterminacy, leaving spectators with the impression that there were always (at least) "two ways of telling a story."[21] Indeed, the lawyer's hyperbole was only the most obvious form of distortion to be found in the transcripts of these trials and it remained far from clear who could reliably narrate the workings of another man's mind. While these trial stories must be approached cautiously and critically, in view of their complicated relationship to the underlying transaction that brought the parties to court, the very fact that the trial participants could not always be taken at their word is an important part of the story to be told in these pages. The surviving sources upon which this study relies, including accounts and commentaries in the popular press as well as treatises and law reports, are themselves fragmentary and filled with self-serving statements and inaccuracies stemming from the infirmities of human memory. They nonetheless constitute a rich repository of information about how the legal system was used to manage the epistemological and ontological problems these cases regularly presented. Much can be learned about the self-understandings of those assembled in the courtroom and the quotidian concerns and crises that animated and punctuated their legal and moral lives by attending to the recurring stories told, arguments made, and rationales offered—concentrating, as Norma Basch has put it, on "the questions they raised instead of which versions triumphed."[22] Following the twists and turns of the capacity contests of the nineteenth century enable us to see not only why they held the attention of spectators within and beyond the courtroom. They also provide a window on the daily distresses, anxious preoccupations, and gnawing fears of those who were supposed to be in charge: the heads of household who were at the center of so many of these trials and those who sat in judgment of them. The opinions of the court are laced with recognition of the "thin partitions"[23] separating the sane from the mad; on occasion, we can catch glimpses of sympathetic identification, as judges seemed to see more than a little of themselves in the men said to be deranged by money-mania, exhausted by competition, mastered by their slaves, controlled by their wives, and ultimately reduced to a "second childhood" in their old age.

These tangled, agonized reflections on the constitution of the legal person provide ample grounds for reconsidering the conventional stories historians have told about the relationship between law and the conditions of freedom in nineteenth-century America. For they have significantly understated how challenging it was to live up to the ideal of the free-standing individual and how routinely the competency of white propertied men was called into question, sometimes even on their own motion. The fact that men and women so often took to the courts—rightly understood to constitute one of "the active centers of social order" during this period, where "leading ideas come together with leading institutions and where a governing elite uses the set of symbolic forms involved to express the fact that it is in truth governing"—to dispute the capacity of men presumed to be in control of themselves, that these claims were thought worth making, and that they proved so difficult to resolve in any satisfactory way calls for historical explanation. The chapters in this part explore what happened when the mind was placed in issue in various fields of private law, highlighting the sorts of civil acts and civil wrongs and the types of circumstances most often giving rise to capacity litigation. Chapters 3 and 4 consider contests involving "unnatural" and "eccentric" wills, which often degenerated into unseemly battles of hired experts as well as the heirs; Chapters 5 and 6 examine challenges to "improvident" contracts and deeds, probing the relationship between love and consent as well as the obligations of kinship and marriage; and Chapter 7 addresses the torts of the insane, reconstructing debates about whether they were to be held to the standards of the reasonable man. Taken together, the chapters highlight the distinct problems insanity posed on the civil side of the docket and the broader questions the cases raised within this liberal legal order: Did the civil law have a character-building function or was the education, discipline, and punishment of individuals better left to the criminal law and other moral authorities? Should the same rules of capacity and responsibility apply in civil and criminal proceedings? Was the state of a man's consciousness always material to his liability?

As we turn from the treatises to particular cases, we will see that the subject of responsibility was eminently contestable. The legal system provided an arena in which the ideal of the sovereign self was tried and reconfigured across time, allowing us to trace the processes by which it became "a primary category of politics," the means by which "the free and independent man" was "made safe for democracy and better suited to the competitive conditions of a fast-expanding capitalism," and the mechanisms used to contain the potential of the individual "to threaten public order and also subvert the very possibility of establishing truth." The law enabled this cultural project even as it broadcast the strains and contradictions entailed in making responsible citizens, the courtroom serving as a forum within which Americans reckoned with their own shortcomings and those of others. Judges fended off the new determinisms as best they could, but they did not simply allow behavior to stand in for the mind in adjudicating capacity and liability. Aware that placing the mind in issue was like opening Pandora's box, they felt compelled both to demonstrate their suspicion of feigning and to hear from all sides before rendering an objective judgment. A basic dilemma continually bedeviled them as they attempted to mark off madness from capacity: "Make the definition too narrow, it becomes meaningless; make it too wide, the whole human race are involved in the drag-net. In strictness, we are all mad when we give way to passion, to prejudice, to vice, to vanity; but if all the passionate, prejudiced, vicious, and vain people in this world are to be locked up as lunatics, who is to keep the key of the asylum?" Committed to individuality and moral order, judges took a pragmatic tack, charting a via media between the extremes of voluntarism and determinism. They remained concerned about whether there was indeed a responsible mind underneath it all because responsibility made no sense to them without it. So they continued to allow the parades of expert and lay witnesses to speak to the question—unwilling or unable to completely shrug off the metaphysical quandaries they presented.[24]

By the end of the nineteenth century, common sense would lose the universality that came from its origin in Common Sense philosophy. Medical jurists frankly admitted the problems of distinguishing the sane from the mad conspicuously in print, with less and less confidence that they could be overcome: "Properly speaking none are absolutely free. Inherited predisposition, educated bias, confirmed habit, hobby-riding, well-fed ambition, and such like, are manacles to impede volition. The free will of a sane man must always be considered in a modified sense, for the ball and chain are hanging at our limbs, as we are paying the penalty for the transgressions of ourselves and our ancestors." Though continuing to hold themselves out as capable of identifying who was "really insane," they acknowledged there was no objective basis for comparison, that every individual was unique, and thus unfit to judge others: "There is no common standard to measure mentality with analogous to the yard stick and bushel in the British Museum. Each man must be gauged by himself, in his antecedent conduct and individuality, for among all the sons and daughters of Adam, no two are alike in body and mind. . . . To expect a uniformity in humanity, and judge that one man must act like any and every other man, is the greatest absurdity. This want of sameness must forever bar the way to finding a general definition of insanity. The conditions are too multifarious for us ever to prove mental *status*, with formulae as definite as those of Euclid."[25]

In the end, a strikingly low level of reasonableness would have to suffice because the one thing upon which judges and juries, legal and medical experts could agree was that rationality is not the norm. For better or worse, the gamblers Rush condemned had won: speculative ventures and money-making mania were too common to count as insane in any serious sense; they had come to be accepted as the stuff of success stories rather than illegitimate side enterprises. Indeed, by the Gilded Age critics as well as advocates had to acknowledge that gambling had become the main show in town.

CHAPTER 3

Unnatural Dispositions

Stat pro ratione voluntas.
Juvenal, *Satirae* VI, 223

BY ALL ACCOUNTS, George Moore was a dissolute bachelor who drank himself to death. In March 1822, a physician "candidly apprised him that his case was a hopeless one and advised him to arrange his temporal affairs." Days before his death, the childless man executed a will disinheriting his three brothers but providing for his female slave, who had lived with him "in a state of concubinage."[1]

Moore's disappointed heirs challenged his will on three grounds: testamentary incapacity, undue influence, and fraud. At trial, they presented testimony that when Moore had contracted a severe fever twenty-five years earlier, he had "conceived an antipathy against his brothers"; he became convinced that they "designed to destroy or injure him, although they attended him constantly in his illness." The fever eventually subsided, but this "unnatural and unfounded aversion" did not. His brothers contended that the drafter of Moore's will, who was not a family member but was among its beneficiaries, took advantage of his deranged state of mind and encouraged his malicious disposition toward his natural heirs. To counter this testimony, the will's proponents called witnesses who maintained that when this document was made Moore displayed sufficient intellect to competently dispose of his estate. The trial court found against the will, and this judgment was affirmed on appeal. In so ruling, Kentucky's highest court did not deny the credibility of the proponents' witnesses. Indeed, the opinion indicated that the court would have had no hesitation admitting the will to record but for two critical pieces of evidence offered by the contestants. First, Moore's concubine, whose emancipation he had secured by way of a recorded instrument set to take effect upon his death, appeared to have "possessed considerable influence over him," particularly in his declining years. Second, he manifested great hostility and suspicion toward his unoffending brothers as he descended into his final illness. The court took these feelings to be "strong evidences of a derangement in one department in his mind" and found them "directly influencing and operating upon the act which is now claimed as the final disposition of his estate." Accordingly, Moore could not be "accounted a free agent in making his will, so far as his relatives are concerned."[2]

Incredulous, the proponents' counsel, Joseph Cabell Breckinridge, moved for a rehearing in a petition that was a tour de force on the perils of the new medical psychology. "In the present case," he asked, "what is the nature of the accusation and proof? The charge is insanity; the proof, that . . . a vindictive misanthrope, in violation of the common charities of life, nurses the sentiments of animosity and distrust against those who expect to profit by his death." Surely Moore was not to be stripped of the "rights of free agency" simply because he exhibited such ill will toward the "natural . . . objects of his bounty." Since "man is a rational and intelligent being" whose "conduct is regulated by motives, which his heart inspires, and his mind controls," the counselor argued, it was more sensible to infer that Moore meant to dispose of his property as he did than to treat his mind as if it were composed of compartments that might be separately deranged. That notion was "at war with the very frame and constitution of our nature," it being a matter of common sense that "the mind of man was a unit." Letting this judgment stand would set a dangerous precedent, Breckinridge warned. For the contestants' doctrine blurred the line between sin and disease, leaving no clear means of distinguishing between "those acts that are prompted by the delusions of the mind, and such as originate in the depravity of the heart." At the same time, it expanded indefinitely the court's "discretionary power, multiplying the occasions of injustice and oppression." Accordingly, Breckinridge appealed to the judges before him to guard the testator's "constitutional freedom" and uphold George Moore's will.[3]

The Kentucky court summarily denied Breckinridge's petition without explaining its ruling. Nonetheless, the issues he posed recurred with disturbing regularity in the decades that followed, as litigation about "unnatural dispositions" seemed to crowd court dockets in every state. From the perspective of judges and jurists, the sheer frequency of this litigation was cause for concern; an article in the *American Journal of Insanity* observed that "last wills have been a prolific cause of imputed insanity." But it was the moral deviancy disclosed in the testimony that truly vexed nineteenth-century judges, steeped as they were in the mental and moral philosophies of liberal Enlightenment thinkers, which posited the existence of "an innate moral sense enabling every man and woman naturally to approve good and abhor evil." Central to the Scottish Common Sense tradition was the notion that all men were endowed with the ability to understand and adhere to the dictates of reason and morality and were therefore responsible for their choices.[4] In line with this belief, as well as with the political economy of the new republic, legislators and jurists expressed their commitment to upholding the sovereign prerogatives of individual property-holders, elaborating legal rules that secured a man's freedom to "do what he will with his own" and allowed his will to stand as the reason for his testamentary disposition.[5]

Yet the judges' words betrayed a concern that liberty might degenerate into licentiousness, particularly in a country that had repudiated so many of the traditional props of social order, and so many hastened to add that the right to dispose of property at death was a creature of statute. Testators such as George Moore brought these anxieties into sharper focus, illustrating the misuses some Americans made of their testamentary freedom, scattering fortunes among the "basest of mankind" and perpetuating "immorality and irreligion" as their legacy. In the protracted, unseemly contests that often ensued, placing matters of household governance into issue along with the minds of testators, judges struggled to square their liberal humanism with the mental and moral infirmities displayed in the trial record. Indeed, some began to wonder whether their optimism about human nature was warranted. The principles of testamentary freedom and natural justice seemed perpetually in conflict, forcing judges to confront the fact that liberty and morality did not necessarily lead all men in the same direction. Isaac Redfield, who had served on the Vermont Supreme Court from 1835 to 1860, captured these strains of thought at the outset of his 1864 treatise on *The Law of Wills*: "The right of testamentary disposition is, unquestionably, one of the results of cultivated social life, and dependent upon municipal law. But it is, nevertheless, an instinctive sentiment, intimately associated with that love of acquisition, and of dominion, which forms the basis, and the stimulus of all social progress; and which, in its normal development, is the sure measure of advancing civilization, and, in its morbid excesses, equally marks the process of declension, and the increase of crime."[6]

The next two chapters examine the efforts of American judges to account for deviant wills over the course of the nineteenth century. Will contests in this formative era have not been carefully scrutinized or systematically connected to broader intellectual and cultural currents of the time. By and large, lawsuits concerning unnatural or unjust dispositions have been seen as material conflicts initiated by opportunistic heirs and resolved by moralistic judges imposing conventional norms of fairness under the cover of the doctrines of testamentary incapacity, undue influence, and fraud. Legal scholars regard this tendency as a persistent feature in the law of wills; some claim that testamentary freedom is a myth within American legal culture.[7] Recent historical work has fortified the impression that the adjudication of testamentary capacity tended to reflect and reinforce conventional morality, though the irreducibly erratic, ad hoc quality of the decisional law is not easily explicable by reference to "the standards of the times."[8] This comes through most vividly in several case studies built upon the close analysis of the local court records as well as published appellate reports in the antebellum South. While these works provide richly textured narratives of the family feuds that played out in courtroom contests about testamentary capacity, the law as they figure it worked mainly to uphold the behavioral norms and power structures of the society within which it was embedded, its ostensibly neutral rules operating to sustain and perpetuate hierarchies of race and gender as well as class.[9]

The strains and conflicts endemic to nineteenth-century will contests arose from a more basic contradiction in the conception of the self upon which the law of wills was premised. Although these contests were certainly about property and the power of those who possessed it, it will be argued in this chapter and the next that the challenges to "unnatural dispositions" are best understood as expressions of deep and abiding tensions and ambiguities in the liberal conception of self-possession. Scholars who present the courtroom as a space where communal understandings of what it was to be a sane testator and a deserving heir governed the outcomes of individual cases have significantly overstated the coherence and stability of the behavioral norms invoked by the participants in these trials. This argument is built upon an analysis of nearly three hundred such contests brought over the course of the nineteenth century, drawing not only on leading appellate opinions identified in legal treatises and works of medical jurisprudence but also on trial transcripts containing judges' charges to the jury, arguments of counsel, and the testimony offered by a parade of lay and medical witnesses. While wills that deviated from societal norms were vulnerable to challenge, the ensuing trials often placed these norms in issue along with the testator's mind, raising fundamental questions about the bounds of human freedom, the dictates of distributive justice, and the very constitution of the self.

These legal battles provide a vantage point from which to assess how the American legal system dealt with the phenomenon of human perversity. Though this problem has long preoccupied criminal law scholars, its manifestations on the civil side of the docket have remained unexplored. To be sure, the moral transgressions alleged in will contests were hardly as extreme as those in murder trials, but they were unsettling in their own way. From the witness stand came stories of alienation of affection within the domestic circle, chronicling how ties of love and trust were rent by sudden gusts of passion, corrosive suspicions, and the machinations of intimates and strangers. However hyperbolic, the statements of witnesses convey a sense of the fluidity of social relations in the new democratic nation and the resulting uncertainty about what constituted proper behavior within the home. In addition, they suggested how widespread depravity and dependency were in a society that held out the moral and material achievements of the "passionless" woman and the "self-made" man as norms.[10] As these domestic disputes spilled into courthouses, they raised metaphysical questions about human agency and accountability that were not easily answered within an Enlightenment framework. If every individual were naturally endowed with the capacity for rational and moral action, how should the court judge a testator who exhibited signs of perversity? Were these best read as deliberately chosen aspects of the testator's character, as proponents were wont to argue? Or were they evidence of some "controlling disease" or other "extrinsic" influence that had compromised the testator's free agency, as contestants often claimed?

The new band of medical men specializing in the diagnosis and treatment of mental alienation promised a scientific basis for judgment. In works of medical jurisprudence, they presented novel classification schemes and urged courts to defer to their expertise in judging mental competence. Members of the bench and bar at first displayed a cautious receptivity to these new ways of accounting for deviant behavior, expanding the meaning of legal insanity to encompass monomanias and delusions short of complete mania or idiocy. Yet as courtroom advocates deployed these medical doctrines to challenge "unnatural dispositions," judges began to fear that they proved too much, implicitly validating a view of human behavior that threatened to undermine the metaphysical basis of legal responsibility within and beyond the testamentary context. The pages that follow chronicle how members of the bench and bar struggled to extricate themselves from this unworkable situation.

The Deviance of the Will

Last wills and testaments have long enabled individuals to deviate from established norms of property transmission. Under English law on the eve of the American Revolution, only married women, children, and "any person *de non sane memory*" were barred from exercising this power. The common law defined incapacitated persons as those who lacked "discretion or judgment," including those who were mad, idiotic, senile, drunkards, and children; persons without "freedom and full liberty," such as slaves and serfs, captives and prisoners, and married women; those who were deaf, dumb, or blind; those who had committed some "heinous crime," including treason, usury, heresy, incest, sodomy, libel, and suicide; and a catchall category of "prodigall persons."[11]

Although all other property owners were statutorily empowered to dispose of their estates in accordance with their "free will and pleasure," the liberty of testation remained limited by both formal and informal norms of reasonableness. Blackstone's *Commentaries*, which promoted the unrestrained transfer and circulation of property, emphasized that testamentary freedom was not a natural right but a creature of positive law subject to civil and municipal regulation. The famous jurist conceded, however, that there were good reasons to doubt the wisdom of the existing laws, which effectively conferred "a power of wantonly disinheriting the heir by will, and transferring the estate, through dotage or caprice of the ancestor from those of his blood to utter strangers." Despite these disturbing instances, Blackstone considered it unduly harsh to curtail testamentary power "on account of some abuses," which were "the natural consequence of free agency, when coupled with human infirmity." On balance, he expected that English testators would make wills tailored to "the exigence of his family affairs, or the justice due to his creditors." If this power were "prudently managed," it would prevent "the too great accumulation of property" and "an excess of wealth in some, and of poverty in others" that would arouse "popular tumults and dissentions," which in ancient Athens "ended in tyranny and the utter extinction of liberty . . . quickly followed by the total subversion of their state and nation." He deemed this consideration "of the utmost importance in this free and commercial country" "whose welfare depends on the number of moderate fortunes engaged in the extension of trade."[12]

The law of inheritance came under sharp attack during the revolutionary era as a potent symbol of the artificial values of aristocracy, a critique exemplified by Thomas Paine's rallying cry in *Common Sense:* "virtue is not hereditary." After independence, state legislatures pronounced it to be "the duty and policy of every republican government to preserve equality among its citizens, by maintaining the balance of property as far as it is consistent with the rights of individuals." The ideological importance of this set of legal reforms was underscored by prominent statesmen in the 1780s and 1790s as they rhetorically cast off the English laws of inheritance as unnatural and unrepublican.[13] The patriot poet and failed lawyer Joel Barlow assimilated great English landlords to the class of "madmen" on account of their dynastic practices. In a similar vein, Benjamin Rush listed "the general unwillingness among us to acknowledge the usurpations of primogeniture" among the indices of American progress, along with "the checks lately given to negro slavery" and "the universal practice of inoculation for the small-pox, and the absence of the plague." Yet Rush privately chided a Congregational clergyman for underestimating the usefulness of traditional English norms: "Where the eldest son or daughter is honored and preferred by parents, a family is never without government in the absence of parents from home, and when these parents are removed by death there is a foundation laid in the habits of the younger children for a continuance of subordination in a family—a circumstance always essential to harmony and happiness."[14]

The limits of egalitarianism in postrevolutionary America were given more explicit public expression in the statutory reforms implemented in the newly established states. Legislators struggled to reconcile a host of competing ends: individual liberty, equality among white men, protection of dependents, and the free flow of commerce. Few called for the reversion of property to the state upon the death of its owner or questioned the right of testation. Most legislators aimed to redistribute wealth within the family in ways that preserved or enhanced the prerogatives of the head of household. It was the father whose authority was shored up by these legal rules, since a married woman rarely owned property in her own right and a widow was entitled only to a life interest in a portion of her husband's estate, while a widower was accorded a life interest in the whole of his wife's estate unless the marriage was childless. Hierarchies of race as well as gender were observed and maintained by rules that defined the legitimate family so as to exclude extramarital relationships and the children resulting from them. Slavery introduced a complicating factor, as the status of mixed-race children derived from the mother rather than the father, deviating from the rule of descent that prevailed among whites. The offspring of a white master and his female slave were persons he disowned as they became his property under the laws of the state. But these provisions left him free to do as he willed with his human possessions insofar as he could choose whether to treat his mixed-race children and their mothers like members of his white family or as saleable commodities. Although ushered in with republican rhetoric, the statutory reforms made in the wake of the Revolution left testators free to dispose of their property in ways that undermined the reformers' vision of a virtuous polity of small landholders.[15]

Deviance was at once the point and the problem of the will. Capricious testators appeared especially threatening in a polity whose viability depended upon its citizens making the right use of their property rights. Jurists and law professors varied considerably in their toleration of eccentricity as they delineated the contours of a distinctly American law of wills in the early republic. Some staunchly defended the testator's untrammeled right to "give his property to whomsoever he pleases, to the complete [disinheritance] of his children; and however unnatural and inhuman this may appear," insisting that any restraint violated "the prevailing spirit and policy of our institutions." Others spoke in more qualified terms, opining that "the law of our nature, by placing us under the irresistible influence of the domestic affections, has sufficiently guarded us against any great abuse of the power of testamentary dispositions, by connecting our hopes and wishes with the fortunes of posterity." Ambiguities as to whether and when the liberty of testators could override "the domestic right of children to property acquired by their parents," particularly if those disinherited were likely to become public charges, were left unresolved. The enactments that impinged most directly on the liberty of testation were those concerning charitable bequests and manumitted slaves at the expense of heirs at law. They were nonetheless construed by judges to be exceptions to the general rule of testamentary freedom, which was said to apply to any property holder of full age and sound mind. As far as the law was concerned, their wills were allowed to stand in place of reason.[16]

Depravity and the Disposing Mind

"Being of sound mind" was a self-description that testators were advised to use at the outset of their wills in order to avoid legal trouble after their death. The subscribing witnesses affirmed that was true by affixing their signatures to the last page of the document. And it was something the proponent had to affirm, if not affirmatively prove, when the will was contested. Sanity was presumed in the common run of civil cases "until the contrary appears." This way of proceeding was said to make practical sense, as wills were more likely than contracts or deeds to be made *in extremis*. The vulnerability of the will was rendered all the more apparent as state legislatures lifted traditional restraints on the liberty of testation, shifting the focus from status to sanity as the key determinant of who could make a valid will.[17]

What had to be true of a testator in order to be deemed of sound mind? In giving concrete meaning to the statutory language, American judges and lawyers had recourse to the "old books" produced by English commentators like Swinburne and Blackstone, who required only "a glimmering of reason." While this standard was regularly invoked by the lawyers for proponents in will contests, their opponents summoned up other precedents indicating that courts required a stronger showing of competence, particularly where the will deviated significantly from the norms of distribution set out in the laws of intestacy, and argued that mental weakness short of a total deprivation of reason ought to suffice when there was also evidence of undue influence or fraud. Judges in the early republic recognized the risks that a more demanding standard of capacity might increase litigation and reduce the leverage of the elderly, who often had to use the threat of disinheritance to secure proper care in their declining years. Yet they were inclined to think that heirs deserved protection against opportunistic friends, relations, and household servants, who had a tendency to swarm the sickbed of the propertied and threaten the integrity of the will-making process. Attempting to strike a middle ground, their decisions collectively provide a portrait of the competent testator whose psychology was concordant with the philosophy of Common Sense.[18]

As a baseline, the default legal person in this doctrinal context had to possess a set of intellectual, volitional, and emotional faculties that enabled him to make a reasonable disposition of his property, even though reasonableness was not legally required for a will to be valid. Courts placed particular emphasis upon the memory; the testator had to be able to appreciate the nature and extent of his estate as well as the identity of those who might justly expect to receive some portion of it upon his death. As he meditated upon these matters, the testator was supposed to be guided by his affections and moral sense, which would naturally move him to bequeath the bulk of his property to his immediate family. In addition, he would not to allow his passions to overwhelm him as he performed this "last solemn act," and he would retain enough mental "strength and vigour" to resist the importunities and detect the subterfuges of scheming relatives and pretended friends. The fact that his body was not as strong or his mind as acute as in other moments of his life was legally immaterial. What mattered most from the standpoint of the bench was that the testator had "the capacity of recollecting, discerning and feeling the relations, connexions and obligations of family" and made the will in question "spontaneously and deliberately," so that it could be deemed an act of "self-possession."[19]

This way of thinking about testamentary capacity encouraged the identification of sanity and freedom with conventional notions of rationality and morality, thereby casting doubt on the competence of those who exhibited irrational, immoral, and impulsive behavior. What led some testators to dispose of their property in ways that appeared completely ludicrous, patently perverse, or downright cruel? Who in his "right mind" would consciously and deliberately choose to act in any such way? Did it not follow that those who deviated from the norms of rationality and morality were less than fully free and therefore less than fully accountable for their actions? The logic of judicial reasoning about the mind of the moral agent seemed to point to the problematic conclusion that the only persons who could be said to be of sound mind were those who would never execute an "inhuman," "unjust," or "unreasonable" will. As the law was reshaped to reflect the optimistic liberal Enlightenment conceptions of individual ability, it had the paradoxical effect of generating serious doubts about the mental competence of those who deviated from this model of the sovereign self.

These doubts were reinforced by professional alienists. In their works of medical jurisprudence, questions of testamentary capacity loomed large, second only to criminal responsibility. The maladies "particularly noticed" in testamentary cases involved either too much or too little volitional power, most commonly classified as "monomania" or "dementia." In this period, the idea of "moral insanity" was part of the general recasting of madness as a "will out of control."[20] For purposes of adjudicating contested wills, the alienists urged revision of the common law's traditional definition of insanity as a cognitive impairment so as to encompass nonintellectual disorders. A testator suffering from the alienation of his "domestic affections" might be "insensible to the impulse of natural motives." Telltale signs of this disorder could be found in expressions of hostility toward loved ones "without any just cause." In making these diagnoses, the medical men suggested that sudden changes of heart and other "unnatural" feelings were in some sense insane. Benjamin Rush, for instance, said that a despondent testator who chose to "bequeath the whole, or the greatest part, of his estate, to a church, or any other public institution, or to a stranger, to the injury of a family of children who had never offended him, and whose necessities, or rank in life, as well as their blood, intitled them to be his heirs, should be considered as morally deranged; and his will should be set aside as promptly as if he had disposed of his estate in a paroxysm of intellectual derangement." In his medical opinion, "the laws, and the voice of nature, in such a case, should silence a volume of reports in favour of a contrary practice."[21]

In subsequent decades medical jurists became more circumspect, seeking to avoid the charge that they had essentially equated sin with disease and left within their schemes no place for ordinary depravity, even as they continued to push for legal recognition of partial and non-intellectual forms of insanity. Following the convention of law writers, they advanced their arguments for reform by way of "hard cases" that presented judges with clashing moral and formal considerations. They concentrated on two recent and high-profile English will contests, *Greenwood v. Greenwood* (1790) and *Dew v. Clark* (1826), "where the charge of insanity rests on some obstinate and long continued feelings of hatred or malice against individuals, and which are evidently groundless." The former was presented by most medical commentators as a specimen of judicial dogmatism, while the latter was read as suggesting a more enlightened perspective.

In *Greenwood*, Lord Kenyon urged the jury to resist the temptation to substitute their own judgment for that of the testator. Though the contestant's lawyer had suggested that they "look first to the act done, and argue up from that to the sanity or insanity of the mind," Kenyon issued a stern corrective: "We must see only whether the will is the will or not of the testator." The question before them was not the justice of its provisions but "whether it was the disposition of this man's mind, exercising the faculties of his mind at a time when in possession of those faculties." They were to allow it to stand unless they found the testator so deranged that he was "prevented from judging who the objects of his bounty should be, according to his own will." Any rule less stringent was really no rule at all: "A multitude of instances there have been where men have taken up prejudices against their nearest and dearest relations. . . . And if once we get into digressions of that kind, then we get upon a sea without a rudder—where will you stop—what partiality will be enough to set aside a will—and what partiality will you give way to, and say the will is good?"[22]

Medical jurists saw *Greenwood* as an obvious case of insanity wrongly decided by a judge in vain pursuit of an unattainable ideal of legal certainty. They were heartened to find that "more enlarged and correct views prevailed in the able and elaborate judgment" rendered by Sir John Nicholl in *Dew v. Clark*. The testator in this case was portrayed by his virtually disinherited daughter as insanely deluded about her moral character as well as his own. Although he was said to conceive of himself as the most perfect and benevolent of fathers, he denounced her as "an abandoned profligate, vile and irreclaimable" despite her exemplary behavior and subjected her to menial labor and brutal floggings for imaginary offenses. Though he was eventually declared insane and placed under a guardianship, this ruling was prompted by a paralytic attack nearly three years after the date of the will. The question was whether the testator was insane at the crucial moment when the instrument was executed.[23]

Nicholl's opinion began by sounding the same cautionary notes as Lord Kenyon about the importance of distinguishing caprice and injustice from testamentary incapacity. But he followed the interpretation of *Greenwood* presented by Lord Erskine in his famous speech in *Hadfield's Case* that partial insanity was a recognized basis for setting aside a will. Nicholl ratified Erskine's "wide distinction between civil and criminal cases," in that the will of a person shown to be insane might be set aside without proof of a direct casual connection between the disease and the disposition, though this was required "to deliver a man from responsibility for crimes." In elaborating what it meant to be insane as a matter of law, Sir Nicholl considered broader societal conceptions of the meaning of madness and looked to the work of medical as well as legal writers. He located insanity in a deluded imagination and argued that what distinguished those who were insanely deluded from those who were merely mistaken or mentally weak was their "pertinacious adhesion . . . to some delusive idea in opposition to plain evidence of its falsity," often accompanied "by an apparent insensibility to, or perversion of, those feelings which are peculiarly characteristic of our nature." In short, insanity consisted in "the belief of facts, which no rational person would have believed."[24]

Finding after a painstaking review of the evidence that the testator's beliefs about himself and his daughter clearly fit this description and that he them held throughout his life, nothing remained but to pronounce the will null and void. But before arriving at this conclusion, Sir Nicholl deemed it necessary to rule out the possibility that it had been executed during a lucid interval. In a passage verging on self-parody, he explained that the only way that this testator could have been found lucid, given all the other evidence in the record, was if he had made an officious will in favor of the daughter he so insanely hated—if, in other words, he had behaved like rational men. Having said this, he was all the more anxious to avoid any implication that he was allowing his compassion for the unoffending child to divert him from his judicial duty. So he ultimately decided the case according to the more exacting but no less circular test of the criminal law. He held the will invalid only because it was "the direct unqualified offspring of that morbid delusion, proved . . . to have been ever present to the mind of the deceased, as to the character and conduct of his daughter—being, if I may so term it, the very creature of that morbid delusion put into act and energy."[25]

Papering over the confusion did not make it disappear. Although *Dew* quickly gained recognition on both sides of the Atlantic as the leading case on the subject of testamentary capacity, it was more effective in setting the terms of courtroom disputations than providing a rule of decision.[26] Although the renegotiation of the boundaries between disease and depravity is a familiar feature in the historiography of criminal law, the secularization and medicalization of sin also had a profound impact on civil cases concerning wills. The concept of a monomania concerning a single topic or relative was a potential goldmine for disappointed heirs and the lawyers who worked for and against them. It was also a potent challenge to the traditional common law of capacity and the assumptions about human nature and psychology upon which it was premised. In opening the door to delusion and making it the test of testamentary capacity, Nicholl sought to bring the law of wills into greater alignment with medical science without making a mockery of the principle of testamentary freedom, exposing but not resolving the internal contradictions upon which this liberal legal order was built. As they were reluctantly drawn into family feuds, the American judges who used *Dew*'s criterion of delusion became entangled in the same sorts of logical and metaphysical conundrums. Alive to the intricately intertwined questions of property and personhood placed in issue during the course of these trials and mindful of the vision of human autonomy that was at stake, they endeavored to chart a course forward, ever more conscious as they did that *Dew*'s test of delusion left them more or less rudderless, just as Lord Kenyon had apprehended.

The Offspring of Delusion

"In the name of God," Mason Lee declared he was "of perfect mind, memory, and understanding" when he executed his last will and testament in July 1820. Lee bequeathed the whole of his $50,000 estate in equal parts to the states of South Carolina and Tennessee, disinheriting his surviving nieces and nephews as well as his illegitimate sons. In order to leave no ambiguity about his intentions, he declared that it was his "will and desire that no part or parcel of my estate shall be enjoyed, or in any wise inherited by either or any of my relations, *while wood grows or water runs*," and enjoined his executors "to contend with them either in law or equity, to enforce this my will, by employing the *best Charleston lawyers*, at the expense of my estate; or in any other way, *again, again, and again*." Lee died a short time after making this will, and when its contents were revealed a challenge was filed by his heirs-at-law on ground of "partial insanity." Relying on Lord Erskine's argument in *Hadfield's Case*, they claimed that "the grand defect of his mind was in relation to those objects that stood nearest to him by the laws of nature; and that under this disease of mind he had made this singular disposition of his property, and that this delusion must avoid the will."[27]

To make their case, the contestants offered a biography of Mason Lee designed to show that he "had not any good cause for disliking his relations." According to their witnesses, Lee was raised in "decent society" in North Carolina and manifested "no very striking peculiarities" until he was struck by lightning at the age of thirty. Then he abruptly began to act very strangely, moving to Georgia, where he inexplicably killed a black man, and fleeing to South Carolina. Lee's management of his property was ridiculous and his business transactions no more sensible; he concocted a number of bizarre and unsuccessful moneymaking schemes and extended long credits without charging interest. He wore shoes and hats with holes in them, as he believed that would enable him to drive out the devil. All the while, he appeared constantly wracked with suspicions that his relatives were bewitching him. He took shelter in a "miserable hovel," perpetually fighting off imaginary assaults of all sorts of evil spirits, as well as "the gravel," a form of liver disease. To the end of his life, he believed that his afflictions were caused by his relatives, who "desired him dead, to get his property." Laboring under this delusion, Lee had determined to make a will "in favor of no human being," to which no court could give effect, as it so plainly "spake the language of insanity."[28]

The proponents' witnesses predictably offered a counternarrative. Drawn from a higher social station and better acquainted with the testator, they depicted him as "eccentric" but nonetheless "sane and perfectly capable of managing his business." Though the bargains he struck looked at first to be "whimsical" and "foolish," they often "turned out to be the best that could have been made." His eccentric mode of dress reflected his "avarice" or "pride." As for his visions of devils and witches, they were likely produced by the "ardent spirits" he regularly imbibed. In addition, there was reason to believe that Lee's suspicions of his relatives were based in fact, for some of them had plotted to have him seized and carried to Georgia to stand trial for murder. The subscribing witnesses to Lee's will all swore to his complete sanity and sobriety at the critical moment of execution. Indeed, he exhibited a striking degree of mental clarity in his final days, insisting that he was "not so credulous" as to believe in bewitchment and that he "knew his disease was the gravel, which would be the cause of his death."[29]

Characterizing the case as one of "great difficultly," the trial judge declared that the proponent was entitled to the benefit of the doubt in his charge to the jury: "A rational state of mind is the natural state of every man, and until there is full proof of insanity the law presumes that every man is in a rational state when he does any act either civil or criminal." His review of the evidence strongly implied the contestants had failed to meet this burden. Nodding to Lord Erksine's "celebrated speech" without using the word delusion, the judge recognized that if a person were found insane "in the legal sense of the word," "all his civil acts were void, whether they could be traced to the malady or not." The judge further advised that the law would validate the will of a confirmed lunatic if it were shown to have been made during a lucid interval. With these authorities in view, he pointed the way toward a verdict in favor of Lee's will. Although the testator's purported belief in evil spirits might be regarded as a "symptom of a disordered mind," the belief was "not of itself any proof of it"; many persons who were "above all suspicion of insanity," including those "distinguished for their wisdom," held similar convictions about the supernatural. Moreover, Lee's peculiarities could be "traced to other causes than insanity," particularly his habitual intoxication. Finally, he acknowledged that there were cases where the will itself was "so irrational" as to provide "intrinsic evidence" of the existence of insanity. But Lee had clearly enumerated reasons for his disposition, "some of which appeared to be well founded, and to justify his belief that [his relatives] had treated him ill." So instructed, the jury found in favor of the will, and the verdict was summarily affirmed on appeal.[30]

The validation of Mason Lee's will illustrates the continuing strength of the common law presumption of sanity, even as Erskine's doctrine of delusion was increasingly deployed by American lawyers in suits seeking to set aside unnatural dispositions. A survey of American law reports reveals that judges initially treated the hypothesis of partial insanity with a fair measure of caution, tending to favor alternate explanations that ascribed deviant wills to such causes as singularity, old age, ill temper, and intemperance.[31] But the doctrine of delusion was gaining traction, and the George Moore will case was added to *Dew* and *Greenwood* in the treatise literature under the general heading "*Monomania—Hatred against relatives.*"[32] Moreover, courts signaled their growing receptivity to the new medical psychology by liberalizing the rules of evidence applying to medical witnesses, allowing them to offer their opinions concerning the testator's sanity even when based solely upon the trial testimony of others.[33] Movement in this direction was quite gradual and halting, however, as courts endeavored to distinguish the province of the medical expert from that of the judge and jury and to contain the disruptive potential of scientific evidence, lest the "truth . . . be lost in the learned contest of discordant opinions."[34]

The gradual incorporation of these medical concepts and their implications for everyday adjudication are exhibited in the 1839 Pennsylvania case of *Boyd v. Eby.* The dispute centered upon a codicil to the will of James Neal, which redirected the bulk of his estate from his closest relatives, Samuel and William Boyd, to a religious denomination. The contestants claimed that Neal had fallen into a "partial delirium," during which he "contracted prejudices and erroneous notions" with respect to Samuel Boyd, for whom he had previously "entertained a high regard and affection." Though the delirium soon passed, Neal "continue[d] to cherish . . . these antipathies and perverted impressions," and he composed the disputed codicil while under their influence. Finding sufficient proof of mental derangement to overcome the usual presumption of sanity, the trial judge instructed jurors that the proponents carried the burden of proving that the testator's mind "had shaken off the disease, and had become generally sound, not only upon some particular subject, but entirely." In terms reminiscent of *Dew*, he distinguished a delusional state of mind from mere error or prejudice:

> A person may form erroneous opinions in his youth, . . . or in sickness when afflicted with disease, or under the influence of bad associations or ardent spirits; and he may retain such prejudices and errors, and act upon them when he comes of full age, is restored to health, is introduced into better company, or becomes sober; so a man I would suppose might possibly retain prejudices or erroneous impressions, after he is restored to his right mind, which had their origin in delusions occurring under the influence of intemperance or perhaps partial delirium, or at least under a partially disordered state of intellect.

Thus, Neal's prejudice could be taken as evidence of his insanity only so long as he remained insane. If he persisted in exhibiting this prejudice after his mind otherwise recovered its equilibrium, it was no longer an insane prejudice. It was effectively incorporated into his character, and he was to be held accountable for any act performed under its influence. So instructed, the jury returned a verdict in favor of the codicil.[35]

The Pennsylvania Supreme Court, however, found that a reversal was warranted because the trial judge had erred "in drawing a distinction between the insane delusion itself, and the impressions or prejudices occasioned by such delusion, and in supposing that the former might cease and the latter continue." The court insisted that "the presence of absurd prejudices, of groundless antipathies, of silly and chimerical hatreds, originating in acknowledged insanity, is the only evidence we can have of the existence of the delusion." When a person first makes a will leaving most of his property to his nearest relations and then "becomes lunatic, and in the paroxysms of his insanity, and in connection with them, imbibes the most violent antipathies against one of those relations . . . without just cause or foundation," he was rightly considered insane on the subject of this relative. If this insane delusion exerted such a hold on his "thinking faculties" that the codicil was its "direct offspring," then it was invalid.[36]

In so ruling, the court begged the question of what constituted insanity in the first place and generated a host of other questions. Why should erroneous impressions or prejudices "contracted" in delirium be treated any differently from those formed in youth, in sickness, or under the influence of bad associations or alcohol? What grounds existed for distinguishing insanity from these other conditions and situations? Did they not also operate as constraints on a testator's will? Was a will made under such constraints actually the testator's will?

The ambiguities in decisions like *Boyd* generated more litigation, as parties tested the limits of the doctrine of partial insanity.[37] With great aplomb, contestants insisted that the perversities of the testator's will were unmistakable signs of mental incompetence, while proponents worked just as assiduously to normalize the disposition in question, reminding courtroom audiences that tensions and hostilities were sadly endemic within the family circle.[38] Given the protracted and acrimonious nature of these trials, presiding judges often betrayed their exasperation in their instructions to the jury. They acknowledged the difficulties entailed in marking "the borders between reason and sanity," which were exacerbated by the fact that jurors had to rely upon "evidence furnished through the uncertain medium of other minds." For better or worse, the jury's verdict did not necessarily bring the case to a close; appeals frequently followed, and appellate judges struggled to maintain some semblance of a uniform rule of law even as medical experts contended ever more strenuously that each case had to be considered on its own facts.[39] Most disturbing was how routinely family members seemed to be driving one another to distraction or insanity. The testimony offered by a witness in an 1838 case illustrates what judges were up against: "He does not think that the testator was crazy, but that his health and age and family affairs had destroyed his mind."[40]

"I Never Knew Any Human Being Who Was of Sound Mind"

In the face of this litigation, which threatened to render the freedom of a man to do what he willed with his property "insecure and comparatively delusive," a number of judges harkened back to the traditional common law of capacity.[41] The most widely noted decision to this effect was the high-profile 1841 New York case of *Stewart's Executor v. Lispenard,* involving the will of the nearly imbecilic Alice Lispenard, which favored the testatrix's brother over her other legal heirs and was upheld on appeal by the state's highest court. In an elaborate but unofficial opinion, Senator Gulian Verplanck invoked the "ancient rule" that a person with "any glimmering of reason" may make a will and that proof of a "total deprivation of sense" is required before it is set aside. Admittedly, this rule set the threshold of testamentary capacity rather low, but it had the virtue of being "clear and definite . . . and therefore wise." Verplanck explained:

> Taking mankind such as observation shows us human nature to be, can any other than this be a safe, prudent, just, or politic rule? When we observe the strange incongruities of human character . . . when, in ordinary life, it often happens that the most sagacious and prudent in many of the affairs of business, are yet in some point of domestic conduct, or in some one matter of opinion or action, guilty of absurdities such as the feeblest minds could not commit, one might almost adopt the startling conclusion of Dr. Haslam, who, after years of professional observation of the phenomena of mental disease . . . , in answer to the customary question, "Was Miss B. of sound mind?" replied: "I never knew any human being who was of sound mind."

The senator maintained that establishing "a standard of intellect or information beyond the possession of reason in the lowest degree, as in itself *essential* to legal capacity," would "exclude females, ignorant persons, and persons laboring under violent and painful disease, from the power of testamentary disposition." He also worried that "proofs of wild speculations or extravagant and peculiar opinions, or of the forgetfulness or the prejudices of old age," might be held sufficient to "shake the security of property, and wrest from the aged and infirm that authority over their earnings or savings which is often their best security against injury and neglect."[42]

While similar concerns were aired in other courtrooms, *Lispenard* attracted far more criticism than praise.[43] By the 1840s the presence of delusion was widely accepted as a distinct basis for setting aside a will.[44] Perhaps the best indicator of this development comes from the *Lispenard* decision itself. In a passage frequently ignored by the case's detractors, Verplanck expressly recognized that an otherwise competent testator might be incapacitated by the force of a "morbid delusion," referring effusively to "the luminous and elaborate judgment of Sir John Nichol [sic], in Dew v. Clark," as well as "the excellent work of our countryman, Dr. Ray, on the 'Medical Jurisprudence of Insanity.'"[45] Indeed, the senator went so far as to suggest that proof of eccentric or absurd behavior when offered in connection with an unreasonable will might provide conclusive evidence of a disabling delusion, rendering the document void. Thus, even as *Lispenard* purported to hew to the traditional common law authorities, the decision was clearly influenced by the new medical psychology.

The doctrine of delusion proved exceedingly troublesome because of its circumscribed nature. It caught on because it seemed to enable judges to avoid drawing a line between weakness or eccentricity and testamentary capacity. A testator could be declared incompetent with specific reference to his will, without calling his general competence into question and thereby unsettling the security of market transactions. The criterion of delusion was also appealing because it had the ring of an intellectual disorder that could be comprehended as part of the common law's cognitive test of capacity. Its legal effects were far easier to contain than those of the amorphous concept of moral insanity, which seemed to pose a more direct challenge to free will. Yet upon closer inspection, the symptoms of delusion identified by doctors and lawyers in will contests almost always included disordered feelings as well as thoughts, delusion in its essence amounting to a loss of control over the process of thinking. Indeed, the monomaniacal testator was described as a person whose mental world was governed by ruling passions that did not answer to the dictates of conscience and had taken reason hostage. It was also quite common to find the delusion figured as an alien invader that captured the will and moved the afflicted to take wholly unintended acts. Either way, the concept of monomania seemed to provide courts with a scientific basis for finding a testator incompetent without needing to rule on the justice or rationality of his will. A judge could set aside an unnatural disposition simply because it could not have been the testator's act: the delusion did it.

It soon became obvious that the test of delusion was not as determinate as it promised to be. Rather than offering an objective means of resolving will contests, the alienists themselves became the center of legal controversy. They sparked disputation among members of the bench and bar about how much weight their diagnoses ought to be accorded relative to the testimony of family physicians and laypersons familiar with the character of the testator. The medical man called to the stand to speak to the subject of mental soundness seemed always on the verge of invading the province of the jury, so courts required attorneys to frame them in the form of hypothetical questions.[46] Because the alienists called by each side were constrained to answer only with reference to slanted renderings of the facts, they appeared to be disagreeing among themselves. That tarnished their public image, as they were made scapegoats for difficulties that were not fairly attributable to them alone. These disputes reflected strains internal to the medical profession as well as between doctors and lawyers, all of whom laid claim to scientific authority. But their ruminations about whether and how far the new medical psychology should be allowed to reshape the conceptions of the default legal person involved more fundamental concerns. Though these will contests were always about property, reflecting the material interests of the parties and the professions, the surviving transcripts, often thousands of pages long, provide the historian with a running commentary on the constitution of the self and the meaning of freedom.

In addressing the deceptively simple question of "will or no will," trial participants unwittingly exhibited the utter want of a common sense about what it was to be a rational actor. Their judgments about personhood were freighted with assumptions about race, gender, generational relations, and social justice, all of which had implications far beyond the outcome of the case at bar. In them, it is possible to detect growing doubts about "man's power over himself to prevent or control insanity," as well as worries about the bounds of state power over the determination of individual wills.[47] What is most intriguing about the questions asked and answered in case after case is the extent to which they betray an anxious identification with the monomaniac and a certain attraction to "what the world calls phrensy" on the part of Americans who cherished their liberty but were at least as ardent in their quest for reassurance that they lived in a rational, moral, and comprehensible universe.[48]

"Who Are the Really Insane?"

Proceeding against the backdrop of growing political polarization and a looming sectional crisis, antebellum will contests dramatically underscore the lack of consensus among professionals and laymen as to the very constitution of natural justice. In their submissions to the court, litigants painted skewed portraits of the departed for their own strategic purposes. However distorted, their biographical accounts nonetheless provide telling indicators of what the parties and their lawyers took to be the behavioral signs of mental competence. As these competing storylines were elaborated in the courtroom, judges and jurors struggled to determine the truth of the matter.

A survey of the rulings published in law reports and featured in treatise literature reveals that midcentury courts were especially perplexed by two sorts of cases: those alleging that the will was the offspring of a monomania on the subject of religion or politics; and those contending that the testator's disposition was the product of "illicit intercourse" with a woman other than his wife. These cases placed judges in the unenviable position of deciding what forms of belief and conduct were so far beyond the bounds of reason that they signified the absence of sanity or free will. As they wrestled with this conundrum, judges were mindful of the broader doctrinal and ideological implications of their rulings. They were reluctant to brand any particular religious or political belief insane as a matter of law, disclaiming any intention to impose orthodoxy from the bench. They were even more wary about drawing inferences of insanity from proof of immoral conduct, appreciating that arguments to this effect might prove every criminal *non compos mentis*. But judges were moved by the plight of the excluded heirs and their appeals to the ideal of natural justice. Even in decisions upholding the testator's will, judges hinted at the circumstances that might lead them to rule otherwise and inspired future contestants to embellish their tales of disinheritance.

Contests involving wills with large bequests to religious associations posed peculiar problems because religious liberty was constitutionally protected. Jon Butler has aptly described the inventive religious culture that developed in the early nineteenth century as "a unique spiritual hothouse."[49] Indeed, in extreme cases these affinities might even supersede the ties of birth and marriage. So multifarious were religious persuasions and so fervent were their adherents that charitable bequests to religious sects at the expense of the natural heirs were sometimes alleged to be evidence of mental impairment.

One of the earliest of these cases, *Chandler v. Ferris* (1834), concerned the will of a Delaware man that bequeathed his entire estate to a vocational school for "male children of the African race."[50] Chandler's heirs contended that he was afflicted with a series of monomanias late in life, leaving him "peculiarly subject to the management of" William Lloyd Garrison's antislavery society. The will itself bore out this point, they argued, for it was made "in favor of a class of people toward whom Thomas Chandler was known to have entertained antipathies, and for an object not only wild and visionary, but in our state of society and political condition, wicked in its character and dangerous in its tendency." In response, the proponents called upon medical experts who diagnosed the testator as merely "asthmatic" and lay associates who attested to his business capacity and affirmed that he had long had "the amelioration of the condition of the blacks at heart." Though the jury charge was measured, requiring that Chandler "knew what he was about" and was not "deprived . . . of his free agency," the verdict was against the will.[51] No appeal was taken from this judgment, but in other contests in which there were further proceedings, judges were pressed to clarify what constituted an insane delusion. For instance, in the 1840 Kentucky case of *George Weir's Will*, a jury had set aside a will manumitting all the testator's slaves, and the claim on appeal was that the testator's so-called "melancholy mania"[52] was distinguishable from legal insanity. The court admitted it was a difficult case, since the testator's anxiety about his spiritual condition was extremely intense and debilitating, but finally ruled out the charge of monomania "on the subject of religion or social obligation," as the testator's "theological principles" appeared "altogether sound and orthordox [sic]," at least from the perspective of his Presbyterian minister. The provisions of his will were provident, rational, and fully consistent with his character, "being in principle an emancipator."[53]

Nonetheless, some on the bench questioned the wisdom of judging sanity on the popularity of a belief or the social status of other believers, particularly in view of the religious diversity and sectional strife that increasingly marked American society. "How many in the community would declare a millerite, or a mormon, or an abolitionist unsound in mind?" one New Jersey judge asked. Public opinion could hardly provide a cohesive or determinate basis for legal judgment without violating individuals' civil rights. "If every man is to be deemed insane because he differs from another in political sentiments," a Maryland judge pointed out, "the whole nation could be proved to be in that condition." The same could be said of various religious creeds.[54]

Perhaps to avoid passing directly on the truth or falsity of a testator's beliefs, a number of courts focused instead upon their psychological effects. The 1856 Massachusetts case of *Woodbury v. Obear* provides one such example, involving a testator who had disinherited his nephew under the impression that his kinsman had not only neglected but tried to poison him. During the course of the trial, the testator was shown to have believed in witches and ghosts and his ability to communicate with "departed spirits." On this evidence, a jury returned a verdict against the will, finding it was the product of an insane delusion that the executor had magnified and manipulated to his advantage through the use of undue influence, and this ruling was affirmed on appeal. Without addressing the rationality of the testator's religious views, Chief Justice Lemuel Shaw confirmed that they had compromised his capacity. "A person by artful, false and repeated surmises and insinuations, operating upon a sensitive and excitable mind of another, may foster and exasperate, if not create, an insane delusion, and at the same time and by the same means obtain such an influence over him as to induce him to make a will, or do any other act, which he would not have done but for the existence of the insane delusion, and the undue influence concurring with it." The emphasis was not on the content of the will but the testator's want of free agency in making it.[55]

"An Indecent Trust"

The same strains and tensions can be traced through the decisional law concerning "iniquitous wills" allegedly arising out of "meretricious" relationships. A substantial number of these contests involved wills bequeathing some portion of the testator's estate to his concubine and their illegitimate children. In such cases, contestants tended to argue that the relationship itself stood as evidence of the testator's mental unsoundness and that the influence exercised by a slave woman was presumptively undue. Although arguments along these lines often persuaded jurors to set aside the will, appellate courts were disinclined to affirm their verdicts.[56]

An especially vivid illustration of these tendencies is found in the protracted contest regarding the will of William B. Farr, a lifelong bachelor who directed that the proceeds of his estate be used for the benefit of his slave "mistress," a "bright mulatto" called Fan, and their son Henry, who was "nearly white." At trial, Farr was depicted as "a man originally of strong mind" whose mental faculties had been "enfeebled by hard drinking" and a "stroke of the palsy" late in life. The proponents contended that his capacity to will nonetheless remained intact to the end, making much of the fact that Farr expressed his desire to benefit Fan and Henry before as well as after his health declined. According to the contestants, Fan "had the influence over him of a white woman and a wife." The testimony they adduced figured the Farr household as a topsy-turvy place where the master did the slave woman's bidding under the threat of physical as well as psychological coercion.[57] This claim was in keeping with the general idea that the law was an instrument to restore the proper hierarchy in social relations, but out of keeping with the legal presumption that a man could do what he wished with his own.

Litigation concerning Farr's estate dragged on for years as judges and jurors repeatedly clashed over whether the testator was "a rational and moral civil agent." After three successive jury verdicts overturning the will and as many appeals, the case again came before the appellate court, which resoundingly reversed the decision, seeking above all else to distinguish immorality from insanity.

> Perhaps no man has ever existed who was so entirely self-willed as to be wholly uninfluenced by the opinions and wishes of those with whom he was connected. . . . It has happened, and will happen again, that a mistress may so captivate the affections of her paramour, that he shall give her his whole estate, to the exclusion of his lawful wife and children. Such an act all would condemn, and concur in denouncing as immoral and improper the influence which produced it; yet, if it be done under the influence of affection merely, however unworthy the object may be, such wills have been, and must be, supported, so long as the law allows a sane man to dispose of his property according to his own wishes.

This court held that Farr's 1828 will was indeed such an act and suggested that the motive which led to it was not entirely disreputable. The judges read the document as an expression of a father's love, intended to secure for his son "that position in society which is the consequence of freedom and wealth."[58]

As political conflict over slavery intensified, Southern courts only grew more adamant in upholding wills of this sort, resisting the idea that bondswomen could rob masters of their free agency. In the 1849 Georgia case of *Potts v. House*, for example, Judge Joseph Lumpkin flatly rejected the contestants' argument that a slave's influence over his or her master could categorically be held to indicate "such moral degradation" as should induce the court to avoid his testamentary act. A similar judgment was rendered by a South Carolina court in the 1856 case of

Jolliffe v. Fanning (1856), which refused to find the testator insane on account of the fact that he allowed a drunken, "saucy" bondswoman "to occupy a level with himself" and "become the mother of his children."[59] Though midcentury judges were often given to moralizing about these sorts of relationships, they nonetheless strenuously upheld the right of the testator to make what was in their eyes an unnatural disposition of his worldly goods. These and similar cases attest to the contradictions in which courts were caught when they sought above all to defend white men's rights over their property.

Significantly, judges took similar positions in contests involving extramarital relationships between white men and white women, though they tended to treat both parties with greater sympathy and delicacy. The 1850 Alabama case of *Dunlap v. Robinson*, for example, upheld the will of a bachelor who devised the whole of his estate to the married woman next door and her children, who were almost certainly his. Following the rule in *Farr*, which he described as a "much stronger case" of impropriety, the judge refused to raise a presumption of insanity or undue influence solely on the presumption of an "adulterous connection" between the testator and a beneficiary of his will. Even if the testator were "guilty of the enormity attributed to him," the judge was prepared to validate his will, for neither "morals" nor "public policy" stood in the way of an unmarried man's effort to provide for his illegitimate children. After all, he reasoned, "it would certainly not tend to mitigate his offence, should he have a spurious offspring dependent on her or her husband for support, to cast them pennyless upon the world."[60]

In antebellum courtrooms, the "rational and moral civil agent" remained the ostensible model of the competent testator even as judges affirmed the wills of those who deviated rather far from this ideal. In rationalizing these rulings, appellate judges often strained to show that the will was not as absurd or unjust as it first appeared. This method of reconciling the principles of testamentary freedom and natural justice worked in many cases involving religious eccentricity and sexual misconduct. Even when the will was downright "monstrous" or "revolting," judges still tended to favor a man's freedom to dispose of his property. These decisions were rarely reached without misgivings, though judicial resolve grew firmer as contestants urged recognition of the medical concept of "moral insanity" as an independent basis for setting aside a will. This unfortunate choice of words all but identified depravity with disease. By and large, the deployment of this diagnosis in the courtroom only heightened judicial skepticism of medical science.

Monomania in the Moral Sense

What contestants meant by "moral insanity" was not always easy to discern, though most used it to refer to an impairment of the nonintellectual faculties. These arguments were chiefly drawn from the writings of medical jurists, who were increasingly inclined to criticize the judicial fixation on the "test of delusion." As physicians repeatedly reminded their legal brethren, the moral faculties, "like the intellect, being connected with the brain, are necessarily affected by pathological actions in that organism." On the basis of their clinical observations, they advised that the "abnormal condition thus produced may exert an astonishing influence on the conduct, changing the peaceable and retiring individual . . . from the calm and quiet of his lawful and innocent occupations, into a career of shameless dissipation and debauchery, while the intellectual perceptions seem to have lost none of their original soundness and vigor." Yet they hastened to add that only those who were "practically conversant with the insane" could accurately determine the extent of the impairment in any given case.[61]

One of the first and most prominent will cases in which the concept of moral insanity was mobilized was the spectacular 1849 New Jersey case of *Trumbull v. Gibbons*. Thomas Gibbons, the testator, was not only a notorious "libertine and debauchee" but also a spectacularly successful steamboat magnate, having prevailed in the landmark 1824 U.S. Supreme Court case of *Gibbons v. Ogden*. A year later he drafted his last will, leaving nearly all of his considerable estate to his son William on the condition that he would never transfer so much as "one cent" to his brother-in-law, John M. Trumbull, or any of Trumbull's heirs.[62]

In arguing against this "unholy" document, the excluded heirs conceded that "general insanity did not exist" but insisted that Gibbons labored under "a monomaniacal feeling against Trumbull, or under deception and influence" by William. The defenders of the will scoffed at this appeal to "moral insanity . . . not coupled with delusion." While recognizing that this kind of insanity was "much in vogue just now," they maintained that it would not have constituted a valid excuse had Gibbons committed a criminal act under its influence. To bolster their case, the proponents summoned two medical men to attest to the soundness of Gibbons's mind when he executed his will. Finally, the proponents offered a perfectly rational explanation for its provisions; they contended that this document was the outgrowth of an ugly family feud set off by the indecent indulgences of Gibbons himself. According to the proponents' witnesses, Gibbons "kept lewd women in his house" and drove out his wife, daughter, and son-in-law, who had remonstrated with him about his deplorable conduct. The infuriated Gibbons then retaliated with a pamphlet "containing the foulest and most unnatural charges upon his wife and daughter, and upon John M. Trumbull." Trumbull then sued Gibbons for libel, emerging triumphant and $15,000 richer.[63]

The judge was partial to these arguments, hinting to the jury that nothing in the record amounted to testamentary incapacity, undue influence, or fraud. Yet, reflecting the new medical psychology, he reminded the jury that the crux of the issue was not Gibbons's "general capacity" but rather his alleged susceptibility to monomania and other "extrinsic influence." The judge made short work of the idea of undue influence on account of the overwhelming evidence suggesting that Thomas Gibbons was "in no wise dependent upon his son" and that he was "a man over whom . . . no human being had any control." It remained possible that the testator was a monomaniac on the subject of Trumbull and his children and that William "artfully administered to this delusion." This instruction encouraged the jury to associate monomania with delusion, rather than to consider the moral form of the disease.[64]

Taking the evidentiary record as a whole, the judge admitted an attraction to the hypothesis of insanity: "These documents . . . certainly exhibit a painful, humiliating, mortifying spectacle of human passion and human depravity; it would seem well nigh incredible that the author of those productions could be sane; . . . that he should spread upon his will the record of his deep malignant feelings toward the offspring of his own loins, his own flesh and blood, and thus perpetuate the record of his own and his family's infamy, are calculated to create the impression, if not the hope, that the author was a maniac." But it was important for the jurors not to indulge in such wishful thinking, for "the inquiry with you will be, was the man deranged, in the appropriate technical sense of the word, or was he merely the victim of unbridled passion? Was reason dethroned, or had passion seized the rein and acquired mastery?" The judge presumed "that there is a line, broad, clear, and well defined, though to our imperfect senses ofttimes imperceptible, between the maniac, the man irrational and irresponsible, and he whose soul is seared by the burning lava of human passions." He implied that Gibbons's antipathy toward the Trumbull family was merely "the bitter hatred which vice bears to virtue, the keen resentment which licentiousness ever manifests against that purity which is its reproach." Ultimately, the question for the jury was not "is this a fair will, a just will, an equitable will, the will of a right thinking man and a kind hearted father, but is it Thomas Gibbons' will?"[65]

The jury answered in the affirmative, and its ruling was upheld on appeal. Judge Carpenter, writing for the New Jersey Supreme Court, averred that the "power of disposition belongs equally to the good and to the bad, and wills cannot be set aside merely because unequal or unjust." That the "motives" animating this testamentary act were "uncharitable, anti-christian, or even impious" was not the court's concern. Having all but severed questions of natural justice from those of capacity, the judge made the issue of moral insanity seem almost beside the point. Misconstruing the contestants' argument as a claim that Gibbons suffered from an intellectual disorder, which he described as a "hallucination of mind . . . towards Trumbull and his family, a causeless and unwarrantable dislike amounting to monomania," he proceeded to apply the standard of insane delusion prescribed in *Dew.* What he found was not mental incompetence but "a sad instance of the extent to which family feuds may be carried" when there was "on the one side, an imperious and haughty temper sustained by wealth and power, and restrained by no softening influences from moral or religious principles," while on the other there was "great imprudence on the part of a daughter and son-in-law in dealing with the errors of an uncontrollable and violent parent, upon whom they were dependent." The family's "successive bitter quarrels" were more than sufficient to "account for the provisions of the will . . . without any necessity to resort for explanation to monomania or any other form of insanity."[66]

Judicial resistance to any further expansion of the legal definition of insanity grew stronger in the 1850s, as some judges questioned whether the "test of delusion" itself ought to stand. They were prompted to do so as they looked across the Atlantic, where the *Dew* doctrine seemed to be subject to increasingly liberal readings by judges who had rejected the concept of moral insanity.[67] The decision that produced the greatest alarm was rendered by Lord Brougham in *Waring v. Waring* (1848). Presuming that the mind is "one and indivisible" rather than a collection of distinct "compartments," Brougham argued that "partial insanity" was a misnomer, for a monomaniac's disease always existed even though its symptoms were not always visible. Therefore, he insisted on a strong presumption against wills of monomaniacs, even where they were "as officious and as rational in every respect, as any disposition of property could be.[68] American jurists sharply criticized the decision in *Waring,* which came to stand for the doctrine of "insane on one point, insane on all." Judges continued to distinguish between "partial" and "general" insanity and to hold that it was the contestants' burden to prove that the will was a manifestation of an insane delusion. Some called attention to the "absurd and dangerous consequences" of adopting the *Waring* rule.[69]

Connecticut's highest court expressed these apprehensions forcefully in rejecting a will challenge that relied heavily upon Brougham's opinion. Invoking the authority of Isaac Ray, Ellsworth repeated the doctor's misgivings about differential standards of civil and criminal capacity. His concern was not with the narrowly cognitive standard of the criminal law but with the broadening of the definition of testamentary incapacity effected by *Waring*:

> Were we to decide that men cannot make contracts nor dispose of their estates, however sensible and shrewd, because they fancy some things to exist which do not, . . . our courts would ere long present the spectacle of a plentiful harvest to the profession or the affairs of society must be arrested from uncertainty and fear. What would be the condition of those who happened to have dealings with a jealous husband, a suspicious neighbor, an infatuated lover, a deceived and half crazed demagogue, a Hindoo worshipping an idol, a sincere and enthusiastic but deluded follower of Mahomet, or a modern spiritualist with his "harmonial philosophy" and "aerial spheres?" Are these men to be read out of society as insane on all subjects, and rendered powerless to provide for themselves and their families?[70]

The judge voiced his reservations about scientific claims regarding insane delusions. In view of the "many discordant views and theories" advocated by putative experts and the remarkable ease with which their perspectives were "stretched and distorted to save life or defeat a hard will," Ellsworth doubted that the new medical psychology would be able to furnish the court with "certain and satisfactory" rules for resolving civil and criminal cases. Drawing on his forty years of experience at the bar and on the bench, he concluded that these cases were best determined by putting "two plain questions of common sense": asking the court to determine, as a matter of law, the degree of capacity essential in a given case, and asking the jury to determine, as a matter of fact, whether that capacity existed.[71]

Though framed as a solution, Ellsworth's decision largely restated the problem that bedeviled courts as they moved away from the traditional common law of capacity. When judges recast the standard for legal competence in terms of a "rational and moral civil agent" and recognized the concept of partial insanity, "unnatural dispositions" became far more vulnerable to challenge. While judges insisted as a matter of principle that a man had a fundamental right to dispose of his property as he wished and that the absurdity or injustice of a will was no basis for setting it aside, in practice judges and jurors acted inconsistently and often disagreed. The resulting ambiguity mainly served to advertise the fact that Americans did not share a common conception of natural justice or of competent personhood.

The introduction of medical psychology into the courtroom only seemed to make matters worse. In all too many cases, experts appeared "arrayed against each other," forcing judges and jurors to "fall back upon their own knowledge of human nature."[72] These contests revealed that individual judgments as to what was rational and moral could vary widely, even among intimates. Again and again, judges were forced to acknowledge that "what is meritorious in the eyes of one man, is hateful to another."[73] That recognition left them with no objective means of determining a testator's competence. Courts treated delusion as evidence of testamentary incapacity only where it clearly compromised the testator's mastery over his own mind. All the while, judges formally rejected the doctrine of moral insanity even as they recognized emotional and volitional impairments as bases for setting aside a will. But this illogic was more a casuistic stratagem to maintain a distinction between disease and depravity than an effective way of drawing the line between deviance and mental unsoundness. The distinguishing characteristics of the accountable actor were hardly as "broad, clear, and well defined" as the judges suggested, and their resistance to the hypothesis of moral insanity only underscored the poverty of the Common Sense theory of legal responsibility.

What was at stake for these officers of the court was the legitimacy of their professional enterprise, which was centrally concerned with apportioning legal accountability on the basis of mental ability. They found it possible to incorporate monomania into the common law of capacity, which focused on cognitive functioning. It was more difficult to admit the idea of a "lesion" of the affections, will, or moral sense, for it raised the specter of materialism and threatened to leave the law without a metaphysical basis for responsibility. To deny the existence of moral monomania was to affirm the idea that some part of the mind was inalienable, ensuring that every man had within himself an absolute moral guide. It amounted to affirming the existence of a benevolent God, who had provided humans with the moral capacity to obey His laws and a conscience to know when they fell short. Yet assuming the truth of this proposition only heightened the problem of human perversity. There appeared to be no way to explain why any sane person without intellectual impairment would consciously choose to disregard such tutelage from within. The problem became even more acute after the Civil War, when judges and jurists worried about capacity suits fueled by the rise of "a new aristocracy of wealth" and a set of scientific theories that left even less room for individual will and less reason for confidence in human judgment. The most problematic cases of all were those involving the wills of rich men and their greedy children, which provided a telling indicator of the manipulability and vulnerability of the ideal of autonomy at the heart of the American law of inheritance. These trials at once reflected and engendered a crisis of faith in the ethos of personal achievement that drove the process of accumulation.

CHAPTER 4

The Eccentricity of the Will

Is this a reality, or is it only phenomenal to us?

John Ordronaux, *The History of Medical Jurisprudence* (1868)

THE PRACTICE OF ATTEMPTING to break wills by claiming the insanity of the testator was a source of growing consternation among American judges during the late nineteenth century. Testamentary litigation swelled court dockets and excited the attention of the popular press, largely because of the vast amounts of money at stake and the social prominence of the families entangled in these disputes. The challenge to the will of the self-made millionaire Henry Parish that played out in the New York courts after his death in 1856 pitted the testator's wife against his surviving brothers.[1] The married but childless man had suffered a massive stroke in a Wall Street counting-room in 1849. Suffering permanent paralysis of his vocal cords and the left side of his body, he lived out his remaining years under the watchful eye of his wife, Susan, and her brothers, one of whom was his physician. Depending on whose story was believed, she was either a selfless helpmeet who was uniquely capable of interpreting the wishes of her still mentally vigorous husband or a grasping virago whose wealthy husband was mentally dead. During those years several codicils were added to an 1842 will, significantly increasing the share of the estate that would go to the testator's widow instead of his brothers. Mrs. Parish's lawyer characterized these revisions as expressions of his gratitude for the tireless attentions of "my dear wife," while the contestants condemned them as "*larger and yet larger* invasions of her husband's Will." As the proponent told the story, the stroke enabled this man and wife to perfectly embody the common law doctrine of coverture; it was "as if they indeed were one person, and the apoplectic blow had fallen upon her with him . . . her voice and lips obedient to the impulse of his will, no longer master of the motions of his own." The contestants argued that the stroke had reduced him to the status of a "domesticated man" with no more mind than that of "your horse, or your dog" and that she was the real author of the testamentary acts attributed to him.[2]

"The long-lasting Parish Will Case," which was litigated over the course of six years, featured virtuoso performances by the some of the best attorneys ever to drain a testator's estate. Testimony from a colorful cast of witnesses "of every degree of social standing and intelligence" provided a tantalizing glimpse into the intimate lives of the very wealthy and those who served them. To the reporters in attendance it unfolded like a "domestic romance"; the protracted courtroom proceedings were recounted in a dramatic series of episodes by newspapers across the country. Not as well suited for popular consumption but certainly causing a stir within the legal and medical professions was a 600-page volume of medical opinions by leading physicians, including Isaac Ray, John Watson, and Luther Bell, who had been asked to provide written assessments of the mental competency of the testator on the basis of the 12,000-page trial transcript, which included the testimony of the testator's personal physicians. While lamenting the fact that no autopsy had been ordered in a case that was so obviously "destined for future litigation," the specialists concluded that the testator's apoplectic attack was the result of a severe organic disease of the brain that had destroyed the integrity of his mind and that his subsequent behavior constituted "an entire transformation of his personal character" that left him "permanently and irrecuperably disabled from executing any document of binding force."[3]

Although none of this material was formally introduced into evidence or incorporated into the official record, the majority decision finally rendered by the New York Court of Appeals in 1862 was in accord with the medical opinions: five judges voted to set aside the codicils on grounds of testamentary incapacity, while one did so on the alternative basis of undue influence.[4] Two dissented because this judgment necessarily implicated Mrs. Parish in a monstrous fraud, which they dismissed as utterly inconceivable because of what it implied about the men in the case. "Women have no doubt existed who were sufficiently vile," the dissenters observed, but they "certainly had never known . . . one who . . . could have practised her wiles with such success as utterly to subvert the moral sense of a whole family, consisting of such men as her brothers are admitted to be; and . . . to 'draw in,' . . . and make '*dupes*,' of lawyers, ministers and financiers, among the most eminent which the country affords."[5] Having died before this ruling was announced, Mrs. Parish was spared any insult it might have caused. An even more unflattering popular account, likely authored by the contestants, was offered for sale in its wake, which promised to be "as rich and racy as a novel" and to prove "interesting, entertaining and instructive to all classes of the community, especially to DOCTORS, MERCHANTS, LAWYERS, HEIRS AND EXECUTORS," but also to "the rich, and those who are anxious to be rich."[6]

That there was some truth in this advertisement is evinced in the medico-legal literature of the 1860s, which recognized the Parish will case as of "peculiar importance to those interested in the jurisprudence of insanity," especially "the vexed question of testamentary capacity." Many hailed the appellate court decision as a legal landmark, definitively overruling *Lispenard* and setting the bar higher than a mere "glimmering of reason"; the ruling required an active mental power that would enable the testator to form a "rational judgment" about the disposition of his estate. The published medical opinions were praised as providing new and important scientific insights into mind-body relations. Some even saw this ruling as a sign that lawyers and doctors were converging in their thinking about mental unsoundness, just as the pioneers of medical jurisprudence had envisioned.[7]

The appearance of Isaac Redfield's *Treatise on the Law of Wills* in 1864 was another hopeful sign, its subtitle announcing that it encompassed "the jurisprudence of insanity" as it pertained to the question of testamentary capacity. A former chief justice of the Vermont Supreme Court who had also taught medical jurisprudence at Dartmouth, Redfield drew explicitly upon his experience on the bench and the writings of medical jurists, quoting approvingly from the work of Ray in particular. But it was equally apparent that he placed practicality above scientific exactitude and was chiefly concerned with remedying the unruly state of the law across American jurisdictions, especially with respect to the presumption of sanity and the legal definition of mental unsoundness. While Redfield saw the infirmities of Coke's classification of persons *non compos mentis*, he had little use for the alternative schemas proposed by medical writers. Instead, he selectively incorporated elements of the new medical psychology into the traditional rule structure of the common law of capacity. He carved out considerable space for the alienists' concepts of dementia and monomania, moral as well as intellectual. Figuring these disorders as involving too much or too little will, he was as concerned as his medical brethren about abuses of liberty and tended to identify sanity with self-control. Yet his discussion of the medical literature was shot through with doubts and misgivings about the doctors' supposed science, for he questioned whether their appearances in court did anything to clarify the law of insanity.

Redfield observed that "medical experts, . . . of late, are beginning to be regarded much in the light of hired advocates, and their testimony, as nothing more than a studied argument, in favor of the side for which they have been called." The accumulated frustrations of his years on the bench spilled out onto the page as he cast them as mercenaries who were themselves teetering on the edge of monomania: "When we consider the conflicting character of testimony coming from experts; and often its one-sided and partisan character; and above all, the tendency of the most mature and well-balanced minds, to run into the most incomprehensible theorizing and unfounded dogmatism, from the exclusive devotion of study to one subject, and that of a mysterious and occult character, we cannot much wonder that some of the wisest and most prudent men of the age are beginning to feel, that the testimony of experts is too often becoming, in practice, but an ingenious device in the hands of unscrupulous men."[8]

Redfield's doubts about the legal value of these paid experts earned him hostile reviews in medical journals. With varying degrees of pique, medical writers insisted that these conflicts resulted from the adversarial character of legal proceedings, which did not allow them "to place themselves in an impartial attitude."[9] Taking the criticism rather personally, Isaac Ray oscillated between self-pity and outrage as he presented his side of the story. "He attends the trial and spends many a weary day in listening to evidence," Ray observed in the third person, as if to underscore that this grievance was shared by other medical experts. "At last he takes the stand himself, where he is badgered by lawyers till his head swims, and he retires with a strong suspicion that he has been making a fool of himself, and damaging his own side." He took particular umbrage at the suggestion that all this was done for financial gain, for the sum the medical expert usually received for all this time and trouble was "scarcely enough" to cover his expenses. Indeed, the professionals who could most justly be said to "sell their services without respect to the merits of the cause" were lawyers.[10]

Ray's more fundamental point was that conflict was endemic to the pursuit of knowledge and happiness in a democratic society. He insisted that "we have no right to regard such diversity of views as the fruit of a mercenary or partisan spirit rather than that honest difference of opinion which may prevail among men of equally eminent attainments," slyly revealing Redfield to be the true dogmatist. "To require all men to agree in opinion on matters of physical science . . . is entirely out of place in an age which boasts of its free inquiry and exults in its diversity of belief. What would become of our author's own profession when tried by such a test? He cannot deny the uncertainty of the law, and he must be familiar with overruled decisions." Inconsistency of character was one of the hallmarks of insanity, so opinions were likely to be especially variable in judging this phenomenon. But that was all the more reason why courts and counselors should recognize and respect "the rightful function of the expert," who has "devoted himself exclusively to the study of insanity—who, for twenty or thirty years, has lived under the same roof with hundreds of afflicted fellow-men, observing the strange and infinitely diversified manifestations of their disease."[11]

In other words, diversity was to be celebrated in the courtroom and contained within the walls of insane asylums in the name of human liberty, with delusion and dogma proving elastic enough terms to apply to professional men who disagreed about what it means to have a sound mind. Beneath the surface of this turf battle between doctors and lawyers lay a more basic contradiction with which they were all struggling even as they blamed one another for their difficulties. Some saw the source of this conundrum quite clearly, at least when they were not defensively responding to others' criticism. John Ordronaux, a graduate of Harvard Law School as well as the National Medical School and professor of medical jurisprudence at Columbia Law School, displayed great insight in an 1868 article published in the *American Journal of Insanity*:

> It is this extreme difficulty of determining what amount of individual dissimilarity any person shall be allowed to exhibit in his opinions and conduct, as against a certain arbitrary and conventional standard, having only a local or temporary character; it is this difficulty of determining how far a man has a right to be himself, without incurring the imputation of being insane; which renders the doctrine of monomania so illogical. For, in its strictest application, it is sufficient for any one to be unfashionable in garb, demeanor or opinions, to be at once decreed insane; and the only standard of mental health recognized therefore would be one never originally created, viz.: entire uniformity in all things between men.[12]

Combining the perspectives of law and medicine more "stereoscopically" than his predecessors, Ordronaux was peculiarly well-placed to perceive the blind spots of both of his chosen professions. He was more inclined than most to interrogate the philosophical assumptions about human rationality that shaped the adjudication of civil and criminal responsibility as well as the medical theories of insanity, problematizing inconsistencies in thought and practice that others tended to treat as too obvious, metaphysical, or worrisome to warrant saying out loud. His reasoning about mental soundness started from the premise that "no two minds are alike" and "the angle of vision determines the parallax of the object viewed," so "that a mental act may wear a very different aspect to two minds beholding it simultaneously, but from different standpoints." On some subjects, especially religion, "the stigma of delusion is attached without any other reason than that our prejudices are opposed" to a given set of opinions, but if this were to be made the ground of testamentary incapacity, "then mental competency before the law is simply a question of mental majorities, and all nonconformists are lunatics."[13]

Seeking to improve the adjudication of these matters, Ordronaux became the chair of the nation's first state-level lunacy commission in 1874. Designed as a quasi-judicial body to supplement but not displace the jury trial, it was among many reforms undertaken during these years to clarify the legal status of the insane. The task of "measuring the intellectuality of man with reference to a determination of his *civil* or *criminal* responsibility before the law" was, he acknowledged, more intricate and perplexing than any other undertaken by the legal system. While living under a government of laws "based upon universality rather than individuality of features in mankind," he observed, "each member of society is not only permitted, but invited and stimulated by educational aids to develop his individuality." Although the law presumed that "every one has his homogenous humanity underlying his heterogeneous personality," it contented itself "with prescribing rules for the aggregate mass rather than the individual unit" in order to ensure that "the unit is never extinguished in the mass." While the individual was to be judged "objectively, in all duties of reciprocal obligation," in all else he was to be considered "subjectively, in all self-regarding acts." Ordronaux's effort to impose order on this self-contradictory situation came to an abrupt halt when he was forced to resign a decade later. His fate was taken by some as a sign of the intellectual and moral bankruptcy of forensic science, though it is fairer to say that he placed himself in an impossible position.[14]

Members of the bench came to doubt that much enlightenment would come from psychological medicine. Jurists were especially reluctant to credit the theories of the "materialistic psychologists," who assumed that all mental life had a biological basis, because their view suggested that all acts were the result of physical necessity and the very idea of free will might itself be a delusion. These psychologists could not provide the guiding light in everyday adjudications, for they left no principled basis for holding anyone accountable.[15] Rather than choosing another medical theory, jurists selectively appropriated scientific concepts and categories in an effort to construct a "psychological law" that served the practical needs of judicial administration. The particulars of this law were most fully elaborated in the courtroom, where American judges daily confronted challenges to eccentric wills disposing of ever greater fortunes.

As judges surveyed their dockets, they observed that the rich were often peculiar as well as disputatious and implied that singularities were normal in a society where religious freedom, political liberty, economic competition, and prospects for financial gain were so extensive. Though the plight of excluded heirs sometimes elicited sympathy, judges were more inclined to lament the opportunism exhibited by the participants in these lawsuits. That doctors were willing to validate litigants' self-serving diagnoses led judges to regard their testimony with skepticism and even scorn; one acidly suggested that there ought to be a "presumption of irrationality in the case of all medical experts." While voicing a preference for "men of good common sense" who were personally acquainted with the habits and character of the testator, judges were unwilling to defer entirely to the judgment of nonprofessional witnesses or jurors, well aware of the proclivity among laymen to impose their own conceptions of justice upon the testator's will. With growing insistence, Gilded Age judges declared that "the law is not a medical or a metaphysical science. Its search is after those practical rules which may be administered, without inhumanity, for the security of civil society."[16] Toward the end of the century, courts adopted frankly pragmatic models of legal personhood, drawing a distinctly legal definition of sanity and human agency. They supplied a way of thinking about autonomy and accountability that proved effective both inside and outside the courtroom in an era when the universalistic morality of Common Sense was losing its appeal.

The Legal Test of Insanity

Just as the New York Court of Appeals was issuing its final ruling in the Parish will case, Amos Dean was finishing a set of articles for the *American Law Register* on the "Unsolved Problems of the Law as Embraced in Mental Alienation." Writing from the borderlands "between the known and the unknown," he observed that scientists had yet to arrive at a working definition of insanity that was "sufficiently comprehensive" to include its myriad varieties, "yet so distinctive as to create the proper limitation." Indeed, experts appeared hopelessly divided about whether the disorder was "a mental or moral disease, having its seat in the mind or soul," "a bodily disease to be referred to . . . the brain," or some combination of the two. Yet Dean insisted that it was possible to critically assess the law's treatment of mental alienation on the basis of its symptoms rather than its causes.[17] Like other members of the elite, he found a strange sort of comfort in the notion that insanity was positively if paradoxically correlated with human progress: "Man in his primitive state is rarely ever insane. The Caucasian is about the only variety that can lay claim to this malady, and, even in that variety, it is very little prevalent in despotic governments. It is in those that are free, in which mind can come freely into conflict with mind, in which every chord of this curiously toned instrument is kept constantly strung, that every possible variety of mental derangement is of the most frequent occurrence."[18]

Americans could no longer whistle in the dark as they contemplated the relationship between insanity and civilization during the Civil War. When antebellum alienists drew these connections, it was part and parcel of a broader critique of Jacksonian society and carried the promise that the asylums they were superintending would cure the disease. As these institutions became the site of scandal, alienists were increasingly figured as tyrannical inquisitors in popular exposés, subverting the principles of free government rather than insulating their charges from the corruptions of civilization. Moreover, the mad-doctors themselves became acutely aware of the fragility of their own sanity and the "thin partitions" separating their own minds from their patients' lunacy.[19] Amidst the political and social strife surrounding Reconstruction, even the most sanguine betrayed doubts about whether all citizens were capable of withstanding "the unrestricted trials of freedom." The extension of new personal and property rights to married women as well as African Americans and the influx of immigrants intensified these worries. Anxieties about mental health were exacerbated by social conflicts that were, in turn, projected onto marginalized groups. As asylums became overcrowded with chronic cases and increasingly served custodial rather than curative functions, mental diseases seemed to map onto and harden social differences. According to Gilded Age medical treatises, the leisured classes were especially prone to neurasthenia, and some doctors suggested that the accumulation of wealth amassed by the era's robber barons was itself pathogenic.[20]

The law of wills was suffused with cultural concerns about the interconnections among mental, moral, and material progress. Indeed, Redfield's 1864 treatise defended the right of testamentary disposition in the most ambivalent of terms. While this right was "one of the results of cultivated social life, and dependent upon municipal law," it was also "an instinctive sentiment, intimately associated with that love of acquisition, and of dominion, which forms the basis, and the stimulus, of all social progress; and which, in its normal development, is the sure measure of advancing civilization, and, in its morbid excesses, equally marks the process of declension and the increase of crime." This theme shaped Redfield's discussion of partial insanity, in which he tried to clarify the indistinct boundary between mental disease and mere eccentricity. "The eccentric man is aware of his peculiarity, and persists in his course from choice, and in defiance of the popular sentiment, while the monomaniac verily believes he is acting in conformity to the most wise and judicious counsels, and often seems to have lost all control over his voluntary powers, and to be the dupe and victim of some demon." Indeed, "one of the most unequivocal evidences of insanity, in many persons, is entire surrender of their wills, and the apparent submission to chance direction, or the caprices of others, or often to imaginary whisperings, which they seem to regard as the voice of supernatural wisdom and power." Troublingly, this "passiveness of the will" was often found in "persons of the strongest understandings, and the most self-reliant."[21]

Yet in the very next breath, Redfield declared that moral insanity was more or less irrelevant in testamentary matters. "This form of insanity is important, chiefly, in the administration of criminal jurisprudence." In a footnote, he explained that "we do not . . . intend to recognize that absurd development of moral obliquity, which allows the possessor to commit crime without compunction, as insanity. If that were allowed, there would exist a too ready excuse for crime. The act itself would always afford satisfactory evidence of the existence of the malady." But only a few pages later, he approved "moral mania" as a ground for setting aside a will where it was "to any extent the offspring of the perverted state of the affections."[22]

The ambiguities and inconsistencies that riddled *The Law of Wills* did not escape the notice of reviewers. But most attributed them to the uncertainty inhering in the jurisprudence of insanity rather than any fault of the jurist, though Oliver Wendell Holmes might have had these pages in mind when he complained of Redfield's "habit of moralizing, which is notably out of place among the rules and precedents of courts."[23] It is nonetheless easy to see why this treatise sold as well as it did, regularly appearing in the briefs and arguments of attorneys on both sides of will contests. Moreover, attorneys continued to think it worth trying to use moral insanity to break wills, even as leading alienists increasingly distanced themselves from the doctrine in the 1860s.

The suit filed by the disappointed nieces and nephews of Margaret Blydenburgh, a New Hampshire woman who never married and died when she was nearly 74, touched off a broader medico-legal debate about the proper test of insanity that had lasting consequences. They challenged her will on the usual grounds of testamentary capacity and undue influence, and a jury returned a verdict for the proponents on both grounds. On appeal, the contestants took issue with the instructions to the jury, which provided that "mere moral insanity; insanity of the moral nature, that is, disorder of the moral affections and propensities, will not, unless accompanied by insane delusion, be sufficient to invalidate a will, or incapacitate a person to make one." The appellate court upheld this instruction. Writing for the court, Judge Sargent referred to the passages of Redfield's treatise the contestants had cited in their brief as well as ones they had not, including the portion indicating that moral mania was "important chiefly in the administration of criminal jurisprudence." He observed a growing divide between legal and medical definitions of insanity, for delusion was "essential to the legal idea of mania" though physicians did "not attach the same importance to this feature of the disease."[24]

The exigencies of the courtroom largely dictated this approach, for without delusion as the test there would be "no fact which is tangible as a matter of proof in a court of justice, upon which it would be safe or wise to act, and thus disturb those numerous testamentary dispositions of property which are made by those whose moral sense may be none of the keenest, or whose affections may not run in the same channel with those of their neighbors." As Sargent saw it, moral insanity was not a manageable standard, for there seemed to be no way to adjudicate matters of feeling and moral sensibility.

> We all have likes and dislikes . . . for which we might not be able to give an intelligible reason, or one that would be satisfactory to another person, who did not see with our eyes and hear with our ears, and the operation of whose mind might not be like ours in every essential particular, and yet are we all insane because we dislike somebody that someone else likes, and because we make a will according to these peculiarities of our views, must it be set aside? Better make a law that all a man's property should be divided equally among his relatives, without regard to the peculiar views or preferences of the deceased owner, and prohibit the making of wills altogether.

So long as the rule of law allowed "a man to do what he will with his own," the court concluded, "he may exercise his individual privilege of having preferences and prejudices as between friends and relatives and even children, without his being called to give any reason further."[25]

The sole dissent came from Judge Charles Doe. His abiding concern was with simplifying the common law, which had become overrun with "arbitrary" rules, including the presumption of sanity. In preparing his opinion, he consulted Ray's treatise and then the doctor himself, initiating a correspondence that matured into a long-term collaboration to rid the law of any fixed rule defining mental disease.[26] The test of delusion was really only "a *dictum* concerning a matter of fact" that had regrettably been "received as a final determination of a question of law."[27] To defend its continued observance "on the ground of convenience," as had the majority, was entirely unacceptable. "Innocent persons cannot be punished as criminals, nor can property and guardianship be disposed of by invalid writings, merely because it is difficult for the court to give to the jury a scientific definition of a pathological fact, which it is the duty of the court not to give." Doe contended that the law could not partition itself off from medical science: "That cannot be a fact in law, which is not a fact in science; that cannot be health in law, which is disease in fact." He concluded that the jury should have been instructed only that "a will cannot be produced by any form of mental disease."[28]

The simplicity of Judge Doe's approach held a certain appeal, and he managed to persuade the other members of the New Hampshire Supreme Court to adopt his preferred instruction for criminal cases a year later.[29] But in those involving property rather than liberty or life, judges in New Hampshire and other states continued to adhere to the test of delusion laid out in *Dew*.[30] Physicians' position in legal proceedings became at once more circumscribed and more contradictory. Although they continued to enjoy the special privilege of offering their expert opinions, the scope of their authority was narrowed considerably. Judges generally held that medical experts were not to testify regarding matters of "mere mental or moral philosophy" or of "common knowledge" upon which jurors might form their own opinions. But they were still required to speak only to hypothetical cases rather than the one at bar. As a result, presiding judges often discounted or dismissed their words as "theoretical speculations" bearing only indirectly, if at all, upon the practical issues before the court. Some judges insinuated that these experts were only pretenders to knowledge and insisted that the essence of the mind and the nature of its operations were simply beyond "man's mental vision." Others more tactfully differentiated the purposes of medical and legal science, suggesting that the alienists' findings were of limited utility in the courtroom. Because they "treat the subject as philosophers and as healers," these medical men included within their definitions of insanity "many persons whom the law would punish as criminals if they violated the law, and whom the law would declare competent to make a will." But courts must inquire "how far society can afford to make insanity an excuse for crime, and at what point it is best for the general good, to say that a man shall not be allowed to make a will."[31]

What No Rational Person Would Believe

The 1865 New York case of *American Seamen's Friend Society v. Hopper* elaborated an unapologetically legal definition of delusion that a growing number of American jurisdictions subsequently adopted. Charles Hopper had made a small fortune by investing the proceeds of his trade in real estate but became convinced that those around him were conspiring to cheat, imprison, and poison him. The will disposing of his $100,000 estate provided modestly for his widow and some of his heirs and directed that substantial sums go to two charitable societies, violating the terms of a recently enacted statute restricting the amount a testator could leave to a charitable organization if he had a surviving spouse or children. Hopper's disgruntled heirs claimed that these dispositions were signs of a deluded mind skillfully practiced upon by the drafting lawyer and an "extremely vicious" and "drunken" attending nurse, both of whom stood to gain under the will.[32]

To support their claims, the heirs detailed the process by which Hopper's affections were alienated from his wife and other relations. "About the year 1856, or somewhat earlier," he suddenly began to fear that his relatives, along with "several clergymen of the city of New York," were conspiring with his wife to "break up his marital connection with her." His public accusations grew more lurid over time; he alleged that the clergymen were "continually engaged in illicit amours" with his wife and that "she had been diseased by one or more of them, and had communicated the disorder to him." All the while, he remained convinced that his relations were plotting to cart him off to a lunatic asylum, seize his property, and "effect his death by chloroform or by violence." Indeed, he was wont to attribute any "trifling accident" to his supposed enemies, rendering him blind to the very real wrongs perpetrated by his lawyer and nurse, who kept his family from him as he lay dying after an accidental fall onto a hot stove. Only four days before his death, the will was executed in the presence of the conniving lawyer, two doctors, and a close business associate. Two of these witnesses testified against his competency. The third confessed that he hardly knew the man, who had "only answered in monosyllables," but Hopper appeared to be "the most God-forsaken man he ever saw."[33]

The proponents countered that this case amounted to nothing more than a marriage gone wrong, largely because of the testator's intemperance. Friends and relations testified to a successful suit for separation brought by Hopper's wife in 1859 on account of his "cruel treatment" after an incident in which he was arrested and charged with assaulting her. All of his relatives took his wife's side in that case, and this perceived betrayal was the real source of his alienation from them. Hopper's animosity toward the clergymen was rooted in his disbelief in revealed religion: he had become convinced that ministers "embraced the profession for selfish purposes, and employed it for base ends, especially in regard to the female members of their congregations." To refute the contestants' case, the proponents presented a train of shopkeepers, mechanics, retailers, and medical men, most of whom were only casually acquainted with the testator. These witnesses described Hopper as "coarse and profane in his conversation," "headstrong" and "willful" in personality, and "much addicted to the use of ardent spirits." Still, they affirmed that he was quite capable of conducting business when sober, his manner exhibiting "nothing extravagant or peculiar."[34]

At the conclusion of this testimony the surrogate summarily issued an order denying probate on grounds of testamentary incapacity, and the proponents' appeal was denied. The majority opinion focused on the question of whether Hopper's mind "was warped or deluded in respect to the natural objects of his bounty." Surveying the history of his relations with his family, the court found that most of the testator's reasoning was sufficiently grounded in reality that he evaded the class of legal incompetents. What made him delusional, and therefore incapable as a matter of law, was his conviction of the "improbable" intercourse between his wife and one of the "venerable" clerics, as both were obviously too old to engage in such acts.[35]

The New York Court of Appeals affirmed the judgment. Chief Justice Denio reduced the case to a single issue: whether the testator's "conduct and declarations" in the last years of his life "were simply the manifestations of an excitable, coarse, ill-regulated and suspicious mind, made more intense by his habits of intemperance," or were instead "the consequences . . . of an insane delusion." Taking *Dew* as the applicable standard, he determined that most of the testator's suspicions were indeed groundless. But the outcome turned on whether his belief in his accusations was "feigned or purely imaginary." If the testator uttered the "gross imputations" upon his wife and relatives "by way of personal abuse, in order to gratify a depraved and malicious disposition, or for the purpose of defaming or otherwise injuring them in the estimation of their acquaintances and the community," this mental condition would not meet the standard of testamentary incapacity. What proved decisive was not the patent irrationality of the testator's beliefs but the fact that the testator's mind appeared to be "constantly occupied" with unfounded apprehensions of infidelity and conspiracy "to the exclusion of almost every other subject." Recalling Redfield, Denio concluded that these delusions had come to dominate his mind. Finally, he added that the drafting lawyer and drunken nurse exerted sufficient undue influence to fortify his delusions and entitle the contestants to a verdict.[36]

Despite the invalidation of this testament, *Hopper* actually stands in defense of the autonomous will. This reading of the decision might seem counterintuitive because the doctrine of insane delusion applied by the court appears to expand the class of incapable testators to encompass those afflicted with controversial diseases such as emotional and moral insanity. Yet the *Hopper* court did not deem morbid affections and impulses insane without accompanying proof of a delusion so compelling that the testator was not the author of his will. So long as the testator's volition was not totally extinguished, he was "sane and competent" in the eyes of the law. Accordingly, the lesson judges most often drew from *Hopper* was that courts ought not to mistake "perverse opinions and unreasonable prejudices" for "mental alienation." The decision counseled them to be vigilant in distinguishing between insanity and "mere eccentricity of conduct, harshness of temper, revengefulness of heart, or a depraved, cruel, and malicious disposition." Courts frequently invoked it as an authority in upholding wills, and many more reached similar conclusions without any such reference, displaying a growing inclination to expand the boundaries of what counted as rational, or at least not insane, belief.[37]

The 1869 New York case of *In re Forman's Will* vividly illustrates this tendency. The testatrix, Anna Maria Forman, lived out her last days in an insane asylum, although the parties disputed whether she had lost her mind before or after her husband, Enos Forman, placed her there. Having been awarded only $1,000 of his wife's $150,000 estate under the instrument propounded as her will, Enos was the contestant in the case. As he saw it, the hypothesis of insanity was the only explanation for this disposition. Before a skeptical surrogate, he and a host of lay and medical witnesses detailed the onset and manifestations of Anna's delusional behavior. According to their version of the story, Anna had suddenly and unaccountably become convinced that her husband, "in league with the cook and servants," was plotting to poison her food. Her insane distrust led her to insist upon sleeping apart from her husband and locking him out of her room. The contestant's attorney presented her denial of her husband's conjugal rights as compelling proof that Anna suffered the sort of morbid feelings and "'incapacity to struggle against delusions' that constitutes 'unsoundness of mind'" as a matter of law. The proponents balked at this conclusion. According to their witnesses, while she had come from an affluent and respectable family, her husband was an unremarkable man who did nothing but manage "his wife's property." It was only natural for Anna to respond with anger and fear when Enos, upon learning the provisions of his wife's will, arranged to have her committed. By challenging this will, Enos confirmed Anna's worst fear: that he had married her for her money.[38]

The surrogate admitted the will to probate, and an appellate panel was even more decided as to the proper verdict. Justice Sutherland declared that the evidence did not support a finding of incapacity. With *Hopper* as a guide, he expressly delimited the bounds of legal incompetence to exclude the medical theory of "moral insanity," which he was inclined to think had no place in civil or criminal cases save where it operated to "impair the intellect." "The question is not whether these feelings towards her husband, at the time, &c., were unreasonable, excessive or unjustifiable morally, or even whether they amounted to, or showed moral insanity as to her husband; but the question is, whether these feelings were insane—whether the contempt, distrust, hatred and fear, which she had of and for her husband, at the time of the execution of the two papers in question, was insane contempt, insane distrust, insane hatred, insane fear; or, in other words, the contempt, the distrust, the hatred, the fear, of an insane wife towards her husband." For a feeling to be insane, it had to "proceed from, or originate in . . . insane delusion." Little in the record supported a verdict of mental alienation. A wife might "trust or fear her husband unreasonably, or love or hate him excessively, without" being "crazy." Moreover, what Anna had often said of Enos might well have been true: "A man could smile, and smile, and be a villain."[39] Her husband's actions made this statement seem plausible; while protesting that he was seeking a reconciliation, he had her confined to an asylum after she barred his way to her bedroom. Because the justice could not know Enos's heart, he refrained from adjudicating the truth of Anna's accusations. Without passing on the rationality or morality of her will, the court concluded that she retained sufficient control over her thoughts and actions to be deemed legally competent.[40]

As courts narrowed the legal definition of delusion, they expanded the bounds of testamentary freedom, in some cases seemingly at the expense of natural justice. Illustrations of the effects of this reasoning abound in late nineteenth-century law reports. The 1873 *Chafin Will Case* provides an especially illuminating example. The testator, Ephraim Bradley Chafin, was a peculiar man by any standard. He espoused odd notions on "mechanical and scientific subjects," placed great stock in "clairvoyants, fortune tellers, and spiritual mediums," and professed to have the capacity to "live without committing sin." Chafin expressed total contempt for his closest relations. Believing that his wife had been unfaithful, he divorced her. He continually maintained that his children were not only illegitimate but also "transgressors" in their own right, which rendered them doubly "unworthy of his bounty." Still, no one questioned his sanity during his lifetime. His children raised the issue only when they discovered that he had devised the bulk of his estate to the American Bible Society, leaving each of them the obligatory sum of one dollar. A county court refused probate of the will, and when a jury trial was had in the circuit court, the verdict was against it as well. On appeal, however, the Wisconsin Supreme Court ruled the verdict to be against the clear weight of the evidence. In the opinion of the court, the very eccentricity of Chafin's will definitively proved that it was, in fact, his will. Its provisions were exactly the sort one would have reasonably expected him to make. The evidentiary record showed Chafin to be "a man of most positive character and most intense convictions" who was "entirely unreserved in the expression of his opinions and feelings." Though the court recognized that his mind was "undisciplined" and that he was prone to be "visionary and illogical," it read these traits as evidence that he was an "independent" and "original thinker."[41]

Applying a series of tests "recognized by science and approved by the judgment and experience of mankind," the court identified two main bases for distinguishing Chafin from those who were truly insane. First, the insane did not reason on the subject of their delusions and could never be convinced of their absurdity. But Chafin's "peculiar opinions and conduct" were "the results of processes of reasoning," and he was apt to revise them upon discovering the error of his ways. Second, the insane often flitted from one delusion to another, but Chafin's character and opinions never underwent any "great changes." "Once having conceived a dislike for his former wife and her children, such dislike continued to the end of his life. . . . In a word, he was always consistent with himself, and his opinions and conduct seem to have been the natural and logical result of his character, disposition and temperament." To illustrate this last remark, the court returned to the will itself: "Who that knew the rugged nature of Chafin, and his settled dislike, almost hatred, of his children, could suppose for a moment that he would do otherwise than disinherit them? . . . Who that knew his persistence could doubt that this general idea would control him in the final disposition of his property?"[42]

Here, the court nearly restated the definition of insane delusion found in *Hopper*, though the opinion did little to clarify how controlling ideas that compromised a testator's free agency were to be differentiated from those that constituted his will. Under what circumstances should a court view behavioral consistency as a sign of mental health, rather than an indicator that the testator was under the dominion of an insane delusion? Was the reasonableness of the will, in fact, the true basis of the appellate court's reversal in this case? The judges seemed to construe the legal definition of insane delusion so narrowly as to exclude most forms of human perversity. But they took pains to show that the disputed document's provisions made sense in the context of the testator's life. In other words, the judges enforced a rule of reasonableness even as they claimed only to be effectuating Chafin's will. They gave broad scope to the principle of testamentary freedom, while still preserving courts' power to adjudicate borderline cases and protect vulnerable individuals from the worst impositions.[43]

The *Chafin* court exhibited a judicial approach typical of Gilded Age will contests. Appellate judges' opinions generally followed a three-step reasoning process. First, they wrote expansively about the testator's right to "give his own to whom he will, irrespective of the taste or judgment of any human being"—assuming, of course, that he was sane and free of any constraint. These declarations had an embattled tone, as judges deplored the many abuses of legal process perpetrated by disappointed heirs and enabled by the courts. In the interest of preserving this "sacred" right, judges construed the doctrines of insane delusion and undue influence quite strictly. A ruling founded upon anything less than "a conscientious conviction of actual incapacity" was "a disgraceful outrage on justice and a plain violation of the oath under which the conclusion is asserted." Second, they illustrated what it took to establish actual incapacity, largely by negative examples. In the eyes of the law of wills, "a sound and disposing mind is not inconsistent with a very considerable degree of eccentricity," "moral depravity," and "dissipation." Only those forms of delusion or duress that deprived the testator of his free agency warranted setting aside a will. Judges often concluded that the evidence failed to meet this standard of proof, from which it followed that the will in question ought to be upheld, however far it deviated from conventional ideas about justice.[44] Then they summoned evidence to show that the will was, in fact, a perfectly reasonable disposition, if not from the view of the jury or bench, then at least in the testator's own mind. They could thus sustain the idea that freedom and rationality were intrinsically related.[45]

These rulings encouraged contestants to exaggerate the alleged monstrosity of the testator's acts to convince the court that they were actually irrational, and judges continued to struggle with cases involving evidence of religious or sexual deviance. Yet in most cases, particularly those appealed to courts of last resort, the wills were upheld. Ardent believers in the doctrines of "Modern Spiritualism" were generally deemed capable of making valid wills, even where there was proof that the testator consulted with the "spirit world" via a medium in the course of drafting the document.[46] Judges were equally disinclined to invalidate the dispositions of those so given to licentiousness or vulgarity that they appeared to have "no idea of the moral obligations of kinship." As courts repeatedly held, the law "does not require any particular grade of moral rectitude" to establish testamentary capacity or dispel any suspicion of undue influence. However lamentable, the "grossest immorality" and "considerable intelligence" could coexist. The more deviant the will seemed, the more courts interpreted it in relation to the testator's life history. But they were ultimately prepared to accept perversity as an irreducible aspect of the human condition. "We have to deal with the human mind and heart as we find them," judges remarked.[47] Even some medical writers concurred with this proposition: "Prejudices! if it were not for prejudices, not a man on earth would be sane, not a man on earth would *be*."[48]

"There's Millions in It"

As discouraging as this line of precedent was meant to sound, contestants proceeded undeterred. Indeed, the problem of determining what constituted a valid will grew only more troubling as the stakes of these courtroom battles were raised to unprecedented heights by the wealth of a new class of businessmen who were both revered and reviled. Their children mirrored their acquisitive spirit by bringing suit when they did not get what they thought they deserved, apparently feeling no shame in exposing to "the public gaze the secrets of a parent's domestic and private life; to belittle his intelligence and his virtues; to distort his providence into meanness; to magnify his eccentricities into dementia; his social foibles into immorality; his business differences into dishonesty and treachery; and to ascribe his diseases to obscene practices."[49]

These were the words of Surrogate Delano C. Calvin, who presided over "The Great Vanderbilt Will Case" challenging the testamentary capacity of the richest man in America, Cornelius J. Vanderbilt. At the time of his death at the age of 82 in 1877, Vanderbilt was known above all else for his indomitable will. His accomplishments inspired celebrations of his business acumen as well as more critical appraisals of the ways he made his millions. Hordes of reporters and messengers from the stock exchange stood vigil outside the Vanderbilt residence for daily briefings about the bedridden old man for months before he died, because "a slight change in his condition, a little fever, or headache more or less, could affect men's fortunes by thousands of dollars."[50] His long-anticipated death hardly affected the financial markets, but journalists found a fresh news angle by reporting that speculation was rife about the contents of Vanderbilt's will and the likelihood of a legal challenge.[51] No sooner was the document unsealed than headlines announced with an air of inevitability: "Of Course. Vanderbilt's Will to Be Contested. Some of the Relatives Not Satisfied, Intend to Make Trouble." The relatives were the sister and brother of the chief beneficiary, Vanderbilt's eldest son, William, and their feud over their father's estate entertained the nation. This dispute was the cost of dying rich, as the newspapers told the story, for there was "no will which cannot be broken by a discontented heir and a couple of sharp lawyers." These professional men were said to know just how to poke holes in the most carefully crafted document and to be equally adept at using the threat of public embarrassment as part of their litigation strategy. Unless and until the quarreling siblings came to terms, reporters assured their readers, there would be a scandalous will contest that effectively placed the testator's character on trial: "his sanity, his kindness, his natural affection, his sense of justice, his morality, his habits."[52]

Owing in no small part to the press's enthusiasm, this was precisely what happened. For the next two years, two weeks, and four days, the testamentary capacity of the late, great Cornelius Vanderbilt was "litigated over" and "cartooned upon" in the court of public opinion as the parties made their cases before Surrogate Calvin. The contrasting portraits of the dead millionaire painted for these multiple audiences—an exemplary entrepreneur or a mental wreck undone by insatiable avarice—were both exaggerated by lawyers who had made a specialty of these lucrative trials. The Commodore seemed to "have been something of a prophet," as he was heard to say more than once, "When I die there'll be hell to pay."[53]

The lawyers for the contestants elicited embarrassing testimony about the dead man's private life, manifestly seeking to compel a favorable settlement. The medical history elicited from the physicians who had taken part in the autopsy was alternately too graphic and too tedious for public consumption, most papers providing abbreviated coverage under such arresting headlines as "The Commodore Dissected" and

"Vanderbilt's Bodily Infirmities Ruthlessly Dragged to Light." Journalists visibly strained to sensationalize the "Painful Diseases that Immense Wealth Could Not Cure" and to spice up "His Sick-Bed Talk" to keep their audiences interested. This was no small feat, as the doctors read from and elaborated upon a written autopsy report, placing particular emphasis on the maladies that afflicted his urinary and intestinal tracts. The portions that found their way into print went into excruciating detail about what his scrotum looked like under a microscope, how "peritonitis" might have affected his bowel movements, and whether this condition was the immediate cause of his death. Within the confines of the courtroom, these revelations seemed to bore more than they shocked: the proponent's lawyer was observed to be "sound asleep" as the doctors droned on. The sheer tedium of it all was confirmed in a widely reported display of "funereal wit" on Surrogate Calvin's part, inspired by a medical witness's testimony on "the meaning of the term chronic in a medical sense." Upon hearing the doctor state that it connoted a slowly progressing disease, Calvin was said to have "yawned and ejaculated, 'In other words, this trial seems to be chronic.'"[54]

Even as laughter reverberated throughout the courtroom, the contestants were allowed to continue questioning medical authorities about Vanderbilt's bodily infirmities. Only after most of this evidence had been presented did one of the proponent's lawyers, Henry L. Clinton, raise a formal objection, taking issue with the autopsy's failure to include any examination of the testator's *brain.* "To attempt to prove a man's insanity . . . by the condition of his bladder and rectum two years after he made his will" was simply absurd. He contended that none of the medical evidence was even remotely material absent actual proof of the impact of the testator's physical disorders on the operations of his mind at the time the will was executed. Although agreeing with Clinton's assessment of the order of proof, Calvin allowed the lead counsel for the contestants, Daniel Lord, to finish his examination of the expert witness then on the stand. But they did little to advance the case that he was trying to make for the invalidity of Vanderbilt's will. Indeed, the more they elaborated on the bodily disorders afflicting the testator, the more impressive his mental strength was made to appear. The proponent's counsel skillfully elicited an admission to that effect from these experts, who uniformly affirmed that he remained "quite self-possessed" and "clear-minded" to the end, even when he was in agony.[55]

Shifting ground in the face of these damaging assessments, the contestants emphasized that they had never meant to claim "general insanity" but rather to assert that Vanderbilt was a monomaniac, laboring under a circumscribed set of delusions about the spirit world and the efficacy of spiritual medicine, and that he was pathologically avaricious and vain. The witnesses testifying to his dealings with infamous sisters Victoria Woodhull and Tennessee Claflin and other purported mediums and magnetic healers brought Clinton to his feet, objecting that belief in clairvoyant power "had no bearing on the question of insanity or undue influence unless it was supposed to be a delusion," an opinion "that would open up the whole theory of human belief for discussion."[56] Calvin admitted the evidence but then struck it from the record after it had been aired in open court and published in newspapers across the country.

Pressed to establish what the endless parade of witnesses who detailed the testator's foibles had to do with the question of his mental soundness, the contestants declared without anything approaching medical authority that "morally and religiously his mind was a howling wilderness. He didn't content himself with worshiping Mammon alone, though he was certainly a zealous devotee at the shrine of that meanest of all spirits that fell; but he indulged in other follies that are sure to demoralize the mind and weaken it, while they corrupt the understanding. Where such things are carried to such an extent, no man under their influence can be called a sane man." One medical expert called to the stand averred that if the facts were as the contestants alleged, Vanderbilt was a monomaniac "on the subjects of the accumulation and acquirement of wealth," while another more colorfully concluded that he suffered from "autocracy—a desire to rule and govern everybody!" In case that did not suffice, they crafted a "conspiracy story" to persuade the court that the will was the product of undue influence and fraud. According to this account, William had duped his father into believing that his younger brother was an inveterate gambler and whoremonger who was hardly fit to manage his own affairs, let alone have anything to do with the family business.[57]

The proponents put on less of show, calling a respectable array of businessmen, ministers, lawyers, and physicians who testified to the unfailingly rational manner in which Vanderbilt had governed himself as well as his domestic and business affairs to the end of his life. On their testimony, the testator was a benevolent and shrewd patriarch who carefully trained and tested "Billy" before allowing him to "step into his shoes," while protecting but not overindulging his incorrigibly spendthrift son Cornelius Jr. The testator's much younger second wife, who was painted as a gold digger by the contestants, came off as Vanderbilt's better half as the proponents' witnesses detailed the philanthropic organizations that she encouraged him to benefit by way of his will, which was of course his alone.[58]

They called an eminent set of medical experts to address the issue of mental soundness. Their key witness, the prominent alienist John P. Gray, voiced the skepticism about moral insanity that he articulated a few years later when called by the prosecution during the celebrated trial of President James A. Garfield's assassin, Charles J. Guiteau. Queried about the details of the autopsy commissioned by the contestants, Gray stated that he could not infer from this postmortem examination the existence of any mental unsoundness or enfeeblement. He resoundingly answered in the negative the carefully framed question: "In medical science and classification is there known any such form of insanity as a desire for accumulating wealth followed by large accumulation?" These answers were ridiculed in the press, for they left "the impression that in the opinion of doctors only the men who want to be rich and fail are crazy." Something closer to contempt emanated from Lord as he likened Gray's refusal to offer a diagnosis to the scriptural declaration that "all things are possible," a literary allusion meant as a swipe at the false piety of Clinton, the proponent's lawyer. Clinton shot back that "all things were possible, excepting, perhaps, that the contestants would get through in this case." "What!" Lord erupted, "at $1,000 a day?" to which Clinton rejoined "You want it prolonged until you have made that much out of it." The rap of the surrogate's gavel ended this round of verbal sparring, which was terminated by Calvin's stern assessment that "both sides had got more than they had earned."[59]

As if on cue, but really because a settlement had been reached out of court, both sides pronounced themselves done, shook hands, and left the courtroom, followed by spectators and newsmen who filed reports that the sensational trial, with its "strange mingling of farce and more serious business," had finally "ENDED AFTER MANY DAYS."[60]

Although the parties had reached a settlement, Calvin delivered a hundred-page opinion affirming the validity of Vanderbilt's will. This literary performance aimed to speak to a wider audience as the surrogate spelled out the reasons and authorities supporting his ruling in self-justifying and self-congratulating prose. Posing as the protector of "the memory of the decedent" and the reputations of countless others impugned during the trial, he promised to give the public a distillation of the facts actually proven by counsel, as distinct from the preposterous "imputations of social, domestic and business delinquencies" made in arguments and testimony that were widely publicized but never admitted into evidence. In drawing these distinctions, he took credit for excluding as much "prurient and defamatory matter" as he could, consistent with "the rights of all the parties engaged in this unseemly revelation of family secrets."[61]

Calvin contended that the very right of testamentary disposition had been on trial. Indeed, he suggested, the case had excited so much publicity because it was about more than rich men; it also concerned "those of moderate means, and those who, by years of toil and prudence, have accumulated small savings in the fond hope of providing therewith for the necessities and comforts of infirm and invalid children and parents, as well as of an affectionate and faithful wife." The surrogate aligned himself with this more sympathetic cast of characters, contrasting their family relations with those of the litigants, who were all too eager to waste their parent's estate and stain the family reputation out of spite. Calvin emphasized that the court was not "to *make* a testamentary disposition of other people's property, or to *revise* a decedent's will upon the principles of justice or equity." Instead, it was his statutory duty to give effect to the voluntarily drafted wills of all sound-minded testators, however "illiberal and unjust" they might appear to those who survived them. This was a republican country, and it remained the right of the father to make an "undutiful will." In confirming this rule of law, however, the surrogate never quite confronted the extent to which he was encouraging the growth of a new aristocracy of wealth that threatened to undermine the producer ethos and middle-class way of life that he championed at the outset of his decision.[62]

Training his attention on the authenticity rather than the fairness of Vanderbilt's testamentary disposition, Calvin conceded that while reasonable people might disagree as to the "propriety" of his "ambition to perpetuate the great railroad enterprise to which he had devoted so much of his business, life and energy as a monument to his great business skill and success, and as to the good taste of boasting of it," it was not unusual, judging from "the common level of commercial incentives and hopes," and it certainly did not make him insane. Anyone wishing to keep his name alive in this fashion would have been almost crazy not to pick William as his successor. Although "many wise and just men" might hold that his unequal treatment of his other children "betokened a lack of parental affection and justice," these shortcomings were of no moment as a matter of law. In view of how often "*gross injustice* and *reprehensible cruelty* manifest themselves in men who are in all other respects mentally and morally responsible for their conduct," Calvin reasoned, evidence to this effect could not alone support a finding of testamentary incapacity. Moreover, the contestants' charges of undue influence and fraud were even less plausible; the testimony established that the testator showed "a very vigorous mind and strong nature" even as he lay dying, his chief deficiencies being the want of "education and culture and a delicate respect for the opinions of his fellow-men." Given that these characteristics appeared to be very much in evidence in the contested will, there was all the more reason to find in the proponent's favor.[63]

All that remained, in the surrogate's judgment, was to draw a few morals from the fabrications that the contestants had tried in vain to pass off as the truth. In their spectacularly unsuccessful attempts to smear the reputation of the testator's widow, they had presented an object lesson "to those who are prone to assail the private character and revel in promiscuous defamation *as a means of intimidating parties and coercing compromises.*" Calvin congratulated himself for maintaining the dignity of the proceedings and minimizing the number of damaging disclosures made by litigants who were disconcertingly insensible to the moral demands of "filial and fraternal duty." He supplied a happy ending that in retrospect appears to be wishful thinking: "When the passions which have been excited by this protracted and acrimonious controversy shall have subsided, and a kindlier spirit pervades the minds and hearts of those who initiated this proceeding, and they reverently turn to the record their father has made upon the business annals of his time, and perchance cast their eyes over the record of this proceeding, they will rejoice that it is preserved so clean, in spite of all their efforts to tarnish it."[64]

The stories that were retold by the newspapers, in contrast, registered a pronounced ambivalence about "the one-man power" wielded by Vanderbilt during his lifetime and bequeathed to his eldest son by way of his will.[65] Though the dynastic ambitions of this "splendid accumulator" may not have constituted sufficient evidence of insanity as a matter of medicine or law, the selfish aim of "founding a family on a money basis" was taken by both lay and professional commentators to present a serious public health threat, which they cast as "the curse of great wealth."[66]

According to the profusion of articles and editorials published on the subject during the last quarter of the nineteenth century, this scourge was visited upon rich men and their families with distressing frequency. Editorialists described the materialistic behavior of Vanderbilt and his bickering heirs as typical of the millionaire class, whose fortunes "were earned in misery, and have left misery behind them." An insatiable appetite for money—"not for the sake of hoarding, nor for the sake of using it for the improvement of the race, but for the joy of holding it, increasing it, and making it grow"—drove men like Vanderbilt to accumulate riches even though success brought "innumerable anxieties," as such men were constantly harassed by begging letters and fraudulent schemes that ultimately robbed them of their "confidence in humanity." Unable to trust even their own flesh and blood, men burdened by large estates faced death with the added terror of knowing that all their faults and foibles would be exposed and magnified during the course of a postmortem legal contest if they dared to make charitable bequests as they saw fit, or otherwise to defy the wills of their children, whose moral sensibilities had been dulled by living amidst plenty "they had no hand in accumulating." So fashionable had capacity contests become in the Gilded Age that they appeared to be an unavoidable aspect of "the natural law of mortality," sure to be perpetuated by "speculative lawyers" who could extract huge fees regardless of the merits or outcome of any given case.[67]

"Things are getting to that point that we absolutely need a Society for the Suppression of Heirs," or perhaps a "Moribund Millionaire's Club" to check the indefinite multiplication of lawsuits, suggested the reform-minded. The mere threat of a postmortem contest "virtually compels every dying man to give all his property to his heirs." One journalist facetiously stated that legislators might as well declare by statute "that the possession of property worth, say half a million dollars or more, shall be regarded as *prima facie* proof of the testator's insanity, and shall give his next of kin the right to place him in an insane asylum while they seize upon his property," with the further proviso that "the insane man's wishes" with regard to its division "should be as carefully disregarded as possible." Another reasoned that insanity might well be rendered as a perfectly accurate finding in any case in which a rich man actually chose to make a will, a patently irrational act given how likely it was to spell his humiliation in a courtroom after his death.[68]

No Legal Obligation to Right Domestic Wrongs

These considerations do not seem to have affected the estate planning of Hezekiah B. Smith, a well-known industrialist, politician, and exceedingly eccentric inventor. Under the terms of his will, the bulk of his enormous estate would be administered by a board of trustees charged with founding and operating a mechanics' college. After Smith's death in 1887, the will was offered for probate and duly approved by the surrogate but was appealed by Eveline Smith, who claimed to be Hezekiah's widow, and three children she said she had by him. Their petition challenged the will on grounds of mental unsoundness, undue influence, and fraud. The trustees denied Eveline's status as the testator's widow until a trial confirmed their lawful 1846 marriage.[69]

During the ensuing will contest, the evidence showed that while Eveline remained at the family home in Vermont, Hezekiah ventured to Massachusetts and then New Jersey, where he founded an industrial town called Smithville and won election to a variety of state and national offices. There Hezekiah took up with Agnes Gilkerson, an ambitious country girl who ultimately persuaded him to "repudiate" his first family and install her as his wife in his Smithville mansion. The couple anticipated that she would outlive him and carry on his legacy through the institution of the college. After Agnes suddenly fell ill and died in 1881, it was left to Hezekiah to realize their shared vision through the instrumentality of his will.[70]

Whether the testator was in his right mind and free from constraint or imposition when he composed this document was the nub of the dispute. In the will contest, the attorneys followed familiar scripts as they made their cases. The contestants' version depicted Agnes as a "brilliant" and "fascinating" seductress able to manipulate Hezekiah to do as she wished. Indeed, she persuaded him to send her to medical school; upon her return, she convinced him that he "could not procreate a child" and thus "his children could not be his." For the contestants, Hezekiah's belief in this claim was evidence that his will was the product of an insane delusion and of Agnes's undue influence.[71]

The proponents insisted that "the denial [of paternity] was a falsehood in furtherance of the joint and several desires and ambitions of Hezekiah and Agnes." To substantiate this charge, they pointed out that Hezekiah was running for Congress when rumors about his first family began to circulate. To end speculation in the local press, he and Agnes cravenly crafted public statements that portrayed Eveline as a desperate woman of "loose character" who sought to extort money from a prominent and public-spirited man. But in private, the proponents noted, he acknowledged his obligations to Eveline and his children by secretly meeting them and supplying vast sums of money, not only to provide for his first family but also to buy his wife's silence.[72]

The jury returned a verdict against the will on grounds of mental unsoundness alone. On appeal, the prerogative court, in an opinion by Judge McGill, observed that the law "looks upon an inofficious will with suspicion," but added that "if it can be accounted for on other reasonable hypotheses it will not be attributed to mental incapacity." For McGill, the case reduced to the question of whether the testator's public declarations about his first family were rightly regarded as "expressions of . . . sincere conviction" rather than deliberate falsehoods or manifestations of a deluded mind. In weighing these three alternatives, the judge ruled out the first, which would have required the court to find that the testator truly believed he had never lawfully wed Eveline, was convinced that he was infertile, and doubted that her children were his. This could not have been true of Hezekiah, whose "strong common sense . . . had made him rich."[73]

McGill acknowledged it was more difficult to determine whether the testator suffered an insane delusion or perpetrated an elaborate fraud, but ultimately concluded that Hezekiah had acted deliberately. Unlike the insanely deluded, who involuntarily adhere to false beliefs, Hezekiah appeared to have repudiated his first family in order to further an "evil purpose"; he "coldly calculated and willed this course" in a desperate effort to maintain his moral standing in Smithville. Alternatively, Hezekiah's denial of paternity might be more charitably read as an effort to "appease his conscience" and convince himself of something he knew to be untrue. In either event, there was no need to invoke the doctrines of insanity and undue influence, for the will was comprehensible in the broader context of the testator's life. Indeed, the judge could imagine no other way for it to end. Having won so many honors through his "continual and emphatic denials of baseness and immorality," Hezekiah could not be expected to "denounce himself and his paramour as impostors and liars" in his last will. Instead, he played the part of a philanthropist in the hope that he would be remembered favorably.[74]

The judge asserted that it was not the court's place to redress domestic wrongs by means of such doctrines as testamentary incapacity and undue influence. Although the document before him was certainly not a fair will, a just will, or the will of a right-thinking husband and kindhearted father, he was firmly convinced that it was Hezekiah Smith's will. Accordingly, McGill validated this disposition as an expression of sanity and freedom, confirming the "absolute control and dominion which the law gives to every man over his own property."[75]

Gilded Age judges approached testamentary litigation with a significant degree of disillusionment about the moral abilities of mankind. Having endured the trauma of the Civil War and the "shock of Darwin," they lacked their fathers' faith in the "orderliness of the human mind and the world it comes to investigate." They expected that medical experts and laymen would disagree about where to draw the line between sanity and insanity. And they displayed a marked solicitude for the eccentric will, some even positively associating it with human autonomy: "Every man has his peculiarities as part of his freedom . . . , and it would be the mere tyranny of a general opinion, or of an opposite peculiarity, that would set aside a will on their account."[76]

Wills with truly "monstrous" provisions might still be refused probate, but the outer limits of tolerance had become quite wide.[77] Judges continued to acknowledge a broad variety of religious beliefs; some even declared that no theological conviction, however absurd, could, in and of itself, be deemed an insane delusion as a matter of law.[78] All the while, judges were determined to stay as much as possible out of the family feuds that generated so many legal contests, concluding that the "real home life" was "concealed from the public eye, and it is not easy to discover who is really responsible for domestic discord." As they considered the interminable testimony proffered by bickering siblings, shortchanged spouses, profiteering caregivers, and putative experts, judges could hardly believe that nothing but the truth was being told. They regarded it as imperative to circumscribe the grounds upon which such contests could be brought.[79]

With all these considerations in view, they reaffirmed the principle of testamentary freedom, maintaining that legal insanity had to be distinguished from "mere" eccentricity and depravity—from the sorts of oddities and infirmities of human character that were simply too widespread to be allowed to overcome the legal presumption of sanity. In doing so, they exhibited their abiding commitment to the notion of free will, often regardless of medical evidence. Ironically, the more scientists exposed the hereditary and environmental determinants of human behavior, the more judges felt moved to defend the principle of testamentary freedom, to protect the rights of property holders to do as they willed with their own. Those who took this tack might be seen as engaging in forms of denial and evasion that thrived during the Gilded Age. A close reading of late nineteenth-century treatises and cases reveals that jurists were gradually elaborating a set of distinctively legal definitions of what it meant to be sane or insane, free or coerced, capable or incapable, that did not conform entirely to either medical or lay understandings. The more trials eroded their confidence in the science of man promoted by philosophers and doctors, the more they were forced to question the existence of an objective standpoint from which to adjudicate matters of mental soundness. By the last quarter of the century, they had become convinced that medical theories left courts without a means of distinguishing depravity from disease. In the face of this conundrum, judges and jurists worked assiduously to distinguish the eccentric from the insane will, regarding this process as a vital means of safeguarding the ideal of human autonomy against both state and family interference as well as the more distant and disturbing specter of philosophical determinism.

The validation of unnatural dispositions proceeded apace, as appellate judges far more often than not set aside considerations of morals, metaphysics, and medical science and pronounced them "sound" as a matter of law. They recast the model of the competent testator to comprehend a wider array of eccentricity and depravity, which appeared less ideal and more hypothetical in form and function. As judges engineered this reconstruction, they performed important cultural work, philosophically as well as practically. To be sure, those who spoke of sanity and insanity in the legal sense were attempting to bring order to their courtrooms, which were overcrowded with litigants, lawyers, and medical experts all claiming the power to read the testator's mind. But this judicial method also served as a provisional way of coping with existential dilemmas that did not admit of any final resolution. Immersed in the "tangled, muddy, painful and perplexed" world of everyday experience, judges came to appreciate the perversities of human nature and the limitations of their own minds.[80] Lacking the moral certainty of their predecessors, they exhibited a more chastened perspective on the problem of evil that underlay so many will contests.

Eschewing abstract speculation and high-toned moralizing, judges took a relatively permissive stance as they policed the bounds of testamentary freedom. Although the "reasonableness" of the testator's disposition remained an important consideration in borderline cases, judges used this keyword in the broadest possible sense, all but embracing eccentricity as the norm insofar as the testator's will was concerned. But even they were prepared to admit that there were testamentary acts that no sane or rational person would freely perform, and those they stood ready to invalidate. Thus, they remained committed to the onerous and time-consuming task of ferreting out the truly meritorious claims, recognizing that the liberty of the will was sometimes best preserved by finding in favor of the contestant. This picture of everyday adjudication hardly accords with conventional renderings of the last decades of the nineteenth century as a time when courts were adopting more objective standards and bureaucratic procedures. Gilded Age judges did not impose societal norms of reasonableness in order to streamline judicial proceedings or reinforce conventional patterns of property transmission, as the instrumentalist analyses of Legal Realists and more recent scholars have suggested. In handing down their decisions, judges were far from certain that most testators enjoyed anything like perfect mental health. But because the putative testator could no longer speak for himself and these contests seemed so often to degenerate into sordid and wasteful family feuds, those who sat in judgment were inclined to let them stand.[81] They validated apparently perverse wills precisely because of their doubts about the truth of the matter and because of the value they placed on human freedom. In so doing, they evinced awareness that a transcendental realm of truth might be unattainable. From where they were sitting, this inference was almost irresistible.

Speculative Mania in the Age of Contract

> They are gambling as recklessly as he who places his substance on the cast of the die. So completely has this mania seized every one, that the obvious truth, a truth which is as apparent as any other law of nature, that nothing can be sustained without a foundation, is completely overlooked.
>
> James Fenimore Cooper (1838)

ON NOVEMBER 17, 1843, a trader by the name of Dorr bought a large supply of ribbons for which he had no use at a price far in excess of their market value. When he returned the goods to the vendors they refused to receive them, so he auctioned them off at a substantial loss. Guardianship proceedings were instituted the following February, and the court found that Dorr had been "lunatic since November 19th" of the previous year. Undeterred, the administrator of Dorr's estate brought an action after his death to avoid the ribbon transaction on the ground that the merchant had "exhibited marks of insanity by his conduct before and at the time of the alleged sale," which the defendants countered with evidence going to show that "his conduct was not such as to lead to a suspicion that he was insane." Viewing the contract as fully executed prior to the date fixed by the lunacy inquest, the trial judge instructed jurors that the parties' dealings could not be unraveled without "some evidence of fraud, nothing of which was alleged." A verdict was accordingly returned for the defendant and affirmed in 1848 by Chief Judge Bannister Gibson of the Pennsylvania Supreme Court in a characteristically terse opinion that underscored how difficult it was to distinguish merchants from maniacs in this speculative economy.[1]

Insanity was not necessarily incapacitating within the realm of contract law, Gibson emphasized at the outset. "An insane man, like an infant, is liable on his executed contract" not only "for necessaries" but for any "merchandise innocently furnished to his order." Although Dorr made "a wild and unthrifty purchase," it was concluded with strangers who were "unapprised of his infirmity" and not shown to be guilty of fraud or taking unfair advantage. Reasoning by analogy without citing a single authority, he futher noted that the insane were responsible for their torts: a person so afflicted "is liable to bear the consequences of his infirmity, as he is liable to bear his misfortunes, on the principle that where a loss must be borne by one of two innocent persons, it shall be borne by him who occasioned it." This rule was all the more compelling in contractual relations because of the thin, indistinct line that separated the schemes of visionary businessmen from those who were truly delusional about their prospects. "A merchant, like any other man, may be mad without showing it, and when such a man goes into the market, makes strange purchases, and anticipates extravagant profits, what are those who deal with him to think? To treat him as a madman, would exclude every speculator from the transactions of commerce." This consideration mattered supremely because profit seeking had become such an overwhelming preoccupation. "The epidemic in this country is an impatient desire to become suddenly rich by desperate adventure, instead of awaiting the slow but sure approach of wealth from industry and small profits," Gibson lamented. As long as speculation constituted the animating spirit of capitalism, insanity would be a problematic plea that could not easily be credited without threatening the security of economic transactions and raising troubling questions about the limits of accountability.[2]

The association of speculation with commerce and madness developed during the late eighteenth century. The term used to connote philosophical contemplation, but a new sense appeared in Adam Smith's 1776 *An Inquiry into the Nature and Causes of the Wealth of Nations*, where he likened merchants who did not follow any "regular, established or well-known branch of business" but moved incessantly from one to another in single-minded pursuit of pecuniary gain to philosophers "whose trade it is not to do anything, but to observe everything." Seeking to capitalize upon the fluctuations of the market, they were sometimes able to amass "a considerable fortune by two or three successful speculations," but were "just as likely to lose by two or three unsuccessful ones." The moral valence of the speculative merchant and his ventures was thus questionable, not least because of the instabilities that speculation introduced, both in society and in the self.[3]

For many Christian moralists and for exponents of labor theories of value, there was something ethically suspect and almost illusory about the wealth obtained by means of speculation, which they commonly cast as the spoils of parasitic gambling and juxtaposed to the steady and honest gains of farmers and tradesmen, who treated money as a means rather than an end as they produced goods for the sake of their families and the wider public. Enthusiasts as well as detractors recognized the dangers inherent in such chancy undertakings and found vivid illustrations of the ways "speculating madness" could seize upon the minds of enterprising men and induce "a kind of national delirium" in John Law's Mississippi Scheme in France (1719–1720), the closely connected South Sea Bubble in England (1720), and a succession of financial bubbles that likewise burst in the newly established United States, visiting devastation on speculators and "involving thousands of families in the same calamity."[4]

The postrevolutionary Americans who spoke in these psychological terms were not simply using them as figures of speech. The "mania for speculation" did indeed seem to be spreading in the early republic, as we have seen in the case of James Wilson. Benjamin Rush, himself a creditor of the "deeply distressed" jurist, worried that although the universal "love of money" could be a powerful and productive stimulus, this passion was being excited to alarming heights by "an increase in the number and magnitude of objects of ambition and avarice, and to the greater joy or distress which is produced by gratification or disappointments in the pursuit of each of them." Speculative ventures were "fruitful sources of madness in our country," for they "unhinged the judgment, deposed the moral faculty, and filled the imagination . . . with airy and impracticable schemes of wealth and grandeur." Rush observed that many Philadelphians were infected with "*Scriptomania*" in August 1791, when shares in the newly chartered Bank of the United States were initially offered to the public. "The slow and ordinary means of earning money were deserted, and men of every profession and trade were seen in all our streets hastening to the coffee-house, where the agitation of countenance, and the desultory manners, of all the persons who were interested in this species of gaming, exhibited a truer picture of bedlam than of a place appropriated to the transaction of mercantile business." Many went bankrupt, some went crazy, and a few committed suicide.[5]

The haunting implication of the doctor's diagnosis was that the speculative maniac was potentially everyman. While Rush placed his faith in the development of virtuous self-restraint, others reckoned that religion and moneymaking went hand in hand. Struck by "the great number of *churches* and *banks*" in the United States, foreign visitors saw them as "evidence of the greater intensity of both spiritual and material activity here than in older communities." But to many this frenzy was not a sign of social progress. The nationwide "manias" and "panics" that punctuated the nineteenth century left a trail of destitution in the form of "embarrassment," "derangement," and "depression"—words invested with the double meanings of psychological and pecuniary distress. The same "gospel of aspiration" that inspired Americans to undertake all sorts of "improving" ventures unleashed "a feverish, insatiable cupidity" that threatened to "unman" them and push their families to "the brink of want." While ministers and moralists saw these cycles as providential reproofs for the sinful "haste to be rich," the popular press was filled with expressions of agitated bewilderment about the arbitrariness and unreality of the capitalist culture of paper and credit. "It is horrible to see our young men goaded on by the fierce, speculating spirit of the age, from the contagion of which it is almost impossible to escape, and to see them tortured into madness, or driven to crime, by the fluctuating changes of the money-market," Lydia Marie Child lamented in her 1843 *Letters from New York*. She found "the young soul . . . entangled in the great merciless machine of a falsely constructed society," a monstrous steam power "he had no hand in raising" which "whirls him hither and thither," it being "altogether a lottery-chance whether it crushes or propels him."[6]

Asylum registers documented the mental disturbances occasioned by the unpredictable vagaries of the market. Among the leading causes of insanity, "pecuniary concerns," variously described as "loss of property," "want of employment," "dread of poverty," "intense application to business," "stock speculations," and "anxiety for wealth," were second only to "intemperance" and "religious excitement" among male inmates.[7] The medical men who admitted these patients regarded their mental diseases as "a part of the price we pay for civilization." Apprehensively contemplating "the almost absolute freedom from restraint" and social fluidity enabling "masterless" white men to be the architects of their own destinies, they warned of "the wear and tear of mind" that could result from limitless self-seeking. The alienist and vital statistician Edward Jarvis cautioned that "the danger of misapplication of the cerebral forces and the mental power increases" as individuals tend "to aim at that which they cannot reach, to strive for more than they can grasp." Educated to approach life as a competitive race for worldly success, citizens of this commercial democracy were plagued by a restless ambition that often ended in disappointed expectations, unmet obligations, nervous breakdowns, and insanity. In assuming the posture of benevolent patriarchs as well as men of science, asylum doctors tended to treat the mental wreckage they saw all around them with varying mixtures of sympathy and censure, apparently unsure of the extent to which individual sufferers were culpable for the improvident expenditures of "mental capital" that ultimately brought about "bankruptcy in the loss of the wealth of mind."[8]

Given the moral ambiguity surrounding speculative mania, it is perhaps no wonder that Judge Gibson refused to accept it as an excuse from civil liability. In holding the merchant Dorr to the disputed contract despite his imminent lunacy, *Beals v. See* might be read as a specimen of the judicial instrumentalism that scholars have long associated with the antebellum bench, characterized by a pragmatic predisposition to facilitate individual initiatives and promote economic growth by means of a "will theory" of law without getting mired in the metaphysics of mutual assent or passing judgment on the intrinsic fairness of the transaction. Yet aspects of Gibson's decision are incompatible with this historical understanding of private law adjudication, for he betrayed a marked uneasiness about what the legal historian James Willard Hurst called "the release of creative individual energy"[9] and its destructive effects on the minds and morals of his countrymen. Although the merchant's estate was made to bear the loss resulting from his buying frenzy, the opinion of the court did not go so far as to declare the state of his mind immaterial to the question of his contractual liability. Had Dorr's mental condition been known to the other party or taken a more obvious form, Gibson allowed, an inference of undue influence or fraud might have been drawn, thereby invalidating the transaction. Moreover, his ruling spoke only to commercial exchanges that were fully executed, and he designedly left open the possibility that the balance might tilt in favor of the mentally impaired in other circumstances.

Nineteenth-century law reports are filled with contractual disputes placing the mind in issue, some involving parties who were well acquainted with one another and others involving strangers who bargained at a distance. The resulting courtroom confrontations provide illuminating examples of the disorienting effects of capitalism, both for individual minds and in everyday social intercourse.[10] In the course of these proceedings, trial participants supplied telling evidence of the new freedoms, constraints, and dependencies Americans experienced as they lived out the "nervous logic" of an expanding market economy, which undermined established structures of authority and measures of value and destabilized traditional bases of obligation and personal identity. As contract thinking increasingly took hold, encouraging the reconfiguration of social relations along more voluntary lines, the individuals caught up in this transformation were moved to reconsider the ties that bound them to their families and communities as well as those neither near nor dear to them. Yet the new model of contract and ethos of individualism were ambiguous in their social meanings and effects, generating strains and conflicts that found frequent expression in nineteenth-century capacity litigation. These contests posed the threshold question of competency, repeatedly requiring judges to clarify the attributes of the competent individual and the nature and bounds of contractual freedom.[11]

Training attention on the borderlands of capacity, this chapter and the next explore how the law of contracts was mobilized and enforced within nineteenth-century courtrooms as Americans struggled to grasp the elusive subject of liberty. It begins by considering the predicament of postrevolutionary judges and jurists tasked with delimiting the realm of contract and the persons who were capable of ordering their lives through these legal means. The first treatises on the law of contracts were prefaced with expansive pronouncements, figuring it as the foundation of human society, the source of "all rights, all duties, all obligations, and all law," and affirming that "all persons can contract." To venture beyond pages, however, was to enter a maze of qualifications, exceptions, and survivals of traditional status-based rules not easily squared with a consent-based theory. Over time, common law disabilities were rooted out or modified by statute, and relational rules were rationalized anew by judges and jurists manifestly concerned with keeping the norms governing market transactions separate from those that were to be applied in the domestic sphere. Yet even as they endeavored to liberate their countrymen from the "feudal" structures of their English past, they did not simply reinstate disabilities that had been previously justified in terms of status. Instead, litigation presenting the question of who was capable of living in the world of contract most often concerned white propertied men who shared the same social background of many of those who sat in judgment.

To trace the complexities of this doctrinal story, the account that follows centers on the four situations that generated the greatest number of capacity challenges. This chapter focuses on cases involving ordinary business dealings "at arm's length" and those involving the provision of life insurance excluding coverage of the insured in the event of "death by his own hands." Chapter 6 considers attempts to establish and sever "the marital bond" and lifetime property transfers within the family circle for "the consideration of love and affection." As litigants placed the mind in issue in these sorts of cases, they registered how common and yet confusing and even threatening it was for nineteenth-century Americans to deal with relatives and neighbors as well as strangers through the medium of contract. The ensuing trials illustrate how and why American judges, lawyers, and laymen struggled to keep the ways of love and the ways of the market in separate spheres, providing a window on the corrosive and unnerving impact of a burgeoning capitalist economy on social relations and identity formation. These developments forced reconsideration of the conception of independence presumed and ratified by the law of contracts.

Competency, Competition, and the Agreeing Mind

At the time of the American Revolution, the term *competency* was still commonly understood to refer to an economic rather than a mental condition, connoting the possession of sufficient property to make a living "without superfluity" or the need to work for others. The pursuit of this form of competency was conceived as a collective family endeavor; the aim was to achieve independence at the level of the household, its members working together—typically but not always under the authority of a male head of household—to secure "free access to the means of production," thereby enjoying "the privilege of managing their own working lives." Postrevolutionary Americans sought a propertied independence that provided insulation from the economic vicissitudes that increasingly marked their everyday lives as they became embedded in the complex interrelations of an expanding market economy. In this turbulent era, marked by political revolution, generational tensions, social dislocation, and geographic mobility, a competency proved ever more difficult to obtain and was only precariously held. Its security hinged upon a tacit level of cooperation within and between households that were all the while being drawn into a competitive "race of life," which gradually yet profoundly changed how Americans thought about their economic fortunes and the meaning of self-government. These changes were reflected in the shifting usages of the term *competency* itself, as it acquired an individuated sense, denoting "a degree of skill or capacity" that was "sufficient to survive in an industrializing world." Indeed, it was increasingly understood to refer to a psychological attribute that was not necessarily tied to the ownership of productive property, save that of one's self, implicitly bounding the term so as to exclude slaves and married women, as well as others regarded as "dependents."[12]

Tellingly, the dictionaries and lexicons of the day point to the Latin root that *competency* shared with *competition*. The root *competo* was said to have two distinct but related meanings: "to seek together with another" and "to be suitable or fit, to agree." The first conveyed the notion of solidarity among contenders, while the second signified a baseline capability that qualified one to be in contention. They were joined together in definitions of competition as a common pursuit among comparative equals who met a threshold level of capacity which might be measured in terms of "mental endowments or attainments" as well as or instead of "worldly goods." Competency in the mental sense often referred to specialized knowledge that qualified its possessor to seek or occupy a post in one of the learned professions or in business. So conceived, the word set certain limits on competition. The felt need to moderate the pursuit of wealth that was expressed through these shifts in meaning was elaborated in public discourse. By midcentury, anxious ministers, moralists, and medical men waxed nostalgic about a simpler agrarian past when "our notion of a 'competence'" had been "more rational and less luxurious" and "we were more disposed to stay our hand when that competence was gained" instead of plunging "madly forward . . . into the hot strife and race of competition." The incessant "go-aheadism" that had come to characterize nineteenth-century America, impelling men to devote their lives to "dollar-hunting" and women to "breeding dollar-hunters," was "straining the mental fabric" of the nation "to its breaking point"—so much so that "a comfortable living" was now almost a contradiction in terms.[13]

The market-addled merchant embodied the perils of a speculative economy, and judges who registered misgivings about the morality of the marketplace cast doubt upon the conventional historical narrative of the "triumph of contract" in nineteenth-century America. These accounts portray members of the bench and bar as "the shock troops of capitalism," deploying their technical expertise in legislatures and courts with the aim of adapting the law to entrepreneurial ends, devoted as they were to the ideas of "rugged individualism" and "a free market in which no-holds-barred competition would generate maximum growth."[14] Scholars have argued that liberal notions of contractual freedom operated "to reinforce existing social and economic inequalities" and to perpetuate status hierarchies of race, gender, class, age, and disability by representing them in cases and commentaries as natural, reasonable, just, or necessary features of the social order.[15] Gibson figures as a key exemplar of this worldview because of his decision in the 1839 case of *McFarland v. Newman*, which enforced *caveat emptor* and argued that the imposition of any greater responsibility upon sellers "would put a stop to commerce itself in driving every one out of it by the terror of endless litigation." This ruling has been cast as a leading illustration of a concerted and largely successful juridical movement in antebellum America to replace a paternalistic, equitable conception of contract with a subjective, will-based alternative that promoted self-reliance and free enterprise by holding individuals to the terms of their bargains, however "hard" or "unequal," in the absence of deliberate fraud.[16] This view fails to capture the apprehensiveness with which judges and jurists regarded the spread of the market and the competitive ethos it engendered, which Gibson himself expressed in *Beals*.

The law of contracts, as it was presented by its earliest American expositors, was a normative system designed to discipline rather than simply facilitate the dealings of market actors, effectively setting the ground rules of the competitive game of life as it was to be played in this democratic republic. To be sure, law and morals were not coextensive in the minds of these professional men. Yet, like the law of wills, cases and commentaries about the law of contracts displayed the continuing force of "natural justice" and traditional equitable principles, as well as the systematized precepts of "moral science" and the everyday ethics of "common sense."[17] Theophilus Parsons prefaced every edition of his treatise from 1853 to 1873 with an expansive vision of his subject: "The Law of Contracts . . . may be regarded as including nearly all the law which regulates the relations of human life. Indeed, it may be looked upon as the basis of human society. All social life presumes it, and rests upon it; for out of contracts, express or implied, declared or understood, grow all rights, all duties, all obligations, and all law. Almost the whole procedure of human life implies, or rather, is, the continual fulfillment of contracts." In other words, men made society as they made contracts, but they were not entirely free to set the terms as they willed; some terms were given by law because they were deemed necessary to "good order and prosperity." As Parsons succinctly and yet rather ambiguously put it, "*contract* is coordinate and commensurate with *duty*" insofar as courts were guided by the principle "that whatsoever it is certain a man ought to do, that the law supposes him to have promised to do." Although jurists were alive to the dangers of empowering judges to write their own prejudices and biases into the law, most held that agreements had to be read in light of certain "principles of reason and justice," the ultimate aim being "to find in a contract a meaning which is honest, sensible and just, without doing violence to the expressions of the parties, or making a new contract for them."[18]

Moreover, historians have failed to accord as much prominence to the baseline concept of mental competency as did the judges and jurists who drew and redrew the boundaries of the world of contract.[19] "Every contract, to be valid in law, is made between parties having sufficient understanding, and age, and freedom of will, and of the exercise of it, for the given case," James Kent stipulated in his *Commentaries on American Law.* This standard excluded married women and slaves, who were commonly cast by law writers as properly subordinated to the master of the household; they had "no will of their own," and their assertion of self-will would disrupt the domestic and social order. The mental prerequisites for making a contract were reiterated ever more insistently in treatises devoted to the law of contracts. Indeed, one jurist held that "a man who is not perfectly master of his reason is incapable of giving a serious and valid assent to a contract or agreement thereby to bind *himself*; because such assent is an act of understanding, of which persons so circumstanced are morally incapable, their actions being the result of an *irresistible* impulse, the power of self-government being wanting." Yet while "full capacity" was "absolutely necessary" to the validity of a contract, the law presumed its existence and treated claims of "mental inability" as "exceptions to the general rule." Only total insanity was recognized as excusing the disabled party from fulfilling the obligations to which he had agreed.[20] But the meanings of insanity grew wider and more ambiguous in its significance within the field of contract law as the status-based disabilities of the traditional common law were recast in terms more compatible with liberal humanism over the course of the century.

The practical meaning of the ideal of mutual assent was mainly illustrated by way of negative examples and lists "of persons incapable of contracting."[21] Parsons's *Law of Contracts* identified the classes of persons partially or wholly disabled from making a contract: infants and minors; married women; bankrupts or insolvents; *non compos mentis*; drunkards; spendthrifts; seamen; aliens; slaves; and "persons under duress." With two significant exceptions, this categorical structure remained constant through successive editions of the work.[22] Parsons added a state-by-state summary of the statutory changes made with respect to "the rights of the married woman" as legislators engaged in the delicate task of removing "old rules" deemed "oppressive and unjust" without doing "great injury" to the marital relation by turning husbands and wives into "bargainers with each other." The challenge was to modernize the law without undermining mutual confidence and encouraging them to become "as watchful against each other, as careful for good security; as strict in making terms, and in compelling an exact performance of promises or conditions, and as prompt to seek in litigation a remedy for supposed wrong, as seller and buyer, lender and borrower usually are."[23] The ambivalent process of liberalization was also evident in Parsons's treatment of slaves, which he introduced in every edition through 1866 with the observation that slavery was "in derogation of natural right," existing only insofar as it was instituted by positive law. In carefully coded language, he suggested that "the courts of the country" upheld slavery in order to guarantee the rights of property. Significantly, the subsection Parsons devoted to "the capacity of slaves to contract" was almost entirely concerned with the ways their personhood was recognized by the criminal law, insofar as injuries to them were punished. In considering "the liability of the master for the slave," he observed that "a slave cannot enter any binding contract *with his master*; nor can he, while yet a slave, appear as a suitor in a court either of law or equity, to enforce any alleged contract against any person."[24] As for the marriage of slaves, Parsons noted it constituted only "cohabitation with the consent of the master," which was not a legal contract unless the master's consent was meant to "operate as a manumission, as in the case of a devise to a slave."[25]

The mental alienation of the insane placed them in a still more complicated relationship to the liberalizing legal order. The presumption of sanity was nearly conclusive under the traditional common law, for an old English maxim provided that "no man shall be allowed to stultify himself, or plead his own disability." Joseph Story commented: "How so absurd and mischievous a maxim could have found its way into any system of jurisprudence, professing to act upon civilized beings, is a matter of wonder and humiliation." Isaac Ray shared neither the surprise nor the mortification of this "distinguished jurist," whose lament he quoted as evidence of the peculiar infirmities of "the science of law." If the law were to be rightly reformed, Ray submitted, there could be no hard-and-fast rule with respect to "the plea of lunacy in avoidance of contracts" because mental diseases were not all equally disabling or apparent to the untrained eye. "Much as the law is bound to protect the interests of the insane, it is no less required to protect those who deal with them, unacquainted with their mental condition."[26]

This conflict of equities was all too familiar to Ray's contemporaries on the bench. No sooner had they emancipated themselves from the doubtful authority of the time-worn English maxim than they found themselves mired in vexatious lawsuits that required them to articulate reasonable, practical rules that could be applied to those who claimed they were mentally unequal to the competitive enterprise of contracting. Although few doubted it was "the more enlightened policy" to allow the plea, thereby bringing the law of contracts into greater alignment with the fundamental precept of mutual assent as well as the needs of the "weak and incapable," most found it considerably more difficult to decide who ought to bear the burden of their incompetence. In giving a man the "liberty" to "plead his own insanity," these judges well appreciated that they were implicating the interests of the sane party, opening up the door to fraud, and threatening the security of transactions. The decisional law recorded their conflicting impulses to regulate the world of contracts and to leave the parties to their own devices. Their task was immeasurably complicated by the volatility of an ever more pervasive market. Enabling individuals to disable themselves to avoid contractual liability might have encouraged opportunistic behavior, but in adopting such a permissive stance American judges effectively expanded their jurisdiction over market dealings as well as those within the family circle. Whether genuine, feigned, or merely exaggerated for purposes of litigation, the claims of incompetence made before the bar provided members of the bench with occasions to impose a modicum of moral order on this bewildering economic lottery, lest the processes of self-making and moneymaking become hopelessly confused. Law reports illuminate the doctrinal ways and means by which judges endeavored to institute a set of ground rules for the market that were imbued with notions of fairness and yet distinct from those supposed to be observed in the home, with the ardent hope of preserving the family as a sacred precinct of love where trust could be safely reposed, with confidence in the returns on emotional investments.

At Arm's Length

Adjudicating the matter of contractual incapacity was an especially fraught enterprise in the entrepreneurial culture of a boom-and-bust economy. Proceeding against the backdrop of acrimonious political struggles over bankruptcy legislation, the litigants who pled incapacity to escape civil liability placed a great deal more than their minds in issue. While reformers debated the underlying causes of financial panics and depressions, some tracing them to dissolute debtors and heartless creditors and others blaming the fiscal policies of short-sighted politicians, those who entered pleas of incapacity presented more fundamental problems of moral and legal accountability. These litigants sought to be released from the obligations of contract by pointing to mental rather than market failures, to defects that were individuated and yet located outside of the conscious, choosing self. Moreover, they tended to work within the legal system, their submissions to the court following out the logic of the jurists' will theory and the implications of the new medical psychology without questioning the socio-legal structures of the emergent liberal capitalist order.

But things were not always as they seemed in this society of placeless men and paper fortunes. The records of these capacity contests are filled with expressions of anxious discontent about the debilitating stresses of making a living in the capitalist market. The misgivings voiced by litigants, lawyers, witnesses, and judges arose from the lived experience and perceived limits of contractual freedom. Contrary to conventional depictions of the nineteenth-century law of contracts as a depersonalizing force, asserting an individualism that paradoxically de-individuated its subjects, the participants in these trials problematized rather than ratified the presumption of sanity. Judges were also committed to looking beyond the four corners of purported agreements to determine if there had been, in fact, a meeting of minds. To this end, they routinely engaged in probing inquiries into the power dynamics of the parties' dealings as well as the mental history of the alleged incompetent. At stake was the legal significance of independence: who could acquire it, how it was gained and lost, and what rights and obligations attached to those who were above or below the threshold of competence it was supposed to set.

In this field of doctrine, as in the law of wills, judges were generally receptive to the teachings of the new medical psychology but found it difficult to apply them in the courtroom. A handful of judges clung to the traditional common law requirement of a "total deprivation of reason," primarily on instrumental grounds. Yet courts in most jurisdictions insisted that something more was required than a "glimmering of reason." In reformulating their standards, judges emphasized the need for a free and knowing assent even as they held to the proposition that mental weakness was not, in and of itself, disqualifying. What was essential to contractual capacity was the ability "to see things in their true relations, and to form correct conclusions" in the course of business dealings; the party in question had to have "a moderate comprehension of his immediate duties and relations, and of the value and uses of his property," as well as the power to provide "a direction to his acts by his own will."[27] These statements closely resemble the standard often set for testamentary capacity, which likely reflect the extent to which such contracts were read as means of avoiding postmortem contests. Nonetheless, it passed as a truism that greater mental strength was needed to make a contract than to execute a will. Isaac Redfield opined that because a contract of sale necessarily involved at least two parties with "some degree of antagonism between their interests and efforts," "it is somewhat more difficult to see clearly the just bearing of all the relations presented, than under the common circumstances of making a will, where one is left free to act upon his own perceptions." While in some instances the testator was "beset by an army of harpies, in the shape of hungry expectants for property, altogether more perplexing than the ordinary circumstances attending a disposition of property by sale," a will was revocable until the death of the testator, whereas a contract or deed could take effect immediately, dispossessing the owner upon execution of the deal. Courts therefore applied a more exacting test of capacity where lifetime transfers were concerned.[28]

Because it was not possible to contract "in solitude," questions of contractual capacity were almost always tangled up with those of undue influence. In addressing these issues, judges had recourse to traditional equitable principles originally elaborated to shield expectant heirs who were regarded as especially vulnerable to imposition. The protective doctrine announced in the 1731 English chancery case of *Osmond v. Fitzroy* was a common starting point in nineteenth-century American decisions, invoked in support of the general proposition that courts would not "measure . . . people's understandings or capacities," as well as the key exception of confidential relationships, where judicial intercession on behalf of the mentally weaker party might be warranted.[29] The reach of this doctrine was qualified by an 1826 English case involving the scandalously perverse Earl of Portsmouth. Given how many men were "perfectly sound in mind on every point but one" and how difficult it was for strangers to perceive these debilities, the court suggested that the insane person's family and friends ought to bear a measure of responsibility for restraining him from making inadvisable contracts.[30]

As these precedents were applied to a broader array of putative incompetents in nineteenth-century America, the litigants and their trial stories exhibited the fluidity of social relations in the world beyond the courthouse and the complex ways the world was being reordered by means of contracts. Seeking to channel the enterprising energies of rising generations without denaturing the home as a space of love, nurture, and repose, judges elaborated distinct rule structures to regulate "arm's length" dealings as distinct from confidential or fiduciary relationships. As was true in the testamentary context, judges were guided by preconceptions about the "natural objects" of a property owner's bounty and jealously scrutinized lifetime transfers made to those standing in relations of trust and confidence to the grantor, most commonly where the grantee served as guardian, trustee, attorney, physician, or spiritual advisor, but also where the connection was adulterous or otherwise meretricious in character. As concerned as they were with protecting mentally weak testators who might not have been found *non compos mentis*, the application of this rule was extended still further where *inter vivos* transactions were involved. Judges widened the range of the relationships that counted as confidential to include those between siblings, parents and children, and husbands and wives. While testamentary dispositions within the family circle were generally treated as presumptively valid, lifetime transfers to the same parties by deed or contract were treated with considerable wariness. Many jurisdictions raised a presumption of unfairness and required the party claiming the validity and benefits of the transaction to affirmatively demonstrate that it was "righteous." To meet this burden, the court needed to be satisfied that "the weaker was not unduly impressed by the natural influence of the stronger, or the inexperienced overreached by him of more mature intelligence," and that the transaction was "fairly conducted, as if between strangers."[31]

As if between strangers. With these question-begging words, judges referred to common law rules for dealings "at arm's length," a gesture that not only signified a want of closeness between two parties but also constituted a measure of fairness and a means of keeping one from exercising a controlling personal influence over the other.[32] To determine whether or not the disputed transaction resulted from an abuse of confidence or power, courts put strangers in the place of the actual parties and imagined what the process of negotiation and the terms of the deal would have looked like had there been no ties of blood, affection, or friendship, no bonds of trust or personal obligation, and no asymmetries of power or habits of obedience in their relationship. The question was not whether the complainant "'knew what she was doing,'" but "'how was she rendered willing?'" Delving into these thought processes almost unavoidably entailed assessing "people's understandings and capacities," and the underlying principles of fair dealing that warranted the intervention of courts were broad enough to support their extension to any and all transactions where one party occupied a position of dominion or trust with respect to the other. Although the sane were never held to be more powerful than the insane as a general matter, many judges verged upon such a position in pronouncing that "those who from imbecility of mind are incapable of taking care of themselves are under the special protection of the law."[33]

This inconsistent way of treating disparities in mental ability—adjudging them immaterial in one breath only to admit their relevance in the next—reflects the divided minds of American judges and jurists struggling to reconcile the conflicting imperatives of liberty and equality that were built into their doctrines of contractual freedom. Positing a world of competent individuals who were capable of exercising the liberty of contract, judges allowed them to decide for themselves what constituted adequate consideration. "Indeed, from the fluctuation of prices, owing principally to the gambling spirit of speculation, that now unhappily prevails, it would be difficult to determine, what is an inadequate price for any thing sold," Joseph Story opined in his frequently cited *Commentaries on Equity Jurisprudence.* Yet while the merchant of "sanguine and ardent temperament and imagination" was not to be relieved from the obligation of his contract "merely from its being a rash, improvident, or hard bargain," Story allowed that "if the same contract be made with a person of weak understanding"—whether arising from "temporary illness, general imbecility, the natural incapacity of early infancy, the infirmity of extreme old age, or those accidental depressions, which result from sudden fear or overwhelming calamities"—"there arises a natural inference, that it was obtained by circumvention or undue influence." Invoking this authority and offering his own gloss, an antebellum Maryland judge blurred the line distinguishing the intrepid speculator from the incompetent dupe as he declared it to be "the peculiar duty of a court of equity to protect the rights and interests of persons of weak understanding and feeble judgment, and who are disabled by distress of mind, arising from pecuniary troubles, or overwhelming calamities, from properly managing and disposing of their property." But the lack of guideposts marking competency off from incompetency often rendered it problematic to rule against the sane party, particularly where he was a stranger without any reason to suspect the other party's mental debility. Having assumed a protective jurisdiction over a class of persons so ambiguously defined, how were courts to ensure that the shield thus extended did not become a sword in the hands of those it was intended to protect?[34]

Struggling to meet these competing commitments, judges only made matters worse by adopting doctrinal rules that varied rather significantly from one jurisdiction to the next. Here the most technical and yet consequential difference of opinion concerned whether the contract of a person found to be *non compos mentis* was void or voidable. With a certain logic on their side, a minority of jurisdictions staunchly maintained that one with "no mind" could make no contract. Holding that the instrument was void *ab initio* meant that neither party was bound; from this line of reasoning it followed that "the world" could take advantage of the fact of incapacity and the insane party could not elect to ratify the transaction if and when he was restored to his right mind. In order to avoid those implications, most courts treated the contracts of persons *non compos mentis* as voidable at their option.[35] Judges were similarly divided in cases where the sane party claimed to have proceeded in good faith and complete ignorance of the debility. Although a few courts declined to take such factors into account, firmly holding that "the fairness of the defendant's conduct cannot supply the plaintiff's want of capacity,"[36] most endeavored to find a middle ground when thus confronted with the conflicting equities of sane and insane parties, recognizing that the outward signs of mental incapacity were not always as discernible as the indicators that one was dealing with an infant or a married woman.[37]

Determining the contractual capacity of monomaniacs proved especially challenging, as they labored under pronounced yet circumscribed delusions and were capable of performing acts of apparent shrewdness and discernment. As in the testamentary context, most courts were disinclined to adopt the rule "insane on one point, insane on all," deeming it to be perilously overinclusive. "Were a monomaniac precluded from executing contracts relating to topics to which his monomania does not extend, the business power of the country would be seriously impaired, since some of the most efficient business men have been monomaniacs on special topics," Francis Wharton observed in his survey of the decisional law. Judicial reluctance to set aside the transactions of those fitting this description is most clearly illustrated by negative examples. The vulnerability of the monomaniac in the competitive world of contract moved some courts to relax the evidentiary rules applied in testamentary litigation, relieving plaintiffs of the requirement to show that the contract was the direct offspring of an insane delusion.[38] But most held it to be necessary that the mental disease "directly affect" the disputed transaction in order to warrant setting it aside.[39] This distinction made all the difference in the Maryland case of *Thornton v. Appleton*, involving an old woman named Sarah Appleton whose capacity to execute a promissory note in 1843 was litigated after her death by her warring children. The testimony indicated that in 1835 Appleton rather abruptly began to display "marked indications of insanity, on particular subjects." She "pretended to be poor" even though she was in possession of property estimated to be worth nearly $30,000, and she became convinced that money she had advanced to her eldest children had been stolen by them instead. Descending more deeply into delusion as she advanced in age, Appleton purported to be various biblical characters, "the Messiah, and afterwards, the Living God." Yet the reviewing judge entertained the possibility that the note in question had been executed during a lucid interval, as testimony indicated that Appleton was able to go on and off "her insanity track" and negotiate business dealings skillfully. Because the contested note benefited one of her younger children and was executed after she became insanely alienated from the elder ones, however, the judge was convinced that it had been "made after these peculiar delusions had paralyzed the intellect and the affections; and when the power to contract was in abeyance."[40]

Ironically, the cases that presented courts with the greatest difficulties were those in which the fact of mental incompetence was not in dispute; the sane party simply contended that he was ignorant of the other party's disability at the time their agreement was made. This claim was most plausibly made where the sane party was a second-hand purchaser with no knowledge of the parties to the original transaction, though it could be maintained with respect to many face-to-face transactions as well. Since mental disease was both real and recondite, it was not clear which party ought to prevail. Judges writing at midcentury began voicing greater solicitude for the plight of the sane and innocent party, as well as more pronounced concern about the security of commercial transactions. Most judges sought a more balanced approach to the conflicting claims of sane and insane parties, inclining toward a rule first elaborated in a leading 1848 English decision in *Molton v. Camroux*:

> We are not disposed to lay down so general a proposition, as that all executed contracts bona fide entered into must be taken as valid, though one of the parties be of unsound mind; we think, however, that we may safely conclude, that when a person, apparently of sound mind, and not known to be otherwise, enters into a contract for the purchase of property which is fair and bona fide, and which is executed and completed, and the property, the subject-matter of the contract, has been paid for and fully enjoyed, and cannot be restored so as to put the parties in statu quo, such contract cannot afterwards be set aside.

This ruling suggested that the issue of legal capacity ought to be resolved by reference to the apparent rather than the actual mental condition of the party in question. As the English ruling was increasingly adopted and applied in American courts, judges strained to assure themselves and the public that they were not violating the hallowed ideal of mutual assent.[41]

One of the most thoughtful decisions on this score was the Vermont case of *Lincoln v. Buckmaster* penned by Chief Justice Isaac Redfield in 1860. The case involved a sale of horses to a monomaniacal trader with the peculiar habit of "buying the most forlorn and desperate class of horses all over the county, with a view to the market, and that in great numbers." Although the seller had been advised of the buyer's infirmity before the deal was concluded, evidence was adduced that he had proceeded in good faith. In the judge's estimation, however, the buyer's mental condition left him "wholly incapable of making a binding contract, as much so as an infant, or a married woman." There was no denying that lunatics were often legally obliged to adhere to agreements they were theoretically incapable of making, as in the cases of *Beals* and *Molton*. But, Redfield reasoned, these decisions were "chiefly for the protection and support of the lunatic, or his family, or to prevent serious injustice to those who have dealt with him, having no means of knowing or learning his incapacity." In other words, the liability of a lunatic ought to be limited to those goods and services that were clearly of benefit to him or converted to his use without permission or any fault on the part of the owner. With these principles in view,

Chief Justice Redfield concluded that the contract before him could not be enforced because the business arrangement was "positively detrimental" to the buyer, whose mental defect could have been discovered by "a prudent and careful man." Having failed to measure up to this standard, the seller had only himself to blame, for the loss he sustained was ultimately the result of "his own foolhardy rashness and folly . . . in not making proper enquiry and examination into the affair."[42] In the space of a single opinion, the default legal person was cast in relation to the reasonable man in such a way as to imply that the perspective of the latter might have some bearing on the constitution of the former.[43]

By the last third of the century, the doctrine formulated in *Molton* and refined in cases like *Lincoln* had become the majority rule in cases involving dealings at arm's length. The "modern" doctrine, as declared by these courts, was that the contracts of lunatics were voidable but not wholly void and that these contracts would generally be upheld where the other party proceeded in good faith and in nonnegligent ignorance of the incapacity, unless the parties could be placed in *statu quo*.[44] This rule never enjoyed uniform recognition, however. A number of jurisdictions, including the federal courts, consistently held to the position that all the contracts of insane persons were absolutely void.[45] As Justice Stephen Field instructed a jury while riding circuit in 1867, an insane person's civil act was no more to be regarded as his own act than if he were "dead at the time of its execution." While the instrument in question in that case was a power of attorney executed by a Pennsylvania asylum inmate named John Hall, authorizing the sale of real estate in California, Field generalized beyond these facts of the matter as he located the insane entirely outside the world of contract. On his analysis, it made no difference that the land had passed into the hands of multiple purchasers by the time Hall's wife and children brought suit to recover the property, not long after the death of the deranged man.[46]

There were, to be sure, many reasons for thinking Hall had lost his mind sometime before the instrument was executed, which might lead us to suspect the gentlemen of the jury would have found for the plaintiffs regardless of how they were charged by the justice. Once a devoted husband and devoted father, Hall accountably stopped attending to his family and their needs, instead spending most days planting and then digging up flowers and vegetables in his garden without stopping for meals, "giving as an excuse that he was obliged to work for his living." He was convinced that "he owned everything he saw in the stores" and did not understand why he could not "help himself to what he liked." Nor could he be made to stop believing he was "the Creator" and insisting everyone address him as such. Any hope of recovery was dashed soon after he was admitted to the Pennsylvania asylum, where he grew more restless and nonsensical, spending his remaining days "weaving wire and fish bones into his arms and legs . . . very much as a woman would darn a stocking."[47]

Confronted with the spectacle of a head of household so completely unmanned, the jurors likely did not need to deliberate long before returning with a verdict pronouncing Hall *non compos mentis.* But when this case was appealed to the U.S. Supreme Court, the parties engaged in a learned debate about whether the contracts of a lunatic were void or voidable, both sides invoking Blackstone and summoning up even older precedents, with little said about the practical implications of ruling one way or the other. In the opinion of the court delivered by Justice William Strong, the jury's judgment was affirmed, effectively leaving the defendants rather than the insane man's dependents to bear the burden of his mental breakdown. In this ruling, the members of the bench might be read as assuming the role of judicial patriarchs, conceiving of themselves as "public custodians of the family," in line with the general tendencies of domestic relations law in this period. It is nonetheless striking that the opinion categorically asserts that "a lunatic, or a person *non compos mentis,* has nothing which the law recognizes as a mind," rendering him "incapable of executing a contract, deed, power of attorney, or other instrument requiring volition and understanding."[48]

Although Strong cast the court's decision as the most protective as well as the most principled way of handling the case of an incompetent adult, it was far from clear this was so. For if the contract were void, the sane party was no more bound by its terms than the insane party. Yet there was a certain cultural logic to his seemingly formalistic judgment. Strong understood the threat that insane persons posed to the world of contract and sought to rule them out altogether, though he did so without addressing any of the problems of definition that had long plagued the jurisprudence of insanity. The limitations of this approach were most clearly revealed in a set of cases where the capacity to break rather than make a contract was brought into question, as judges were required to grapple with men who appeared to have been maddened more directly by the ways of the market.

A Premium for Suicide

Under the headline "Melancholy Occurrence," newspapers in upstate New York reported the death of Hiram Comfort, a Catskill merchant who "put a period to his existence" on June 25, 1839, by jumping from the steamboat *Erie* into the Hudson River. Comfort had been accompanied on board by several friends, who hoped the journey would cure him of the "mental derangement" he appeared to suffer as a result of "business difficulties." His drowning was pronounced a suicide in the popular press and regarded with compassion after the panic of 1837 had pushed many heads of household to the brink of despair.[49]

The circumstances surrounding Comfort's death were subject to greater scrutiny with the filing of a civil suit in 1841 by the administrator of his estate, seeking recovery on a $5,000 life-insurance policy, which the merchant had purchased from the Farmers' Loan and Trust Company several months before embarking upon the *Erie*. The policy contained a "saving" clause rendering it void if the insured died "by his own hand." Determining Comfort's death a suicide, the insurance company maintained it had no obligation to pay a death benefit. Comfort's administrator pleaded that "he was of unsound mind, and wholly unconscious of the act," so the exclusion clause was inapplicable. While the insurance company maintained that the mental state of the insured was immaterial, the trial judge construed the phrase in question, though "somewhat indefinite and equivocal," as referring to "a criminal act of self-destruction," which could be performed only by one "in the possession and enjoyment of his mental faculties." Court-appointed referees found that Comfort "threw himself into the Hudson River . . . while insane, for the purpose of drowning himself, not being mentally capable at the time of distinguishing between right and wrong." On the basis of this report, judgment was entered against the insurance company.[50]

This decision held up on appeal. Writing for the majority, Judge John Willard affirmed that the exclusion clause "imported a criminal act of self-destruction," in part because it was listed alongside exceptions "in consequence of a duel, or by the hands of justice, or in the known violation of the law." He then offered a short disquisition on the metaphysics of responsible agency that demonstrated why Comfort's death was not attributable to him. "An insane man," whom this judge defined as "incapable of discerning right and wrong, can form no intention. His acts are not the result of thought or reason, and no more the subject of punishment than those which are produced by *accident*." Because insanity propelled Comfort overboard, the insurer was just as liable for his death as if it were the product of duress. "Can a man be said to do an act . . . when he is compelled to do it by irresistible coercion?" Willard asked rhetorically. "Can it make any difference whether this coercion came from the hand of man or the visitation of Providence?" To the dissenting judges, this line of analogical reasoning seemed based upon faulty premises. The factual record had not established that Comfort's willpower had been completely vanquished by mental disease, nor did legal responsibility necessarily entail the capacity to distinguish right from wrong. They read the evidence to show that he consciously, voluntarily, and intentionally cast himself overboard with a full understanding of the consequences. If this were not "'dying by his own hand' within the spirit and intent of this clause of the policy," it would be "difficult to attach any legal significance to such language."[51]

The difference of opinion exhibited by the members of the appellate bench in *Breasted* extended well beyond New York. Although juries displayed a pronounced solicitude for plaintiffs in these civil suits, reviewing judges appeared less easily swayed, with some expressing unease about the distorting effects of sympathy and error during the trial proceedings. Yet when called upon to construe the suicide exemption clauses, these judges appeared unable to arrive at any settled consensus regarding the bounds of coverage. Though professing a common concern with divining the intent of the parties, they diverged considerably in their interpretations of the state of mind that meant an insured could be deemed to have died "by his own hand" or "committed suicide."

Conflicting judgments about the mental prerequisites of the suicidal person reflect broader cultural shifts in thinking about rational and responsible behavior in nineteenth-century America as the fledgling life-insurance industry marketed a new means of securing against the "fatal chances of life." Although a man's fortune could be made or unmade by unpredictable forces beyond his control, he might provide his family with "a certainty against their future want" through "the agency of a life policy." Insurers' advertising campaigns endeavored to convince the public at large that buying their product was not just a prudent measure but an ethical imperative. The head of family who failed to do so was "criminal in his neglect," exhibiting a degree of selfishness that was likely to elicit an even harsher rebuke when he was finally called to judgment before his Maker. One insurer used the emblem of the pelican piercing her own breast in order to draw blood to nurture her young as its company logo, appearing along with the motto "I live & die for those I love." Men like Comfort seemed to have taken the insurers' ethos of familial responsibility to its logical limit, estimating that they would be worth more to their families dead than alive.[52]

Their actions brought the culture of insurance into courtrooms in the form of contract suits, requiring courts to determine whether their ways of exiting the world also took them outside the bounds of coverage under the terms of the policies. Faced with the possibility of forfeiture, the intended beneficiaries—most often the dependents and creditors of a white propertied man—deployed a tried-and-true legal strategy in pleading his insanity. It had played well before coroners' juries in an earlier era when suicide was punished with ignominious burial and property confiscation. Yet the insanity plea took on a different cast when it was raised in nineteenth-century insurance litigation. The plea was intended to answer a charge that the alleged suicide had violated the terms of a contract rather than the criminal code, and the threatened forfeiture redounded to the benefit of the insurer rather than the state. The task of construing the policy terms in such cases was further complicated by the fact that suicide had all but ceased to be a punishable offense in most American jurisdictions by midcentury, though a few states enacted new provisions criminalizing attempted and assisted suicide. Ambivalence about the suicide was also evident in the society at large. Although ministers and moralists continued to condemn self-murder as a mortal sin, a host of medical men, statisticians, and social reformers pointed to the biological and social roots of the self-destructive impulse. In so doing, they sparked a wide-ranging public debate about the sanity of suicide that spilled over into the courtroom.[53]

In the immediate aftermath of the *Breasted* ruling, insurance companies sought to clarify the meaning of the suicide exclusion clause or modify its terms, emphasizing that it was meant to apply to all forms of self-destruction, "sane or insane." But these changes did not have the effect that insurers sought. They only shifted the interpretive battleground, encouraging more litigation about the relationship between consciousness and liability. Ironically, these courtroom disputations soared into metaphysics, essentially pressing courts to determine whether an act of self-destruction could sensibly be performed by one suffering from "a total eclipse of the mind." No amount of careful redrafting on the part of insurers could insulate them from litigation that placed the mind of the insured in issue, effectively presenting the question of what constituted the *self* in self-destruction.[54]

The U.S. Supreme Court confirmed the enforceability of clauses excluding coverage in cases of "suicide, sane or insane," in its 1876 decision in *Bigelow v. Berkshire Life Insurance Company*. Justice Davis reasoned that if insurers were "at liberty to stipulate against hazardous occupations, unhealthy climates, or death by the hands of the law, or in consequence of injuries received when intoxicated, surely it is competent for them to stipulate against intentional self-destruction, whether it be the voluntary act of an accountable moral agent or not."[55] The qualifying words "sane or insane" were understood to apply to any act of self-destruction where the insured "was conscious of the physical nature of his act, and intended by it to cause his death, although, at the time, he was incapable of judging between right and wrong, and of understanding the moral consequences of what he was doing." Yet this construal of the clause did not appear to embrace the more severe case of mental incapacity presented by the plaintiffs, who claimed that the insured was "so unsound of mind" when he fatally shot himself as to be "wholly unconscious" of the act he was committing. Assuming the truth of this proposition, Davis nonetheless released the insurer from liability for the death, as he took these words to confess that the insured "intentionally took his own life," understanding the physical nature and consequences of turning a loaded pistol upon himself, remaining unconscious only of "the great crime he was committing" because "his darkened mind did not enable him to appreciate the moral character of his act." In reaching this conclusion, Justice Davis only deepened the ambiguity about what "insane suicide" meant, as his opinion expressly reserved judgment on the question of whether there might be some forms of mental unsoundness debilitating enough to render the death an accident as a matter of law.[56]

The very words that insurers inserted into their policies to remove the "shadowy and difficult" subject of mental soundness "from the domain of controversy" provoked litigation and generated conflicting decisions about what distinguished an "insane," "nonfelonious," or "involuntary" suicide from an "accidental death." As they confronted this new definitional borderland, plaintiffs seeking to recover deftly shifted their forensic tactics. Most pursued one of two strategies. The first was to flatly deny that a suicide had occurred at all and maintain that the death was a naturally occurring, wholly inadvertent, or essentially mysterious event, thereby leaving it to insurers to overcome the common law's presumptions in favor of sanity and against suicide.[57] But where the defending company was able to summon up substantial evidence to the contrary in the form of a suicide note or a coroner's report, the plaintiff often insisted that appearances of "a self-inflicted death" were deceiving because the fatal act was in fact the product of mental illness rather than the conscious will of the insured; it was contended that the disease rendered the death an accident. Defense counsel sometimes found it expedient to emphasize the correlation between insanity and suicide, making the most of any known eccentricities of the insured in order to fortify the conclusion that he had indeed committed the "unnatural" act.[58] Yet in so doing, insurers risked overplaying their hand, for they only prompted plaintiffs to posit ever more extreme diseases of the mind that had completely vanquished the insured's mental and moral faculties. It was difficult to see what was left of the concept of individual agency when the putative actor was conceded to be "wholly bereft of reason and without the power to control his will." Holding such a man legally responsible for the consequences of his acts both deviated from the norms of "civilized" jurisprudence as plaintiffs understood them and strayed from the insurers' own deterrence-based justification for the suicide proviso, premised as it was upon the capacity of the insured to respond to the threat of forfeiture.[59]

While sympathy for plaintiffs remained as pronounced as ever in the jury box, members of the bench were considerably less resolute and unified in their interpretations of these policy clauses. The main lines of judicial conflict were aired in the 1875 New York contest of *De Gogorza v. Knickerbocker Life Insurance Company*, in which a divided bench addressed the ultimate boundary case: an insured "wholly bereft of reason" at the moment he discharged the contents of a pistol into his mouth, "so that the mere act of self-destruction was wholly involuntary."[60] In the judgment of a bare majority of the five-member panel, the mental condition of the insured was entirely immaterial under the terms of the policy, which was rendered void by the fatal act. The only way to give "legal effect" to the phrase "sane or insane," they reasoned, was to exclude all evidence pertaining to the insured's state of mind. It seemed apparent to these judges that the clause was intended to insulate the insurers from "death by insanity," a contingency that they held to be importantly distinguishable from a "pure accident."[61] The coherence of this line of analysis was sharply challenged by the two dissenting judges, who maintained that the death of an insured "by his own hand, sane or insane," necessarily entailed the existence of an intentional actor capable of designing and carrying out this final act. A person who lacked the mental power to comprehend or control his behavior in such a basic sense could "no more be said to act than an automaton." Nor was it clear why "an unintentional death of an insane man by his own hand" should be treated any differently from that of one who was sane; in either circumstance, the death "would properly be classified with accidents." If the insurer wanted to be excused from liability "in case the brain of the assured became so diseased and his mind so disordered that he should unconsciously or unintentionally, or from an irresistible impulse, take his own life," then, the dissenters suggested, the policy ought to explicitly say so.[62]

Judicial advice of this sort was greeted with consternation on the part of insurers and their advocates, who cynically surmised that the true basis of decision was an "unwritten law of 'hardship'" slanted in the beneficiary's favor.[63] Jurists surveying the legal landscape from a somewhat more objective standpoint lent a measure of credence to such assessments. While finding that "the various decisions of the English, Federal and State courts, cannot, by any process of mental legerdemain be twisted into even the semblance of uniformity," they confirmed the general propensity of American judges to "sail round" the exclusion clause in order to find for plaintiffs "if any shadow of a rule of law can be found to support the ruling."[64] Worn down by and too often beaten in these legal contests, insurers increasingly came to the conclusion that the suicide exclusion clause was more trouble than it was worth.

An 1885 survey of the industry revealed that most companies offered policies that either made no mention of suicide or merely excluded it for an initial period after purchase ranging from one month to five years.[65] Moreover, a significant number of insurers self-reported their general tendency to make full payment on policies in cases of suicide unless there was unmistakable evidence of fraud.[66] The fact that this was now their customary practice was something that companies endeavored to publicize in a variety of ways, most boldly in the form of newspaper advertisements that sought to drum up business with boasts such as "no claims in dispute" and "not a case litigated."[67] This shift occurred as legislation was enacted in several states barring the defense of suicide in insurance litigation save where it could be shown "that the insured contemplated suicide at the time he made his application for the policy."[68] In other jurisdictions, it remained unclear whether intentional self-destruction would lead to the denial of benefits if the policy was silent on the matter. This ambiguity pressed to the fore a question that had always lurked uncomfortably on the margins of the legal discourse: was sane suicide an insurable risk?

The fullest answer to this question was provided by the U.S. Supreme Court in the 1898 case of *Ritter v. Mutual Life Insurance Company of New York*, which concerned an apparently prosperous Philadelphia businessman, William M. Runk, who enjoyed a sterling reputation before fatally shooting himself in October 1892, nearly a year after he had purchased $75,000 in life insurance from the defendant, whose policies contained no express exclusion in the event of suicide. News of the shooting was initially greeted with shock and incomprehension among those who knew him well, but a motive for his action soon emerged. Runk had fallen into desperate financial straits over the preceding five years by speculating in the stock market using funds he embezzled or obtained under false pretenses from the dry-goods firm of which he was a member, as well as from a local charity and a wealthy aunt. As his losses multiplied, he took out additional policies on his life so that he had a half million dollars of insurance by the time of his death.[69]

At trial, the presiding judge interpreted the law as denying recovery to the estate of the dead man if he killed himself intentionally, understanding the moral character and physical consequences of the act "as a sane man would." In an attempt to prove the contrary, the plaintiff elicited testimony from his intimate friends and relations that he was uncharacteristically "nervous" in the last days of his life, upon the basis of which they opined that his mind was "unbalanced." On cross-examination, however, these witnesses were compelled to admit that their convictions about his mental condition were formed only after his death. The jury charge all but ruled out the hypothesis of insanity, strongly suggesting that "the natural worry and distress occasioned by his unfortunate circumstances, and the contemplation of self-destruction as a means of relief," were sufficient to account for his unusual behavior and appearance. Even more decisive in securing a jury verdict for the defendant were the suicide notes entered into the record, painstakingly written by Runk in his final hours with the intent that they be delivered after his death to his executor, aunt, and several associates at his firm. Evidently seeking to avoid meeting with disgrace in his lifetime, the self-condemned man acknowledged his misdeeds and avowed his intention to fulfill his financial obligations by killing himself. As he poignantly put it to his business partner: "This is a sad ending of a promising life, but I deserve all the punishment I may get. Only I feel my debts must be paid. This sacrifice will do it, and only this. I was faithful until two years ago. Forgive me. Don't publish this."[70]

On appeal, the members of the Supreme Court confirmed that the jury had been properly instructed on the subject of insanity and warranted in concluding that the insured suffered from no such impairment at the time he took his life. The more vexing legal question presented was whether sane suicide was indeed a defense to liability under a policy containing no exclusion clause to this effect. Answering in the affirmative for a unanimous bench, Justice Harlan advanced two distinct rationales, one grounded in the principles of contract law and the other based upon public policy. First, he defined life insurance as a business arrangement constructed upon the basis of actuarial tables "showing at any age the probable duration of life." Was it not, then, an implied condition of any life-insurance contract that the insured "will leave the event of his death to depend upon some other cause than willful, deliberate self-destruction?" A similar condition was regularly implied in the case of both fire and marine insurance, and the grounds for doing so seemed only stronger where life rather than property was intentionally destroyed by the insured. "To hold otherwise," Harlan submitted, "is to say that the occurrence of an event upon the happening of which the company undertook to pay was intended to be left to his option. That view is against the very essence of the contract." Justice Harlan further provided that had the parties actually entered into an agreement expressly covering the risk of deliberately self-inflicted death, it would have been deemed unenforceable by any court of justice, "in that it tempted or encouraged the assured to commit suicide in order to make provision for those dependent upon him, or to whom he was indebted," thereby constituting a threat to public welfare. Underscoring the dangerous consequences of removing the restraint against crime and fraud provided by the penalty of forfeiture, Harlan concluded that a policy that was silent on the subject of suicide had to be read to exclude coverage.[71]

As for the fate of others who took their lives for the benefit of those they loved or counted as creditors, the judicial record remained quite mixed. The rule announced in *Ritter* met with far more criticism than approval in state courts. "The history of insurance makes difficult the argument that the exception is not now expressed because it is necessarily implied," a New Jersey judge observed in an especially pointed decision allowing recovery in a case of sane suicide. State judges also balked at "the supposed analogy" that Harlan drew between property and life insurance, pointing out that the latter was not a contract of indemnity but "an arbitrary agreement to pay a fixed sum upon the happening of an inevitable event, to wit, the death of the insured, without regard to the value of his life or the loss sustained by the assured." Moreover, it was far from obvious that public policy always dictated the discouragement of suicide in a country where "the paternal theory of government" did not prevail. Though a democratic polity had an interest in the preservation of the lives of all its citizens, this interest was not rightly regarded as paramount over all others, and it was difficult to see why the state ought to be "more concerned to prolong a life that may be worthless to the public than to secure to creditors their just demands, or to afford a maintenance to wife and children." To allow recovery where the suicide risk had not been expressly excluded from coverage was hardly the threat to communal welfare that Harlan made it out to be, at least in the estimation of those members of the bench who took there to be "no public policy more useful than that which holds contractors to performance."[72]

Living in an age when suicide was so often associated with "pecuniary embarrassment," nineteenth-century American judges were impaled on the horns of a dilemma. A ruling that a death was self-inflicted might reduce the intended beneficiaries to penury. But allowing compassion for the dependent family to decide the matter was problematic. To require payment on the disputed policy not only facilitated a fraud on the insurer but also rewarded and even encouraged a monstrous form of financial planning. These clashing considerations help to account for the accumulating mass of inconsistent decisions in cases where the insurer's defense of suicide was met by the beneficiaries' plea of insanity.[73]

In this maze of rulings it might be possible to discern the outlines of what one scholar has aptly described as "the order of equity, if not the equity of order."[74] Yet this begs the question of what equity meant to nineteenth-century judges, implying greater uniformity of thought about justice than was expressed in their opinions. The law reports indicate that the judiciary remained deeply conflicted about how to allocate the burden of loss between insurers and beneficiaries in cases of self-destruction. The alleged suicide had a destabilizing effect on the doctrinal landscape. Embodying market failure as well as moral hazard, this figure confounded conventional moral and legal categories.[75] Though he seemingly took charge of his own destiny, this figure appeared a rather crazed confidence man who could be counted among the casualties of capitalism, a haunting emblem of an economic order in which everything could be bought and sold.

It was precisely because the suicide appeared both deliberate and deranged that judges struggled with the issue of liability. Their clashing opinions reveal tensions and contradictions at the core of the nineteenth-century ideal of the responsible provider.[76] In accounting for the death of a broken man like Comfort, members of the bench could hardly ignore evidence of careful planning motivated by a profound sense of duty to his family and creditors. Yet to credit the actor with such acts of self-sacrifice was, ironically, to dispossess him of the capacity to fulfill his obligations as a husband, father, and businessman. For the designated beneficiaries to recover under the life policy, the death had to be attributed to circumstances beyond the control of the erstwhile head of household. Only by denying that the insured had any choice about how and when he came to his end could courts ensure that he met the expectations of his family, creditors, and community. In so ruling, however, judges risked undermining this model of responsible manhood, as their decisions might well be read as inducements to suicide, fatally tempting those who had fallen on hard times to liquidate their sole remaining asset—life itself—rather than endure its trials with unflinching fortitude.

Faced with this dilemma, members of the bench betrayed doubts about the moral agency of the insured, though most tended to locate the source of the constraint within the diseased body or mind of the actor rather than the surrounding social circumstances. At the same time, courts did not rule out the possibility of entirely voluntary suicide. Indeed, the sane suicide appeared to be a nearly indispensable character in this jurisprudence. Personifying both the spirit of capitalism and its debasing effects, his willful death indicated the moral limits of the enterprise of life insurance and illustrated how hell-bent some men were upon dying in "a state of solvency" instead of living through bankruptcy.

CHAPTER 6

The Consideration of Love

> Our souls, after all, are not our own. We convey a property in them to those with whom we associate, but to what extent can never be known, until we feel the tug, the agony, of our abortive effort to resume an exclusive sway over ourselves.
>
> Nathaniel Hawthorne, *The Blithedale Romance* (1852)

ON JUNE 21, 1882, less than a year after the death of his wife, William Jarvis, a seventy-two-year-old music teacher, entered into an antenuptial contract with Jane L. Conner, an artist he had met a few months earlier. In consideration of their agreement to marry, as well as "the mutual affection existing between them," Jarvis was to convey $10,000 worth of mining company bonds to Conner "on or before the day of their said marriage," which was to take place "within a reasonable time hereafter." By early September 1882, he was dead. After trying and failing to obtain the bonds from Jarvis's son-in-law, Lee Stanley, who was appointed administrator of the estate, Conner filed suit in state court. Stanley insisted that the conveyance of the bonds was conditional upon the marriage. The trial judge agreed with this reading of the contract, but the appellate court reversed the decision, conceiving of her consent to marry as valuable consideration and faulting Jarvis for failing to "consummate his engagement" before he died. "It was not for her to seek him," the court ruled, taking into account "the modesty of the sex" and the marital opportunities Conner had foregone during the period she had waited for her intended to make good on his promise.[1]

But what if she had actually not been as passive as the court assumed? So Stanley argued during the ensuing trial on the merits, maintaining that Jarvis was insane and incapable of making the alleged contract, which was the product of Conner's undue influence. According to this account, Jarvis was a "mental wreck" by the time he made Conner's acquaintance. After the loss of his only child (Stanley's wife) twenty years before, the bereaved father had sought solace in Spiritualism. The defendant's witnesses called him a monomaniac, testifying to his reliance on "the supposed spiritual advice" of mediums in his business affairs even when it was manifestly to his detriment. His forfeiture of autonomy was all the more troubling during his wife's last illness. Informed by a medium that she would soon die, he refused to supply her with medical attention or nourishment. Her death left him more of a mark than a match for a woman like Conner. Though he had initiated their relationship by offering her money "to be developed as a medium," it was she who insisted upon the antenuptial contract. She had placed him under lock and key in his own house for two hours in order to extract his signature, complained after the fact that he was an "old fool," and described him as "crazy."[2]

With this evidence in view, the appellate court determined there was more than enough in the record to support the trial court's findings of incapacity and undue influence. It was not so much the content of Jarvis's beliefs as his want of control over them that led the court to this conclusion. Even more compelling was the confidential nature of Conner's relationship to Jarvis, which gave rise to a presumption of undue influence that she had failed to disprove. "The rule applies with peculiar force to the relation of one and his priest, confessor, clergyman, or spiritual adviser, and certainly with no less force to the relation between one who is a firm believer in, not to say a monomaniac upon, the subject of spiritualism, and the medium in whom he has confidence, and upon whom he habitually relies." The members of the bench regarded Conner as a matrimonial adventuress rather than a discarded lover; her attempt to capitalize on the affectionate gratitude of a vulnerable confidante would not be consummated by the law.[3]

Poised on the threshold of matrimony and purporting to be able to mediate between this world and the next, Conner stood as a potent threat to many things that her judges would have considered sacred. Spiritualism was the subject of intense controversy, at once titillating and troubling popular audiences while skeptical scientists and moral reformers looked on with mounting disdain. The stories about the late Cornelius J. Vanderbilt's liaisons with Victoria Woodhull and Tennessee Claflin told during the postmortem contest over his will were generally treated with levity by the press, but spiritualists' belief in "elective affinities" threatened the security of marriage. In the early nineteenth century, some religious enthusiasts had abandoned a wedded spouse to form an intimate relationship with a soul mate and justified their scandalous conduct on the basis of spiritual affinities. After the mass carnage of the Civil War, grieving widows seeking to communicate with the dead contributed to the increasing popularity of Spiritualism. The spectacular new technologies of "materialization" deployed in séances and larger, more profitable venues that entertained curiosity seekers were targeted by fraud prosecutions. But mediums and followers continued to convene around parlor tables in "family or home circles," taking the advice of the spirits seriously in ordering their business affairs and personal lives even though this exposed them to the risk of being denounced as social pariahs or railroaded into insane asylums. The linkages between Spiritualism and insanity were substantiated by neurologists, who pronounced women to be especially susceptible to "mediomania" and ascribed the disease to an abnormal positioning of the uterus. In this view, all "ultraisms"—"Mormonism, Mesmerism, Fourierism, Socialism, oftener Spiritualism"—had the same cause and resulted in deviant sexual behavior.[4] While this diagnosis implied a degree of mental unsoundness that impaired agency, social purity crusaders cast adherents as "free lovers" whose anarchic forms of sexual commerce imperiled the home as well as the nation-state.[5]

In pronouncing against the antenuptial agreement in *Conner v. Stanley*, the California court delimited the bounds of rational choice with respect to beliefs as well as spouses. The decision quickly acquired the status of a leading case in late nineteenth-century treatises. Yet the opinion begged more questions than it answered about the consideration of love. If there was nothing inherently objectionable about agreeing to marry for money, what circumstances rendered the exchange invalid? While Jarvis's age and mental condition figured prominently in the court's analysis, they did not amount to disabilities as a matter of law. Conner was not shown to be guilty of any intentional wrongdoing, whether in the form of illicit sex, fraud, or duress. The deciding factor was the confidential nature of the relationship between the man and his medium. The intimacy of their association raised a presumption against the validity of the transaction, paradoxically inclining the court to doubt the mutuality of the affection and assent expressed on the face of the alleged contract. Indeed, the judges showed themselves to be of two minds about the interplay between affection, attraction, and trust in prenuptial negotiations, treating them as both vital and vitiating elements in the formation of a contract.

The extent to which the emotions aroused by close relationships might compromise individual autonomy and erode the material basis of the household and communal life is strikingly illustrated in Nathaniel Hawthorne's *The Blithedale Romance*. Affection not only makes a father concerned to provide for the welfare of his children; for better and for worse, it also joins like-minded people together in nearly indissoluble knots. The dilemmas inherent in the myriad pulls of individualism, family, and community in early nineteenth-century American society are especially charged in the romance's fictional setting, a utopian experiment based on the free association of creative, high-minded men and women whose devotion to their inspired visions makes it difficult to get the prosaic but necessary tasks of farming and housework done. The excesses to which good people are liable are dramatized by a male character's credulous belief in Spiritualism, as a young woman who serves as a passive medium is manipulated by a designing man. The economic disaster that follows is as much the result of this leader's delusion as of the others' neglect of labor. Yet the verdict of Hawthorne's narrator is ambivalent. For all its follies, Blithedale farm expressed people's aspirations as well as their frailties. All human associations are tinged by self-interest; conversely, all notions of interest are shaped by personal attachments. In the world of the novel, drawing a clear line between idealism and delusion is impossible; so is maintaining a strict boundary between the sentimental family and the heartless business of financial transactions.[6]

Love and self-interest proved no less confounding to judges who had to consider contractual dealings within the family circle and among other sorts of intimates. Indeed, judges' determined efforts to contain their effects eveal the extent of the difficulty they encountered. As a general rule, they distinguished "natural affection" from "valuable" consideration, with the implication that the former was insufficient to sustain a promise at law or a decree for specific performance in equity. "For most practical purposes, it has no place in the law of contract," William Herbert Page went so far as to say in his 1905 treatise. Though this declaration exaggerated the legal consensus, it epitomizes the separate doctrinal realms that many nineteenth-century judges envisioned and tried to maintain, concerned as they were with insulating intimate relations from those of the market. They treated economic transactions between parties in confidential relationships as presumptively suspect, requiring positive proof that they were not tainted by undue influence. This standard was almost diametrically opposed to that which obtained in the testamentary context, where dispositions to the natural objects of one's bounty were generally regarded with favor. This doctrinal distinction was premised upon the notion of a possessive individual who knew he could not take his property with him when he died but was not expected to give it away during his lifetime, even or perhaps especially to those he loved. In deciding these sorts of cases, courts proceeded upon "the natural assumption that a living person having, it is to be supposed, a need for his property, or at least a desire to retain it, during life, will not part with it without a measurably adequate equivalent." Though it was in accordance with "the exigencies of mortality" for a testator's property "to pass from him to others selected by himself, according to the dictates of his affections," considerations of "friendship, trust, and confidence, affection, [and] personal obligations" were treated as impairments that tended to compromise the exercise of contractual freedom.[7]

To be sure, love was not disabling in the same sense as insanity. What rendered it problematic was its association with dominion: judges thought that it created or reinforced power imbalances in personal relationships, generating suspicions that the parties were not dealing with each other as free agents "on a plane of equality," which judges took to be a precondition for the formation of a valid contract. Though the tensions between affect and assent were everywhere to be found in agreements between intimates, they appeared in sharpest relief in capacity contests within the sphere of "domestic relations." Sharing nineteenth-century cultural elites' sentimentalization of the home, judges described it as a private sanctuary from the "selfish and calculating world" that was governed by the "gentle influences" of love rather than law. But they recognized the home was constituted by and maintained through the instrumentality of contracts that subjected the parties to laws that were not entirely theirs to alter as they wished. When men and women entered the married state, they and their progeny acquired rights and duties that emanated from natural law and subjected them to state regulation. Assuming the posture of judicial patriarchs, members of the bench spoke of marriage as a "civil status" and a "procreative institution" more emphatically as legislatures granted married women a degree of control over their property and liberalized the law of divorce over the course of the century. They pronounced the marital bond "no more a contract than 'fatherhood' or 'sonship'"; some even drew analogies between the union of man and wife and "selfdom, slavery, or apprenticeship." The subordination it entailed was precisely why the institution was deemed objectionable by an increasingly vocal chorus of women's rights advocates, while male and female free lovers sought liberation from its constraints. Judges could neither validate nor ignore the reformers alternative visions of gender and sexual relations, apprehending as they did the dangerous appeal of these egalitarian ideals and unconventional practices, which threatened to derange minds, households, and the wider social order.[8]

Anxious to insulate the natural and salutary dependencies of the home from the corrosive individualism of the market, members of the bench wielded the law of contract as a mediating device, straining to distinguish domestic relations from other sorts of consensual arrangements. The love they envisioned as governing the hearth was domesticated by a distinctly American law of the family, expressive of their dual and dueling commitments to nuptial freedom and domestic harmony. Conundrums about the subject of contract appeared most vividly in two sorts of capacity suits where love was involved: in order to secure release from the bonds of marriage, and to set aside agreements to care for aged and infirm members of the household. The family histories recorded in these disputes confronted judges with the darker side of intimacy. Witnesses recounted sudden gusts of passion and emotional reversals that wreaked havoc within the sheltered space of the home, sometimes issuing in shocking acts of violence, sexual perversity, and cruelty, other times in more insidious abuses of trust, and still other times in wounding displays of indifference. Although these domestic scenes were dramatically reconstructed for forensic purposes by narrators whose reliability was the more to be questioned the closer they were to the party whose competence was in dispute, the problems they brought to the surface were pressingly real, concerning as they did the nature and interrelations between love, power, identity, and personhood. Those who fell under the rule of love were not easily distinguished from the insanely deluded, and both of these sorts of "affections" impinged upon the sovereignty of the individual in ways that proved exceedingly difficult to comprehend within the nineteenth-century American law of contracts.

Insanity as a Ground for Divorce

Shortly after the marriage of John and Susanna Hamaker in January 1853, the husband discovered that his wife was not the woman he thought he had married. They had not spent much time together during their engagement, so it was only when they were both living under his roof that he began to notice signs of insanity. Her "absent-mindedness, and causeless paroxysms of anger and other passions" eventually became unmanageable, and he had her committed to the state hospital for the insane. Or so Mr. Hamaker claimed in the petition he submitted to an Illinois state court in 1855 praying for a divorce on account of her mental illness, which was alleged to have existed without his knowledge before their marriage and grown worse over time so that it was now incurable. A general denial was entered in response by a conservator on Susanna's behalf, and a master proceeded to take evidence from an array of relatives, neighbors, and medical men, which uniformly supported the husband's position. To know her was to be terrorized by her, on the witnesses' accounts, as she often seemed on the verge of harming someone, even though others made every effort to appease her. She appeared to have taken after her mother, who had long been afflicted with a similar sort of insanity. Susanna frequently threatened the life of her unoffending husband and hid a butcher's knife near his bed. Most of her planned assaults were thwarted, but she seriously wounded a woman boarder and set fire to the house. Her violent actions displayed a purposefulness that she failed to apply to her wifely duties to take care of her husband and keep house. Andrew McFarland, the superintendent of the state hospital, testified that Susanna was "probably incurably insane" and her dementia had quite likely been in existence previous to the marriage. Two other practicing physicians who heard all of this testimony concurred with his assessment. The presiding judge, however, summarily dismissed the case, and an appellate panel proved no more sympathetic to the husband's plea.[9]

In the opinion of the court, the insanity of the wife was no cause for divorce. Strictly construing the governing statute even though it accorded judges greater discretion, Chief Justice Walter B. Scates held that a release from the bonds of marriage was to be allowed only for common or canon law causes and those specified by statute: precontract, consanguinity, affinity, corporeal infirmity or impotency, adultery, cruelty, desertion, conviction of a felony or other infamous crime, or habitual drunkenness.[10] "The pitiable misfortune of the defendant" was no reason "for casting her off from her only domestic stay and support." Recognizing that a marriage, like any other contract, could be rendered void for "want of sound mind," Scates reviewed the evidence and found that, although suffering "occasional paroxysms of insanity," "in the intervals she was capable of all the duties of a citizen or a wife." More to the point, the plaintiff had failed to prove that the marriage was contracted during an episode of insanity. The husband's real complaint, as the judge heard it, was that he had been "cheated and defrauded" by the concealment of this infirmity before the marriage. But that offense would, at most, warrant the recovery of damages from those who had misled him, not a rescission of the marriage contract, "unless, indeed, the law guarantees to every husband a rational mental standard for the mind of a wife." "If there be a period during the marital relation, when, more than at any other, the tenderest care, support and watchfulness of an affectionate husband is demanded, it is while the wife is helpless from sickness or insanity. To make this misfortune, the greatest that can befall us, the ground of the next greatest wrong and injustice, would be truly adding insult and injury to providential misfortune." Yet even as he affirmed the judgment, Scates seemed to dissociate himself from the law of marital dissolution he was applying, which was putatively designed to promote "procreation and the nurture of children" but took notice only of the bodily health of prospective parents and neglected to attend to the soundness of their minds. "If there be here incongruity, inconsistency, irrationality," he concluded, "we can only say, we do not make, but interpret and apply the rule."[11]

Pleas for release from the bonds of matrimony were not readily granted, for the marriage contract was not "merely a thing of bargain between men and women." The terms of this contract were set by the state; consenting parties were transformed into husbands and wives with specified duties, many of which were legally enforceable until they were parted by death. Married men and women acquired new legal personalities that could not be voluntarily shed, even or perhaps especially when one or both became discontented with their own assumed identities or the other party's behavior.[12] The permanency of this union did not mean there was no way out. In postrevolutionary America, the freedom and mutuality of assent were at least as important to marriage as any other contract.[13] Judges and jurists took it to be "a self-evident principle" that the relation could not be valid unless both parties were "capable in law of consenting" and that their consent was not obtained by fraud or force.[14] "All contracts are vitiated by such a worm at the vital part," Joel Bishop declared in his influential 1852 *Commentaries on the Law of Marriage and Divorce*, "and to this rule the contract of marriage is no exception." Yet he immediately added that certain "peculiarities" had to be kept in view in assessing the validity of marriage contracts, because "the parties take each other for better, for worse, for richer, for poorer, to cherish each other in sickness and in health; so that a mistake, resulting either from accident, or, generally, from fraudulent practices, in respect to the character, the fortune, or the health of a party to a marriage, does not vitiate the marriage."[15] Indeed, despite their commitment to demystifying and modernizing marriage, few members of the bench and bar were prepared to treat it just like any other contract, animated as so many of them were by a felt need to preserve the sanctity of this union and to ensure that it remained distinct from business relations forged in the market.[16]

These tensions in legal thinking are apparent in early nineteenth-century laws of marriage and divorce, especially regarding *who* could enter into and exit from marital relations. As permissive as American judges proved to be regarding "common-law marriages," they did not as readily accept desertion as a grounds for divorce despite the lower classes' acceptance of this practice.[17] Members of the bench were not eager to exercise the new powers to dissolve marriages that were increasingly conferred upon them by state legislatures. Indeed, these measures were conflicted concessions to the custom of permanent separation; they attempted "to bring extralegal dissolutions under the aegis of state government," largely to protect vulnerable women and children.[18] Although the statutory provisions varied considerably across jurisdictions, divorce was everywhere understood as "a public process allowed only for public reasons" arising from the misconduct of one of the parties that constituted a serious breach of their matrimonial vows. Insanity did not fit this description, and in most states the offenses so recognized were initially limited to adultery, desertion, and cruelty. By midcentury many statutes had been revised to encompass a wider range of wrongs; the most common additions were habitual drunkenness and incarceration for crimes, while some legislators authorized divorce on grounds of "gross neglect of duty" or for "other causes" left to the discretion of the court. As in the case of *Hamaker*, some courts simply read these omnibus clauses out of the statute. Justice Joseph Story questioned their constitutionality: "A man has just as good a right to his wife as to *the property* acquired under a marriage contract. He has a legal right to her society and her fortune; and to divest such right without his *default,* and against his will, would be as flagrant a violation of the principles of justice as the confiscation of his own estate."[19]

At the same time, judges like Story anxiously emphasized that the acquisition of a wife or husband was not simply like that of any other form of real or personal property. As Norma Basch observes, "By the 1850s, when access to a divorce was becoming ever easier and the number of decrees was rising, divorce served as a lightning rod for deep-seated tensions over the positive and negative implications of freedom. . . . It is worth remembering that fault divorce placed a man and a woman in an adversarial setting that implicitly tested their relative authority." Judges made it abundantly clear that they were aiming not only to secure the prerogatives of husbands but also to enforce certain obligations and duties of care that applied to both spouses, even or perhaps especially if the one did not provide the other with the companionship or fortune that had been expected at the time of the marriage ceremony. The sorts of fraud that could vitiate a marriage were defined quite stringently by courts so as to exclude "all those deceptive acts to which the sexes, too frequently, have recourse, with a view to obtain, what they consider, an advantageous marriage connection," whether "by setting off their person, characters, tempers, circumstances and connections, in too favorable a light; or by professions of ardent affection, which they either may not feel, or not in a degree equal to what they profess." However inconsistent such representations were with "truth and sincerity," they could not be recognized as grounds for rescission—a contractual remedy that restored the parties to their original positions—without degrading marriage, "which is a main pillar, on which society itself is founded, to a level with the most trifling of bargains."[20]

Similarly, attempts on the part of the wary to hold prospective spouses accountable for their financial commitments by means of contract did not prove legally effective. While a prudent buyer might obtain an express warranty from a seller when he purchased land, slaves, livestock, or commercial goods, no such analogue was recognized between parties contracting for marriage.[21] Qualities that did not go to "the essentials of marriage" could not be secured by private agreement without compromising the concept of matrimony as American judges and jurists understood it. As Bishop summarized the doctrine:

> If the man should expressly agree with the woman that he would be to her a husband only on the condition that she should prove to be so rich, so virtuous, so wise, so healthy, of such standing in society; and should finally consent to celebrate the marriage on her false and fraudulent representations that she possessed the stipulated qualities, while in truth she was destitute of them, still when he comes to be married he says to her in effect and in law, "I take you to be my wife, whether you have those qualities or do not have them, whether you have deceived me or have not deceived me." In other words, he waives the condition. To carry such a condition into the marriage relation would be contrary to its spirit and purpose, and against good morals. It would be suffering a connection which might prove to be a prostitution, resulting in the birth of illegitimate children, the corruption of virtue, and the disrepute of the marriage relation.[22]

The jurists' concern was to differentiate the marriage contract from the short-term contracts for sexual services that constituted prostitution, which was generally seen as an unholy mix of the commercial and the intimate.

But was it fair to presume that a man consented to the lifelong bondage that was entailed in being married to a woman whose mental illness not only compromised her capacity for marital companionship but robbed her of her *self*, so she was no longer the person he had married? Was mental alienation a "conjugal risk" both parties assumed as a matter of law, as they did the risk of physical illness and debility? In cases where the validity of a marriage arose collaterally, courts sometimes seemed to imply it was not. As one Kentucky court declared in a decision denying dower to a plaintiff on account of the want of capacity in her supposed spouse, "If there be no reason or volition, there is no mind which can make a valid agreement. A person of 'unsound mind' . . . is, as to all intellectual purposes, dead; and such a thing, destitute of intellectual light and life, is as incapable as a dead body of being a husband or a wife, in a legal, rational or moral sense."[23]

Most state legislatures denied formal recognition to insanity as a cause for divorce, both because they remained under the sway of the fault paradigm and because they did not want to open the door any wider to fraud and collusion. Yet their responses to individual petitions revealed ambivalence about the plight of the sane spouse. In one especially prominent Ohio case, a lawyer with an epileptic wife, whose periodic fits were deemed by experts to have grown so dangerous as to require confinement, was sympathetically cast in a committee report recommending that his bill for divorce be granted, as she was unable "to perform any of the duties of the marital relation, or to derive any benefit or satisfaction from the performance of those duties on the part of her husband." Indeed, their childless, loveless arrangement was hardly worthy of the name of marriage: "*She* is a prisoner in the asylum, and in all probability will remain a prisoner for life. *He* is worse than a prisoner, out of doors—a freeman, who ranges up and down with the invisible shackles on his soul, of a union that was entered into under a misapprehension of facts, a union that has brought nothing but gloom and misfortune, a union that does no good in any quarter and produces only evil continually." Wedlock, indeed.[24]

While all of the participants in this debate insisted that the marital bond served as "the safeguard of civilization and advancement," they disagreed sharply as to whether this institution was purified or fatally threatened by the recognition of "mental causes" of divorce. On one side were those who insisted that "the parties are under an obligation by their marriage vow, to adhere to each other, and particularly under circumstances of affliction and misfortune." On the other side were those who contended that it was "equally hard that a husband should be compelled to pass his life with a human being who might be insensible to all the sympathies, and dead to every purpose of the marriage relation." As the judiciary committee of the state of New York pointedly asked in 1849:

> A marriage had with one insane, is void. Why should not, on the same principle, the fact of subsequent insanity, if incurable, work the same result? There is nothing left on which to base such a relation; the body remains but the mind is flown. That light only which could nourish the connection is extinguished forever. Should the law bind together the mentally dead to the living? It is well settled, that insanity is transmissible or hereditary. The law should be so construed, as to remove every inducement to the extension of so deplorable a calamity. In this, the whole body of the people have a direct interest.[25]

While the legislators did not act on this recommendation, their counterparts in Michigan decided in the same year to authorize divorce in the case of incurable insanity, with the requirement that the husband make adequate provision for the care and support of his former spouse. But most states were disinclined to venture into such "shadowy and doubtful" psychological territory, as it was so difficult to distinguish cases of actual mental illness from those that merely manifested the "smothered hatred, and love turned to the reverse" which the parties to marriage were required to endure.[26]

Without challenging the fault paradigm within which these lawmakers were operating, medical jurists called attention to cases of partial insanity that underscored how hard it was to disentangle evidence of disabling mental illness from that of incompatibility. "Within a few years," Isaac Ray observed in 1844, "a class of cases has made its appearance, exceedingly embarrassing to the medical jurist":

> The woman, after preparing for a union, to which her head and heart had apparently fully consented, and going through the marriage ceremony with the utmost propriety, manifesting all the while nothing unusual in her deportment, immediately after imbibes an insuperable aversion towards her husband, shuns his company, and perhaps refuses to live with him. In some of the cases, other singularities of conduct soon appear, one after another, till at last the woman becomes a subject of unequivocal insanity. In others, however, this strong repugnance towards the husband continues to be the principal, if not the only symptom, of mental disorder, but so closely do they resemble the former in other respects, that we can have no hesitation in regarding them as merely varieties of the same affection.[27]

At that time, a wife had no right to refuse to have sexual intercourse with her husband, though given the absence of contraception the advocates of "voluntary motherhood" asserted this right.[28] Physicians regarded feminine repugnance to sexual relations as simultaneously normal and pathological, a state aggravated by "the crowd of new thoughts and feelings" a woman experienced upon becoming a wife. The question was "not so satisfactorily settled" as a matter of law, which turned on whether the insanity was clearly manifest before the wedding.[29] Ray thought it might not be "strictly just" to condition legal relief on such a showing, though he recoiled "from the idea of depriving a woman of her protection and support, at the very moment when the severest of earthly calamities has overtaken her, merely on the strength of what we may call a pathological abstraction." Ultimately, Ray was unable to decide what was to be done when madness destroyed the consortium that defined the marriage relation and yet demanded dutiful care from the sane spouse.[30]

In view of the symbolic significance of marriage as "the irrevocable contract that made all other contracts possible" in this "shifting, competitive world," members of the bench worked to particularize the substantive and procedural rules so as to protect the vulnerable and prevent fraud in both the making and breaking of marital contracts.[31] Articulations of the requisite mental threshold sometimes amounted to the basic capacity "to take care of his or her own person and property," though some judges allowed those under guardianship to marry.[32] The judicial tests that enjoyed the widest application and strongest approval on the part of commentators trained attention on the specific qualities of mind one needed to possess in order to "have a real appreciation of" what it meant to be married, providing that "while it is in some degree of the head, it is primarily and chiefly of the heart." The capacity deemed essential to the validity of a marriage contract, unlike other civil contracts, depended "more on sentiments of mutual esteem, attachment, and affection, which the weakest may feel as well as the strongest intellects, than on the exercise of a clear, unclouded reason, or sound judgment, or intelligent discernment and discrimination." For this very reason, however, the weak-minded might fall below the bar of legal competence, given their susceptibility to fraud, coercion, and more subtle forms of influence strong enough to vitiate their consent. Exactly how much influence was excessive or how little mental capacity was disabling had to be determined case by case. As Bishop put it, "the question is not altogether of brain-*quantity* or of brain-*quality*, in the abstract; but it is, whether or not the mind could and did act rationally regarding the precise thing in contemplation."[33]

To be legally cognizable, a claim of the incapacity to marry had to relate to the moment when the contract was supposed to have been made. The vision of marriage as a meeting of two capable and willing minds was powerful enough to incline courts to entertain capacity challenges brought by the sane as well as on behalf of the insane spouse, treating the marriage contract as void *ab initio*. To be sure, suits met with a more receptive bench when they were brought on behalf of the alleged incompetent, and success often seemed to hinge upon a fairly compelling showing of unfair dealing as well as incapacity.[34] Moreover, a sane spouse filing for divorce on grounds of adultery, cruelty, or desertion might be thwarted by an insanity plea. This legal strategy proved quite effective in excusing these forms of civil wrongdoing, testifying to the judges' commitment to marriage as a lifelong endeavor. Yet even or especially in decisions requiring that the parties remain married, members of the bench consciously or inadvertently drew attention to the gap between the cultural ideals of matrimony and the lived experiences of the miserable husbands and wives before them. The more they saw of these marriages, the more they were moved to rethink what the sane and innocent spouse should be made to bear in cases of postnuptial insanity, out of concern not only for the sane spouse's well-being but also for the fitness of the race.[35]

To make sense of this change over time, consider the stories told by litigants in annulment suits. Petitions commonly played on cultural fears about mercenary motives and the threat they posed to the sanctity of marriage. More often than not, the insane spouse was cast as the injured party, a rich but unsuspecting character whose guilelessness stemmed from a mental disorder that would have been readily apparent to even the most casual observer. Indeed, in some instances the existence of mental unsoundness had already been established by means of a formal inquisition that resulted in the appointment of a guardian who had been circumvented by the gold-digging defendant. Although the methods of these confidence men and women varied, their devious plan almost always featured a clandestine marriage ceremony hurriedly performed without the knowledge of any relative or friend and rarely preceded by any sort of courtship. Defendants typically met these charges with professions of true love for or sincere attachment to the petitioner, whose alleged mental illness they completely denied, minimized into eccentricity, or said was punctuated by a lucid interval during which the marriage was contracted or ratified. Their counternarratives sometimes figured the bride and groom as a star-crossed pair, thwarted at every turn by disapproving family and friends who were shamelessly animated by selfish pecuniary interests or unalloyed spite, which explained why they had not been invited to the wedding and exposed the real motives behind the capacity contest.[36]

Successful suits usually featured substantial evidence of imposition as well as incapacity, as can be seen in a pair of North Carolina cases decided by Chief Justice Thomas Ruffin in 1843. Both were instituted by the committee of the alleged incompetent to set aside a marriage *de facto* with a person who did not travel in the same social circles. The first involved a middle-aged man by the name of Reese Johnson, who had been adjudged "of unsound mind . . . from his infancy" and placed under guardianship upon arriving at the age of majority in 1827. Those who had known him through the years described him as "ignorant of the most common things in life," including "the days of the week." His pretended wife Ann was depicted as a shrewd adventuress who knew him to be entitled to an estate valued at $3,000 and "procured a marriage" with him in September

1841 with the assistance of two male confederates. The justice of the peace who married them recounted the suspicious signs that marked the occasion, especially the comment by one of Ann's accomplices as soon as the ceremony was over that "Johnson was *non compos mentis*." The would-be Mrs. Johnson stood on her pleadings, which represented her as the victim of a smear campaign, spearheaded by Reese's greedy uncle and given a respectable patina by a local Presbyterian minister, to keep the newlyweds from living happily ever after. From all that Chief Justice Ruffin could see, their misgivings about this union and pursuit of legal redress were warranted. The evidence before him showed that Reese lacked sufficient mind to understand and assent to a contract of such "great importance" and that the defendant made it with "a consciousness of the wickedness of bringing it about." The court therefore pronounced Reese "free and divorced from the said Ann."[37]

Ruffin performed a similar act of emancipation in the case of Letitia M. A. Crump, a woman "of most respectable parentage" who was married in 1826 to Colonel John Crump, "a gentleman of fortune and character." By all reports, she performed her wifely duties conscientiously, moving in the best circles and bearing five children by the time she was thirty. But then she was struck with puerperal mania, and her condition was seriously aggravated by the death of her husband in 1836, leaving her with a substantial estate she could not manage. Upon being found a confirmed lunatic in April 1837, she was put under the guardianship of her brother, who placed her in the household of Littleton Harris, a respectable and trusted friend of the family. All went well until October 1839, when, in view of the impending nuptials of one of his children, Harris sent Letitia to stay temporarily with a neighbor, who passed her off to another neighbor for a single day. During that brief time, the neighbor's son, Henry Morgan, secured a license as well as a willing magistrate and wed the woman in a remote field before a small gathering of his family relations, but none of hers. Although Henry was a young man "of the age of twenty or a little more, without education, standing, property, or expectancy," he insisted before the court that he was "actuated by his attachment to her for her personal attractions, amiable disposition, and mental accomplishments" and admitted "he did not regret the favorable opportunity of making a proposal at his father's," which she had freely accepted. But to Ruffin, her acceptance of this suitor's attentions and proposal appeared to be "acts of madness in themselves." "Possessed with a fury of animal passion" when left to her own devices, Crump insanely looked forward to the gratification of these impulses upon the return of her dead husband, voicing this expectation even after her makeshift wedding to Henry. "'I wish'—she said—'the Colonel would come.'"[38]

As he released this deluded woman from the bonds of marriage, Ruffin made no mention of what was to become of the child born to her sometime after the supposed marriage and before this suit was filed in August 1841. Although the defendant tried to persuade the court that this constituted evidence of ratification and that it was "best for all parties" to keep this family together, Ruffin pointedly rejected these lines of argument. He affirmed that if he had any discretion about whether to annul this marriage, which he insisted he did not, there was no good reason for "leaving this person and her property" in the power of one "whose motives and conduct from the beginning to the end have been most flagitious." Yet in other cases, judges' concerns about the impact of a decree of nullity upon unwed mothers and their innocent offspring figured prominently. Illegitimacy continued to carry negative social and legal consequences, even as state legislatures worked in halting but significant ways to revise bastardy laws so as not to visit "the sins of the parents" upon the unoffending products of their unlawful intercourse.[39]

These clashing legal, social, and economic considerations were all in evidence in an 1859 Georgia divorce suit brought on behalf of Richard N. Westbrook on the ground of his mental incapacity at the time he was married to his second wife, Catherine, in 1848. Formally declared a lunatic in May 1849, he was placed under guardianship and committed to an asylum. The superintendent testified that his condition was incurable, and the defendant did not dispute the point. The main bone of contention between the parties was the judge's instruction to the jury, which authorized them to grant a total divorce to Richard, yet required that their verdict be framed so as to treat Catherine's child by Richard on equal footing with his children from a former marriage as far as the distribution of his estate was concerned, and allowed that they might accord Catherine some portion of the property "if they saw proper so to do." The verdict made provision for her as well as her son. The plaintiff appealed, contending that neither Catherine nor her child were entitled to any of Richard's property because his want of capacity rendered the marriage void, with the implication that "the parties have been living together in a state of concubinage, and not of wedlock, and that the offspring of this unlawful connexion is a bastard."[40]

Writing for a divided court, Judge Joseph Henry Lumpkin refused to authorize such an outcome. He read his state's recently enacted divorce statute as designed to ensure that nullity suits did not cast off unsuccessful female defendants "like Hagar and Ishmael, with only a morsel of bread and a bottle of water, to starve in the wilderness, while the husband and father have a plenty to spare." Georgia's reformed provisions enabled jurors to punish a woman guilty of fraud by turning her away penniless "as a punishment for her conduct" without penalizing "the guiltless progeny," but there was no evidence of wrongdoing in the case at bar, and the defendant was certainly not blameworthy simply because she was poor and her husband was rich. "Do mercenary matches never take place, in this our day and generation, except among the insane?" he asked rhetorically. "Such a conclusion, I regret to say, would almost stultify our race. Love matches! They exist only in the creation of novelists. They are rarely known in actual life."[41]

While no more starry-eyed about the moral economy of marriage, the dissenting judge took issue with the majority opinion, maintaining this was not really a divorce case even though it had been filed under a statute that recognized "mental incapacity at the time of marriage" as one of the grounds for marital dissolution. The claim of the plaintiff who stood before them was that it was impossible for him to have married anyone because he was as incompetent to enter this legal relation as "an infant five years old; a slave; a person with a living wife or husband." To talk of divorce in these cases was simply nonsensical, tantamount "to talk of death, when there has never been any life." The judge acknowledged that his reading of the law might operate to "'bastardize the issue,' as the expression is, and leave it and the mother, without provision, from the father." But he minimized "the evil of these things, as compared with the evil of holding, that all persons laboring under 'mental incapacity' to marry, may yet marry and (by consequence) make any other contract—that idiots, lunatics, infants old enough to say yes, slaves even, may marry or make any other contract." While conceding that there might be "cause for sympathy" with the child, he insisted "there can hardly ever be any cause for sympathy with the parent. The fact will be, that in nine of the cases out of every ten, the parent was a fortune hunter, and acted with open eyes." Expressing confidence that "marriage will never invade the idiot or the lunatic, who is without fortune," the judge held an action for nullity to be the proper way of extricating the mentally incapable from these situations and ensuring that the legal category of contract, and marriage more particularly, encompassed only those who were capable of meaningful consent.[42]

This position was taken by sane spouses who sued to set aside their marriages, typically claiming to be victims of fraud perpetrated by the insane person's relatives. Few succeeded, even where it could be shown that the insanity had been deliberately hidden by the family during a brief and well-orchestrated courtship. Consider, for example, the case of William Smith, a Mississippi man who alleged that he had married a woman within several months of meeting her, only to learn that she was "the victim of hereditary insanity" and had been afflicted with the disease since childhood, a secret well guarded by her mother. After she had nearly killed their newborn child, William, who had young children from his previous marriage, concluded that it was no longer safe to cohabit with her. Relatives and physicians presented enough evidence of mental disturbance before and after the marriage to make the court wonder how a suitor could have failed to notice her symptoms during their courtship. But instead of refusing William's petition because he failed to establish his ignorance of her diseased condition, as the statute required, the court ordered them to stay married because he had not shown that she was insane at the moment they exchanged their vows, which would have been almost impossible to do without undermining his claim of ignorance.[43]

Sane spouses were all the more unlikely to be released from the bonds of marriage in cases where they had endeavored to live with the situation for a substantial period, usually from some mixture of financial motives and social considerations, often with the hope that a stable home life would produce a recovery. So Mrs. Elizabeth Rawdon would discover when she filed for divorce from her husband Isaac in 1854, nearly thirty years after they were married in 1826. Though she asserted in her petition that Isaac's insanity had developed "in 1822 or '23" when "a severe attack of brain-fever" left him with "his reason dethroned," she contended that he appeared to have recovered by the time she met and married him. He was a "generally intelligent and sensible man," but she soon noticed "many strange things in his conduct." About six years into their life together, "he suddenly became greatly concerned about the subject of religion" and displayed "such indubitable proofs of insanity" as to convince her that "his mind was permanently deranged." During violent paroxysms "he evinced a disposition to shed blood," which she managed to contain when it was directed at their slaves. Tragically, she was unable to prevent him from killing their only child. After cutting his throat, erecting a scaffold, and burning the body, he explained "'that he offered his son [as] a sacrifice to God, as Abraham had offered his son Isaac." Her husband was subsequently committed to a lunatic asylum, where he remained when the suit was brought. Because she had "slumbered on her known rights" for over twenty years, the court held that she could not now divorce him, even though it was conceded that his medical history provided reasons to doubt his mental malady had "entirely healed" at the time of the marriage. Although there was "no living offspring" to suffer by a judicial sentence of divorce in the case at bar, the court apprehended that "the rule, if we adopt it, may in some future proceeding, illegitimate a household," so the woman was left married to an insane man, her status fixed for the broader public good.[44]

The judicial commitment to marriage was likewise pronounced in divorce actions brought on grounds of desertion, cruelty, and/or adultery, where insanity was pled as a defense to allegations of marital wrongdoing. These cases provide further illustrations of the perils of suffering too long with the problem of an insane spouse. The more intolerable the situation became, the greater the judicial inclination to read the filing of a suit as a blameworthy evasion of the marital duties of care and protection. No case taught this lesson more clearly than *Tiffany v. Tiffany*, a divorce action filed in December 1888 by an aggrieved wife who charged her husband with "such inhuman treatment as to endanger her life." He was adjudged insane in February 1889 and committed to the Iowa Hospital for the Insane at Independence by a court-appointed guardian. In answer to the divorce petition, the guardian pled an insanity defense. According to expert testimony, the defendant was afflicted with a chronic form of dementia rooted in "hereditary predisposition," which developed as a result of "an injury to the head, excessive venery, and domestic infelicity." He was now permanently insane, greatly enfeebled in body as well as mind, and "incapable of self-support." Convinced that the defendant's offenses against his wife and children must have "originated in a diseased mind, and were the result of insanity," the court dismissed the plaintiff's suit as an indirect attempt to procure a divorce on the ground of insanity, emphasizing that Mr. Tiffany's illness not only released him from responsibility for his abusive behavior but also increased his wife's responsibility for him:

> The marital relations impose upon each spouse the duty of care and protection of the other when in disease. If disease impairs the mind, the obligation is not discharged, but is rather increased in force; for a diseased mind requires even more care for one so afflicted than a simple physical ailment, which does not affect the mind. Those nervous diseases and old age, which by the overthrow of the will and self-control, and the impairment of the mind, producing distorted and false views of the acts and conduct of a spouse or other of the family, and rendering the subject incapable of self-protection, would indeed leave him in a pitiable condition, if these afflictions would justify his wife in casting him off, and gaining from the law exemption from the obligations of the marriage contract imposing the duty of kindness, tenderness, and care.

Lest he be misread as imposing a disproportionately heavy burden on wives, the judge declared that allowing insanity as a cause of divorce "would bring the heaviest affliction and burden upon women who have, added to the general diseases of humanity, peculiar diseases of the body and nerves, which produce impairment of the mind and will." For the sake of other women, though not Mrs. Tiffany, "the spirit of Christian civilization of the day will admit nothing of the kind, and the law will enforce marital obligations in harmony with that spirit."[45]

Harmony proved difficult to come by in the crucible of the courtroom, where the deeds and misdeeds of husbands and wives were recounted with such inflated rhetoric as to strain credulity. The portraits of complaining spouses as "perfect" helpmeets and unfailing providers often verged on the ridiculous, and the insanity pleas raised in response tended to be at least as stylized and hyperbolic. Though the terror or misery of the one spouse and the madness of the other might be established beyond a reasonable doubt, judges were confronted with the perennial problem of distinguishing depravity from disease as a matter of law, as divorce statutes generally required a showing of the defendant's guilt and the plaintiff's innocence, and even that the plaintiff had not done anything to enable or provoke the offense of the defendant. The scenes from troubled marriages were strategically presented in court by their respective lawyers to effectuate their clients' ends, but the resulting performances must have seemed so implausible as to render it questionable whether fault was a viable concept in the adjudication of divorce. Simply pronouncing that insanity was not a cause of divorce did not make it so.[46]

Ironically, the cases that prompted the most thorough rethinking of the fault paradigm were those involving the greatest marital wrong: adultery. Although insanity was initially accepted as a defense to a divorce action on grounds of adultery,[47] Chief Justice John Bannister Gibson arrestingly suggested otherwise in the 1847 case of *Matchin v. Matchin*. His decision focused on the harm to the husband and essentially disregarded the want of culpability of the demented wife. While crediting the proof of moral insanity because she had confessed her crime to a relation of her husband without evincing any consciousness that she had done anything wrong, Gibson insisted it was no defense in this action. "The offence is a social, as well as a moral one," he explained, holding that it was more grievous to the sufferer when committed by the wife than the husband, "whose transgression cannot impose a supposititious offspring" on his spouse. Since the primary purpose of a divorce action was to relieve a man from the responsibility to treat another man's children as if they were his own, "the preventive remedy is to be applied without regard to the moral responsibility of the subject of it." Surely no court could allow the woman to raise a plea of "*nymphomania*" or "*erotic mania*" in defense of her act, however irresistible it might have been. Indeed, fault had nothing to do with why she was barred from raising an insanity defense in this civil action. "The great end of matrimony," Gibson explained, "is not the comfort and convenience of the immediate parties." Rather, its paramount purposes were "the procreation and protection of legitimate children, the institution of families, and the creation of natural relations among mankind; from which proceed all the civilization, virtue, and happiness to be found in the world," and therefore it is "a *political status* subject to the power of the state."[48]

When deployed by injured husbands and their lawyers in subsequent cases, this line of argument did not meet with much success. The 1858 Vermont case of *Nichols v. Nichols* is more representative of the views of the nineteenth-century bench. In this case, the plaintiff's attorney made a florid and learned argument concluding with the assertion that it would strike at "the foundation of the marriage relation to place a man in a position where he may be compelled to '*keep a corner in the thing he loves for others' use*,' and surrender his bed and house for a 'nest to hatch a brood of strangers to his blood.' Every sane mind revolts at this possibility." Writing for the court, Chief Justice Isaac Redfield declared it was the counselor's argument and the *Matchin* ruling that were "truly revolting to all just sense of propriety and decency." He agreed with the defendant's lawyer that "there is no adultery when there is no will" because of mental derangement. However right it was to punish adultery, that argument could not be made with any force against "a party *morally* and *legally* guiltless." Interposing himself as the protector of such will-less women, he suggested that men like the plaintiff were actually to blame. The alleged adultery of the wife "might fairly be regarded as superinduced by the consent or connivance of the husband, since he has the right, and is bound in duty, to restrain the wife, when bereft of reason and the power of self control, from the commission of all unlawful acts, both to herself and others. . . . It was in the power of the husband always to guard against such consequences. And if he failed in this duty, he surely could not ask the court to visit the consequence of his own misconduct upon the unfortunate being, whom having sworn to love, comfort, honor and keep, in sickness and in health, till death, he had chosen to abandon to the short charity of a proverbially heartless world, in the hour of her utmost necessity." Indeed, an insane wife was "at the mercy of every base man" and all the more vulnerable because "in many cases sexual propensity is more or less excited during insanity, and the liability to such contingencies proportionally increased. In such cases, for the husband to seek for the dissolution of the marriage relation, must argue great weakness or great depravity." Moreover, to find in his favor would be, in effect, to recognize insanity as grounds for divorce, which Redfield concluded the court was not empowered to do under the laws of his state.[49]

The most fascinating perspective on this vexed question was that offered by the doctor-lawyer-commissioner of lunacy in New York, John Ordronaux, who, after surveying all these cases circled back to and ultimately sided with Gibson's opinion in *Matchin:* "Marriage does not produce omniscience. How then can a man be held culpable for not foreknowing and preventing an act of sexual intercourse committed by his wife and when at a distance from him, without his connivance in that act being first proved?" He suggested the adultery be thought of as a tort and that torts be thought of as acts for which one can be responsible *without* being a moral agent. "If, therefore, we divest ourselves of all idea of crime as associated with adultery, when committed by a lunatic, . . . we shall be forced to the conclusion that upon principle and in analogy to the practice of courts of law and equity, there is no reason why a lunatic should not be a respondent in a suit for divorce. Marriage is a civil contract, and adultery a breach of it, and at law a lunatic is liable on a contract or for a tort." In this last bit of legal reasoning, Ordronaux begged more basic questions about the role of fault in private law.[50]

The impossibility of reconciling the mental threshold for a valid marriage with a spouse's duty to care for his or her mentally unhinged partner seemed insoluble, no matter how assiduously jurists attempted to resolve them by sorting out mercenary motives from considerations of love. As late as 1910 a legal commentator complained: "Will someone be good enough to lay down what the essentials for entering into and continuing in the marriage relation are? If we accept the doctrine which is now unquestioned, that false representations as to chastity, name, family, or fortune of the parties [are] immaterial, and that once married impotency, insanity, and drunkenness are likewise immaterial, then marriage would appear to resolve itself into genteel social imprisonment, without, however, the privilege that ordinary offenders enjoy—the hope of pardon."[51]

Contracts for Care

After suffering a paralytic stroke in 1802 shortly after his wife's death, seventy-nine-year-old Comfort Wheaton began to behave in ways that were out of character, sliding into a routine of drinking and other vicious indulgences entirely at odds with the unfailing propriety this Rhode Island businessman had exhibited over the course of his long and productive life. Family and friends grew alarmed, particularly as Wheaton appeared to be "squandering his estate with a negligence" that threatened to reduce him to want and frustrate the expectations of his heirs. Instead of beginning guardianship proceedings, the family attempted to arrive at an "amicable arrangement" among themselves. This agreement took the form of two deeds, by means of which Comfort conveyed the whole of his estate, estimated to be worth upwards of $8,000, to his son-in-law, Asa Handy, for the stated consideration of $2,178. Both the terms of this transaction and the grantor's mental soundness were contested after he died intestate in December 1810. According to Comfort's eldest son, Caleb, the deeds were intended to provide for the maintenance of their mentally incapacitated father and preserve the residue of his estate for the benefit of his heirs. But Asa, joined by his wife, Mary, claimed the estate as his alone, the conveyances being executed by a grantor of sound mind in exchange for the grantee's payment of the grantor's debts and the provision of suitable support during the latter's lifetime, all of which had been secured by bonds deposited with a trustee.[52]

While the lay and medical testimony presented on the issue of mental competency during an 1821 trial of the matter in federal circuit court was "contradictory to an unusual degree," Justice Story found the disputed deeds to be the product of imposition upon "a mind in dotage." Indeed, the conveyances stood impeached on the grantee's own showing, the consideration hardly being adequate as the grantor had few debts and a short life expectancy at the time this arrangement was made. On such facts, the deeds might well have been held utterly void, but Story took "a more mitigated course," allowing Asa to recover his actual expenses in managing the person and property of his father-in-law. Surveying the record on appeal in 1826, Chief Justice John Marshall of the U.S. Supreme Court was similarly compelled by the proof of Comfort's incapacity. Where there was such a "great and sudden revolution" in conduct, where a man habitually "sober, prudent, reflecting and moral" abruptly becomes so "intemperate, immoral, and childishly whimsical and indiscreet" that his closest friends and relations "think it necessary to put it out of his power to ruin himself," Marshall declared, we must conclude that the old man's "mind had ceased to be the safe guide of his actions."[53]

The want of an agreeing mind was as problematic as it was obvious in the daily affairs of aging patriarchs who outlived their ability to take care of themselves, let alone their households. The onset of a parent's "second childhood" was a delicate moment for many nineteenth-century American families, given the emotional and financial stakes of acknowledging the fact of mental decline. To initiate guardianship proceedings risked touching off a family feud and alienating the person in question, perhaps to the point of disinheritance, for those placed under a potential heir's supervision usually retained the testamentary power to punish the party who had put them in this position.[54] Such concerns may well explain why Comfort's children used the instrumentalities of contract to deal with a father whose incompetence was the very reason for the transaction. It was fashioned as an agreement only in a nominal sense, as Justice Story saw it, "to save the estate, and yet satisfy the scruples of an aged and discontented man." Justice Marshall pointedly remarked that Wheaton was "on ill terms with Caleb" at the time, and this quarrel subjected the disfavored son "in an increased degree, to the influence of Mary and her husband," which added to the reasons for seeing this case as warranting equitable interference on grounds of undue influence.[55]

The readiness with which the court set aside the deeds of "this afflicted old gentleman, finding definitive evidence of incapacity in his proclivity to repeat the same questions, leave the house without any pants on, and break off from coherent conversation into song, tears, sermons, and profane tirades, stands in marked contrast to the treatment of testamentary transfers from parents to the "natural objects of their bounty." While the rights of the elderly and infirm to do as they willed with their property were strenuously guarded by nineteenth-century American judges, a different rule was applied to their deeds and contracts, particularly where they conveyed property in exchange for support and maintenance. These transactions had "to be watched with extreme jealousy," in Story's opinion, and if not held to be "entirely void," they were "at least to be restrained to such effects, as a rational mind would be supposed to contemplate." In sum, Comfort Wheaton's legal capacity was made to turn on the reasonableness of the terms of the alleged transaction, which might even be judicially reformed to reflect what a right-thinking man would have done were he so circumstanced.[56]

What explains this judicial posture? Contracting for care within the family circle was a worrisome practice from the standpoint of the bench because it signaled the breakdown of natural order that was supposed to obtain in the domestic realm. Care*giving* was cast as the norm in family relations, performed by individual members out of feelings of love, duty, and solidarity, without the expectation of pecuniary gain.[57] "To look to contract law and expect a court to adjudicate what one family member owed to another for the work done in maintaining that family must have seemed, by its very nature, an odd and perilous task," Hendrik Hartog has trenchantly observed; to contract with other members of the household was to risk "destroying the very bonds that united a family."[58] Yet, in employing the language of contract with reference to kinship, these cases reveal how intertwined family relations and commodity relations had become.[59] The logics and values of the market shaped conduct and expectations in the most intimate spaces of American life. Financial calculation was applied to intergenerational as well as marital relations.

To a greater extent than historians have recognized, Americans with failing bodies and minds entered into contractual relations to ensure a comfortable old age, many proceeding against legal advice as they ceded control of their estates in exchange for services they were no longer capable of performing for themselves. These agreements were commonly incorporated into the deeds conveying most if not all of their earthly possessions or executed as part of such transactions, formalizing the fact that the property was given not only in consideration of "love and affection" but also in exchange for "the comfortable support and maintenance" of the grantors for the remainder of their natural lives. What was expected of caregivers was often either too vague or overly specific, generating litigation before judges who remained undecided about whether to regard these arrangements as expressions of contractual freedom or their negation. While the grantors displayed "a natural yearning to secure the benefits of filial regard," the irrevocable nature of their deeds gave pause to many members of the bench, as there was something rather obviously dangerous about "giving up the reins too soon." These lifetime transfers were all too easily recast as the product of insanity and imposition in suits brought to set them aside, sometimes by the old folks themselves but more frequently by aggrieved heirs.[60]

Their petitions to the court read like declarations of dependence, recounting the abuses of trust and usurpations of authority the grantors had endured in their declining years, reducing them to pathetic supplicants in the households they had once headed or, worse, to paupers "suffered to wander abroad" and seek a "living" among strangers or end their days in a poorhouse.[61] These melancholy narratives about the loss of self-command elaborated by lawyers acquired a conventional form by midcentury. The first scenes of these stories found the grantor working hard to amass a valuable estate, the main emphasis being placed on the many years of support he had provided to his dependents. Then infirmity struck. A physical or mental illness, the death of a spouse or child, or a catastrophic pecuniary loss destabilized the government of the household. Amidst the confusion, conspiracies were hatched, opportunities seized, and advantages taken of the newly vulnerable patriarch or matriarch, culminating in an act of dispossession executed in the form of a voluntary conveyance that left the grantor completely at the mercy of the grantee. Reposing "the most unlimited confidence" in the grantee, the grantor signed papers while laboring "under an entire misapprehension" as to their nature and effect. Falsely led to believe these documents saved his estate from waste or the depredations of others and ensured he would be properly cared for "in sickness and in health," the grantor was terribly surprised to find himself stripped of all of his property and subjected to the cruelest forms of neglect, reduced in the end to the status of "a vagabond, an outcast, and a slave."[62]

Pleading innocent to any and all charges of wrongdoing, grantees proffered grievances of their own. Though their answers were formulated as a series of denials of the existence of insanity, undue influence, and fraud, most insisted they were the long-suffering parties to these agreements, which they entered at the behest of the complainant from a sense of duty or guilt rather than any hope of personal gain. To the contrary, they had plenty of reasons for thinking the proposed arrangement, which invariably required significant adjustments of the grantee's professional and family life, would be more trouble than it was worth, particularly where the grantor was known to have a fault-finding personality or a loathsome disease. Their tales featured promising careers cut short, marriages contracted or foregone, and existing households reconfigured; ulcerated bodies and degenerating minds; and the failure of others to provide the necessary maintenance and support. These deals were hardly sweetened by revelations that the proffered land was encumbered with debts, which sometimes did not come to light until after the grantee was already overtaxed by the emotional and financial burdens of feeding, clothing, and housing the "helpless" person, who grew more needy and demanding with each passing day. If anyone were consigned to "slavery" in these situations, it was the grantees tasked with providing a comfortable home for one who proved difficult to live with and impossible to please, despite all their diligent labors "night and day," faithfully offering "the help of their hands . . . and the sympathy of their hearts, with that honesty of purpose and unceasing affection that they thought should always actuate the conduct of children towards an unfortunate parent." Having made all these sacrifices, they averred, it would be manifestly unjust to allow the complainant to take back what had been freely and knowingly conveyed. Indeed, if any evidence could be found of the grantor's mental incompetence, it was in his groundless accusations of unfair dealing, not the contract for care.[63]

Ironically, the very existence of an explicit agreement seemed to weigh against its validity in judicial opinions. Judges expressed "a strong dislike of such arrangements" because they formalized domestic relations; services and support were supposed to be offered freely, without expectation of return. The depressing prospects, unnerving insecurities, and dreadful fears that moved the elderly and infirm to enter into these contracts were effectively memorialized in the articles of their agreements, sometimes recognizing the reversals of power that had already taken place within the household—"my dependence upon my son's management"—and giving voice to the reasons the elderly and infirm had for making lifetime transfers of their entire estates—to "'spare me much care and trouble, and save me from further losses, and the destruction of my property.'" That these were, in fact, the reasons why a given grantor had given up the reins so soon might be verified by the doctors, lawyers, and notaries who witnessed the execution of the deed, but the examinations and interviews they conducted and recounted at trial could excite more concerns than were quieted about the voluntariness of a conveyance. As one notary testified, he had asked of the grantor: "'Grandmother, do you know what you are making this deed for?' and she answered: 'I have no one. I have to have a place to live at, and Mr. Stanton is going to take care of me; and if he takes care of me while I live, then he is to have this land.'" The painful clarity of these acknowledgments and the exacting descriptions of the care that was to be provided, while likely intended to avoid subsequent disputes, tended to compound judicial doubts about the capacity and freedom of individuals who violated "those maxims of prudence that enjoin a man, whilst he has breath in his body, to keep the staff in his own hands," signing away their estates in exchange "for those attentions which are ordinarily the gifts of filial love rather than the obligations of contracts."[64]

But in this legal culture, improvidence was one thing, insanity another. As troubled as judges were about the commodification of care, they stopped short of drawing any conclusive presumptions of "insanity or unfair practice" from these contractual arrangements between old and young. They were aware of the economic, psychological, and physical constraints that operated on the aged and infirm, struggling to give legal recognition to these facts without denying the rights of those so situated to make such contracts. In determining what to do, they had recourse to traditional equitable doctrines concerning confidential relations between parents and children. The question was whether these paternalistic precedents, designed to protect impressionable and inexperienced minors, were to be applied to those growing old and infirm in a dynamic liberal capitalist society in which children were not legally bound to support their parents, who retained the power to waste their estates or disinherit their offspring by will. Age-old dilemmas took on new significance in a country where emancipation was defined as the freedom from parental authority, self-sufficiency celebrated as the norm of adulthood, and senility dreaded and denigrated as a loss of self-command. A second childhood was far different from the first; it constituted a distinct form of dependency ending only with death. Those who reached this troubling and troublesome stage of life had already experienced what it was to be grown up, to have some measure of control over their own destinies, and to shape the future of others. Some had done all they could to stave off the degenerating effects of senility by following the regimens widely prescribed by physicians and evangelical health reformers, while others slid into habits of dissipation or chronically overworked their minds and bodies so that they became old before their time. Whatever the cause, the men and women who had descended into a second childhood were no longer the same people they had once been, though they might display signs of their former selves and some consciousness of the change they were undergoing. Those who expressed this awareness by contracting for care seemed to exercise a degree of foresight, but the terms of these arrangements evinced their vulnerability and often placed them in an even more precarious position, as the signatures of the parties could not fix their feelings or ensure that the love and affection that formed only a part of the consideration did not become an occasion for abuse or deception on either side.[65]

The complex intermixture of financial and emotional motives that led the parties to enter into contracts for care, which clearly marked the fact that they were not on equal footing, proved nettlesome to the judges tasked with determining their validity in contested cases. The home lives of the litigants as they were presented at these trials were shaped by the profit-driven values of the marketplace as well as the inescapable fact of mortality. Within the family circle, young and old managed the stresses, disruptions, and complications introduced by illness and aging through the use of legal instruments that made them into purchasers and vendors of love and attention, effectively domesticating the abstractions of capitalism to suit their needs and interests. As they bargained in the shadow of dependency and death, the parties negotiated or renegotiated who they were to each other as a matter of law, assuming new roles and responsibilities by virtue of their agreements, which they might or might not have been performing already as a matter of fact. The varied and conflicting stories told from the stand brought to light the fluidity and volatility of family dynamics in these trying times. These disoriented identities, changeable minds, unstable alliances, and frustrated expectations help explain why contracts for care were both made and challenged. But for the judges attempting to determine the equities of these situations, the evidence proved positively confounding, not least because it was difficult to find disinterested witnesses who were in the position to know what actually went on in the bosom of any household. Old habits of authority and obedience, of control and trust, were seldom entirely reversed by the ravages of time and disease, so it was not obvious to those who sat in judgment that it was fair to either party to extend to the elderly and infirm the same protective doctrines as applied to children who traded with their parents and guardians. Well aware of the precarious and putative independence of male household heads who relied upon the labor of their supposedly dependent wives and children and fully appreciating the dangers of being overly suspicious or insufficiently vigilant in policing this peculiarly domestic form of commerce, judges issued opinions that reflected the tensions and contradictions in their own ideals of propertied independence and family solidarity.

The most delicate cases were those involving aging patriarchs who petitioned the courts in their own right, disclaiming the deeds they had made to their children. Unlike Comfort Wheaton, whose contracting mind was disputed only after he had died, these men alleged their own incompetence and implicitly cast their flesh and blood as con artists. A complaint to this effect was filed in the Chancery Court of New York in 1822 by John Whelan, a seventy-five-year-old farmer with seven children, a sixty-eight-year-old wife, and a 350-acre farm. Sibling rivalries and marital discord had fractured the family unit: all but two of Whelan's sons had gone away, and his wife had left him and taken up lodgings elsewhere in town. Upon being called to account for her board, amounting to $5 per week, he anxiously sought the advice of his remaining sons, who bluntly informed him they could no longer afford to live with him, given the rate at which their parents appeared to be dissipating their estate, unless the farmstead were transferred to them now rather than by way of his will. A conveyance of all that was left of the father's real and personal property, valued at $9,000, was drawn and executed, along with a mortgage and bond that obligated the grantees to support their parents for the rest of their natural lives. Some witnesses said that John Whelan had expressed satisfaction with the transaction at the time, boasting that it showed, contrary to his wife's accusations, that he had not allowed his sons "to make a negro out of him." But others suggested that the father had signed the papers under the false impression that he was simply ensuring that his property could not be reached by his wife's creditors and that both of them would be supported in their old age.[66]

While there was no gainsaying the imprudence of the arrangement, the chancellor found nothing amounting to fraud and accordingly dismissed the bill, underscoring that this was the price of contractual freedom: "He had power to dispose of his property, and he is not at liberty to revoke his own conveyances from mere repentance." Yet this opinion assumed that the elderly man had enough mental strength to do otherwise, which a majority of the appellate panel doubted, in view of how credulous and labile he had reputedly become in his "second childhood," being most "easily led" by his trusted sons, who did nothing to dispel his patently delusive fears of financial ruin. Transactions of this kind constituted a gross derogation of filial and legal duty, for grantees who were related by blood had to conduct themselves with "all imaginable fairness," while in this case "the partiality of a parent has been artfully made use of to strip him of his property, and to reduce him to a state of dependence and want." In undoing this act of dispossession, the court was hardly infringing upon "the right of alienation" properly understood, for property ownership entailed "the full, ample and uninfluenced enjoyment of it." Whelan had been denied this prerogative by his opportunistic sons, whose attempts to make "a profit of their treachery" should not be rewarded.[67]

Not all complaining fathers won their suits, and it was difficult to tell whether those who did were any better off. Petitioners who recovered their estates were rarely in any condition to manage them, so they remained vulnerable to abuse and neglect or the imposition of the very form of legal guardianship they had sought to avoid by contracting for care. The best interests of the complainant did not formally enter judicial analyses of the validity of these arrangements. Still, concerns about the future welfare of childlike men quite clearly and perhaps unavoidably inflected retrospective judgments of their capacity to contract, tipping the scales toward the defending children when they had carried out their agreement to their own detriment and conducted themselves as faithfully as any sane father had a right to expect.

When confronted with the case of Philip Nace, a seventy-year-old widower seeking to be released from a family settlement, a midcentury Pennsylvania court decided he was bound to live with what he had done. By this agreement, forged with his nine children over the course of two consecutive Saturday gatherings, a son and two sons-in-law were entrusted with the management and control of his entire estate; they were responsible for liquidating his real and personal property, paying his debts, investing the residue in real estate, and applying the interest to his support and maintenance, with the remainder to be divided equally among his surviving children after his death. Sometime after this transfer of property and power, the son was dismissed from the trust, and he was among those testifying on his father's behalf at the ensuing trial. Though Nace declared on the face of the disputed deed that he was moved to make this disposition after a string of "'disadvantageous bargains and undertakings'" and in the midst of family quarrels making him "so much troubled in mind as to be unable of attending to business," the judges took this as evidence of self-awareness rather than overreaching on the part of any of his children. It was always somewhat hazardous for a man "to take off his clothes before he is ready to go to bed," but Nace had been fully apprised of the risks involved by the notary. "If mad, surely there was method in his madness," opined the trial judge by way of explaining why Nace was to be held to his retirement plan against his present will. Having so deliberately given up control of his estate to obtain "freedom from care and responsibility," he did not have the prerogative to change his mind. This ruling was affirmed by an appellate court that was as concerned about the stability of transactions in the home as about the stability of those conducted in the market. The contract in question seemed all the more worthy of validation because it disposed of the estate just as "the law of the land" would have done "if it had taken the property out of the old man's hands."[68]

When an old woman petitioned the court, judicial patriarchs may have more readily assumed a paternalistic posture, given how common it was for women and children to be grouped together as dependents in the prevailing legal and cultural discourse.[69] While evidence that an old man allowed his wife to handle business matters was routinely taken as a telltale sign of his incapacity to contract, judges generally presumed that a woman's nature, education, and life experiences had accustomed her to trusting others when it came to the management of her property.[70] Yet these biases are obscured in suits brought to set aside contracts for care, as courts tended to apply the same formal rules to complaining men and women, which were stated in gender-neutral terms or by reference to a male standard.[71] Equitable principles designed to protect "a man of weak understanding" from "stripping himself of his property" were routinely applied by courts in cases where the dispossessed claimant was a woman without making any explicit adjustment on account of her sex. Judges displayed the same basic ambivalence where the elders contracting for care were widows and "aged maidens," struggling as they did in cases of widowers and bachelors to accord ample protection to the "helpless" party without robbing dutiful caregivers of the just rewards of their labor.[72]

"Where the aged parent turns over his estate to the child upon his filial promise of support and care," observed one South Carolina judge in a 1902 suit brought by a seventy-eight-year-old mother against her erstwhile favorite son, "we are apt to find in too many cases that the child has lost 'the pregnant and potential spurs' to filial duty," calling to mind "the fool in 'King Lear,' I think, who speaks of such a parent as one 'that giveth his children the rod and putteth down his own breeches.'" The plantiff, Susannah Revels, had lost her husband in 1874, when five of her twelve children were still minors. The defendant, Jefferson Davis, who with his mother's guidance grew to be "the man of the family," was "responsible for making the little farm support his mother, sisters, and himself for many years." The witnesses told an all-too-familiar story. Latent domestic tensions erupted in a property dispute between the mother and one of her sons-in-law in 1895, and in the midst of that turmoil the disputed conveyance was made in exchange for support and maintenance. Although the old lady may never have wielded a rod or put on breeches, the court understood her deed as a manifestation of the same basic propensities exhibited by the literary patriarch and his nineteenth-century male counterparts. Like them, she was presumed to be moved by "the freest instincts, promptings, and desires of her untrammeled heart and reason,"

> To shake all cares and business from our age,
> Conferring them on younger strengths, while we
> Unburthen'd crawl toward death

and, like them, possessed of "the right—most highly respected by our law—of disposing of her own as she pleased." The difficult question, as always, was whether the disposition in question was a true expression of the grantor's wishes and not "the result of the skillful and artful touch of the scheming son upon the strings of maternal affection, or of the subtle but potent influence of the strong mind upon the weak."[73]

The partiality of the parent toward one child cut like a double-edged sword so far as the capacity to contract was concerned. Once established as a matter of fact, the existence of such feelings could simultaneously account for the transaction and undermine its validity. According to the trial judge, Mrs. Revels "presented the appearance of a very old and exceedingly feeble woman"; her testimony was filled with "contradictions and inanities," amounting to "a piteous spectacle of complaining, querulous, inconsequent, driveling senility." He nonetheless credited her insistence that "I know what I am doing," uttered at the time she deeded the family farmstead to Jefferson, whose mental capacity was "very little superior to his mother's." This impression was apparently not shared by the circuit judge who reversed the ruling, perhaps because he accorded more weight to the fact that the care arrangement had not been properly inserted into the terms of deed, to the medical testimony diagnosing the woman with "dementia naturalis as to business affairs," or to the evidence that she was found with vermin on her body while residing with the favored son. But the members of the state's highest court were instead inclined to think the suit was really being prosecuted by her other children, whose "love of money" had overwhelmed their sense of filial duty. Finding the transaction in issue to be "reasonable, natural, and fair," these judges left the old lady and her 96½ acres of land in the hands of a child she no longer trusted, the court betraying its own wariness as it conditioned its judgment for the son upon his execution of a deed to his mother that expressly bound him to support her for as long as she lived, or at least lived under what was now his roof.[74]

The "unburdened crawl toward death" held out peculiar terrors for nineteenth-century Americans, who inhabited a culture where property, independence, and personhood were tightly bound together. The loss of control that preceded and presaged the end of life was difficult to confront, yet impossible to avoid, inspiring complex forms of denial, deception, and manipulation.[75] An aging patriarch anxious to escape the indignity of guardianship might go to considerable lengths to hide his infirmities from family and friends, who sometimes played along. An old widow might make inconsistent promises of property to those who swarmed around her or threatened to leave as she declined in health; her inconstancy sometimes seemed a stratagem for keeping family members close and at other times a mark of failing memory. Assurances of care made by the younger generation were also laced with contradictory feelings and mixed motives, sometimes expressing great earnestness but less consideration of what the task might entail and other times manifesting a calculating sensibility all too mindful of the elder's life expectancy and net worth. Negotiated against the backdrop of a market revolution that underminded earlier forms of patriarchal authority, these agreements may be read as indicators of the impact of these economic and ideological transformations on intergenerational relations: a more general depreciation of the value of old age and a concomitant increase in the bargaining power of younger adults. The Lear-like plaintiffs who claimed to have been dispossessed by those who had once been the objects of their care played out this historical process in nineteenth-century courtrooms. The ensuing trials dramatized the material and psychological constraints that operated on the young as well as the old in these inverted households, testing the meaning of free assent as a matter of law and giving the lie to the bourgeois ideal of home as sanctified by a love untainted by the profit motive, a sheltered space where trust could be invested without fear of betrayal.

Confronted with discomfiting stories depicting the dissolution of confidential relationships into a confounding array of confidence games, members of the bench proceeded warily lest their own courtrooms become another staging ground for fraudulent activities. Like the playwrights who adapted *King Lear* for nineteenth-century American theaters by allowing Cordelia and Lear to live, the judges who presided over these courtroom dramas may have felt some pressure to provide a happy ending that accorded with the principles of natural justice, the law of contracts, and the ideology of separate spheres. Yet those who sat in judgment disagreed about what constituted a just outcome in these matters, for the norms they were expected to apply pointed them in conflicting directions. The accumulating mass of decisional law was filled with contradictory directives about how to treat old people entering a second childhood, particularly when it came to their dealings with their own flesh and blood. One set of authorities held these transactions to be presumptively valid, as it was "in accordance with the promptings of nature" for parents to convey property to their children on more favorable terms than that they would to strangers; the acquisition of property by the parent was, after all, largely driven by the aim "to give it to the child, and that child in turn will give to his, and in this way the debt of gratitude we owe to our parent is paid to our children."[76] But another line of argument suggested that a more protective rule should be applied to lifetime as distinct from testamentary transfers from aging parents to their adult children, even or perhaps especially when they were made in exchange for care. The same considerations that conventionally and justly determined the dispositions of a last will—love, trust, and a sense of duty—were sources of suspicion in the context of *inter vivos* transactions. In the case of a disputed care arrangement, the child was required to prove that he or she not only abstained from all forms of duress and deceit but affirmatively guarded the parent's interests, so that they dealt with each other "upon a plane of equality, and at arms-length." In sum, the children were expected to conduct themselves "exactly as a stranger would have done," "to cut off, as it were, the connection which bound [them] to the party giving or contracting," to show they had gained "no advantage" from this family relation, "beyond what may be the natural and unavoidable consequence of kindness."[77]

Ironically, dependence upon the care and kindness of strangers was precisely what most aging parents sought to avoid by entering into support and maintenance agreements with their children. Moreover, courts were no more likely to validate similar arrangements that were made with those beyond the family circle; judges typically read the want of natural affective ties between the parties as grounds for questioning both the sanity and the freedom of the older party. We look in vain for a settled rule. Instead, there is an abiding tension between competing rule structures—one presuming that children were generally trustworthy caregivers, the other that they were prone to selfishness—that ultimately evokes the tragedy of growing old in the age of contract. In the final analysis, these cases illuminate the peculiar sort of identity crisis experienced by aging patriarchs and matriarchs in an expanding market society of placeless men and women. While doctors like Ray debated whether the literary Lear was insane, the words from the play most often taken as a sign of his mental illness surely resonated with those who had to revise their sense of what independence and family connections meant as their minds and bodies were worn down by the strains of life in a mobile capitalist society: "Does any here know me? Why, this is not Lear; does Lear walk thus? Speak thus? Where are his eyes? Either his notion weakens, or his discernings are lethargied—Sleeping or waking? Ha! Sure 'tis not so.—Who is it that can tell me who I am?"

CHAPTER 7

The Responsible Originator

"Is Ahab, Ahab? Is it I, God, or who, that lifts this arm?"
Herman Melville, *Moby-Dick* (1851)

IN THE FINAL HOURS before the brig *Emily T. Sheldon* was wrecked along the coast of Cape Cod on March 22, 1886, members of the crew began to suspect that their captain, William Hays, was not in his right mind. Even after reporting that the vessel was in distress, the steward was unable to rouse Hays from his cabin. Once on deck, the captain gave "irresponsive answers to questions," staggered about in a "dazed condition," and appeared to crew members "either drunk or insane." He could not be convinced that the rudder had sustained any damage, maintaining, "I can't see it, and you can't, I think," even in the face of clear evidence to the contrary. Seeking to save the vessel, the crew attempted to adjust the sails, but the captain threatened to string them up on charges of mutiny. He refused several offers of assistance from passing tugboats; "We are all right," he insisted as he lost control of the *Sheldon.* Even after the brig struck the shore, the captain stubbornly remained at the helm; it took rescuers several hours to coax him into a lifeboat.[1]

The ship was pronounced a total wreck, and litigation to determine who was liable for the loss ensued. During these proceedings, Hays claimed not to remember how the *Sheldon* ran aground. The last action he recalled was instructing his first mate to assume command of the vessel so that he could retire to his cabin after being on duty for three straight days during a violent storm. Exhausted and unwell, he feared he was about to suffer an attack of malaria, so he took fifteen grains of quinine as a preventative measure. The next thing he knew, he was on dry land in a life-saving station with no memory of how he had gotten there. In recounting these events the captain did not deny that he had been in command when the *Sheldon* ran aground, and he even admitted that he "might have said silly things and given silly orders." Yet Hays maintained that he "knew nothing of what occurred, that in fact he was, from some cause, insane, and therefore not responsible for the loss of the vessel."[2]

But was his insanity an excuse? Authority indicating it was not could be readily summoned from the treatise literature. Many commentators bluntly pronounced that the insane were just as responsible for their torts as the sane, with the implication that the default legal person functioned differently (or perhaps not at all) in the law of torts and that sanity was conclusively presumed to exist in cases involving civil as opposed to criminal wrongs.[3] Understanding the primary aim of tort law to be compensation rather than punishment, jurists writing in this vein maintained that liability was triggered by the fact of an injury done, without regard for the motive or mental capacity of the actor who "occasioned" the harm. Although this principle added to the burdens of those struck with "the inexpressible calamity of mental obscurity," it was both equitable and socially beneficial to follow this rule when confronted with a choice between "two innocent persons," for it encouraged those who stood to benefit from the estates of the insane to take appropriate precautions and ensured that no one could evade responsibility by feigning insanity. The fairness and coherence of this approach was challenged by equally prominent jurists, who questioned whether an insane person could be "a juridical cause" in any meaningful sense. To be counted as "a responsible originator," the individual in question had to have the basic capacity for "moral choice." They argued that insanity, whether understood as "a visitation of God" or the result of more proximate physical and moral causes, rendered sufferers incapable of bearing any responsibility for their civil or criminal acts, which were justly relegated to the class of "inevitable accidents" for which no one was to blame.[4]

In placing his mind in issue, the captain of the *Sheldon* inadvertently set these conflicting lines of authority on a collision course. Hays was the first to file suit, seeking to recover on an insurance policy he had taken out with the Phenix Insurance Company as one of fifty part-owners of the ship. The insurer denied liability, contending that the shipwreck was caused by the negligence of the insured and his first mate, which was not among "the perils of the sea" that the policy covered. In the midst of this suit, the captain was sued for negligence by an assignee of this insurer, who succeeded to the rights of other part-owners of the ship, after compensating them for the loss under a separate policy.[5] In the ensuing tangle of trials, which took almost a decade to resolve, the litigants did not dispute that Hays had failed to act the part of "a careful and prudent captain" and that his "bad seamanship and improper navigation" would have been negligent "if done by a sane man." It was the relevance of his mental condition that was at the core of these two trials: assuming he was "not in his right mind" at the time of the wreck, who was responsible for the loss?

In the first case, the answer to this question turned on the meaning of "the perils of the sea." Hays was required to show that the loss arose from this cause rather than his negligence or that of the ship's crew.[6] In construing this policy language, the presiding judge had recourse to Kent's *Commentaries*, particularly a section concerning the common law liability of common carriers, which were exempt from losses resulting from such perils. Drawing the meaning of this crucial phrase from outside the field of contract law, the judge held that an insurance policy that covered losses arising from such perils extended only to losses caused by "natural accidents peculiar to the sea, which do not happen by the intervention of man, nor are to be prevented by human prudence," but occurred "in spite of all human effort and sagacity." In sum, it was Hays's burden to prove that the loss he suffered was "a sea damage occurring at sea, and nobody's fault." Conflicting evidence was presented upon the issue. The insurer suggested that the loss was caused by the captain's voluntary intoxication and his first mate's failure to take charge of the vessel. Hays insisted that he was incapacitated by insanity rather than alcohol and that his impairment was not so obvious as to render his first mate negligent for continuing to obey him. The jury returned a verdict for the captain, awarding him nearly $2,000 in damages, and this judgment was affirmed on appeal.[7]

While this matter was still pending, Hays was required to answer the charge of negligence filed by the insurer's assignee. During the course of this trial, the plaintiff maintained, as a matter of law, that "the sickness or insanity" of the captain was "no excuse and did not free him from liability." He accordingly objected to the introduction of evidence concerning the captain's mental impairment and the jury charge instructing them to find for the defendant if they believed he had "lost his reason" as a result of "circumstances which were providential, and over which he had no control." Declining to characterize this as an "excuse" when pressed by the plaintiff's counsel, the trial judge held that a debility "caused by an act of God, and not by any voluntary act of his own . . . might be such that he could not be guilty of negligence, because he had not the capacity to act." A verdict for the defendant brought the case before the New York Court of Appeals, which in 1894 reversed the lower court's decision and granted a new trial in a split decision, which only deepened the perplexity.[8]

Writing for the majority, Judge Robert Earl undertook a searching inquiry into the law of the case, from which he derived "the general rule . . . that an insane person is just as responsible for his torts as a sane person," with the exception of those for which intention was "a necessary ingredient." Tort law mainly aimed to provide compensation to the injured party "without reference to the purpose or the condition, mental or physical, of the person causing the damage." He accordingly held that Hays was legally bound to exercise "such care as a reasonably careful and prudent owner would ordinarily give to his own vessel," a standard he proceeded to clarify at the behest of "some of my brethren":

> It is not such care as a lunatic, a blind man, a sick man, or a man otherwise physically or mentally impotent, could give. Such a man is not the jural man of ordinary prudence, and he does not furnish the standard. The standard man is no individual man, but an abstract or ideal man, of ordinary mental and physical capacity and ordinary prudence. The particular man whose duty of care is to be measured does not furnish the standard. He may fall below it in capacity and prudence; yet the law takes no account of that, but requires that he should come up to the standard and his duty be measured thereby.

Yet Earl recognized a potential exception to this rule: "If the defendant had become insane solely in consequence of his efforts to save the vessel during the storm . . . it might be claimed that his want of care ought not to be attributed to him as a fault."[9]

So the captain's counsel argued when the case was retried, but this line of reasoning was summarily rejected by the presiding judge. "Given a full legal responsibility on the part of a lunatic for his acts," he wondered, "how is it material what caused his condition?" Writing off Earl's proviso on this score as an expression of lingering "repugnance to a principle of law still felt to be against natural justice," this judge applied the objective standard "with all its logical consequences" and directed a verdict for the plaintiff. Although concededly "a cruel doctrine," it was not meant to convey anything regarding the "personal fault" of Hays, but constituted "a rule which serves the convenience of the public to which individual rights must give way." An intermediate court affirmed this judgment, but it was reversed on appeal. "To our minds," Judge Albert Haight wrote in 1899 for a nearly unanimous bench, "it is carrying the law of negligence to a point which is unreasonable, and, prior to this case, unheard of, and is establishing a doctrine abhorent [*sic*] to the principles of equity and justice." Reasoning from what was essentially the same factual record as that developed during the previous trial, Haight implied that the captain had done all he was legally expected to do under the adverse circumstances that plagued the *Sheldon*'s voyage. The judge pointedly concluded that "impossibility is an excuse in law, and there is no obligation to perform impossible things."[10] This rather ingenious bit of doctrinal reasoning deftly avoided the shoals of the insanity defense and inspired the discontinuation of the suit, which was pronounced "a practical victory" for Captain Hays.[11]

The Standard Man

But what of the jural man of ordinary prudence and the objective standard of liability he represented? Had he triumphed over the default legal person within the domain of tort law, enabling judges to abstract away from vexing questions of mental capacity? Did it matter as a matter of law whether Hays was actually Hays when he navigated the *Sheldon* to her destruction? Was the lunatic obliged to do the impossible? In playing "battledore and shuttlecock" with the case of *Williams v. Hays*, the judges of New York's highest court left the law in a more unsettled state than they had found it. So complained the prominent corporate lawyer William B. Hornblower in an 1904 address on "Insanity and the Law of Torts" delivered to the New York Society of Medical Jurisprudence and published the following spring in the *Columbia Law Review*: "It is a singular fact, and one not altogether creditable to our jurisprudence, considered as a science, that in this Twentieth Century, the question of liability of an insane person for tortious conduct—or rather, for that which would be tortious conduct on the part of a sane person,—should remain to a large extent an open question."[12]

Hornblower, who had just ascended to the presidency of the New York State Bar, harbored little doubt about the right answer: an insane person was not a legal cause and the injuries attributed to him were "'really due to inevitable accident, or the act of God, for which no action lies.'" It made no sense to him to speak of the negligence of a lunatic who lacked the capacity to exercise due care, and he questioned whether one who had lost his reason could be guilty of trespass, since "it might be plausibly argued that if the mind did not go with the act, there was no legal wrong done." To hold a person responsible for failing to do what he was incapable of doing was "certainly shocking to the common-sense of the average individual," yet he could find no definite rule on the subject. Concededly, many treatise writers contended that lunatics were liable for their civil wrongs, and it was "the general understanding in the profession . . . that insanity as a general rule is no defense in an action of tort." But when he traced back the authorities cited in support of this proposition, he found only dicta to this effect in the seventeenth-century English trespass case of *Weaver v. Ward* (1616), in which a perfectly sane soldier was found liable for the inadvertent discharge of his musket. Hornblower concluded: "The true rule and the only rule consistent with justice and reason, and the rule towards which the authorities are evidently tending, is that a person who is *non compos mentis* cannot be held liable for negligence."[13]

True or not, this rule had a messiness of its own, for persons *non compos mentis* were neither as readily identifiable nor as uniformly incapable as Hornblower presumed. They appeared to be as varied and variable in the nature and extent of their disabilities as the sane were in their abilities, and the same could be said of the complex of physical, psychical, and moral causes that were understood to have made them sane or insane. This ambiguity was precisely what rendered the jural man of ordinary prudence such an appealing and problematic figure to so many members of the bench and bar; it was also what made them so ambivalent about allowing this figure to set the standard in civil as well as criminal cases involving insanity. By the time Hornblower spoke in the defense of the deranged captain, the ideal of self-command from which the latter had deviated was itself imperiled. Hays's want of capacity to navigate the vicissitudes of the sea exemplified the experience of many of his fellows on land, who proved unable to weather the booms and busts of a capitalist economy, losing their minds along with their worldly goods and the hope of a manly independence. This fragile sense of selfhood was rendered all the more precarious by the increasing number of accidents that accompanied the mechanization of workplaces and transportation, for while these advances were hailed as manifestations of ingenuity that connected Americans in new ways and expanded the scope of individual liberty, with them came unprecedented daily tolls of human injury. As Jonathan Levy has acutely observed, "The image of the ship on stormy waters became a powerful metaphor for the perils and possibilities of life under capitalism," as risk taking was identified with liberal self-ownership even as it presented a constant threat to individual and social security. This tension lay at "the very operational and moral heart of both capitalism and a rising liberal order" and encouraged the development of new practices to commodify and offload risk. Marine insurance, the fruit of early modern merchant capital, was the earliest form of "risk management." As these practices were adopted on land, they further fractured and diffused responsibility in ways that seriously complicated the process of morally and legally accounting for human loss and suffering in ways that severely strained the concept of an autonomous self.[14]

Entirely unlike Ahab until much later in his voyage, Captain Hays modeled what it was to be a sensible proprietor by contracting with an underwriter before he set sail. Though he owned only a sliver of the *Sheldon* and was merely transporting a cargo of ice along the Atlantic coast, he exercised a measure of prudence and foresight in offloading some of the risks of this journey onto the Phenix Insurance Company, remaining nonetheless responsible to the vessel's co-owners for exercise of due care, both on his part and that of his crew. The policy should have been read to cover the captain's own negligence and that of his first mate as perils of the sea, but his recovery in the first suit and his release from liability in the second both hinged upon his ability to prove he was utterly and yet not too obviously powerless in the aftermath of the storm. Compensation came only with an effacement of individuality as well as agency, ultimately entailing an unmanning of the self so complete that the captain was reduced to a part of the scenery, vividly illustrating the dependencies insurance engendered. Ironically, the captain voiced his derangement with a refusal of assistance that repeated the insurer's own advertising slogan, strategically placed on their trade cards above an impeccably dressed, gray-haired couple, the man displaying the policy with a proud serenity while the woman contentedly leaned on his shoulder as buildings burned at a safe distance behind them: "We're all right—We're in the PHENIX."[15]

If he had ever bought into this idea, Captain Hays must have had second thoughts during the years he spent in litigation. But it was not only those who stood to lose money who resisted his plea of insanity; those who sat in judgment were also remarkably reluctant to recognize this excuse. Some part of their hesitancy is readily explained by the jurisprudence of insanity, which was a morass by the end of the nineteenth century. Just as Lord Kenyon had predicted, the judiciary found itself at sea without a rudder once it abandoned the landmarks of the common law of capacity as civil and criminal dockets became hopelessly swamped with vexing litigation about mental unsoundness, presenting ever more novel claims of partial insanity about which doctors were sure to disagree. It hardly helped that their elaborate classifications of symptoms bracketed matters of etiology, which were especially crucial within the field of tort law, where liability so often turned on questions of causation. Yet their points of agreement were even more unsettling within a field of law that mediated between injurers and their victims. In speaking of insanity as mental alienation and figuring the disease as an invisible agent that invaded the mind, robbing those afflicted of their autonomy and sometimes also their very consciousness of being robbed, these medical men underscored the status of the insane as victims with the capacity both to harm and to be harmed because they had no will of their own. The difficulty of fixing responsibility was magnified by their descriptions of the disease because they fatally blurred the boundaries of the self, the line philosophers like Emerson drew between "the me and the not-me." This stance made it difficult to distinguish the injured from their injurers and conjured up the disturbing possibility that the autonomous will was itself a delusion, from which it followed that the concept of a responsible human originator—the notion of man as an uncaused cause—was a figment of the legal imagination.[16]

In steering clear of the subject of insanity and invoking the standard man as the measure of civil liability, Judge Earl supplied a solution even he was unable to follow to the end of his own decision, because the insane presented what was really only an extreme case of a more general and unavoidable problem. The plea of insanity was simply another way of asking what was to be done about harms that were "nobody's fault." Did legal responsibility depend upon personal blameworthiness, or was it instead determined in accordance with broader considerations of social welfare or by mere expediency? To plead insanity at once perceived to be riven by social, economic, and racial conflicts and ever more interdependent, such that "everybody's mixed up with everybody else," was only to exacerbate the confusion about causal relations, not least because the increasing incidence of the disease was associated with the advance of civilization."[17] The last quarter of the nineteenth century has long been identified as a period of social and intellectual upheaval that occasioned a fundamental rethinking of the relationship between divine and human agency and the significance of accidents, ultimately resulting in a profound shift in the conventions of causal attribution. Commonly cast in terms of a "revolt against positivism" or "formalism," this cultural movement was led by a new generation of social scientists and legal reformers whose work underscored the "growing interdependence" that characterized American society. This heightened consciousness of the ways in which life and liberty were imperiled and constrained by the hazardous instrumentalities of an industrializing society, many historians have argued, gradually effected a transformation of American tort law, particularly as it applied to accidents in the workplace and on the nation's expanding network of streetcars and railroads. Confronted repeatedly and concretely with the human costs of economic and technological development, courts and legislatures were pressed to redraw the bounds of individual autonomy in relation to corporate entities, even the state. The sheer number of injuries and fatalities recorded from year to year disturbingly confirmed the vulnerability of ordinary men and women as they conducted their daily affairs, slowly but surely eroding the ideal of "self-reliant individualism" that had informed liability determinations for much of the nineteenth century. Swearing off the metaphysics of causation and proceeding with an actuarial mindset, judges, lawyers, legislators, and bureaucrats sought to enforce an ethic of prevention, and their change in orientation constituted what several scholars have described as a shift from a paradigm of "fault and responsibility" to one of "insurance and risk."[18]

In chronicling the renegotiation of the bounds of individual liberty in "the age of enterprise and accident," historians of American law have documented the emergence of a "social self" along with a new and more pronounced sense of social responsibility. This scholarship has focused on the reconfiguration of status relations rather than the baseline conception of competence as it was drawn and redrawn by the nineteenth-century judges and jurists embedded in the bewildering "chance-world of capitalism." The cases where the capacity to occasion harm was called into question show a more complicated universe of ideas about freedom and fate, which demonstrates that the path toward the pragmatic "objectivism" of Holmes and his followers was paved with considerable ambivalence. In particular, members of the bench and bar could never quite decide whether a "juridical cause" was differently constituted in civil as opposed to criminal cases. Nor did Progressive Era lawyers and judges simply throw off the metaphysical quandaries that had troubled previous generations; states of mind were not summarily ruled out of consideration as they acquired greater facility with statistical modes of analysis and deeper comprehension of the institution of insurance as a means of redistributing risk and responsibility. Instead, we witness a reconstitution of the law of persons, reflecting the extent to which legal responsibility at the turn of the twentieth century remained bound up with the state of a man's consciousness even as jurists recognized the fortuity of being prudent. Indeed, debates about the relationship between consciousness and responsibility only intensified in the early decades of the twentieth century, as jurists were sharply divided on the question of whether the test of liability ought to be subjective or objective. The doctrinal developments chronicled here were tortured efforts to stave off the disturbing notion that we are the inevitable accidents of biology and environment.

Insanity and Inevitable Accident

William Hornblower was right about one thing: the insane were not often made defendants in tort suits, or at least those that were appealed all the way to courts of last resort. The reasons for this are not entirely clear. Surely there were instances in which it was thought too expensive or hard-hearted to litigate the matter. But factors internal to the nineteenth-century legal system also shaped and reflected the ways Americans thought about injury and compensation for loss. The law of torts did not coalesce as a distinct doctrinal realm until 1859, when the first treatise devoted to the subject was published by the American jurist Francis Hilliard, who offered a systematic survey that was organized according to "scientific" principles rather than the traditional common law forms of action. Yet even then, the nature and extent of liability for what he called "private wrongs" remained significantly shaped by relational, status-based rules and standards of care, leaving large zones where there was no one to blame.[19] Nonetheless, jurists worked to organize and rationalize these rules in accordance with more liberal political and economic principles. Infusing old common law maxims with new meaning, they affirmed the individual liberty to "so use your own, that you injure not the rights of others" and delimited categories of harms for which there was no legal remedy because no rights were violated. New emphasis was placed upon fault, in the sense of a failure to exercise due or reasonable care, as a limiting condition. In his 1881 masterwork *The Common Law*, Oliver Wendell Holmes articulated what was by then the dominant understanding of the elite bar: "The general principle of our law is that loss from accident must lie where it falls."[20]

Much depended upon what was meant by the word "accident," and only gradually did judges and jurists begin to speak in terms of a law of accidents. This doctrinal field was a complex, variegated, and deeply conflicted response to the novel hazards and forms of injury Americans experienced and suffered at home, at work, and in public. The doctrine of "inevitable accident" had been understood by early modern English judges as a very narrow defense to liability, requiring the injurer to demonstrate he was "utterly without fault" in order to escape responsibility for the harm. What might fit this description was subject to endless disputation. To succeed, defendants had to show not only that they had committed no negligence but also that the injury was inevitable, beyond their or any human being's power to prevent.[21] By the mid-nineteenth century, this stringent rule had been displaced by a looser one that focused more on the desirability than the possibility of prevention. Chief Justice Lemuel Shaw's decision in the 1850 Massachusetts case of *Brown v. Kendall* is commonly taken as a key expression of this shift, requiring only the exercise of "that kind and degree of care which prudent and cautious men would use, such as is required by the exigency of the case, and such as is necessary to guard against probable danger." Unless the defendant was shown to have fallen short of this norm, he was not "in fault" and, the harm resulting from his act was to be deemed "a pure accident" for which he could not be held liable. In line with this ruling, courts applied this criterion to streetcars and railroads, redefining inevitable accident as "an act that ordinary human care and foresight are unable to guard against," rendering any resulting harm "the misfortune of the sufferer" and providing "no foundation for legal responsibility."[22]

As tort liability came to turn on fault in this sense, with negligence setting a new baseline, it might have been expected that the harmful acts of the insane would be assimilated to the legal category of inevitable accidents. The equitable doctrine concerning two innocents existed in uneasy tension with the new fault-based standards articulated by judges like Shaw. Yet even as judges and jurists seemed to disclaim the "ancient" rule that a man acts at his peril, it continued to apply to the insane. Indeed, the status of the lunatic was left unchanged as the doctrine of negligence assumed growing importance as an organizing principle within the field of tort law, judges simply restating the dicta from *Weaver v. Ward* without attempting to square it with the principle of fault. Such pronouncements continued to be made most often in this same form of dicta, as judges were seldom called upon to rule directly on the question.[23] Indeed, the insane were most likely to make appearances as sources of analogy and distinction in suits brought against other classes of persons, especially those in subordinate positions such as children, married women, slaves, and sailors, entities such as corporations and municipalities, and nonhuman agents such as wild and domestic animals, to say nothing of man-made machinery. It was precisely because of their want of reason that the insane were drawn into these courtroom disputations, their deployment as limiting cases at once reflecting and generating uncertainty about whether the standard set by the reasonably prudent man was premised upon the capacity to care in the first instance, or otherwise adjusted in recognition of differences in mental ability. And it was the very bluntness of the rule with respect to lunatics that seemed to provoke controversies about whether and when parents, guardians, husbands, masters, owners, and the state could be held to account for the torts of those who were in their charge, control, or care.

More often than not, references to the insane confused the grounds of civil responsibility more than they clarified them, as can be seen in the leading 1874 case of *Brown v. Collins*, decided by Judge Charles Doe. This case involved two horses, thrown into a panic by a passing train engine, escaping the control of the defendant who had been in the exercise of "ordinary care and skill" in navigating the wagon they were drawing, at least until it careened into the plaintiff's lamppost. While noting that a long line of English authorities stretching from *Weaver* to *Rylands* imposed "absolute liability without evidence of negligence," even where the defendant was a lunatic, Doe suggested most American courts had cast aside this time-worn rule as incompatible with "those modern, progressive, industrial pursuits which the spirit of the common law, adapted to all the conditions of society, encourages and defends." In following suit and allowing the losses to lie where they fell, the decision of the court was added to the string of authorities supporting the principle that there could be no civil liability without personal blameworthiness. Yet the last lines of the judge's opinion made such a citation problematic, as he expressly and tellingly reserved judgment on the question of liability where the defendant labored under the influence of some form of mental disease. "Whatever may be the rule or exception, or reason of it, in cases of insanity," Doe evasively concluded, it was clear that the defendant whose conduct was in issue was "as innocent as if the pole of his wagon had been hurled on the plaintiff's land by a whirlwind, or he himself, by a stronger man, had been thrown through the plaintiff's window."[24]

To speak of insanity even when it was not directly in issue was not only to test the extent to which status continued to be determinative of questions of liability for harm. It was also to bring to the fore questions about the distinguishing features of civil and criminal law, the most fundamental of all being whether they proceeded upon the same underlying model of the responsible agent.

The Capacity to Harm and Be Harmed

Although the decisional law was filled with morally loaded terms like "innocent" and "wrongdoing," judges were at pains to emphasize that these words carried different meanings when they were used on the civil as distinguished from the criminal side of the docket. They articulated their operating assumptions by repeating one of Lord Bacon's maxims, "that there was a distinction between answering *civiliter et crimialiter* for acts injurious to others; in the latter case the maxim applied, *actus non facit reum nisi sit rea*; but it was otherwise in civil actions, where the intent was immaterial if the act done were injurious to another."[25]

In the limited number of cases where insanity was asserted as a defense to liability, the receptivity of the court turned on whether intention was perceived to be an element of the civil wrong sought to be redressed. The more the plaintiff's complaint sounded in trespass, the less likely judges were to allow evidence of mental unsoundness to enter into the assessment of responsibility. Thus an allegedly insane man was held to account for the ox he had strangled in an 1845 Vermont case, the court simply declaring it to be "a common principle, that a lunatic is liable for any tort which he may commit," even though the damaging conduct was "not punishable criminally" and might have been done "by mistake, or without design," and notwithstanding the fact that the plaintiff knew he was insane.[26] The same distinction was drawn between civil actions and criminal prosecutions by a Maryland judge in an 1870 decision holding a congenital idiot civilly liable for burning down his neighbor's barn, the opinion of the court simply stating this had always been the rule.[27] On the occasion of another barn burning by an armed and mentally disturbed man in 1887 that had a more tragic outcome, as the man perished in the fire after fatally shooting the owner's wife, his sister-in-law, the responsibility of lunatics for their torts was confirmed by an Illinois court. "However justly this doctrine may have been originally subject to criticism, on the grounds of reason and principle," the members of this panel concluded it was "now too firmly supported by the weight of authority to be disturbed." While there was certainly "an appearance of hardship in compelling one to respond for that which he is unable to avoid, for want of control of reason," considerations of public policy proved more compelling, for "there is more injustice in denying to the injured party the recovery of damages for the wrong suffered by him, than in calling upon the relatives or friends of the lunatic" to provide for his "efficient custody and guardianship" so as to prevent such harm from occurring.[28]

But even as this liability rule was said to be settled, fin de siècle courts continued to admit that "there may be an exception . . . in the case of an inevitable accident" without clarifying whether and when a lunatic might be accorded this excuse. In 1891 a New Hampshire court charged with determining whether an insane defendant could be made to pay compensatory damages for a fatal shooting declared the fact of insanity to be immaterial and proceeded to rule in the plaintiff's favor, with but a nod to Doe's opinion in *Brown* and no indication of what it was that distinguished the deranged shooter from the wagon driver who was adjudged an "innocent" instrument of destructive forces beyond his control.[29]

The plea of insanity was more readily accepted as a defense to civil liability in cases where "malice, and therefore intention" were considered necessary "ingredients" of the wrong or grounds for imposing punitive damages. Evidence of mental unsoundness was admitted as a matter of course in slander and libel actions, though judges differed as to whether they were doing so because it constituted a complete defense of liability or simply mitigated the damages. While the outcome of the lawsuit was likely to be the same regardless of how such evidence was treated, judicial ambivalence on this score must be read against a backdrop of growing contention about the significance of "malice" on the civil as distinct from the criminal side of the docket, with opinions differing as to whether it connoted a malevolent mental state or was better understood as a technicality or legal fiction in the common run of cases.[30] Those adopting the former view more or less tracked popular usage in conceiving of malice as "a wrong feeling in a man's mind," including but not limited to the "corrupt or wrong motive" of "personal spite or ill-will." By contrast, those who insisted it had a specialized meaning in civil actions understood the word to denote nothing more or less than "a wrongful act, done intentionally without just cause or excuse," a few going so far as to suggest that determinations of liability generally turned on the objective tendency of the act rather than the subjective motive, purpose, or intention of the actor.[31] Yet though it is possible to trace an increasing inclination on the part of jurists and judges to speak of malice in less moralistic and more technical terms, words like "evil" never entirely disappeared from the discourse, and opinions continued to be rendered after the turn of the twentieth century exonerating insane defendants simply and solely because of a want of personal blameworthiness.[32]

No case better displays this judicial orientation than the action for slander brought by Florida Gibson against Bettie H. Irvine, a married woman, allowed to be sued in her own right. An answer to the petition came by way of two court-appointed guardians *ad litem*, who defended on her behalf by contending that the words complained of were either not spoken by Mrs. Irvine at all or uttered while she was "laboring under a pronounced and well-defined monomania or delusional insanity upon the subject of her husband's relations with women," which rendered her incapable of knowing or understanding what she said with reference to the complainant. On appeal from a jury verdict for Gibson, awarding her the startling sum of $30,000, the question was whether the trial judge had erred in refusing to instruct the jury that "insanity or monomania" was a complete defense to liability. Answering in the affirmative in a 1904 decision, the court confirmed that "legal malice certainly cannot be imputed to one who in law is incompetent to harbor an intent," implying it would be a miscarriage of justice to impose civil liability "for the thoughtless babbling of an insane person." Though it would be for the jury to say, on retrial, whether Mrs. Irvine and her words fit this description, the panel found the evidence in the record sufficient to prove that she was "totally deranged" at the time the words were uttered. With undisguised sympathy, the court characterized the mental disease as the harmful agent insofar as it "controlled her actions, dominated her will, and wrecked her mind," thereby robbing her of the capacity to be malicious. Should the jury see the matter in the same way, she was to be released from civil liability, regardless of the extent to which her delusional statements were recognized and discounted as such by those who heard them. "Insanity, however viewed anciently, is in modern times deemed a visitation from God, a disease or malconstruction of the mind," the court reasoned, mixing old and new conceptualizations of mental disease as it proceeded to judgment, ultimately pronounced in the form of a rhetorical question: "If God does not hold accountable for their misdeeds those whom he suffers to be thus afflicted, shall his creatures, entrusted with the enforcement of human laws, refuse to excuse their ostensible evil doing?"[33]

Judges and jurists displayed considerably more confusion and conflict when it came to the question of whether a lunatic could be guilty of negligence. While no appellate cases seemed to have passed directly on the question, debates among midcentury jurists exposed an unresolved ambiguity about what it was to be negligent as a matter of law: did it describe a state matter of law: did it describe a state of mind or was it essentially an objective standard, applied without any reference to an actor's personal qualities? Although antebellum alienists might have been expected to take the lead in advocating a subjective standard, even the most vehement medical critic of the common law of capacity, Isaac Ray, essentially took the tort law as he found it, reflecting that while it was "hard" for a lunatic "to suffer for actions committed while utterly unconscious of their nature, it would manifestly be the height of injustice to make another suffer, who was equally innocent and perhaps equally unconscious of the act." One of the earliest American jurists to oppose this view was the Boston lawyer Theodore Sedgwick, who contended in the 1852 edition of his *Treatise on the Measure of Damages* that the imposition of negligence liability presupposed that "the act punished is that of a party competent to foresee and guard against the consequences of his conduct," which obviously could not be said of lunatics.Although this might have been taken to follow from the fault principle that judges articulated in negligence cases involving other sorts of persons, they tended to vacillate between objective and subjective formulations, as they did with the element of malice, reflecting a felt need to articulate uniform standards that could be consistently applied across cases that nonetheless did not impose liability upon the blameless.[34]

These conflicting imperatives ran through charges to juries, which were routinely instructed to apply the negligence rule by reference to the circumstances of case before them. It was, to be sure, every individual's duty "to employ the faculties nature has given him" to avoid injuring others and suffering harm himself. Nonetheless, judges emphasized that "the measure of 'reasonable care' must of course depend upon the circumstances of the particular situation" and the rights and obligations that the parties possessed and owed to one another.[35] In the course of evaluating the behavior of the parties, jurors were allowed, and sometimes actually encouraged, to take into account such variables as gender, age, maturity, intelligence, physical and mental health, and economic circumstances insofar as they impinged upon an actor's ability to exercise due care. As wary as judges were about laying down particular standards of conduct for certain classes of persons, even those most committed to the maintenance of an objective norm admitted the salience of "differences existing by nature" as well those growing out of "different occupations, modes of life, education and experience." How exactly these constitutional and environmental factors were to be weighed in the assessment of liability was left for jurors to determine, in recognition of the fact-intensive nature of the question of what constituted reasonable care. It is nonetheless striking to find that an actor's personal characteristics were far more readily and fully taken into consideration when he appeared before the court as a plaintiff alleged to be guilty of contributory rather than primary negligence.[36]

Though this asymmetry in law of negligence was maintained across jurisdictions, surprisingly little was provided by way of systematic explanation or analysis of it in law reports or treatise literature. Instead, we find blunt judicial pronouncements that contributory negligence was not imputable to certain classes of persons. In turn, treatises catalogued the special treatment accorded to the mentally incompetent, along with women, children, drunkards, and those deprived of one or more of their senses, when they were charged with contributing to their own injuries.[37] Upon closer inspection, this realm of doctrine remained remarkably unruly. Judges equivocated about the legal significance of human difference and social inequality, never making it quite clear whether more or less care was to be required of such "exceptional" persons on account of their perceived weaknesses and disabilities. "Sex is certainly no excuse for negligence," Judge Cooley declared in the course of adjudicating a claim of contributory negligence on the part of a thirteen-year-old girl killed at a railroad crossing. The specific question before the court was whether the trial judge erred in instructing the jury that the law "did not expect or require the same degree of care and prudence in a woman as in a man," or "of a child as of an adult person." While the charge was "unquestionably correct" with respect to her age, "the difference in sex" presented a more complicated matter. The analysis began with the citation of a case in which a male defendant was charged with a higher standard of care in view of "probable deficiencies" of the female plaintiff with whom he collided while both were driving horses on a public highway. This precedent might have been taken to imply a lower standard of care for women, but Cooley suggested otherwise by referring to two other cases in which the female plaintiffs, also injured while driving horses, were denied recovery because they failed to take the sorts of precautions "a woman of common and ordinary prudence" would have taken, in view of her "natural timidity and inexperience with dangers." Although these cases were summoned up to demonstrate that the law did not categorically demand less care on the part of women than men, the judge stopped short of holding that they were required to conform to the same standard as a general rule. In one breath, he declared "no person of any age or sex is chargeable with legal fault who, when placed in a position of peril, does the best that can be done under the circumstances," but in the next, he added the proviso that "the legal requirement is only the observance of ordinary care," which he further allowed might be different in the case of women. The only exception was those who availed themselves of the opportunity they now enjoyed to enter the same "occupations of life" as men. Women who chose such a career path and obtained employment as surgeons, engineers, or the like could not "claim any privilege of exemption from the care and caution required of men," he insisted, closing his opinion with words suggesting this exception was actually the rule: "The rule of prudent regard for the rights of others knows nothing of sex. Neither can sex excuse any one for the want of ordinary care when exposing one's self to known and obvious perils."[38]

Judicial opinions addressing the contributory fault of other disabled classes of persons were likewise shot through with ambiguities and contradictions. With respect to age, courts resisted any generalization about the elderly[39] but generally held children to a lower standard of care than adults.[40] There were significant variations in the formulations of the rule with respect to minors, some judges evaluating the plaintiff's conduct by the relatively objective measure of his years, others suggesting the child could be fairly judged only from a wholly subjective standpoint, in view of his own capacity to act with discretion, and still others vacillating between these two positions even in a single decision.[41]

Even sharper divisions arose as to the nature and extent of parental responsibility for injuries to their children occasioned by third parties. A minority of state courts followed the English rule in imputing the negligence of a parent or guardian to the child, most influentially stated in the 1839 New York case of *Hartfield v. Roper,* involving an unattended two-year-old plaintiff run over by sleigh and horses driven by the defendant. While acknowledging that a child of such tender years was as "incapable of personal discretion" as "a hopeless lunatic," the court nonetheless regarded it to be "a mistake to suppose . . . he is, therefore, above all law." Just as the lunatic was "liable personally for wrongs which he commits against the person and property of others," so too was the child, and it seemed to follow, by the somewhat convoluted reasoning of the court, that when the latter "complains of wrongs to himself, the defendant has a right to insist that [the complainant] should not have been the heedless instrument of his own injury. He cannot, more than any other, make a profit of his own wrong."[42] This doctrine of "infantile responsibility" was, however, not one that was widely accepted in the several states, some going so far as to attack it as "harsh and repugnant to justice," and most preferring the rule expressed by an 1850 Vermont court in the oft-cited *Robinson v. Cone*: "We are satisfied that although a child, or idiot, or lunatic may, to some extent, have escaped into the highway, through the fault or negligence of his keeper, and be so improperly there, yet if he is hurt by the negligence of the defendant, he is not precluded from his redress." Assuming the defendant knew "that such a person is in the highway, or on a railway," this court provided, "he is bound to a proportionate degree of watchfulness, and what would be but ordinary neglect in regard to one whom the defendant supposed a person of full age and capacity, would be gross neglect as to a child, or one known to be incapable of escaping danger."[43]

Cases involving the contributory negligence of the insane began to appear in law reports in the 1850s. One of the earliest, *Willetts v. Buffalo and Rochester Railroad Company,* was brought by the administrator of Washington Willetts, a thirty-year-old confirmed lunatic who had been ejected from the train he was riding while temporarily separated from his father and then was struck and killed several hours later by the very train his father was riding as he searched for his missing son. There was no question in the judge's mind that "the calamity was occasioned" by what would have been "the negligence of the deceased" had he been sane.

Recognizing that he was not, the railroad's liability turned upon whether the conductor had sufficient notice of this passenger's lunacy. The court found that he did not. Willetts had exhibited no signs of insanity until after he had been removed from the train, staring at the conductor and his assistant with a "a sort of wild, scared look about his eyes," which they took to be evidence that he was "of the stubborn sort" and the judge conceded was an inference reasonable enough to insulate the railroad from liability. Although this might be seen as requiring the impossible of a lunatic, the judge considered it no more just to require the conductor to act at his peril. He opined that those who were "incapable of diligence should, and usually have, guardians to care for them: upon them the duty of care and diligence is devolved, and their negligence must, in law, be regarded as the negligence of the incapable infant or lunatic when they have been injured, in cases arising between them and third persons acting without notice." The father of the lunatic was at fault for leaving him "exposed to any and all danger that might arise from his condition"; "the responsibility cannot be thrown on the defendants."[44]

Courts nonetheless remained undecided as to the standard of care that was to be applied to insane plaintiffs accused of contributory fault on their own part. On the one hand, there was the 1892 Alabama case of *Worthington v. Mencer*, in which a "weak-minded" track-hand was alleged to have contributed to his own injury by the defendant employer. "On the question of the plaintiff's contributory negligence as affected by his mental condition," the Alabama court at first seemed prepared to enforce a subjective standard, declaring he was "to be held to the exercise of the degree of care of which he was capable." But in the very next sentence, the panel substantially qualified what it had just said:

> If he was merely a person of dull mind, who could labor for his own livelihood, and there was no apparent necessity of putting him under the protection of a guardian to keep him out of harm's way, he is chargeable with the same degree of care for his personal safety as one of brighter intellect, as any attempt to frame and adapt varying rules of responsibility to varying degrees of intelligence would necessarily involve confusion and uncertainty in the law. If, on the other hand, he was so absolutely devoid of intelligence as to be unable to apprehend apparent danger, and to avoid exposure to it, he cannot be said to have been guilty of negligence, because he was incapable of exercising care.

Yet even were the plaintiff able to establish this degree of mental deprivation, he was still not entitled to recovery unless he was further able to show that the defendant had "some notice of the injured person's mental deficiency, and of his consequent helplessness and peril in the circumstances in which he was placed." Because this had not been part of the jury instruction, a verdict for the plaintiff was reversed and the case remanded with the outcome more or less determined, as the court also held that the degree of mental unsoundness he had to show in order to prevail also would have precluded him—the only witness of the injury—from being competent to testify.[45]

Apparently less daunted by the problems presented by a more subjective rule, the U.S. Supreme Court found for the plaintiff in *Baltimore & Potomac R. v. Cumberland*, a 1900 decision affirming an $8,000 award to a twelve-year-old boy severely injured by a passing train while he was engaged in his evening occupation of lighting streetlamps in the city of Washington, D.C. Though the defendant railroad company contended it was entitled to a directed verdict upon the question of contributory negligence, the Court disagreed, in view of the evidence in the record going to show the boy was "dull for his age" and likely "had only the capacity of a child of six or seven." Deeming it unjust to hold the plaintiff accountable "for faults which arise from inherent physical or mental defects, or want of capacity to appreciate what is and what is not negligence," the Court insisted he was only bound to exercise "such faculties and capacities as he is endowed with by nature for the avoidance of danger." Had the plaintiff who initiated this action been "a man of mature age and average intelligence," the Court allowed, it would have been "difficult to escape the conclusion that he was guilty of negligence in crossing this track without taking more careful observations of incoming and outgoing trains." But this was manifestly not true of this particular lamplighter, and so he was entitled to compensation for his injuries. While there was, in the final analysis, "no hard and fast rule applicable to everyone under like circumstances," this was not to say there were as many rules as there were persons. "To an adult, in full possession of his mental and physical powers, one standard may be applied; to a boy, particularly if he be of limited intelligence, another standard; and to an infant not *sui juris* and totally ignorant of danger, still another. Indeed, in the last case the only contributory negligence with which he is chargeable is that of his parent or custodian who permits him to stroll in a place of danger."[46]

With these words, the Supreme Court affirmed that the state of a plaintiff's consciousness was material to the question of his contributory negligence, without any mention of the vexed matter of primary negligence that had been lately and inconclusively addressed in the decisions of New York courts in the case of *Williams v. Hays*. The fact that tort cases placing the mind in issue were so few and far between is at least as puzzling as the variability of the decisions rendered from the bench, particularly in view of the volume of capacity litigation in other realms of civil and criminal law. The matter did, however, generate a rather more searching debate about the relationship between causation and responsibility in the medico-legal literature of the Gilded Age.

"What Is a Juridical Cause?"

The affliction of madness took on a more ambiguous aspect in the last decades of the nineteenth century as the mind-body relationship was subject to searching reexamination by a widening array of specialists in the fields of physiology, psychology, and neurology. Exponents of the new physiological psychology comprehended human behavior in resolutely naturalistic terms, conceiving of mental phenomena—normal as well as abnormal—as part of "a unified Science of Physics." While boldly presenting their research programs as models of what it was to be scientific, they tended to be evasive about the ethical implications of their work, particularly as it concerned "the reality of subjective experience and the nature of moral responsibility." Many took critical aim at the pioneering generation of asylum doctors, accusing them of clinging to an outmoded faculty psychology and standing in the way of medical progress. But they were no more successful in supplying courts with workable means of identifying "the really insane." To the contrary, their pathological schemes were built upon mechanistic and hereditarian theories of human nature that seemed to fatally blur the already problematic line between depravity and disease. In so doing, they obscured as much as they revealed about what distinguished the normal from the pathological, immeasurably complicating the question of who was to be held accountable for the increasing number of Americans reportedly afflicted with this ever more amorphous but nonetheless debilitating condition.[47]

Positioned on the outskirts of the predictable universe that professional men sought to comprehend and control, the insane exemplified the capriciousness and recalcitrance of human nature, embodying the formidable challenges entailed in the cultural project of making responsible persons. "The great law of necessity and humanity" pronounced by Chief Justice Shaw at the height of the cult of curability proved increasingly difficult to uphold during the Gilded Age. State hospitals had become overcrowded with poor and chronically insane inmates, a growing proportion of whom were foreign born, and both public and private institutions were steadily falling away from individuated treatment models as their limited resources were redirected toward the provision of custodial care; they resorted to the use of physical restraints in order to keep the furious from harming more peaceable patients who had to share cramped quarters. These shifts left asylum doctors vulnerable to charges of abuse by former patients, which were confirmed by a vocal chorus of journalists and civil libertarians who insisted that these institutions were nothing but prisons in disguise, rendered all the more offensive given the apparent ease with which the unsuspecting could be "railroaded" into a life sentence without due process of the law.[48]

These graphic and often lurid asylum exposés vied for public attention with no less threatening accounts of the havoc wreaked by patients who "eloped" or were prematurely released from custody.[49] With little assurance that the dictates of necessity and humanity pointed in the same direction, those charged with making and enforcing the law reassessed how best to safeguard public welfare and personal liberty in an industrial society that presented insuperable challenges to the idea of individual autonomy. Reckoning that the probability that a person would harm himself or others could not be quantified on the basis of medical science, legislators left it to members of the legal profession to patrol the permeable boundary between mental soundness and unsoundness and manage the risks to life and property presented by those who lacked the faculties of self-control and sometimes even the instincts of self-protection. As late nineteenth-century American judges and jurists confronted the vast borderland between perfect sanity and raving lunacy and the complex roots of mental disorder in the self, soma, and society, they reconsidered the place of fault in the structure of civil liability and the extent to which causal responsibility necessarily implied the existence of a moral agent.

The more Gilded Age jurists read about the etiology of insanity, the more they realized that this murky territory was fraught with dangerous implications for the legal system, particularly the process of attributing responsibility. Many associated the subject of causation with the famously thorny question of free will and relegated the deterministic doctrines of physiological psychology to "metaphysics," a term that was now synonymous with the vain pursuit of that which was probably unknowable and certainly of no practical import. Yet efforts to bracket all matters of cause and effect were almost invariably attended with strained reasoning and self-contradiction, especially in the context of determining liability for harmful conduct.

"Cause! who can get at the cause? The cause of anything in the present is the whole past!" exclaimed J. H. Balfour Browne, a leading English barrister, whose 1871 treatise on medical jurisprudence enjoyed wide circulation on both sides of the Atlantic. Browne's dismissive tone was belied by his discussion of "the real science of causality in relation to mental disease": "One must enter into a synthesis of causes, and confess that man is . . . half the cause of his own disease, if through any combination of circumstances he becomes insane." The causal connection drawn by Browne did not necessarily imply any culpability on the part of the sick man. His liability seemed to turn on whether he retained sufficient self-awareness and power to return to mental health "by an exercise of the volition" or take appropriate precautions against "any evil consequences which may arise during the continuance of the disease." Yet, as Browne surveyed the formal doctrinal rules applying to civil and criminal proceedings, the inability to avoid injury to oneself or others did not compel a judgment of irresponsibility. Though only "a free and understanding agent" could be subject to criminal punishment in a civilized, liberal polity, civil sanctions might be imposed "consistent with equity and justice" on an individual who was "incapable of guiding his acts in any way" and "utterly unconscious" of the damage done. To this jurist, and most physicians writing within this field, the common law requirement to make recompense in such instances was eminently fair: "Why should a man suffer because he is sane, and have immunity because he is insane?"[50]

The answer turned out to be less obvious to jurists who focused on the law of torts as it crystallized during the last quarter of the nineteenth century. They were fairly evenly split on the question of what the common law required of the insane tortfeasor. Those who, like Browne, held insanity to be no excuse simply rested on the authority of *Weaver v. Ward,* sometimes buttressed with barely elaborated considerations of fairness. "This is necessary," Amasa Redfield and Thomas Shearman bluntly put it in their 1869 *Treatise on the Law of Negligence,* "because otherwise there would be no redress for injuries committed by such persons," or any means of avoiding the "anomaly" of a mental incompetent with "abundant wealth, depriving another of property without compensation." Other jurists contended that holding a lunatic liable for his torts was unjustifiable "on principle," imposing liability without fault. This argument, initially made by Theodore Sedgwick in his midcentury *Treatise on the Measure of Damages,* was advanced more elaborately and systematically in the ensuing decades, as the case of the lunatic became tangled up with broader controversies about the imposition of "absolute liability" upon industrial enterprises, controversies that noticeably intensified in the wake of the 1868 English decision in *Rylands v. Fletcher.*[51]

Typical of this trend was an 1875 article on "The Liability of Persons of Unsound Mind and Infants for Tort Civil Actions," published by Iowa lawyer Timothy Brown in the *Southern Law Review.* "All liability for torts rests upon the basis that the party charged has done a wrongful or culpable act, either intentional wrong or the failure of himself or agent to use ordinary care," "measured by the intellect the actor possesses or is presumed to possess." A person who lacked knowledge of right and wrong could not be held responsible for his civil wrongs, for the law emphatically did not require "impossible things." This rule applied with particular force to sufferers of insanity, whom Brown cast as victims of an "act of God" as much as if they were affected by a "tempest or earthquake," making it difficult to see why a madman's estate should be made to pay for resulting harm.[52]

These questions about the insane tortfeasor proved divisive even within the ranks of legal thinkers who are conventionally portrayed as unanimously adhering to "objective causation." The contours and broader significance of this dispute can be understood by considering the opposing viewpoints of Francis Wharton and Thomas M. Cooley, set out in treatises that were influential at the time and have been recognized by historians as important building blocks in the construction of "a system of private law free from the dangers of redistribution" and insulated from the "infusion of politics."[53] In significant respects these two jurists fit this general description, for both were committed to maintaining clear boundaries between public and private. It is precisely because of their shared concerns with limiting state power and sustaining the fault principle that their divergent views on the responsibility of the insane for their torts warrant attention, for they indicate significant differences of opinion about matters of social ordering and distributive justice that point toward basic ambiguities within the liberal worldview.

Wharton arguably took the more principled position in his 1874 *Treatise on the Law of Negligence.* He limited the universe of juridical causes to those who fit the description of a "responsible voluntary agent," one who was capable of anticipating and avoiding the harmful consequences of his conduct. Those "incapable of reason," by which he meant idiots, maniacs, and infants, manifestly failed to meet this threshold requirement and were deemed to be "conditions" rather than "causes." This tendency to presume "the convertibility of causality with free agency" was certainly of a piece with Wharton's contributions to the medical jurisprudence of insanity, although he refrained from delving into questions of partial insanity and graduated responsibility as he took up the subject of negligence, contemplating only extreme forms of mental deprivation as bases for excuse from liability for civil wrongs. In this doctrinal context, insane persons were summoned to the fore mainly as a negative reference point in the discussion of what constituted a "responsible cause" in the field of jurisprudence. While "materialistic" scientists and philosophers such as J. S. Mill might define the cause of an event as "the sum of all its antecedents," he argued, judges had to "discriminate between the antecedents by which an event is conditioned." Given the "juridical and moral purposes" of this work, it was necessary to eliminate all those antecedents that were "mechanical and irresponsible," retaining only the ones that were "moral, responsible, and capable of being molded by law." From this narrower class of causes the single, "responsible originator" was then to be chosen in accordance with even more exacting criteria: "He must either design the event, and it must have resulted from his design; or, if attributable to his negligence, it must result, by the force of ordinary natural laws, directly from that negligence."[54]

Although the adjudication of responsibility was premised upon the regularity and legibility of the operations of the physical universe, Wharton insisted that the jurist's supremacy over scientists was "required by the good of society and by the will of God." By this time, jurists had ample reason to doubt the utility of experts in courtroom proceedings where the issue of insanity was involved. All too often, they were summoned to offer proof of the "non-responsibility of particular manias," and some betrayed a conviction that "all crimes presuppose insanity." The failure of these medical experts to "speak coherently on any issue involving the moral relations of physical facts" was symptomatic of the basic inadequacy of the scientific doctrine of causality as a tool of governance. One needed only to pause to consider the "practical communism" this doctrine effectively underwrote, he cautioned; its "leveling of all antecedents to the same parity" encouraged making "the capitalist" the responsible party solely on account of his ability to pay for injurious occurrences to which he could be linked by the most tenuous of connections. If tort liability were made to depend upon wealth, Wharton warned, the recklessness of the unpropertied was sure to increase and bring about "ruin which otherwise would have been averted," and it was only a matter of time before entrepreneurial activity ceased altogether so there were no capitalists left to sue. Piercing the veil of the corporation too often written off as a soulless entity, he traced the damaging effects of such an eventuality from the highest to the lowest levels of the interdependent society of late nineteenth-century America. For, in truth, the derided population of "bloated bond-holders" consisted mainly of "professional men of small incomes, and widows and orphans" with no other means to support themselves, and no class would suffer more from curtailment of industrial growth than the laborers who counted on wages from the companies shuttered by lawsuits.[55]

Accentuating the material stakes of the legal doctrine of causation, Wharton left it to the common sense judgments of members of the bench rather than the expertise of philosophers or scientists to determine who was to be counted among the moral causes in any given case and to identify the responsible party. This approach was to be preferred, in his estimation, precisely because it did not pretend to a false objectivity about causes and effects in the realm of human activity. The appeal of common law adjudication was that it closely tracked the evolving moral sense of the community and its conventions of causal attribution. Wharton did not worry that the conventions adopted by American judges facilitated economic development, but his *Law of Negligence* was neither a straightforward brief for laissez-faire capitalism nor an unequivocal argument for the orthodox ideal of a neutral state, recognizing as he did the need for the law to make special allowances for those "incapable of reason." The classes of irresponsible persons were rather narrowly drawn, and it was consistent with the notion of a minimalist state to let the losses resulting from their harmful acts lie where they fell.

Yet from a victim's standpoint, this neutrality could seem more like bias than impartiality on the part of the courts, and some suggested that this judicial norm of noninterference effectively sanctioned the uncompensated expropriation of property. Although Wharton never directly addressed this argument, he would probably have considered it confiscatory and more basically uncharitable for a court to impose liability on a mentally incompetent defendant, for he held the state to a different standard in its dealings with those who were unable to care for themselves. "One of the cardinal duties of Christian civilization is the protection of the helpless," he averred, and infants and insane persons were properly treated as wards of the state who could do no wrong on account of their civil incapacity. Logic and justice required that the protective shield of the law be extended to cases where they were victims as well as perpetrators of harm, so they were insulated from the charge of contributory negligence that might have applied to those of full age and sound mind and assured that the neglect of their parents and guardians would not be imputed to them. In view of the burdens that nature and society had already inflicted on unfortunates, there was surely no good reason to hold them financially accountable for injuries they did not legally cause, at least from the standpoint of a jurist so deeply committed to a fault-based conception of civil as well as criminal liability.[56]

This was precisely where Cooley begged to differ from Wharton in his 1879 *Treatise on the Law of Torts*, which more sharply distinguished this field of doctrine from other areas of public and private law. Though he shared Wharton's sense that infants and other mental incompetents were deserving of the paternalistic solicitude of the state insofar as their contractual dealings and criminal liability were concerned, he treated the civil wrongs they committed quite differently. When a suit was brought to recover damages for these sorts of harms, Cooley explained, the law commanded a focus on "the injury done, and not commonly the purpose, or mental or physical capacity of the person or agent doing it." Passing over the question of whether one incapable of reason could be sensibly said to be a responsible cause of any injury, he took it to be "just that the consequences of the unfortunate occurrence should fall upon the estate of the person committing the injury, rather than upon that of the person who has suffered it." This doctrine enjoyed wide acceptance among commentators and judges, including Earl in *Williams v. Hays*. Though there might be "some appearance of hardship in imposing upon a person already visited with the inexpressible calamity of mental obscurity an obligation to observe the same care and precaution respecting the rights of others that the law demands of one in full possession of his faculties," Cooley pronounced this view a misperception resulting from a failure to apprehend the object of the law of torts, which was compensation rather than punishment. In this realm of doctrine, the question of responsibility was reducible to a matter of public policy to be settled by reference to the "general welfare," with no need to discriminate as between defendants suffering from mental disease as opposed to moral perversion.[57]

With mental incompetents firmly placed within the class of potential tortfeasors, Cooley enumerated several policy considerations in favor of holding them responsible for the injuries they unintentionally visited upon others. First, he observed that this liability rule was consistent with the approach most states took in the financing of mental hospitals, which was to require a patient with means to cover the costs of his own care. Holding such a person to account for his torts would also provide "an important stimulus" to preventative action on the part of "those who have a personal or family interest in him, or who might be entitled to succeed to his estate if it were preserved"; the rule encouraged "competent and responsible guardians . . . to guard both them and the public against such injuries as would be likely to result from their condition." Yet another reason for adopting this rule stemmed from the well-known difficulty of determining whether and when the condition of incompetence existed;

juries were frequently "urged on and impelled by public passion and clamor to find in the freaks of delusion the evidences of criminal intent and depravity, and to convict and punish those who are only deserving of compassion." The temptation to simulate incapacity "for purposes of mischief and revenge" would be especially strong in a prosecution for a civil wrong, for the defendant stood to gain full immunity if successful, and otherwise put at risk nothing more than the amount of damages proved by the plaintiff. While "evils of this sort" were probably "inseparable from the administration of the criminal law," Cooley suggested, they had "no necessary place where only civil redress is given," so it seemed to him "better to exclude them by an invariable rule that mental disease or infirmity shall be no defense to an action for tort."[58]

Cooley maintained that "strict justice" demanded that a party wronged at the hands of an insane person be justly compensated, even though the injury done was "in the nature of a misfortune rather than of a fault." But he hastened to add that the imperative to compensate did not necessarily require that the responsibility shouldered by the mentally incompetent be the same as that of other persons. Instead, he allowed that incompetency of this sort might have a significant bearing on the extent and even the existence of tort liability, particularly in cases where some form of "personal abuse" was alleged. The difference was greater still where malice was an element of the tort. It was a "monstrous absurdity" to impute this state of mind to one who was manifestly "incapable of harboring an intent." Cooley extended this reasoning to negligence actions, conceding the relevance of capacity in determining whether any neglect of duty or want of due care on the part of the injured party contributed to the harm and defeated recovery. With qualifications such as these riddling the law of torts as Cooley rendered it, the reader could only wonder what remained of the his "invariable rule."[59]

It was with the aim of reconciling these competing conceptions of the founding principles of legal responsibility that Oliver Wendell Holmes intervened with his lectures on *The Common Law* published in 1881. "Some middle point must be found between the horns of this dilemma," he insisted as he sought the "common ground" of civil and criminal liability. The solution Holmes famously figured in the form of the reasonable man was meant to confirm that the law did indeed "determine liability by blameworthiness" in an objective sense, by reference to "what would be blameworthy in the average man, the man of ordinary intelligence and prudence." He applied this standard to both criminal prosecutions and civil actions, it being the purpose of the common law as a whole "to induce external conformity to rule," though an individual's claim to justice might be overruled in pursuit of this communal end. If anything, he counterintuitively suggested, it was in the redressing of civil rather than criminal wrongs that "the condition of a man's heart of conscience" was more likely to be taken in account, personal culpability being the most frequently cited reason for redistributing an existing loss from one individual to another.[60] Nonetheless, Holmes pointed to an overriding judicial tendency, especially pronounced in those fields of civil and criminal law that were most directly concerned with "establishing standards of conduct," to formulate "tests of liability" that were "external, and independent of the degree of evil in the particular person's motives or intentions." As he put it in one of the most frequently quoted passages from *The Common Law*:

> The standards of the law are standards of general application. The law takes no account of the infinite varieties of temperament, intellect, and education which make the internal character of a given act so different in different men. It does not attempt to see men as God sees them. . . . In the first place, the impossibility of nicely measuring a man's powers and limitations is far clearer than that of ascertaining his knowledge of law, which has been thought to account for what is called the presumption that every man knows the law. But a more satisfactory explanation is, that, when men live in society, a certain average of conduct, a sacrifice of individual peculiarities going beyond a certain point, is necessary to the general welfare.[61]

Often overlooked in conventional restatements are the exceptions the jurist then proceeded to delineate in order to "illustrate the rule, and also the moral basis of liability in general." Anyone possessing a peculiarity or defect that was distinct enough "that all can recognize it as making certain precautions impossible, will not be held answerable for not taking them." But it remained unclear whether Holmes took this position because the want of blame was so obvious as to be uncontroversial, or only insofar as the impairment was so prominent as to provide competent persons with adequate notice of the need to adjust their conduct accordingly. While saying nothing about women, Holmes readily instanced blind men and infants as classes of persons whose differences warranted special treatment when they appeared before the bar as injured parties, and perhaps also (here he was not as sure) when they were summoned to answer the charges of injury to others.[62] Insanity, by contrast, was adjudged to be "a more difficult matter to deal with," and the jurist determined that "no general rule can be laid down about it." Many of those afflicted remained "perfectly capable" of meeting the behavioral expectations set by the law. But where the mental disease was sufficiently pronounced, "manifestly incapacitating the sufferer from complying with the rule which he has broken," Holmes concluded that "good sense would require it to be admitted as an excuse." So it seemed that the impaired state of a man's mind was immaterial to his liability, save where it appeared to deprive him of "a fair chance to avoid bringing the harm to pass."[63]

What would keep these "well-known exceptions" from swallowing Holmes's general rule of liability was not easily discerned in *The Common Law*, which warned that those who fell below the threshold of "ordinary intelligence and reasonable prudence" acted at their peril but still promised to shield some among their number from responsibility for the injuries they caused or brought on themselves. The principles that were to guide judges and jurors remained obscure. Here we can detect the jurist's own ambivalence about those who appeared constitutionally incapable of exercising due care toward themselves and others. To be sure, the work communicates a tough-minded message about the evils of governmental interference, particularly in view of Holmes's insistence that the state was not "a mutual insurance company" that undertook to provide "a pension for paralytics" or otherwise insulate unfortunate individuals against accidents of birth and subsequent mishaps that impaired their capacity for self-government. Yet he came close to contradicting himself as he further extended his argument against state redistribution of losses "irrespective of fault" to the case of a person who injured another "in a fit." Imagining himself in such a condition visiting harm upon his neighbor, Holmes suggested that it would have been no more justifiable for a court to require him to compensate the injured party than "to compel me to insure him against lightning." Whether or why the "gifts" of ordinary intelligence and prudence ought to be treated as any less fortuitous the jurist never quite said.[64]

All of this theorizing about tort liability shows that there was nothing amounting to an orthodoxy about what constituted a juridical cause among legal thinkers. Their conflicting and internally conflictual writings register deep fault lines in fin-de-siècle conceptions of responsible agency. Although leading commentators were rarely detained very long in their consideration of the problem of mental deficiency within this field of doctrine, few were able to rest easy with the blunt pronouncement that the sane and insane were to be treated alike in suits brought to redress civil wrongs. Many shared Cooley's pragmatic impulse to cordon off the domain of tort law so as to spare members of the bench the sorts of embarrassments that accompanied the plea of insanity in other civil and criminal trials. Even Wharton, who was schooled more than any other American jurist of the day in the vagaries of mental illness, did not venture to address anything but the most severe cases of mental derangement, which utterly effaced the agency of sufferers and thereby warranted their categorization as acts of God or inevitable accidents. Yet, as Holmes observed, insanity was a uniquely problematic phenomenon, so subtle and variable in its manifestations and effects as to defy classification and seemingly require the case-by-case analysis that his objective standard was meant to obviate. The dilemma he set out to resolve in *The Common Law* was only restated, however evocatively, in such a fashion as to beg the question of how the risks and burdens associated with being of unsound mind were to be apportioned as between afflicted individuals, their families and neighbors, the state and society.[65]

So insanity remained among the "anomalies" of the law of torts at the turn of the twentieth century, reflecting general uncertainty about the relationship between consciousness and liability in American legal culture. The confused state of the law was expressed with peculiar poignancy in a set of wrongful death suits concerning railway passengers who were driven to insanity and then suicide after suffering injury at the hands of railroad companies. In almost all of these cases, the railroad was held blameless, as the death was adjudged too remote from the concededly negligent conduct of the railroad. In marked contrast to the conflicting and conflicted decisions involving the life policies of insane suicides treated in Chapter 5, these self-destroyers were bluntly deemed the agents of their own undoing.[66] Thus the Supreme Court held in an 1881 case involving a successful middle-aged merchant who "became much disordered in mind and body" as a result of a railroad collision and allegedly took his life in order to escape "the phantasms, illusions, and forebodings" that had "prostrated all his reasoning powers." "The argument is not sound which seeks to trace this immediate cause of the death through the previous stages of mental aberration, physical suffering, and eight months' disease and medical treatment to the original accident on the railroad. Such a course of possible or even logical argument would lead back to that 'great first cause least understood,' in which the train of all causation ends."[67] A New York court followed suit in a 1903 case where less than three months transpired between the collision and the passenger's death, which the evidence tended to show was induced by mental disturbance, ultimately moving him to strangle himself with a napkin. Making much of the fact that he locked himself in his bedroom before this was done, the court adjudged the self-killing to be his choice, if not his fault: "It may be said that he is forced to the deed by his disordered faculties. Some contend that we are all slaves of destiny. Our subject brings us near to the vexed theological problem as to free will and predestination. Without attempting to pursue these inquiries too far, we are of the opinion that the voluntary, willful act of suicide of an insane person, whose insanity was caused by a railroad accident, and who knows the purpose and physical side effect of his act, is such a new and independent agency as does not come within and complete a line of causation from the accident to his death."[68]

These cases dramatically revealed the continuing difficulty judges experienced as they attempted to characterize the responsible self and the extent to which they remained on the horns of the dilemma from which Holmes had promised to deliver them in his *Common Law.*

Subjective or Objective?

The madman continued to lurk on the margins of legal personhood along with other stock figures such as the idiot, drunkard, married woman, seaman, and spendthrift, standing ready as sources of analogy and potential bases of legal exemption or disqualification. Among these categories of persons, those "of unsound mind" proved most difficult for late nineteenth-century jurists to delimit. The outlines of this category grew only more indeterminate over time, a trend that was, ironically, exacerbated by the rise of the new medical psychology. Those seeking clarity or simply taking advantage of ambiguity helped to generate troubling levels of capacity litigation, not only in the familiar context of criminal prosecutions but in a wide array of civil actions as well. Positive judicial pronouncements that a man was free to "do what he will with his own" paradoxically authorized endless streams of disappointed heirs to challenge conveyances and last testaments on grounds of mental incapacity and undue influence. Moreover, as American jurisdictions threw off the "ancient" English rule that "no man shall be allowed to stultify himself, or plead his own disability," multitudes pleaded their incompetence so as to avoid legal arrangements ranging from commerce to matrimony. Both before and after *Williams v. Hays*, any tort litigant could plead insanity in order to escape liability for punitive damages, intentional torts, and contributory negligence. With cases like these clogging court dockets, there was surely good reason to wonder whether the law's twin presumptions of sanity and freedom were actually warranted. American judges and jurists did not allow these doubts to overwhelm them in the waning decades of the nineteenth century. They did not simply take the objective way out, conclusively presuming everyone was as competent as the reasonable man. Instead, they continued to call upon the default legal person to resolve questions of mental competence arising in private law, endeavoring to take the state of a man's consciousness into account so far as practicably possible.

By the end of the century, the default legal person that American judges deployed in civil contests was a somewhat denatured version of its former self. Still, these judges neither returned to the traditional common law standard of a "glimmering of reason" nor embraced a wholly objectified model of a "reasonable man." Instead, they persisted in defining legal competence in terms of the "capacity to reason," while emphasizing that the irrationality of the act in question, whether a will, contract, deed, or tort, would almost never constitute sufficient proof, in and of itself, of the irresponsibility of the actor. In remaining more or less open to pleas of civil incapacity, American judges confirmed that the legal system did not oblige its subjects to do impossible things and committed themselves to maintaining a certain correspondence between consciousness and culpability.

The figure of the default legal person makes it clear that nineteenth-century American judges were not simply or solely concerned with maximizing individual liberty or stimulating the development of capitalism. The capacity suits that formed a regular part of the courts' work were quite taxing, sometimes dragging on for months or years and invariably raising an array of unsettling issues that not only threatened the security of marketplace transactions but also challenged basic assumptions about domestic relations and the constitution of the self. Although it was formally only the mind that was placed in issue by civil claimants, the ensuing proceedings almost unavoidably presented courts with broader questions of generational equity, social welfare, and human psychology, all the while providing judges with ample grounds for reconsidering how far medical science could be made a part of common law without undermining the traditional basis of legal responsibility.

The final judgments rendered in nineteenth-century capacity contests left many of these issues unresolved. Judges were primarily concerned with specifying how much "mind" a person had to possess in order to be held accountable for a given civil act or wrong, recognizing as they did that internal states of consciousness could be only imperfectly gauged by means of external behavioral signs. In and through their rulings, they developed ways of modeling competence that retained a certain appeal within American legal culture, even as faculty psychology was displaced by new sciences of the mind. Despite these advances, a gray area between the uncontested competence of the reasonable man and the clear incompetence of the individual falling below the threshold set by the default legal person remained. Those who populate this murky middle ground continue to bedevil judges and jurists, eluding objective measure. This situation is only to be expected within a legal system that treats mental derangement with such ambivalence, leaving its practitioners unable to make up their own minds about whether lunatics ought to be pitied or penalized.

Conclusion

> And madness is in their hearts while they live, and after that, they go to the dead.
>
> Ecclesiastes 9:3

"ALL WILL END WELL," repeated Benjamin Rush in letter after letter, almost as if writing would make it so. With an unshakable belief in the absolute sovereignty and goodness of God, an unswerving conviction regarding the righteousness of the republican cause, and an abiding confidence in its eventual triumph, the doctor confronted mounting evidence to the contrary with a cheerfulness that his contemporaries and later biographers have described as bordering on the perverse. Though Rush sounded increasingly pessimistic as his countrymen became "absorbed in the love of money," his faith in the benevolence of the universe intensified. "It is the prerogative of man to bring evil out of good, but it is the prerogative of God to bring good out of evil," he assured a dispirited compatriot in the spring of 1788. "The last thing I can believe is that providence has brought us over the Red Sea of the late war to perish in the present wilderness of anarchy and vice," he affirmed to another a few months later. "We are advancing through *suffering* (the usual road) to peace and happiness." His quarrels were always with his fellows, not his God, and even after his retirement from politics he remained committed to the task of fitting the minds of Americans for the responsibilities of citizenship in the new republic.[1]

Feeling that he acted freely even as reason told him that his part in the drama of life was divinely scripted and environmentally determined, Rush lived out the contradictory logical and psychological implications of the Common Sense philosophy he helped to propagate. His career exemplifies the profound shift in moral consciousness over the century following 1750, as men and women in the United States and Britain, as well as elsewhere in North America and Western Europe, manifested a heightened sense of their individual capacity and personal responsibility to combat the sins they perceived in themselves and the world around them. Although the campaign to abolish slavery was the most successful and momentous of these movements, reformers also committed themselves to the education of the young, the deterrence of crime, the elimination of poverty, and the cure of mental disease. Here Rush made his most permanent mark, taking an affliction that had "been enveloped in mystery" and bringing it "down to the level of all the other diseases of the human body," in order "to show that the mind and the body are moved by the same causes and subject to the same laws." Educated in the precepts of Enlightenment moral and political philosophy as well as psychological medicine, Rush conceived of the madman as the antithesis of the self-possessed liberal legal subject and undertook to rescue him from grasp of the law so that he might be rightly placed under the benevolent dominion of medical science.[2]

Rush's self-consciously heroic measures on behalf of the insane have won him impassioned champions and detractors in equal measure. No critic has been more unsparing than the psychiatrist Thomas Szasz. He cast Rush as a manufacturer of madness, a grand inquisitor in medical garb who prefigured the oppressions of "the therapeutic state" as he diagnosed blackness of skin as a form of leprosy and pathologized those who thought and acted differently than him under the cover of a "benevolent paternalism" that was a mislabel for "human evil," proving that "while he loved liberty, he loved power far more." The historian David Brion Davis has taken a similarly dim view of Rush's career as a mental physician but sees him as more of a tragic figure, appearing in the vanguard of an international movement to abolish slavery whose members were selective in the objects of their moral concern. On this view, "The 'strain for consistency' did not prevent Rush from being both a crusader for freedom and a personal tyrant who imprisoned his son for life in his own mental hospital and who tortured alcoholics and mental deviants for the supposed good of society." Striving to alleviate human suffering and achieve personal and social salvation, such reformers focused attention on the singular evil of slavery while screening out other forms of injustice, effectively if not intentionally giving sanction to the emerging capitalist order and exhibiting a certain blindness to their own infirmities. As Davis trenchantly observes: "There can be no greater disparity of power than that between a man convinced of his own disinterested service and another man who is defined as a helpless object."[3]

The problem of insanity in the age of reason and revolution was nonetheless distinct from that of slavery because the insane were understood to suffer from a different form of alienation than the slave. To be sure, both madness and slavery had for centuries been associated with original sin and regarded as part of the divine order, as punishments or tests of faith, and as integral to the very constitution of authority, subordination, and discipline. Moreover, linking blackness with madness was at least as long-standing; in classical medicine based on the theory of humors, "the melancholic was understood to have a black countenance." And the humanitarian movements that proliferated in the last decades of the eighteenth century extended the boundaries of moral concern to encompass the insane as well as chattel slaves, both of whom suffered the horrors of dehumanization, wrongly treated like animals and cut off from the ties of sympathetic identification. At least metaphorically, Orlando Patterson's characterization of enslavement as "natal alienation" and "social death" might be extended to the insane. Yet the reformers drove home the injustices visited upon enslaved Africans and African Americans by encouraging their white audiences to imagine what it would be like to be robbed of their freedom and treated like mere things, figuring the slaves as innocent victims and the institution of slavery as an obstacle to human progress. This rhetorical strategy was not often deployed in speaking of the madman's loss of reason, which was conceived of as a perplexing derangement rather than a crime. Early eighteenth-century medical writers described the terrain of madness as "a wild uncultivated region, an intellectual Africa, that abounds with an endless variety of monsters and irregular minds." Even as insanity was recast as a physical disease within the emerging field of mental psychology, it remained difficult to identify a victimizer who profited from their suffering and could be called to account for their dispossession. There were, to be sure, sadistic keepers of madhouses and ignorant members of the general public whose brutality and cruel curiosity could be sharply contrasted with the forms of "moral treatment" advocated by Rush and the alienists who superintended America's first insane asylums. But the origins of the condition of insanity were not easily traced back to a particular wrongdoer. Mental disease was commonly described by both lay and medical writers as the result of multiple causes, moral and physical, hereditary and environmental, proximate and remote, though not so far back as to implicate God. More often than not, both sermons and medical tracts placed no small part of the blame on the victims themselves.[4]

Insanity and the Liberal Subject

The insane remained problematically different from the other groups of hapless souls whom reformers tried to redeem from bondage in postrevolutionary America, for many if not all required confinement in order to recover their reason and become part of the polity. Nor did the building of asylums contain the threat posed by this protean disorder, as it appeared to thrive amidst the fluidity and instability of the young republic. Rush underscored this point with peculiar force in a satirical letter to the editor of the *Columbian Magazine* "On the Species of Mania," anonymously published in 1786. He observed that the most prevalent type was "partial madness," which was betrayed by "false judgment, or injudicious conduct upon any subject," though it was manifest most often in the form of religious delusion and financial speculation. Rush elaborated his diagnosis by "naming some of those species which at present prevail in America," writing of them "in the language of our country, because I wish to be understood by men of all classes, and by both sexes, altho' it would be easy to clothe them in more technical and learned terms."[5]

Topping the list was "The Negro Mania," an affliction "now confined chiefly to North and South Carolina and Georgia," whose inhabitants all too commonly "*mistake* their interest and happiness in supposing their lands can be cultivated only by negro slaves." Twenty-five other manias followed in no apparent order, Rush's expansive categories at once mirroring and skewering a society suffering from too much freedom. Misuse of time, money, and material resources were designated as diseases. Some involved ruinous pursuits that threatened death or destitution, such as "The Gaming Mania," "The Pleasure Mania," "The Donation Mania," "The Rambling Mania," "The Land Mania," and "The Machine Mania." Others were simply pointless, vain, or eccentric, such as "The Pride Mania" and "The Dress Mania." Looming largest were manias on the subject of government: the undue reverence for human authority of "The Monarchical Mania," the bigotries and aggressions of "The Ecclesiastical Mania" and "The National Mania," the excessive sensibility of "The Humane Mania," the airy speculations of "The Liberty Mania," and the unwarranted optimism of "The Republican Mania." Here his description verged on self-satire: "Every man, who attempts to introduce a republican form of government, where the people are not prepared for it by *virtue* and *knowledge*, is as much a madman as St. Anthony was, when he preached to the fishes." Indeed, Rush submitted that "every man is mad . . . upon some subject," a conclusion that not only accorded with the classificatory principles of Linnaeus but was supported by the authority of Ecclesiastes. The last lines of Rush's letter read more like a minister's peroration than a scientific demonstration: "How great are our obligations to Christianity, which, by enlightening—directing—and regulating our judgments—wills—and passions, in the knowledge—choice—and pursuit of *duty—truth* and *interest,* restores us to what the apostle emphatically calls a 'sound mind.'"[6] Rush understood the varieties of mania he had delineated as manifestations of human nature, which was as prone to illness as to sin. And he saw recovery from delusion as synonymous with redemption. His devout effort to convince himself that the enlightenment brought by Christianity would cure these myriad maladies suggests that he was certain that the people and the polity could not cure themselves. It is his rueful acknowledgment that "every man is mad . . . upon some subject"—implicitly including himself, on the subject of manias—that resonates most powerfully through the nineteenth century.

Rush's reflections on madness and civilization provide an intriguing window into Americans' struggles to make sense of human freedom, agency, and accountability. Shadowing the sovereign, self-disciplined individual, the vaunted subject of dominant political discourse, were the looming threats of mental alienation and social dissolution. Indeed, frenzied figures unmoored from traditional social structures and ways of being ran riot through the public debate and private correspondence of postrevolutionary Americans—sometimes expressly summoned up, at other times appearing unbidden, but always manifesting their profound ambivalence about the agency of self-governing selves, their own included. To their British cousins they appeared presumptuous "lords of themselves, these kings of Me." To the enslaved, as Frederick Douglass memorably put it, they stood in stark contrast to those who "did not even have the privilege of saying 'myself.'" All the while, the supposedly sovereign—and by definition white male—heads of household failed to see how much their lordly status depended upon their ownership and rule over slaves and other dependents, their sense of self inextricably bound up with the lesser persons they conceived of as not-Me. Theirs was an illusory autonomy, built upon a false sense of their own independence, which ensured they could never live up to their own ideals. In sum, their conceptions of themselves were fatally flawed at their very core, both at the level of the liberal Protestant self and at the level of societal conflicts. When the dominant Self is refracted through its entangled relationships with Others, we see most clearly the perplexities that lay within—and, indeed, that these white propertied men themselves were disturbed by such images, which revealed fault lines, vulnerabilities, and contradictions within their supposedly sovereign selves.

In the new republic, what had seemed common sense dissolved into a bewildering diversity of perspectives even among the propertied white men who were assumed to represent the reasonable and responsible person. Rush's taxonomy of the many species of mania in the new nation proved a prescient listing of the various afflictions that were claimed as excusing conditions in nineteenth-century courtrooms by Americans seeking to disqualify themselves or others from the rights and responsibilities of citizenship. Although the doctor had drawn the bounds of the polity to exclude those deprived of their reason, subjecting them to the curative powers of his profession, they were not so clearly identifiable, nor was it was obvious what should be done with those who were only partially insane. Some remained at large, causing harm to property and life, both their own and that of others. Many married and made commercial contracts, failing at all sorts of ventures. Some raised children but cut them out of their wills, perhaps because they had entered into a second childhood. The insane were not easily isolated and contained, socially or psychically, and those who managed the legal system were required to deal with a myriad of questions about their agency and accountability on a disturbingly regular basis.

While the medical jurists who followed Rush were ostensibly concerned with critiquing the common law of capacity and responsibility, they brought to the surface unarticulated premises about the constitution of the competent and accountable person, unwittingly exposing ambiguities and strains in the liberal humanist conception of the self they shared with members of the bench and bar. Like their legal brethren, they understood human nature to be "essentially good, rational, free, and capable of self-government," but they did not as readily conclude that those who deviated from this norm were morally and legally responsible for their failings. To the contrary, alienists suggested that irrationality and lack of self-control might be manifestations of an underlying somatic disease, especially if these partial or total lapses were out of character. Because their science had not yet advanced far enough to provide visual evidence of the underlying physical locus of the disease, they made do with behavioral signs, contending that they provided compelling evidence of the intrusion of a "controlling" disease that took possession of the sufferer's self.

In positing the existence of this "alien persona," Karen Halttunen has argued, medical men did more than simply exonerate afflicted individuals of culpability for their transgressive acts. They also created "a kind of moral quarantine" that contained the threat such behavior posed to "the liberal faith in human nature." Yet even as they set the insane apart as a social type, distinguishable from criminals, the indigent, and the merely eccentric, alienists also chipped away at whatever sense of security their categories provided, redrawing the social geography so as to underscore that everyone was vulnerable to this mental scourge. In works directed toward popular as well as professional audiences, they filled this vast borderland between perfect sanity and total derangement with scientific categories and accompanying descriptions, drawings, and daguerreotypes which challenged traditional ways of seeing the insane in relation to everyone else. Their writings are replete with references to the "thin partitions" separating the sane from the insane, underscoring a common vulnerability: "Every man is interested in this subject; for no man can confidently reckon on the continuance of his perfect reason." Indeed, insanity was all but identified with the human condition as readers were reminded that "no one is of perfectly sound mind but the Deity." In so doing, alienists extended the jurisdiction of their profession to encompass the whole of the population, which not only begged the question of responsibility but pointed toward the paradoxical and unworkable conclusion that the only *fully* accountable agents were those who were constitutionally incapable of violating the laws of God and man.[7]

In retrospect, the embarrassing and irresolvable contests about capacity and responsibility that played out in nineteenth-century courtrooms were, ironically, the by-product of Enlightenment optimism in the form of Common Sense. Members of the bench and bar were schooled in this way of thinking about selfhood, and it shaped their values and expectations of other people. It also informed the way they revised and renovated the English common law, most notably in setting the baseline of legal capacity in terms of mental ability, in defining an "anthropological minimum"[8] that I have called the default legal person. The mind acquired a new salience as an enlightened and acceptable basis for structuring legal relations and discriminating between classes of persons, on the assumption that mental differences were God-given and that each individual was responsible for his or her own self-development. Yet while they often used the word *man* in the generic sense, American jurists retained many of the status hierarchies that served to subordinate married women, children, and slaves, all of whom were conventionally grouped along with insane persons in the earliest commentaries on American law. These jurists projected a model of competence in their own image and treated departures from this norm as deficiencies or defects. Women were figured as weaker in intellect and will, owing in part to their heightened moral and emotional sensibilities, which justified their subordinate status in marriage. People of African descent and indigenous peoples were regarded as intellectually inferior and wanting in a capacity for self-improvement, which provided the basis for arguing for legal restraints. In postrevolutionary America, many jurists regarded the extreme deprivations of enslavement—the denial of self-ownership, bodily integrity, legal marriage, and parenthood—as necessary to social and moral order; after emancipation, they rationalized the imposition of constraints on the basis of an increasingly biologistic definition of racial superiority and inferiority. All the while, the legal definition of insanity expanded to unmanageable bounds, reflecting and exacerbating widespread confusion and uncertainty about the mental prerequisites for legal personhood. Some reformers contended that the possession of rights ought not to turn solely on the capacity to reason, but more fundamentally on sentience, the capacity to feel and suffer pain, a quality that some extended not only to women, children, and the insane but to animals as well. Others held to the standard of rationality and insisted that they were wrongly classed as wanting in intellectual capacity, considering their rights to be violated precisely because they were treated like the insane.[9]

The courtroom contests in which such claims and counterclaims were aired were undeniably staged performances that exaggerated the characteristics of the parties parties involved. Nonetheless, they provide revealing illustrations of the processes of identity formation and social sorting during the formative era of American law as well as the profession of psychiatry. Indeed, these trials constitute defining moments in the history of legal personhood. The arguments, testimony, decisions, news reports, and critical commentaries produced about what it was to be a self-governing self stand as concrete and revealing instances of what Ian Hacking has provocatively described as "making up people": the phenomenon of naming, describing, and accumulating knowledge about different kinds of individuals, effectively introducing new ways to be—or not to be—a person.[10]

The categories of persons constructed and reconstructed in American courtrooms were neither imaginary nor created only in such venues. Rather, they are telling indications of the multiplicity and historicity of ways of comprehending mental difference and disease and they call attention to the roles played by patients, their families, newspaper reporters, and the broader public as well as doctors, lawyers, and judges in determining who is insane. To be sure, the word *insane* and its cognates had been around for centuries, along with lived experiences of mental debility and disorder. But "monomania" and "moral insanity" were not simply new labels for diseases that had an objective existence long before they were discovered and so named by nineteenth-century alienists. While these specialists drew upon and were greatly influenced by the legal doctrines and folk beliefs they purported to explode, their classification schemes did not map precisely onto the territory covered by previous definitions and diagnoses. To the contrary, their tendency to conceive of these forms of insanity as disease entities, as pathological deviations from a normal state that were curable by scientific means, was expressive of a more general reorientation towards human nature, which was increasingly viewed as dynamic and malleable rather than fixed and embedded in a divinely determined universe. The concept of normality gradually displaced nature in discourse about human kinds in the middle decades of the century as evolutionary ideas began to take hold, marking "a shift in the locus of faith from a God-centered to a human-centered world, from a culture that looked within to a core and backward to lost Edenic origins toward one that looked outward and forward to a perfected future."[11]

Indeed, the alienists' disease entities took on a life of their own. As historian Charles Rosenberg has put it, they came to operate as "social realities, actors in complex and multidimensional negotiations that configure and reconfigure the lives of real men and women." These medicalized concepts worked to naturalize and legitimate conventional ways of understanding and treating human difference and deviance. At the same time, however, they were prone to destabilize and problematize them, particularly insofar as they gave credence to new social and biological determinisms that challenged the notion of self-making itself. As the alienists' taxonomies became part of the cultural lexicon, they profoundly altered "the space of possibilities for personhood," inducing changes in the self-conceptions and behavior of the people so classified. The responsiveness of the labeled to this labeling process made them "moving targets" from the standpoint of clinicians, who were tasked with continually revising their classifications and theories as a result of these dynamics.[12]

The *law* of persons added another layer of complexity to these alienists' efforts to give rules to folly. Though manifestly influenced by the new medical psychology as well as broader social, political, and economic forces, this body of judicial decisions, statutes, and learned commentaries constituted a distinct conceptual scheme with its own purposes, logics, and instrumentalities. Moreover, the modernization of the law of persons *non compos mentis* was inextricably bound up with legal controversies about other traditional status regimes, most notably those concerning slavery and marriage. It is surely no coincidence that the legal definition of insanity underwent a marked expansion in the so-called age of emancipation, supplying conservative elites with new means of rationalizing racial and gender hierarchies and legitimating their own privileged position within a liberalizing legal order. Alienists could be cited to support the proposition that African Americans were not fit to withstand the trials of freedom; asylum statistics might be summoned up to show that abolition had yielded "a beautiful harvest of mental and physical degeneration," that the freedman was "now becoming a martyr to an heredity thus established," destined to die off or revert to primitive savagery. This imagined fate bears striking similarities to that of Native Americans, who represented the continent's indigenous "savages"; these vanquished tribes were now proclaimed to be "vanishing" in the face of competition from white settlers despite futile efforts to "civilize" them. Medical authorities could likewise be summoned up regarding the peculiar vulnerabilities of women, who could not participate in activities that taxed the intellect without running the risk of mental disorder and reproductive damage, though their exclusion from the political arena was usually rendered by conservatives as "a noble sort of disenfranchisement," wholly unlike that of "the pauper, the criminal, the insane," who were "*set aside* as persons not human."[13]

But these group-based theories of mental difference and deficiency were eminently contestable, and the moral valence and legal significance to be attached to the fact of insanity remained exceedingly ambiguous, not least because "the insane" was not as determinate a category of persons as it was sometimes made out to be. Nor could lunatics or people suffering from delusions and monomanias be simply identified with "the dangerous and defective classes," exiled from the human family, or pronounced civilly dead. To be sure, the linkages between insanity, poverty, and crime gained credence with the spread and popularization of the evolutionary theories of Charles Darwin and Herbert Spencer, especially as others ominously spun them out in terms of degeneracy.[14] Yet all the while insanity remained complexly intertwined with civilization, ironically assuming "epidemic" proportions among the white propertied men and women who seemed to have worked the hardest in their separate spheres to conform to the moral prescriptions set out in textbooks and advice manuals. They were the ones whose minds were most often placed in issue in late nineteenth-century capacity contests, presenting the most arresting challenge to law's presumption of sanity as well as the ethos of self-making upon which it was premised.

The Crucible of the Courtroom

To place the mind in issue in American courtrooms was always and unavoidably to beg the question of what it meant to be human. It was also to raise fundamental questions about human difference and inequality, as insanity trials were crucial testing grounds of the liberal faith in the individual capacity for self-government. In the crucible of the courtroom, Americans attempted to forge a common sense of the subject of responsibility, civil as well as criminal. Yet consensus proved maddeningly elusive, for the situations presented were so varied, the causes and meanings of capacity so context-specific, that these cases could not be systematized into a "law of insanity" in any meaningful sense. In fact, many were reluctantly compelled to concur with the leading authorities on medical jurisprudence that "no absolute rule can be laid down" to differentiate insanity from eccentricity or depravity—that "each case must be judged on its own facts." The insane never were or could be as determinate a category of persons as children, married women, and slaves because the mental manifestations of this disease were widely understood to take as many forms as they were individuals; it was commonly said that "the vagaries of insanity are as varied as are our faces," and some acknowledged that the diagnoses of these maladies could be as varied as the number of observers.

Judges took these facts of the matter to heart, accepting them as unavoidable byproducts of the liberal legal order they struggled to maintain, acutely aware that they were not themselves immune to mental disease or exempt from having their perfect reasonableness called into question by others. Because the insane remained a seemingly limitless legal category that defied delimitation, judges thought differently about them as compared with other classes of individuals that were marginal to or excluded from full and independent personhood. The strategies of differentiation applied to these other classes—the tendency to project "the finitude, imperfections, sensuality, self-mockery and depravity of human nature" onto slave and free black people, "thereby amplifying the opposite qualities in the white race" and reaffirming "the vision of classless opportunity" for white men, all the while subjecting Native Americans, married women, and children to similar treatment—did not work when it came to the insane. Because judges knew they were susceptible to insanity in a way they were not to these other conditions, the insane presented more of a direct threat to their self-image. Most courts gravitated toward the notion of a radical and unaccountable change in character as the most serviceable definition of insanity as a matter of law, but this was really no solution, as it did not address the issue of responsibility for diminished capacity or even for character. Judges were skeptical of the notion that self-consistency was a reliable sign of sanity, not only because evangelical Protestants as well as more unconventional religious seekers so commonly experienced new births and changes of heart, but also because there was such a thing as "insane character" that remained as fixed as rationality in the common sense renderings of the default legal person. Their decisions are thus shot through with apprehensions about human nature, insanity as they defined it expressing everything these professional men feared might be universal rather than exceptional. In the end, this was what came of the effort to organize oddity.[15]

Rather than confront the ultimate questions posed by such trials, American judges and jurists equivocated on the subject of legal personhood, pronouncing in one breath that "medical science is part of the common law of the land" only to insist in the next that "the law is not a medical or metaphysical science." Standardizing the legal person proved ever more challenging in an industrializing nation that continued to celebrate its diversity and privilege the ideal of the autonomous individual even as it centralized and bureaucratized its systems of governance, erected new barriers to immigration, and absorbed the deterministic teachings of a new generation of neurologists, psychologists, social scientists, and criminologists, many of whom were downright derisive about the concept of free will. Proceeding in a positivistic spirit, these students of human behavior focused their inquiries on observable phenomenon with the aim of generating empirically verifiable principles that were of practical utility, commanding assent, forging consensus, and reliably guiding social policy. Those trained in these disciplines repudiated the faculty psychology upon which the field of medical jurisprudence was founded, casting philosophical efforts to construct an "Ideal Standard Man" as quixotic at best and favoring laboratory techniques and statistical methods as the most promising means of measuring and making sense of mental abnormality. This way of being scientific appealed to many Gilded Age jurists, including Oliver Wendell Holmes. His 1881 study of *The Common Law* traced the movement from subjective to objective norms, a transformation in American law he equated with the passage "from barbarism to civilization." But the reasonable man he proposed as a standard in the pages of this monumental work was not exactly a statistical subject and as his judicial posture took on the quality of a "detached Olympian skepticism," he expressed in his private correspondence a willingness to leave "a loophole for free will," recognizing that "we don't know whether anything is necessary or not." Musing about the latest philosophical disputations concerning the mind-body relation in a letter to Morris Cohen in 1920, Holmes rendered his settled judgment: "I don't perceive why there is any more right to think away consciousness than there is to think way nerve tissue—the total is the datum."[16]

From the perspective of those who worked at the intersection of law and medicine on behalf of the insane, however, the reasonableness standard was part of the problem they labored to redress in their testimony and tracts on the subject of responsibility. The persistence with which common law judges held to a liberal Protestant conception of the self, allowing the default legal person to stand in for most anyone, was a source of increasing frustration and puzzlement to medical jurists across the century, for the more they worked to bring to light the varieties of mental disorder that lay between the extremes of perfect sanity and raving lunacy, the more courts seemed to strengthen the law's presumption of sanity. Yet the medico-legal literature was far from clear about what distinguished the realm of the normal from the pathological, and most alienists retained strong allegiances to the ethos of self-made manhood even as they documented its debilitating effects.

No one exhibited the self-contradictory position of the medical jurist with greater clarity and vigor than the eminent, albeit controversial, British psychiatrist Henry Maudsley. His 1874 treatise, *Responsibility in Mental Disease*, was a lightning rod on both sides of the Atlantic, as he arrestingly spoke of "the tyranny of organization," a phrase that actually made him sound more deterministic than he really was, for he believed in the inheritance of acquired characteristics and his model of the mind retained "an important, even decisive, role for self-mastery and self-creation."[17] Yet what most concerns us here are the ways he figured the insane in relation to the rest of us, for they illustrate the funhouse mirror effect of the alienist's reflections on the subject. While the general public continued to harbor all sorts of erroneous notions about the insane, expecting them to look like wild beasts and thus prompted to wonder where all the inmates were when they visited asylums, experienced practitioners knew better than to expect that they would find "a new world and a new race of beings" behind their walls. Madmen, as a rule, "were not at all like the pictures which Hogarth painted of them," Maudsley informed his readers, suggesting that a "skilled observer" would instead find man *exaggerated*: "'In such a house the traits are stronger, the colours more vivid, the shades more marked, the effects more startling, because man is seen in all his nakedness, because he does not dissimulate his thoughts, because he does not conceal his defects, because he lends not to his passions the charm which seduces, nor to his vices the appearances which deceive.'"[18] Without pausing here to consider whether any of this was owing to proverbial "cunning of the insane," a topic of great concern in the medico-legal literature of the day and noted elsewhere in this work, his observations beg the question of whether he had lulled himself into a false sense of the legibility of his patients' illnesses.

The misconceptions that Maudsley was most interested in correcting in *Responsibility in Mental Disease* were those that were frustrating the administration of justice in Anglo-American courtrooms. Written for a general readership, his work is a concerted attack on "the metaphysical spirit" that "still inspires the criterion of responsibility which is sanctioned and acted upon by courts of justice in cases of insanity." He lamented the tendency of judges to rely on the "one-sided" method of "mental introspection," each looking only "into his own mind and propounding as philosophy what he thought he observed there," without attending to the insights of physiological psychology, to the progress that scientists were making in delineating "the bodily conditions of all mental action," normal as well as pathological. "The conclusions reached by the observations of self-consciousness in a sane mind are strictly applied to the phenomena of diseased mind," Maudsley complained, "not otherwise than as if it were solemnly enacted that the disorder and violence of convulsions should be measured by the order and method of voluntary movements, and that whosoever, being seized with convulsions, and knowing that he was convulsed, transgressed that measure, should be punished as a criminal." This stance failed to make allowances for those who deviated from the requirements of law and morals "not because they *would* not, but because they *could* not," demonstrating the dangers of generalizing from one's own mental experience. Thinking this way also perpetuated the stereotyping of the insane as raving lunatics, leading members of the bench and bar to characterize the insane mind as nothing like their own. "The ideal madman whom the law creates is supposed to act without motives, or from such motives as it enters not into the mind of a sane person to conceive," Maudsley observed, "and if some one, who is plainly mad to all the world, acts from an ordinary motive in the preparation of an offence, he is presumed to have acted sanely and with full capacity of responsibility." This view was doubly wrong because "the insane have like passions with those who are not insane, and are restrained from doing wrong, and constrained to do right, by the same motives which have the same effects in sane persons" but "these motives are only effective within limits," beyond which "they become powerless, the hope of reward being of no avail, and the expectation or infliction of punishment actually provoking more unreason and violence."[19]

Seeming to apprehend that he had related the insane too closely to the rest of the human family, Maudsley immediately added: "And yet, although in much so like, how different is the madman essentially! Be the change in him what it may, it is plain that he has fallen from man's high estate, that he is no longer one with his kind, that he has lost the highest human attributes—those by which man is what he is among animals. Learned men may dispute concerning the nature and extent of the change; but the wayfaring man, though a fool, cannot fail to perceive it. Nor does the change fail to influence him: deep in his heart there is generated an instinctive feeling of distrust, if not actual repugnance; he recoils in spite of himself from the distortion of humanity." Within the bosom of even the most benevolent and enlightened of humanitarians who had done the most to ameliorate the condition of the insane "there is a dim but deep instinct that this is not a disease which is quite like other diseases, that a man by it 'from himself is ta'en away,' alienated from himself and from his kind, and that he is something of a reproach to the nature of humanity; the result being a vague feeling of antipathy like that which the lower animals display towards one of their kind that has fallen ill." This repugnance might be seen as "curious evidence of the operation of the law of natural selection," to the extent that the mentally diseased were deemed "unfitted for the natural functions of its kind" and "instinctively extruded from companionship." But this was not the story of human progress as Maudsley narrated it. He held that theology, with its notion of insanity as demonic possession, and its successor, metaphysics, which had merely secularized that notion, were to blame for the repulsion so widely felt toward the insane. Maudsley confidently maintained that insanity could and should be medically treated like any other affliction of the body, almost normalizing the disease as he emphasized the physical constraints on all human beings: "The metaphysical notion of man as an abstract being endowed with a certain fixed moral potentiality to do the right and eschew the wrong, is as little applicable to each human being born into the world as the notion of a certain fixed intellectual power would be applicable to each being, whether of good mental capacity, imbecile, or idiot." Yet what he called "emancipation" would only be complete with the full acknowledgment of human limits. "A true reformation would be the *re*-forming of the individual nature," he asserted, "and how can that which has been forming through generations be *re*-formed within the term of a single life? Can the Ethiopian change his skin or the leopard his spots?" While there was a place for education in his scientific project, its first and most important mission was to "determine what is predetermined," there being no way to "make a Socrates or a Shakespeare of every being born into the world."[20]

In sounding these notes, Maudsley marked the distance he had traveled from prescriptive writers even as he strangely echoed them: "When will man learn that he is at the head of nature only by virtue of the operation of natural laws? When will he learn that by the study of these laws and by deliberate conformity to them he may become the conscious framer of his own destiny?" What really distinguishes his perspective is that it bears the imprint of an industrialized society where madmen and criminals were increasingly coming to be seen as social products. He took these classes of person to be "as much manufactured articles as are steam-engines and calico-printing machines," maintaining with greater assurance than many could muster that "there are neither accidents nor anomalies in the universe, but come by law and testify to causality; and it is the business of science to find out what causes are and by what laws they work." For those who found the physicalism of the human sciences in the last decades of the nineteenth century more threatening, and this included most members of the American legal profession, there may have been something strangely attractive about the unruliness of the insane. The ambivalence with which even Maudsley continued to regard the insane may well have arisen from an inability to resolve the paradoxes inherent in the fragile but persistent concept of the unique and autonomous self within a universe that seemed both determined and irreducibly unpredictable.[21]

The problem of insanity as it played out in nineteenth-century courtrooms is ultimately best understood as an episode in the age-old struggle to determine the nature and limits of human freedom and responsibility. The form these trials took owed much to the market culture in which they were embedded and more particularly to the phenomenon that Thomas L. Haskell has termed "interdependence," referring to the growing consciousness of social interconnectedness in this period and the concomitant questioning of the bounds of autonomous action. Freedom and fate became "two sides of the same coin" because the market fosters a debate between formalism and antiformalism, making possible "the emergence of a game of causal attribution whose rules are sufficiently indeterminate that every event has both 'formal' and 'deep' interpretations, and which therefore allows for the emergence of rival elites, each committed to its own mode of explanation."[22] This formulation perfectly describes the game that opposing counselors routinely played with the assistance of medical experts in nineteenth-century capacity contests, helping to explain why they so often devolved into what Charles E. Rosenberg has so aptly characterized as "amorphous sessions in competitive biography."[23] Though audiences within and beyond the courthouse had good reason to view these performances with jaundiced eyes, they are nonetheless revealing from a historical standpoint, suggesting that the self was a precarious possession in nineteenth-century America. The deterministic stories told during the course of these trials shine considerable light on the meaning of individualism in this era, underscoring how difficult it was to live up to the cultural ideal of personal sovereignty. Yet they also double as cautionary tales that remain applicable today. For they illustrate the perils of according priority to deeper explanations, which provide only a different perspective that threatens selfhood if taken too far. As Haskell incisively observes: "When we set about the destructive work of stripping away the masks that shelter someone else's self from the world, we should do so in the full knowledge that we, too, rely on a conception of self that, when stripped of all claims to autonomy, ceases to exist."[24] The law reports of the nineteenth century suggest that judges were ever mindful of this peril, endeavoring in case after case to steer clear of the threatening prospects of determinism and indeterminism.

Although Ecclesiastes was never cited, the path of the law of insanity over the course of the nineteenth century might be read as a confirmation of the madness of mankind. Unable to sustain the certitudes of Common Sense or to completely incorporate medical explanations of human behavior, Gilded Age judges developed a new way of thinking about the old problem of evil, incorporating more and more forms of human perversity into the default legal person that set the baseline of mental competence. As they adopted this stance, these judges knew they had not come close to resolving the puzzles of human freedom and responsibility or warding off the twin threats of solipsism and determinism. They had come to see that rationality was a matter of perspective and to accept that there was much that could never be known about another mind. So they fortified the presumption of sanity even as they recognized that no one has a perfectly sound mind, primarily because of the value they continued to place on the unrealizable ideal of human autonomy. They deployed the presumption of sanity to cover many sins. In so doing, they displayed an acute awareness that a transcendental realm of truth might well be unattainable.[25]

Here they anticipated Oliver Wendell Holmes's famous statement about the "bad man" at the turn of the twentieth century. In the judicial opinions they have left behind, we can see indications that they had grasped what William James later took to be the essence of pragmatism: "The trail of the human serpent is over everything." From where they were sitting, this inference must have been almost irresistible.

Modernity, Mind, and the Law

The letters about the human condition that Holmes and James exchanged never shared anything resembling Rush's confidence in the benevolence of the universe. "I suppose you are sinking ever deeper into the sloughs of the law," James wrote his "dear Wendle" in January 1868 from Berlin, where he was ostensibly engaged in medical study but actually, he confessed, submerged "in the dismalest of dumps." Offering a buoy he surely needed more than his friend Holmes, James half-seriously proposed a new intellectual venture. "When I get home let's establish a philosophical society to have regular meetings and discuss none but the very tallest and broadest questions—to be composed of none but the very topmost cream of Boston manhood." "It will give each one a chance to air his own opinion in a grammatical form, and to sneer and chuckle when he goes home at what damned fools all the other members are—and may grow into something very important after a sufficient number of years." And so they did. As the philosopher Charles Sanders Peirce recalled in 1907, "It was in the earliest seventies that a knot of us young men in Old Cambridge, calling ourselves, half-ironically, half-defiantly 'The Metaphysical Club,'—for agnosticism was then riding its high horse, and was frowning superbly upon all metaphysics,—used to meet, sometimes in my study, sometimes in that of William James." The words and syntax they chose were a deeply significant part of their endeavor to make their ideas clear to each other. So, too, they command our attention as we take stock of what they made of themselves and the subject of responsibility in an era where historians have located "the origins of modern consciousness."[26]

"Metaphysical" was a term of abuse hurled most readily and contemptuously by the practitioners of positive science at all those who found their picture of the universe incomplete. The word had been given new currency at midcentury by the French philosopher Auguste Comte, whose evolutionary account of "the development of human intelligence" identified three successive stages: "the theological or fictive, the metaphysical or abstract, and the scientific or positive." In this sequence, the metaphysical referred to a transitional period in which critical reasoning displaced theological speculation, substituting natural entities for the supernatural deities originally used by the primitive mind to personify causal forces. This shift effectively drained the former deities of "the power and stability" that were "indispensable for their effective authority" and prepared the way for philosophical "manhood," when genuine knowledge was finally understood to be obtainable only from observable phenomena. Although Comte's thought came to most Americans secondhand through the writings of English philosophers such as J. S. Mill and Herbert Spencer, his schema expressed a broader reconfiguration of ideas about science and religion in the late nineteenth century.[27]

A deeply disquieting sense of the arbitrariness of human existence came to pervade the thinking of many educated Americans, gradually but inexorably chipping away at whatever remained of the certitudes of the Common Sense philosophy. Beliefs in the autonomy of the individual and the correspondence of moral and material progress were difficult to square with the facts of life as they experienced them, appearing most conspicuously and troublingly in the form of disabled Civil War veterans, victims of industrial accidents, and corpulent robber barons, none of whom could be confidently said to have gotten what they deserved. There were also less visible but undeniable signs that work and reward were not as closely related as had been hoped. Indeed, the mounting numbers of "mental wrecks" crowding the asylums represented ample reason for thinking that the moral philosophers' ethos of self-determination was self-defeating. Perhaps the most telling statistic was the increasing incidence of "neurasthenia," a new disease popularized by the neurologist George M. Beard's 1881 work *American Nervousness*, in which he declared the malady's "chief and primary cause" was "modern civilization," observing with a strange sort of pride that its main sufferers were "brain workers" who were "most frequently met in civilised, intellectual communities." William James, one of his most famous patients, spoke of the condition somewhat less patriotically as "Americanitis." James questioned whether Beard and others studying neurasthenia were not "mistaking a symptom for a cause," possessed as he was of the painful knowledge that this was "but one factor of a much more complex ailment."[28]

Beard's diagnosis was not completely novel. The pathogenic potential of civilization was apprehended from the nation's founding, and statesmen, ministers, moralists, and medical men all sounded variations on this theme through the century that followed. Yet the "nervous exhaustion" that was particular to neurasthenia manifestly differed from the "passion for liberty" Rush had named *anarchia*. It was deliberately set apart from all the species of mania and phobia that alienists had added to the lexicon in their increasingly strained efforts to diagnose and treat an expanding patient population and address knotty questions of capacity and responsibility when called to the stand and the wider bar of public opinion. Nuerologists like Beard promised deliverance from "the problem of insanity" that asylums and their superintendents had manifestly failed to solve. Drawing inspiration and assurance from European laboratory experiments concerning cerebral anatomy and physiology, American medical practitioners who formed the subfield of neurology exuded a distinctly positivist faith in the lawfulness of universe, believing that the mysteries of the mind could be solved by jettisoning the "transcendental" abstractions of the faculty psychology upon which the jurisprudence of insanity was based.

Relentlessly reductive, Beard so completely exemplified and embodied the tendencies of the era and his chosen profession as to stand as a representative man and an object lesson, almost amounting to a caricature of himself. His life's work blurred the line between the normal and the pathological, constituting an answer of sorts to the question posed as the title of one his earliest popular pieces, "Who of Us Are Insane?" Many more than was commonly thought, he fearlessly reported, as if it were a startling exposé rather than a truism of antebellum medical psychology. By the time he wrote, the fact that insanity was a matter of degree was widely accepted; no one, save God, had a perfectly sound mind. Yet, despite his propensity to overstate the originality of his ideas, Beard was more thoroughgoing in his physicalism than the medico-legal thinkers he claimed to have superseded. Certain that his was "the one science of the future," he set out to breach what Maudsley called "the absolute and unholy barrier set up between physical and psychical nature" and was poised to storm "the mysterious citadel of the will." He optimistically hailed the gradual emancipation of his countrymen from "the slavery to the delusion in the belief in what is called the will" and pressed onward with his scientific endeavor "to study the limitations of the human brain—to analyze and organize its weaknesses, its blunders, and its diseases."[29]

What, then, became of the matter of human responsibility? If "the Free Will question" had been definitively answered in the negative and "our volitional life" proved to be far more constrained than previously admitted, what sense could there be in holding individuals morally or even legally accountable for their actions? Here neurologists hedged and equivocated, some with profound discomfort, others more concerned with keeping up appearances, and still others without seeming to realize they were giving up the game. Though ridicule and criticism of judicial tests of capacity and responsibility came easily to their lips, particularly with respect to the "legal dogma" that insanity was not to be found where there was knowledge of right and wrong, few went so far as to say publically that there was no such thing as human responsibility. Visibly struggling with the ethical implications of their explorations of the complex interrelation of mind, body, and behavior, they anxiously "tread a tightrope between materialism and automatism on the one side and unscientific metaphysics on the other." The more deterministic were their conclusions about the environmental and hereditary influences impinging upon the individual, the more concern they voiced about education and discipline, though increasingly with the aim of recharging or regenerating rather than containing and channeling "the volitional powers." That phrase no longer carried the implication of free will, but indicated the ability to take decisive action, which in some cases seemed to have been depleted to the point of utter prostration. Self-consciously distinguishing their mental models from the Common Sense dualism and moralism, these men of science privileged the results of the laboratory over the products of introspection. Yet even as they recast the brain as a storehouse of nervous energy, they suggested it could be trained like other muscles, implying there were ways and means by which individuals as well as their physicians could prevent insanity and promote mental health. For example, Beard took the "fear of responsibility" as a symptom of neurasthenia and aimed to rejuvenate these "self-made invalids," leaving it to members of the bench and bar to decide who among the mentally ill was to be relieved from responsibility, which he took to be "really a legal rather than a medical word."[30]

Dividing the professional labor in this manner had a ring of false modesty, and it might be regarded as an evasive move characteristic of a generation who felt simultaneously obliged to ask and unable to answer what James spoke of as "the very tallest and broadest questions" about the universe. It is telling that the storied philosophical society whose formation he proposed while he was abroad and on the edge of a mental breakdown—significantly, one that was at least partially brought on by his exposure to the new physiological psychology—proved a rather short-lived endeavor, as the primary site of intellectual work was moving in the last third of the nineteenth century from such informal, clubby gatherings to research-oriented universities. In these decades, clerics were gradually displaced by academic administrators with a more secular orientation, seeking to raise the nation's "stock of talent" and equip their graduates with the competence to be leaders of this complex industrial society. Moral philosophy was no longer considered the capstone of the curriculum within these institutions of higher learning, as their missions were redefined in terms of science rather than theology and restructured in accordance with a more impersonal set of standards, reflecting an altered conception of merit that privileged "exact" knowledge acquired by means of specialized academic training in order to address the proliferating problems of the modern world.[31]

Betwixt and between these momentous changes in the modes of pursuing knowledge and professions in the United States, the members of the Metaphysical Club were drawn together by the same forces that rendered their intellectual association unsustainable. The core group was evenly split between scientists and lawyers who relished opportunities "to spar, or at any rate excite each other to all sorts of ideas and expressions." But it proved increasingly difficult to fit discussions of these sorts into a professional life. Coming of age in an era when so much was perceived to be new and increasingly said to be so in uppercase letters—"The

New South," "The New Education," "The New Thought," "The New Psychology," "The New Woman," "The New Negro," "The New Nationalism," "The New Freedom"—the men of the Metaphysical Club struggled mightily with a perennial problem in American culture which Louis Menand has aptly called "the metaphysics of the relations between fathers and sons." Becoming a professional in the specialized, compartmentalized, scientized sense of the word was one way of managing this perpetual crisis of authority and life's bewildering uncertainties.[32]

This path would have been especially appealing to both Holmes and James, who had grown up in privileged households headed by zealous men whose uncontained, exuberant, almost carnivalesque intellectual energies (expressions of their own forms of rebellion against the stern Calvinism of their youth) propelled their sons into careers with more determinate limits. Unlike his father, a famed conversationalist who was also "one of the last true generalists, crusading all his life against encroaching specialization among lawyers, clergymen, scientists or doctors," Oliver Wendell Holmes Jr. distinguished himself as "a real concentrator of thought." His Civil War experience had taught him the limits of logic and the value of expertise. Obsessed with making his vocational mark by the age of forty, he penned *The Common Law* to enshrine an "external standard" of liability. Holmes heroically endeavored to define objective standards for subjective states but had to acknowledge their limits, given the diversity among individuals and the instability of ascriptive social classes.[33]

William James took longer to find his own groove as a scientist, owing in part to his rather eclectic education before he started his medical training at Harvard in 1861. He was on the front lines of the transatlantic debates about Darwin's theories. Under the tutelage of Holmes Sr., who dodged the sorts of questions about mind, matter, and scientific method that most interested James, he "drifted into psychology and philosophy by a sort of fatality." Yet it was his extraordinary indecisiveness—as compared with most anyone, but particularly his friend Wendell—that ultimately fit James for the academic discipline he successfully carved out for himself. His pragmatism constituted an answer to old and new dilemmas of determinism, built upon the will to believe in free will and a conception of human freedom that doubled as a coping mechanism, constituting a novel way of dealing with the essential uncertainty of the universe and the individual's place within it. Although holding that "certainty generally is an illusion," the tough-minded Holmes was more willing to bet that there was no such thing as free will and found himself less and less interested in arguing with James about it. The two men grew more distant in every way as they both achieved eminence in their increasingly separate professions.[34]

Though the estrangement between Holmes and James may be traced to temperamental differences, the fraying of their friendship and the fate of their philosophical society also reflected deepening strains and fault lines in medico-legal relations at the turn of the century. The stereoscopic vision that Francis Wharton and Moreton Stillé projected in their 1855 *Treatise on Medical Jurisprudence* proved exceedingly difficult to effectuate in courtrooms where the mind was placed in issue. Even the judges who shared the authors' conviction that "medical science is a part of the common law of the land, and is to be treated as such" proved unable to decide whether insanity was properly understood as a question of fact, law, or medicine, and the problem was exacerbated by the doctors' propensity to disagree among themselves. The prospects for realizing the civic ends of medical jurists dimmed all the more with the reorganization of universities, as leaders in the field tried and failed to obtain a foothold in the new university structures. While medical jurisprudence had been one of the nine areas in which William James was examined before he received an MD from Harvard, the number of professorships and courses in the field steadily declined with the reorganization of medical schools in the years that followed, and it never attained the status of a core course in the estimation of law faculty.[35]

Some indication of how the first generation of academic lawyers regarded medical jurisprudence can be gleaned from the reviews of leading texts that Holmes and Green contributed to the *American Law Review* in this era. Holmes bluntly questioned whether the English physician Albert Swaine Taylor's "'Medical Jurisprudence' is, in fact, a legitimate title, either in law or medicine," the union between the two fields striking him as superficial from the standpoint of both theory and practice. Green amplified this judgment in his consideration of the latest editions of works by John Elwell and Isaac Ray: "It is difficult to see how 'medical jurisprudence,' so called, ever came to be considered a branch of law," for however useful it might be for lawyers to know something of other arts and sciences, that was no warrant for composing an entire *jurisprudence* on a given subject like medicine, and readers were not to be fooled into thinking the works under review were true "books of science." He issued this warning: "Any lawyer who rests content with the smattering of knowledge to be got from any medical jurisprudence may have the pleasant feeling that he is astonishing the bystanders by his show of learning; but must also have at heart the unpleasant feeling that he is a humbug." The whole enterprise seemed to him a wrongheaded attempt to unify professionals manifestly aiming at different and sometimes cross-purposes, as medicine revolved around the needs of the individual patient, while law was made to order and protect "society at large." To substantiate this point, Green offered a disquisition on "insanity in its relation to the law," which lampooned the physicians' misplaced criticisms of the common law's differential tests of civil and criminal accountability and underscored the problems of definition: "What is insanity? There is no rule by which it can be measured, so that one can say this is, and this is not insanity. . . . Generally, too, in speaking of insanity one speaks of the 'will;' but the word *will* is perhaps the vaguest and most complex of any in the language." The difficulty with insanity, as Green saw it, is "continually recurring in law" and "pervades all matters of human investigation. All things in nature, all things external, all ideas, all sensations, all emotions, shade into each other by imperceptible degrees. No absolute lines can be drawn. Things are separated from one another by a debatable ground. The difficulty is inherent in the nature of man." His bottom line was exactly what was to be expected from a foe of formalism:

> Insanity cannot be known till we know what sanity is; nor can the laws which govern the modes of mind called insanity be known till we have a well-established psychology. The mind itself is a metaphysical abstraction; it does not exist as an entity. No man knows the nature of it. Mental action, as far as at present known, is dependent on nervous structure. . . . Between the highest and finest intellect and the lowest maniac there are many gradations of infinitely complex modes of mental action. It must be impossible to draw any line upon one side of which shall lie the sane, and upon the other the insane.[36]

The more problematic insanity was seen to be, the more fractious the relations became between and among doctors and lawyers. Medico-legal societies sprouted up in growing numbers in the 1870s and 1880s, seemingly to compensate for the lack of space accorded for their activities within the confines of universities, but they struggled to stay afloat financially and ran aground whenever they attempted any sort of reform of the judicial tests of capacity and responsibility. By the 1890s, the famous Medico-Legal Society of the City of New York had largely devolved into an elite supper club superintended by the corporate attorney Clark Bell, who had to admit that the field was "drowning in a sea of disease conditions and diagnostic categories," which now encompassed "introspective insanity" and "the insanity of doubt." Alienists and neurologists were barely on speaking terms. In 1894 the prominent neurologist S. Weir

Mitchell devoted his keynote address on the fiftieth anniversary of the founding of the American Association of Asylum Superintendents to a frontal attack on asylum medicine. Mitchell's critique helped to initiate significant structural changes in the way mental disorders were conceptualized and treated. The association changed its name to the American Psychiatric Association in 1921, and the *American Journal of Insanity* was reborn as the *American Journal of Psychiatry* in the same year. Confirming this set of developments and suggesting its implications for law, the asylum superintendent William A. White explicitly disclaimed insanity as a medical term in his 1923 treatise on *Insanity and the Criminal Law*. "Insanity is a purely legal concept and means irresponsibility, or incapacity for making a will, or for entering a contractual relationship." When he looked beneath the surface of the related term *responsibility*, self-consciously doing so in the capacity of a professional psychologist, he found that it was not an attribute inhering in the person, but instead "something which is projected upon him by the herd."[37]

The turn of the twentieth century appears to have been marked by a rupture in thinking about selfhood and responsibility. Approaching the subject autobiographically in *The Education of Henry Adams*, the Henry Adams chronicled the evolution of his own thinking about the mind, arriving at the conclusion that sanity was an "acquired habit" and suggesting that "normal thought" was a precarious balancing act as he likened the self to "an acrobat, with a dwarf on his back, crossing a chasm on a slack-rope, and commonly breaking his neck." With a greater sense of historical distance, the sociologically minded jurist Roscoe Pound viewed the nineteenth century as a time when "metaphysical jurists . . . strove valiantly but vainly to put the whole law in terms of the will." In *Law and the Modern Mind*, Jerome Frank added a psychoanalytic gloss, diagnosing their professional work as expressive of unconscious yearnings to "recapture, through a rediscovery of a father, a childish, completely controllable universe." Yet Frank preached self-reliance as a corrective, commending the models of both James and Holmes and paying particular tribute to the latter as "The Completely Adult Jurist." While their renderings of the lawyers, judges, and jurists who have peopled the pages of this book are exaggerated in many respects, there is a measure of truth in the label "metaphysical" as applied to these nineteenth-century men. For in their daily work on the bench and at the bar, particularly when the mind was placed in issue, they wrestled mightily with what were truly existential dilemmas, even as they insisted law was a "practical" science. Their protestations to the contrary notwithstanding, the law reports and treatises in which they recorded their impressions about the cases and controversies of their day show that these men were worrying through age-old conundrums about freedom, determinism, and the grounds of human responsibility.[38]

While their literary remains might not provide historians with the same sorts of insights into law and life that can be obtained from the works of men like Emerson, Melville, James, or, for that matter, Holmes, they are impressive in their own way. The form of closure the law provides does not resolve the conundrums brought to the surface in insanity trials, but this study has shown the significant cultural work these jurists performed. If they do not compare with the penetration and insight of contemporary philosophical and literary works about human freedom and responsibility, they nonetheless modeled a practical way of living with the uncertainty and terrors of everyday existence, particularly the threats that lurked within the mind. Indeed, many of these judges were alive to "all the subtle stratagems, passive as well as aggressive; to all the interpersonal knots and invisible webs of ensnarement which are so much a part of the psychopathology of our everyday lives," insights historians tend to credit only to "poets, novelists, and exceptionally perceptive psychiatrists" but not the common run of common law judges.[39]

Their pronouncements of practicality have misled us into assuming legal thought and practice were not places where much was done by way of deep thinking about the human condition. Mining literary and philosophical sources for the roots of major intellectual movements known under the signs of Pragmatism and Existentialism, we have failed to notice the ways in which these problems were being considered every day in courthouses across the country. Over the course of the long nineteenth century, in a republic united, divided, reunited, and reconstructed, insanity trials were no mere sideshows, though judges understandably tried to ward off the specter of the madman as best they could, supplying through their modes of doctrinal reasoning a means of keeping afloat amidst the tumults of ordinary life. That they did not completely succeed in this regard is amply recorded in nineteenth-century treatises, law reports, and trial transcripts, where we find men and women of all ages wondering out loud what they were to make of the "visitation of God" they renamed "mental alienation," betraying in their own words the same yearnings and doubts found in the works of literary artists like Emerson, Thoreau, and Melville. While it would be too much to say that the metaphysical jurists who presided over these trials and attempted to reckon with the damage monomaniacs did to themselves and others were the heroes of the story this book has told, it is fair to say that more often than not they played the part of Ishmael to Melville's Ahab, buoying up a crazed culture by stopping short of the conclusion the author conveyed through the voice of a supposed idiot, "the little negro" called mad by his shipmates, the cabin boy Pip: "So man's insanity is heaven's sense, and wandering from all mortal reason, man comes at last to that celestial thought, which, to reason, is absurd and frantic; and weal or woe, feels then uncompromised, indifferent as his God."[40]

Notes

Introduction

1. Oliver Wendell Holmes, Jr., "Privilege, Malice, and Intent," *Harvard Law Review* 8 (1894), 5; Holmes, *The Common Law* (Boston: Little, Brown, 1881), 5, 51, 108.

2. Holmes, *Common Law*, 50, 109.

3. Recounted by Charles E. Rosenberg in his *The Trial of the Assassin Guiteau: Psychiatry and the Law in the Gilded Age* (Chicago: University of Chicago Press, 1968), 53–55, 102–103.

4. James Wilson, *The Works of James Wilson*, ed. James DeWitt Andrews (Chicago: Callaghan & Co., 1896), vol. 1, 210.

5. Daniel Walker Howe, *Making the American Self: Jonathan Edwards to Abraham Lincoln* (Cambridge, MA: Harvard University Press, 1997); Jackson Lears, *Something for Nothing: Luck in America* (New York: Penguin Books, 2003), 2–10, 142 (quoting Ralph Waldo Emerson's 1841 essay, "Self-Reliance"). For other studies documenting the pervasive influence of the Scottish Common Sense philosophy in antebellum America, see especially Donald H. Meyer, *The Instructed Conscience: The Shaping of the American National Ethic* (Philadelphia: University of Pennsylvania Press, 1972); Terence Martin, *The Instructed Vision: Scottish Common Sense Philosophy and the Origins of American Fiction* (Bloomington: University of Indiana Press, 1961).

6. Joyce Appleby, "The Radical *Double-Entendre* in the Right to Self-Government," in *The Origins of Anglo-American Radicalism*, ed. Margaret C. Jacob and James R. Jacob (Atlantic Highlands, NJ: Humanities Press International, 1991), 304–312 (quoting Thomas Jefferson); Louis P. Masur, "'Age of the First Person Singular': The Vocabulary of the Self in New England, 1780–1850," *Journal of American Studies* 25 (1991): 189–211, 194 (quoting Fisher Ames).

7. James Kent, *An Address Delivered before the Law Association of the City of New York*, Oct. 21, 1836 (New York: G. & C. Carvill & Co., 1836), 5; Timothy Walker,

Introduction to American Law, 2nd ed. (Philadelphia: P. H. Nicklin & T. Johnson, 1837), 10; Wilson, *Works*, vol. 1, 3; Samuel Warren, *A Popular and Practical Introduction to Law Studies* (New York: D. Appleton, 1846) ; Robert A. Ferguson, *Law and Letters in American Culture* (Cambridge, MA: Harvard University Press, 1984), 24–25, 65; Martin Wiener, *Reconstructing the Criminal: Culture, Law, and Policy in England, 1830–1914* (New York: Cambridge University Press, 1990), 38–45, 52–83.

8. David Hoffman, *Legal Outlines: Being the Substance of the First Title of a Course of Lectures Delivered in the University of Maryland* (New York, 1848), viii; James Kent, "An Introductory Lecture to a Course of Law Lectures. Delivered November 17, 1794," reprinted in *Columbia Law Review* 3 (May 1903), 330–343, 342; Ferguson, *Law and Letters*, 28.

9. Walker, *Introduction*, 2nd ed., 2–3, 200; David Hoffman, *Legal Outlines*, viii; Kent, "Introductory Lecture," 339; Alexis de Tocqueville, *Democracy in America*, ed. Phillips Bradley (1840; reprint, New York: Knopf, 1994), vol. 2, 100–113; William J. Novak, *The People's Welfare* (Chapel Hill: University of North Carolina Press, 1996), 25–29.

10. Walker, *Introduction*, 202–255; Joseph W. Moulton, *Analysis of American Law* (New York: J. S. Voorhies, 1859), 10. See generally Susanna L. Blumenthal, "The Default Legal Person," *UCLA Law Review* 54 (2007): 1135–1265.

11. Wilson, *Works*, vol. 1, 22; Walker, *Introduction*, 227; Hoffman, *Legal Outlines*, 178–210; R. H. Graveson, *Status in the Common Law* (London: University of London, Atholone Press, 1953); Nancy Isenberg, *Sex and Citizenship in Antebellum America* (Chapel Hill: University of North Carolina Press, 1998), 28; see also Martha Minow, *Making All the Difference: Inclusion, Exclusion, and American Law* (Ithaca, NY: Cornell University Press, 1990); Linda K. Kerber, *Women of the Republic: Intellect and Ideology in Revolutionary America* (Chapel Hill: University of North Carolina Press, 1997); Rosemarie Zagarri, *Revolutionary Backlash: Women and Politics in the Early American Republic* (Philadelphia: University of Pennsylvania Press, 2007); Sarah Knott, *Sensibility and the American Revolution* (Chapel Hill: University of North Carolina Press, 2009); Laura F. Edwards, *The People and Their Peace: Legal Culture and the Transformation of Inequality in the Post-Revolutionary South* (Chapel Hill: University of North Carolina Press, 2009), 205–298; Barbara Young Welke, *Law and the Borders of Belonging in the Long Nineteenth Century United States* (New York: Cambridge University Press, 2010), 21–94. For the foundational essay on intersectionality in a legal context, see Kimberle Crenshaw, "Demarginalizing the Intersection of Race and Sex: A Black Feminist Critique of Antidiscrimination Doctrine, Feminist Theory, and Antiracist Politics," *University of Chicago Legal Forum* 140 (1989): 139–167.

12. St. George Tucker, *Blackstone's Commentaries* (Philadelphia: W. Y. Birch and A. Small, 1803), vol. 1, 69–70 (quoting James Sullivan, the governor of Massachusetts); Tucker, *A Dissertation on Slavery: With a Proposal for Gradual Abolition of It, in the State of Virginia* (Philadelphia: Matthew Carey, 1796), 67; see also Walker, *Introduction*, 164, 165, 222, 650–651. On the forms of liberation and domination that the Enlightenment promised and provoked in postrevolutionary America, see Robert A. Ferguson, *The American Enlightenment, 1750–1820* (Cambridge, MA: Harvard University Press, 1997), 22–43.

13. John Carson, *The Measure of Merit: Talents, Intelligence, and Inequality in the French and American Republics, 1750–1940* (Princeton, NJ: Princeton University

Press, 2007), 38–60, 75–97. On the dissemination of racial science in postrevolutionary America, see Winthrop D. Jordan, *White Over Black: American Attitudes toward the Negro, 1550–1812* (Chapel Hill: University of North Carolina Press, 1968); Bruce R. Dain, *A Hideous Monster of the Mind: American Race Theory in the Early Republic* (Cambridge, MA: Harvard University Press, 2002). Accounts extending further into the nineteenth century include William R. Stanton, *The Leopard's Spots: Scientific Attitudes Toward Race in America, 1815–1859* (Chicago: University of Chicago Press, 1960); Ann Fabian, *The Skull Collectors: Race, Science, and America's Unburied Dead* (Chicago: University of Chicago Press, 2010); Nell Irvin Painter, *The History of White People* (New York: W. W. Norton & Company, 2011).

14. For wide-ranging treatments of these developments, attending to the strains and contradictions of legal liberalism, see especially Holly Brewer, *By Birth or Consent: Children, Law, and the Anglo-American Revolution in Authority* (Chapel Hill: University of North Carolina Press, 2005); Laura F. Edwards, *Gendered Strife & Confusion: The Political Culture of Reconstruction* (Urbana: University of Illinois Press, 1997); Edwards, *The People and their Peace: Legal Culture and the Transformation of Inequality in the Post-Revolutionary South* (Chapel Hill: University of North Carolina Press, 2009); Ariela J. Gross, *Double Character: Slavery and Mastery in the Antebellum Courtroom* (Princeton, NJ: Princeton University Press, 2000); Gross, *What Blood Won't Tell: A History of Race on Trial in America* (Cambridge, MA: Harvard University Press, 2009); Linda K. Kerber, *No Constitutional Right to be Ladies* (New York: Hill and Wang, 1998); James D. Schmidt, *Industrial Violence and the Legal Origins of Child Labor* (New York: Cambridge University Press, 2010); Amy Dru Stanley, *From Bondage to Contract: Wage Labor, Marriage, and the Market in the Age of Slave Emancipation* (Cambridge: Cambridge University Press, 1998).

15. This discussion of the cultural significance of private law owes much to the work of Hendrik Hartog, particularly his evocative studies of marriage and care work. See Hendrik Hartog, *Man and Wife in America: A History* (Cambridge: Harvard University Press, 2000); Hartog *Someday All This Will Be Yours: A History of Inheritance and Old Age* (Cambridge, MA: Harvard University Press, 2012).

16. Tocqueville, *Democracy in America*, vol. 2, 159; Carson, *Measure of Merit*, 39. On character discourse see Karen Halttunen, *Confidence Men and Painted Women: A Study of Middle-Class Culture in America, 1830–1870* (New Haven, CT: Yale University Press, 1982); Judy Hilkey, *Character Is Capital: Success Manuals and Manhood in Gilded Age America* (Chapel Hill: University of North Carolina Press, 1997).

17. A realization that would prove deeply destabilizing to William James, one of the era's most sensitive and knowing observers of mental breakdown, including his own. See Robert D. Richardson, *William James: In the Maelstrom of American Modernism* (New York: Houghton Mifflin, 2006), 117–122.

18. David J. Rothman, *The Discovery of the Asylum: Social Order and Disorder in the New Republic* (Boston: Little, Brown & Company, 1971), 123; Alison Winter, *Mesmerized: Powers of Mind in Victorian Britain* (Chicago: University of Chicago Press, 1998), 46–47; Benjamin Reiss, *Theaters of Madness: Insane Asylums & Nineteenth-Century American Culture* (Chicago: University of Chicago Press, 2008), 1–22.

19. Jeffrey Sklansky, "The Elusive Sovereign: New Intellectual and Social Histories of Capitalism," *Modern Intellectual History* 9 (2012); 233–248. For a

sampling of some of the new directions being pursued by historians of capitalism, see Michael Zakim and Gary John Kornblith, eds., *Capitalism Takes Command: The Social Transformation of Nineteenth-Century America* (Chicago: University of Chicago Press, 2012).

20. Oliver Wendell Holmes to Morris Cohen, July 21, 1920, "The Holmes-Cohen Correspondence," in *Portrait of a Philosopher: Morris R. Cohen in Life and Letters*, ed. Leonora Cohen Rosenfield (New York: Harcourt, Brace & World, 1962), 325.

Part I: The Testimony of Consciousness

1. Benjamin Rush to John Adams, November 17, 1812, in Benjamin Rush, *Letters of Benjamin Rush*, ed. L. H. Butterfield (Princeton, NJ: Princeton University Press, 1951), vol. 2, 1166–1168.

2. Benjamin Rush, "An Account of the Influence of the Military and Political Events of the American Revolution upon the Human Body," *Medical Inquiries and Observations* (Philadelphia: Thomas Dobson, 1794), vol. 2, 263–278; Benjamin Rush, "Address to the People of the United States on the Defects of the Confederation," *American Museum* 1 (January 1787): 8–11; Rush to Richard Price, May 25, 1786, *Letters*, vol. 1, 388–390. Rush treats the phenomenon of dreams, understood to be "the result of mental disease," in *Benjamin Rush's Lectures on the Mind*, ed. Eric T. Carlson, Jeffrey L. Wollock, and Patricia S. Noel (Philadelphia: American Philosophical Society, 1981), 647–683. For studies placing his analysis of dreams in broader cultural context, see Mechal Sobel, *Teach Me Dreams: The Search for Self in the Revolutionary Era* (Princeton, NJ: Princeton University Press, 2002); Merle Curti, "The American Exploration of Dreams and Dreamers," *Journal of the History of Ideas* 27 (1966): 391–416. On Rush's life and works more generally, see Donald D'Elia, *Benjamin Rush: Philosopher of the American Revolution* (Philadelphia: American Philosophical Society, 1974), 1–113.

3. Louis P. Masur; "'Age of the First Person Singular': The Vocabulary of the Self in New England, 1780–1850," *Journal of American Studies* 25 (1991): 189–211; Richard McKeon, "The Development and the Significance of the Concept of Responsibility," *Revue Internationale de Philosophie* 11 (1957): 6–8, 23; Thomas Haskell, "Responsibility, Convention and the Role of Ideas in History," in *Objectivity Is Not Neutrality: Explanatory Schemes in History* (Baltimore: Johns Hopkins University Press, 1998), 282–283; Jay Fliegelman, *Declaring Independence: Jefferson, Natural Language, & The Culture of Performance* (Stanford, CA: Stanford University Press, 1993), 140–147. See generally Gordon S. Wood, "Conspiracy and the Paranoid Style: Causality and Deceit in the Eighteenth Century," *William and Mary Quarterly*, 3rd ser., 39 (1982): 401–441. On the colonial background, see Jon Pahl, *Paradox Lost: Free Will and Political Liberty in American Culture, 1630–1760* (Baltimore: Johns Hopkins Press, 1992).

4. Alexander Hamilton, James Madison, and John Jay, *The Federalist Papers*, ed. Clinton Rossiter (New York: Penguin, 1999), 350–358, 391–403. See generally Charles R. Kesler, "Introduction," *The Federalist Papers*, xxii–xxxi; Fliegelman, *Declaring Independence*, 147–150; Gordon S. Wood, *The Creation of the American Republic* (Chapel Hill: University of North Carolina Press, 1969).

5. Herbert J. Storing, ed., *The Complete Anti-Federalist* (Chicago: University of Chicago Kansas, 1981), vol. 1: 131, 139, 142, 148, 173, 180, 242, 266. See generally Cecelia M. Kenyon, "Men of Little Faith: The Anti-Federalists on the Nature of Representative Government," *William and Mary Quarterly*, 3rd ser., 12 (1955): 3–43; Isaac Kramnick, "The 'Great National Discussion': The Discourse of Politics in 1787," *William and Mary Quarterly*, 3rd ser., 45 (1988): 3–32; Saul Cornell, *The Other Founders: Anti-Federalism and the Dissenting Tradition in America, 1788–1828* (Chapel Hill: University of North Carolina Press, 1999).

6. Mark A. Noll, *America's God: From Jonathan Edwards to Abraham Lincoln* (New York: Oxford University Press, 2002); Nathan O. Hatch and Harry S. Stout, eds., *Jonathan Edwards and the American Experience* (New York: Oxford University Press, 1988); Norman Fiering, *Jonathan Edwards's Moral Thought and Its British Context* (Chapel Hill: University of North Carolina Press, 1981); E. Brooks Holifield, *Theology in America: Christian Thought from the Age of the Puritans to the Civil War* (New Haven, CT: Yale University Press, 2003); Allen C. Guelzo, "From Calvinist Metaphysics to Republican Theory: Jonathan Edwards and James Dana on Freedom of the Will," *Journal of the History of Ideas* 56 (1995): 399–418.

7. Thomas Reid, *Essays on the Intellectual and Active Powers of Man*, 2 vols. (Edinburgh, 1768; repr., Philadelphia: William Young, 1793); William E. Channing, *Self Culture* (Boston: Dutton and Wentworth, 1838), 13–14.

8. Henry May, *The Enlightenment in America* (New York: Oxford University Press, 1976), 356; Alexis de Tocqueville, *Democracy in America*, vol. 2 (Boston: C. C. Little & J. Brown, 1841), ch. 13; [Henry W. Bellows] "The Influence of the Trading Spirit Upon the Social and Moral Life of America," *The American Review: A Whig Journal of Politics, Literature, Art, and Science* 1 (January 1845): 94—98; Richard B. Latner, "Preserving 'the Natural Equality of Rank and Influence': Liberalism, Republicanism, and the Equality of Condition in Jacksonian Politics," in *The Culture of the Market: Historical Essays*, ed. Thomas L. Haskell and Richard F. Teichgraeber III (Cambridge: Cambridge University Press, 1993), 189–230. On the shifting connotations of "competency," see Daniel Vickers, "Competency and Competition: Economic Culture in Early America," *William and Mary Quarterly*, 3rd ser., 47 (1990): 3–29.

9. Isaac Ray, "Criminal Law of Insanity," *American Jurist and Law Magazine* 14 (1835): 253–254; Isaac Ray, *A Treatise on the Medical Jurisprudence of Insanity* (Boston: Charles C. Little and James Brown, 1838), 100.

Chapter 1: Common Sense and Common Law

1. James Wilson, *The Works of James Wilson*, ed. Robert Green McCloskey (Cambridge, MA: Harvard University Press, 1967), vol. 1, 81.

2. Ibid., vol. 1, 81, 124–129, 197, 212–213.

3. On Wilson's treatment of women, see Jan Lewis, "'Of Every Age Sex & Condition': The Representation of Women in the Constitution," *Journal of the Early Republic* 15 (1995): 359–387; Rosemarie Zagarri, "Morals, Manners, and the Republican Mother," *American Quarterly* 44 (1992): 192–215. Wilson's thinking exhibits "the feminization of ideas about public virtue" analyzed in Ruth H. Bloch, "The Gendered Meanings of Virtue in Revolutionary America," *Signs* 13 (1987): 37–58.

4. Through numerous popularizers and systematizers, Reid's works became known in America soon after their publication in Edinburgh. American reprints of the works themselves were also common. See, e.g., Thomas Reid, *Essays on the Intellectual and Active Powers of Man*, 2 vols. (Edinburgh, 1768; repr., Philadelphia: William Young, 1793).

5. Wilson, *Works*, vol. 2, 751. On the influence of the Scottish Enlightenment philosophy within American legal culture, see Robert A. Ferguson, *Law and Letters in the American Culture* (Cambridge, MA: Harvard University Press, 1984), 186–194; David T. Konig, "Jurisprudence and Social Policy in the New Republic," in *Devising Liberty: Preserving and Creating Freedom in the New American Republic*, ed. David T. Kong (Stanford, CA: Stanford University Press, 1995), 178–216. For a study tracing its influence on Wilson in particular, see William Ewald, "James Wilson and the Scottish Enlightenment," *Journal of Constitutional Law* 12 (2010): 1053–1114.

6. Thomas L. Haskell, "Persons as Uncaused Causes: John Stuart Mill, the Spirit of Capitalism, and the 'Invention' of Formalism," in *The Culture of the Market: Historical Essays*, ed. Thomas L. Haskell and Richard F. Teichgraeber III (Cambridge: Cambridge University Press, 1993), 441–502; Gordon S. Wood, "Conspiracy and the Paranoid Style: Causality and Deceit in the Eighteenth Century," *William and Mary Quarterly*, 3rd ser., 39 (1982): 401–441. On the liberalization of American Protestantism, see Nathan Hatch, *The Democratization of American Christianity* (New Haven, CT: Yale University Press, 1989); E. Brooks Holifield, *Theology in America: Christian Thought from the Age of the Puritans to the Civil War* (New Haven, CT: Yale University Press, 2003); Mark A. Noll, *America's God: From Jonathan Edwards to Abraham Lincoln* (New York: Oxford University Press, 2002).

7. Thomas Reid, *An Inquiry into the Human Mind on the Principles of Common Sense*, ed. Derek R. Brookes (Edinburgh, 1764; repr., Edinburgh: Edinburgh University Press, 1997), 163; Reid, *Essays*, vol. 2, 399–401.

8. Henry May, *The Enlightenment in America* (New York: Oxford University Press, 1976), 346–358; John Carson, *The Measure of Merit: Talents, Intelligence, and Inequality in the French and American Republics, 1750–1940* (Princeton, NJ: Princeton University Press, 2006), 47 (quoting Noah Porter); Daniel Walker Howe, *Making the American Self: Jonathan Edwards to Abraham Lincoln* (Cambridge, MA: Harvard University Press, 1997), 107–135. On the reception of Common Sense philosophy in postrevolutionary America and the "theistic mental science" built upon its premises, see Noll, *America's God*, 93–113; Holifield, *Theology in America*, 173–196. On the mobilization of mental philosophy as a tool of the liberal state in nineteenth-century European societies struggling with the unsettling effects of political and economic change, see Jan Goldstein, *The Post-Revolutionary Self: Politics and Psyche in France, 1750–1850* (Cambridge, MA: Harvard University Press, 2008); Mary Poovey, *A History of Modern Fact: Problems of Knowledge in the Sciences of Wealth and Society* (Chicago: University of Chicago Press, 1998). This inquiry draws on the methods and insights of scholars engaged in what Lorraine Daston has called "historical epistemology"; see Daston, "The Moral Economy of Science," *Osiris* 10 (1995): 3–24.

9. Louis P. Masur, "'Age of the First Person Singular': The Vocabulary of the Self in New England, 1780–1850," *Journal of American Studies* 25 (1991):

189–211; Warren I. Susman, "'Personality' and the Making of Twentieth-Century Culture," *Culture as History: The Transformation of American Society in the Twentieth Century* (New York: Pantheon, 1984), 271–285; Carson, *Measure of Merit*, 11–60. Howe, *Making the American Self*, 107–156, suggests greater congruency between the logic and lived experience of democratization, arguing that nineteenth-century American culture exhibited "a tendency to expand the number of people who were entitled to an autonomous self" (109).

10. For a wide-ranging historical treatment of the idea of common sense as it has figured in elite politics since the eighteenth century, see Sophia A. Rosenfeld, *Common Sense: A Political History* (Cambridge, MA: Harvard University Press, 2011).

11. James Willard Hurst, *Law and the Conditions of Freedom in the Nineteenth-Century United States* (Madison: University of Wisconsin Press, 1956); Morton J. Horwitz, *The Transformation of American Law, 1780–1860* (Cambridge, MA: Harvard University Press, 1977); see also Lawrence Friedman, *A History of American Law* (New York: Simon & Schuster, 1973; repr., 2005); William E. Nelson, *The Americanization of the Common Law* (Cambridge, MA: Harvard University Press, 1975); Craig Haney, "Criminal Justice and the Nineteenth-Century Paradigm: The Triumph of Psychological Individualism in the 'Formative Era,'" *Law and Human Behavior* 6 (1982): 191–235.

12. For a comprehensive overview and incisive synthesis of this body of scholarship, see Barbara Young Welke, *Law and the Borders of Belonging in the Long Nineteenth Century United States* (Cambridge: Cambridge University Press, 2010).

13. Joel Peter Eigen, *Witnessing Insanity: Madness and Mad-Doctors in the English Court* (New Haven, CT: Yale University Press, 1995), 79. See also David Rothman, *The Discovery of the Asylum: Social Order and Disorder in the New Republic* (Boston: Little Brown, 1971); Martin J. Wiener, *Reconstructing the Criminal: Culture, Law, and Policy in England, 1830–1914* (Cambridge: Cambridge University Press, 1990).

14. Michael Meranze, *Laboratories of Virtue: Punishment, Revolution, and Authority in Philadelphia, 1760–1835* (Chapel Hill: University of North Carolina Press, 1996), 4; cf. Christopher L. Tomlins, *Law, Labor, and Ideology in the Early American Republic* (Cambridge: Cambridge University Press, 1993). These interpretive strains can be traced back to tensions and ambiguities in Michel Foucault's own renderings of the relationship between law and discipline over the course of his career. See Jan Goldstein, "Framing Discipline with Law: Problems and Promises of the Liberal State," *American Historical Review* 98 (1993): 364–375; Ben Golder and Peter Fitzpatrick, *Foucault's Law* (Abingdon: Routledge, 2009).

15. While Foucault dismissed "philosophical theories of the mind, passions, or body" as a site for examining the processes by which the modern subject was constituted, Jan Goldstein has compellingly illustrated how the theory of the French philosopher Victor Cousin functioned in nineteenth-century France as a structure of power/knowledge and a technology of self in the Foucauldian sense. Jan Goldstein, "Foucault and the Post-Revolutionary Self: The Uses of Cousinian Pedagogy in Nineteenth-Century France," *Foucault and the Writing of History*, ed. Jan Goldstein (Oxford: Blackwell, 1994), 99–115.

16. Karen Halttunen, *Confidence Men and Painted Women: A Study of Middle-Class Culture in America, 1830–1870* (New Haven, CT: Yale University Press,

1982), 1–32; Perry Miller, *The Life of the Mind in America: From the Revolution to the Civil War* (New York: Harcourt, Brace and World, 1965), 99–265.

17. Charles Page Smith, *James Wilson: Founding Father, 1742–1798* (Chapel Hill: University of North Carolina Press, 1956), 3–20; Thomas Boston, *Human Nature in Its Fourfold State, Primitive Integrity, Entire Depravity, Begun Recovery, and Consummate Happiness or Misery* (Falkirk, Scotland, 1787); James Harper, John Eadie, and William Lindsay, *Lives of Ebenezer Erskine, William Wilson, and Thomas Gillespie: Fathers of the United Presbyterian Church* (Edinburgh: Fullarton, 1849), 186.

18. James Wilson to Bird Wilson, August 4, 1798 in *The Documentary History of the Supreme Court of the United States, 1789-1800*, ed. Maeva Marcus and James R. Perry (New York: Columbia University Press, 1990), vol. 3, 282–283; Smith, *Wilson*, 388. See generally Ewald, "James Wilson and the Scottish Enlightenment," 1062–1065, 1081–1114; Mark David Hall, *The Political and Legal Philosophy of James Wilson, 1742–1798* (Columbia: University of Missouri Press, 1997).

19. Perry Miller, *Errand Into the Wilderness* (Cambridge: Belknap Press, 1975), 55; Norman Fiering, *Jonathan Edwards' Moral Thought and Its British Context* (Chapel Hill: University of North Carolina Press, 1981), 6–7; Norman Fiering, "Irresistible Compassion: An Aspect of Eighteenth-Century Sympathy and Humanitarianism," *Journal of the History of Ideas* 37 (1976): 200. See generally Theodore Bozeman, *Protestants in an Age of Science: The Baconian Ideal and Antebellum American Religious Thought* (Chapel Hill: University of North Carolina Press, 2011); Herbert Hovenkamp, *Science and Religion in America, 1800–1860* (Philadelphia: University of Pennsylvania Press, 1978), 19–36; Noll, *America's God*, 233–238; Holifield, *Theology in America*, 174–180. On the natural science of psychology as it was reconfigured in the eighteenth century, emphasizing shifts in disciplinary matrices, see Gary Hatfield, "Remaking the Science of Mind," in *Inventing Human Science: Eighteenth-Century Domains*, ed. Christopher Fox, Roy Porter, and Robert Wokler (Berkeley: University of California Press, 1995), 184–231.

20. On the multivalent nature of this discourse about the human sciences, see Roger Smith, "The Language of Human Nature," in *Inventing Human Science*, 88–111; Ludmilla Jordanova, "Sex and Gender," in *Inventing Human Science*, 152–183; Robert J. Richards, *Darwin and the Emergence of Evolutionary Theories of Mind and Behavior* (Chicago: University of Chicago Press, 1987); Carson, *Measure of Merit*.

21. Smith, "Language of Human Nature," 89, 97; Fiering, "Irresistible Compassion," 204 (quoting Bishop George Berkeley); J. A. Passmore, "The Malleability of Man in Eighteenth-Century Thought," in *Aspects of the Eighteenth Century*, ed. Earl R. Wasserman (Baltimore: Johns Hopkins University Press, 1965), 21–46. For a comprehensive historical assessment of the significance of the new moral philosophy, which emphasizes "its close reconsideration of the philosophical anthropology of Christianity in light of nonreligious experiential evidence," (6), see Fiering, *Jonathan Edwards's Moral Thought*.

22. Jonathan Edwards, *A Careful and Strict Enquiry into the Modern Prevailing Notions of that Freedom of the Will*, ed. Paul Ramsey (New Haven, CT: Yale University Press, 1957); Allen C. Guelzo, *Edwards on the Will: A Century of American Theological Debate* (Middletown, CT: Wesleyan University Press, 1989), 50, 53, 73. See generally Fiering, *Jonathan Edwards' Moral Thought*; George M. Marsden, *Jonathan Edwards: A Life* (New Haven, CT: Yale University Press, 2003).

23. James Dana, *An Examination of the Late Reverend President Edwards's "Enquiry on Freedom of Will"* (Boston, 1770), v; Allen C. Guelzo, "From Calvinist Metaphysics to Republican Theory: Jonathan Edwards and James Dana on Freedom of the Will," *Journal of the History of Ideas* 56 (1995): 399–418.

24. Noll, *America's God*, 53–157; Hatch, *Democratization of Christianity*, chap. 2; Edmund S. Morgan, "The American Revolution Considered as an Intellectual Movement," in *Paths of American Thought*, ed. Arthur M. Schlesinger and Morton White (Boston: Houghton, Mifflin, 1963), 11–33; Ferguson, *Law and Letters*, 3–86.

25. Rosenfeld, *Common Sense*, 4, 56–89. See generally Gladys Bryson, *Man and Society: The Scottish Inquiry of the Eighteenth Century* (Princeton: Princeton University Press, 1945); David Fate Norton, "From Moral Sense to Common Sense: An Essay on the Development of Scottish Common Sense Philosophy, 1700–1765" (PhD diss., University of California–San Diego, 1966); Richard B. Sher, *Church and University in the Scottish Enlightenment: The Moderate Literati of Edinburgh* (Edinburgh: Edinburgh University Press, 1985); Stephen A. Conrad, *Citizenship and Common Sense: The Problem of Authority in the Social Background and Social Philosophy of the Wise Club of Aberdeen* (New York: Garland, 1987); Peter J. Diamond, *Common Sense and Improvement: Thomas Reid as Social Theorist* (New York: Peter Lang, 1998); S. A. Grave, *The Scottish Philosophy of Common Sense* (Oxford: Clarendon Press, 1960); Paul B. Wood, "Science and the Pursuit of Virtue in the Aberdeen Enlightenment," in *Studies in the Philosophy of the Scottish Enlightenment*, ed. M. A. Stewart (Oxford: Oxford University Press, 1990), 127–149.

26. These works, which circulated separately as well as in volumes of collected works, were *An Inquiry into the Human Mind on the Principles of Common Sense* (1764), *Essays on the Intellectual Powers of Man* (1785), and *Essays on the Active Powers of Man* (1788). On the philosophical and historical significance of Reid's writings, see generally David Fate Norton, *David Hume: Common-Sense Moralist, Sceptical Metaphysician* (Princeton, NJ: Princeton University Press, 1982), 152–191; Knud Haakonssen, *Natural Law and Moral Philosophy: From Grotius to the Scottish Enlightenment* (Cambridge: Cambridge University Press, 1996), 182–186; ed. Terence Cuneo and René van Woudenberg, *The Cambridge Companion to Thomas Reid*, (Cambridge: Cambridge University Press, 2004). Gideon Yaffe, *Manifest Activity: Thomas Reid's Theory of Action* (Oxford: Oxford University Press, 2004).

27. Reid, *Essays*, vol. 1, 572; Barbara J. Shapiro, *A Culture of Fact: England, 1550–1720* (Ithaca, NY: Cornell University Press, 2003); Louise Marcil-Lacoste, *Claude Buffier and Thomas Reid: Two Common-Sense Philosophers* (Kingston, Ontario: McGill-Queen's University Press, 1982), 92. See also Julia Rudolph, *Common Law and Enlightenment in England, 1689–1750* (Woodbridge, Suffolk: Boydell Press, 2013).

28. Reid, *Inquiry*, 21; Thomas Reid, *The Works of Thomas Reid* (Charlestown, MA: Samuel Etheridge, Jun'r, 1815), vol. 3, 109–110.

29. Reid, *Inquiry*, 19–20, 68–69, 98, 170; Reid, *Works* (1815), vol. 3, 76. Reid often figures common sense and reason as female adversaries, though reason appears to be overmatched by common sense, "who never fails at last to triumph over those who wage with her." Philosophy, when personified, is also gendered female. Reid, *Inquiry*, 268.

30. Reid, *Works* (1815), vol. 3, 102, 132–156.

31. On Reid's treatment of the free will problem, see generally James A. Harris, *Of Liberty and Necessity: The Free Will Debate in Eighteenth-Century British Philosophy* (Oxford: Oxford University Press, 2007), 179-202; William Rowe, *Thomas Reid on Freedom and Morality* (Ithaca, NY: Cornell University Press, 1991); William Rowe, "The Metaphysics of Freedom: Reid's Theory of Agent Causation," *American Catholic Philosophical Quarterly* 74 (2000): 425–446; Timothy O'Connor, "Thomas Reid on Free Agency," *Journal of the History of Philosophy* 32 (1994): 605–622; Timothy O'Connor, *Persons and Causes: The Metaphysics of Free Will* (New York: Oxford University Press, 2000); Douglas McDermid, "Thomas Reid on Moral Liberty and Common Sense," *British Journal for the History of Philosophy* 7 (1999): 275–303.

32. Reid, *Works* (1815), vol. 3, 170–172.

33. Apparently at Reid's direction, later editions of these two works were published together under the general title *Essays on the Powers of the Human Mind* (1803). James A. Harris, "Reid and Hume on the Possibility of Character," in *Character, Self, and Sociability in the Scottish Enlightenment*, ed. Thomas Ahnert and Susan Manning (New York: Palgrave Macmillan, 2011), 45n8.

34. Reid, *Works* (1815), vol. 4, 24.

35. Ibid., 86, 130, 157, 236; see also Yaffe, *Manifest Activity*, 105–107.

36. Thomas Reid, *The Works of Thomas Reid* (New York: E. Duyckinck, Collins and Hannay, and R. and W. A. Bartow, 1822), vol. 3, 200.

37. Ibid., 203.

38. Ibid.

39. Reid, *Works* (1815), vol. 4, 258, 260, 267. Intriguingly, Reid held that a treasonous act would be excused if "extorted by the rack," but not if gotten by the "greatest bribe" (260). He explained: "The love of money, and of what is called man's interest, is a cool motive, which leaves to a man the entire power over himself: but the torment of the rack, or the dread of present death, are so violent motives, that men, who have not uncommon strength of mind, are not masters of themselves in such a situation, and therefore what they do is not imputed, or is thought less criminal" (260).

40. Ibid., 259, 261, 267. He did concede that human judges could not easily determine whether and when passion was completely irresistible and admitted that criminal courts excused only those who were truly insane.

41. Reid, *Works* (1822), vol. 3, 39–41.

42. See Rosenfeld, *Common Sense*; Haakonssen, *Natural Law*. On the ethic of responsibility, see Jackson Lears, *Something for Nothing: Luck in America* (New York: Viking, 2003); Haskell, "Persons as Uncaused Causes." In "Conspiracy and the Paranoid Style," Wood blurs the distinctions between various theological and philosophical renderings of the basis of human responsibility, painting with overly broad brushstrokes the process by which human agency gradually displaced divine agency. More particularly, he erroneously reads Reid to agree with Edwards in viewing the will as "necessarily determined" by motives, quoting a passage from *Essays on the Active Powers* that insists this was *not* the common sense of the matter; see esp. 401, 417.

43. On the transmission of the Scottish philosophy to the colonies, emphasizing it was "not a monolithic system of ideas" and was not incorporated wholesale

to the exclusion of other intellectual systems, see Peter J. Diamond, "Witherspoon, William Smith, and the Scottish Philosophy in Revolutionary America," in *Scotland and America in the Age of Enlightenment*, ed. Richard B. Sher and Jeffrey R. Smitten (Edinburgh: Edinburgh University Press, 1990), 120; see also Norton, "From Moral Sense to Common Sense"; Noll, *America's God*, 10, 93–137; Holifield, *Theology in America*, 127–156; Howe, *Making the American Self*, 50–77; Donald H. Meyer, *The Instructed Conscience: The Shaping of the American National Ethic* (Philadelphia: University of Pennsylvania Press, 1972); May, *Enlightenment in America*; Douglas Sloan, *The Scottish Enlightenment and the American College Ideal* (New York: Teachers College Press, 1971); Daniel W. Howe, "John Witherspoon and the Transatlantic Enlightenment," in *The Atlantic Enlightenment*, ed. Susan Manning and Francis D. Cogliano (Burlington, VT: Ashgate Publishing Co., 2008), 61–80; Ewald, "James Wilson and the Scottish Enlightenment."

44. Among the numerous works that have documented the widespread influence of Scottish Common Sense philosophyamong statesmen and educators in postrevolutionary America, this account relies in particular upon Bozeman, *Protestants in an Age of Science*; Carson, *Measure of Merit*, 44–60; Merle Curti, *Human Nature in American Thought* (Madison: University of Wisconsin Press, 1980), 70–146; Rand Evans, "The Origins of American Academic Psychology," in *Explorations in the History of Psychology in America*, ed. Josef Brozek (Lewisburg, PA: Bucknell University Press, 1984), 29–48; Alfred H. Fuchs, "Contributions of American Mental Philosophers to Psychology in the United States," *History of Psychology* 3 (2000): 3–19; Holifield, *Theology in America*, 173–196; Hovenkamp, *Science and Religion in America*, 3–36; Daniel Walker Howe, *The Unitarian Conscience: Harvard Moral Philosophy, 1805–1861* (Cambridge, MA: Harvard University Press, 1970); Kuklick, *Churchmen and Philosophers*, 128–145; Terence Martin, *The Instructed Vision: Scottish Common Sense Philosophy and the Origins of American Fiction* (Bloomington: University of Indiana Press, 1961); May, *Enlightenment in America*, 346–358; Meyer, *Instructed Conscience*, 35–52; Noll, *America's God*, 233–238; Rosenfeld, *Common Sense*, 136–180; Dortothy Ross, *The Origins of Social Science* (Cambridge: Cambridge University Press, 1991), 36–37.

45. James McCosh, *The Method of Divine Government Physical and Moral* (1850), quoted in Meyer, *Instructed Conscience*, 57. See also Allen C. Guelzo, "'The Science of Duty': Moral Philosophy and the Epistemology of Science in Nineteenth-Century America," in *Evangelicals and Science in Historical Perspective*, ed. David N. Livingstone, D. G. Hart, and Mark A. Noll (New York: Oxford University Press, 1999), 267–289.

46. See Jay Fliegelman, *Prodigals and Pilgrims: The American Revolution against Patriarchal Authority, 1750–1800* (Cambridge: Cambridge University Press, 1982); Haskell, "Persons as Uncaused Causes," 441, 457.

47. The Scottish Common Sense philosophy first gained a foothold in American colleges under the auspices or effective control of the Presbyterian Church, which amounted to two-thirds of those in operation as of 1851. By 1825, Common Sense textbooks had supplanted Locke at both Yale and Harvard. Evans, "Origins of American Academic Psychology," 33–34.

48. Joseph Haven, *Moral Philosophy: Including Theoretical and Practical Ethics* (Boston: Gould and Lincoln, 1859); Meyer, *Instructed Conscience*, 3–4. Haven, who was professor of mental and moral philosophy at Amherst College, had

published a text on mental philosophy two years earlier. On the formative role of the Scottish Common Sense philosophy in the development of these academic disciplines, see Evans, "Origins of American Academic Psychology"; Guelzo, "'Science of Duty,'" 272–273; Wilson Smith, *Professors and Public Ethics: Studies of Northern Moral Philosophers before the Civil War* (Ithaca, NY: Cornell University Press, 1956). For surveys of a representative sample of moralists, highlighting their varied religious backgrounds and differing orientations toward moral philosophy, see Meyer, *Instructed Conscience*, 13–22; Fuchs, "American Mental Philosophers," 5–19. On the extent to which Southern moral philosophers followed the main outlines of Northerners and simply excised antislavery elements, see E. Brooks Holifield, *The Gentlemen Theologians: American Theology in Southern Culture, 1795–1860* (Durham, NC: Duke University Press, 1978).

49. Thomas C. Upham, *Elements of Mental Philosophy* (New York: Harper & Brothers, 1841), vol. 1, iii.

50. Thomas C. Upham, *Elements of Intellectual Philosophy* (Portland, ME: William Hyde, 1827); Thomas C. Upham, *Elements of Mental Philosophy* (Portland, ME: S. Coleman, 1831); Thomas C. Upham, *A Philosophical and Practical Treatise on the Will* (Brunswick, ME: Joseph Griffin, 1834). These works were reprinted in numerous editions, some of them abridged.

51. Upham, *Treatise on the Will*, 236, 246–247; Thomas C. Upham, *Outlines of Imperfect and Disordered Mental Action* (New York: Harper & Brothers, 1840), 19; Upham, *Elements of Mental Philosophy*, 411. Upham noted at the outset that this subject had been "almost totally neglected, except by a few learned and philosophical writers of the medical profession." Upham, *Outlines*, iii. See M. C. Madden and E. H. Madden, "Thomas Upham on Relations and Alienation," *Transactions of the C. S. Peirce Society* 19 (1983): 240–248.

52. Upham, *Outlines*, 21, 56–57, 63–64.

53. Upham, *Treatise on the Will*, 298.

54. Francis Wayland, *The Elements of Moral Science* (New York: Cooke and Co., 1835), 68–74, 89.

55. In the 1838 tract, *The Limitations of Human Responsibility*, Wayland distanced himself from what he perceived to be the excesses of the abolitionist movement, even though he maintained slavery was a moral evil. Francis Wayland, *The Limitations of Human Responsibility* (Gould, Kendall, & Lincoln, 1838). For a discussion of the genesis of this work and its place in the debates over slavery that were increasingly dividing colleges, denominations, and congregations, see Deborah Bingham Van Broekhoven, "Suffering with Slaveholders: The Limits of Francis Wayland's Antislavery Witness," in *Religion and the Antebellum Debate over Slavery*, ed. John R. McKivigan and Mitchell Snay (Athens: University of Georgia Press, 1998), 196–220.

56. Meyer, *Instructed Conscience*, 3 (quoting Francis Grund's *The Americans in the Moral, Social, and Political Relations* [1837]).

57. Halttunen, *Confidence Men and Painted Women*, 9–10, 21–22, 27; William A. Alcott, *Young Man's Guide* (Boston: Lilly, Wait, Colman, & Holden, 1833). Nor were these manuals directed only to young men. See, for example, Edwin H. Chapin, *Duties of Young Women* (Boston: George W. Briggs, 1848).

58. Catherine E. Beecher, *A Treatise on Domestic Economy* (Boston: Marsh, Copen, Lyon, and Webb, 1841); Catherine E. Beecher, *The Elements of Mental and*

Moral Philosophy, Founded upon Experience, Reason, and the Bible (Hartford: n.p. 1831). Initially circulated anonymously, the latter text was promoted it for use in the classroom. See Kathryn Kish Sklar, *Catharine Beecher: A Study in American Domesticity* (New Haven, CT: Yale University Press, 1973). For a probing exploration of the ways women were schooled in female academies and seminaries, including their engagement with moral philosophy, see Mary Kelley, *Learning to Stand and Speak: Women, Education, and Public Life in America's Republic* (Chapel Hill: University of North Carolina Press, 2008).

59. Carson, *Measure of* Merit, 56-60; Howe, *Making the American Self*, chap. 8. As Louis Masur incisively observes, "Intellectuals in New England approached the question of the self from three different yet interconnected perspectives: deny it, improve it, or rely on it." Masur, "Vocabulary of the Self," 197.

60. Howe, *Making the American Self*, esp. chaps. 4, 5, and 9; Halttunen, *Confidence Men and Painted Ladies*, esp. chap. 2. There is an extensive literature concerning the concept of the self in nineteenth-century America. Classics in the field include John Cawelti, *Apostles of the Self-Made Man* (Chicago: University of Chicago Press, 1961); Richard Rabonwitz, *The Spiritual Self in Everyday Life* (Boston: Northeastern University Press, 1989); Mary Kupiec Cayton, *Emerson's Emergence: Self and Society in the Transformation of New England, 1800–1845* (Chapel Hill: University of North Carolina Press, 1990); Sacvan Bercovitch, *The Puritan Origins of the American Self* (New Haven, CT: Yale University Press, 1975). For more recent work, see Thomas Augst, *The Clerk's Tale: Young Men and Moral Life in Nineteenth-Century America* (Chicago: University of Chicago Press, 2003); Jesse F. Ballenger, *Self, Senility, and Alzheimer's Disease in Modern America* (Baltimore: Johns Hopkins University Press, 2006); James Block, *A Nation of Agents: The American Path to a Modern Self and Society* (Cambridge, MA: Harvard University Press, 2009); Wilfred M. McClay, *The Masterless: Self and Society in Modern America* (Chapel Hill: University of North Carolina Press, 1994); Scott Sandage, *Born Losers: A History of Failure in America* (Cambridge, MA: Harvard University Press, 2005); Jeffrey Sklansky, *The Soul's Economy: Market Society and Selfhood in American Thought, 1820–1920* (Chapel Hill: University of North Carolina Press, 2002).

61. Richard Hildreth, *A Theory of Morals: An Inquiry Concerning the Law of Moral Distinctions* (Boston: Little and Brown, 1844), 3.

62. David Brion Davis, *Homicide in American Fiction, 1798–1860: A Study in Social Values* (Ithaca, NY: Cornell University Press, 1957), 16; see also Karen Halttunen, *Murder Most Foul: The Killer and the American Gothic Imagination* (Cambridge, MA: Harvard University Press, 1998).

63. Upham, *Treatise on the* Will, 292; Upham, *Elements of Mental Philosophy*, 455.

64. Beecher, *Elements*, 254.

65. For biographical studies exploring Wilson's engagement with Common Sense philosophy, see Robert Green McCloskey, "Introduction," in *Works of James Wilson*, 1–48; Stephen A. Conrad, "Polite Foundation: Citizenship and Common Sense in James Wilson's Republican Theory," *Supreme Court Review* 1984, (1984): 359–388; Ewald, "James Wilson and the Scottish Enlightenment"; Hall, *Political and Legal Philosophy of James Wilson*; Shannon C. Stimson, "'A Jury of the Country': Common Sense Philosophy and the Jurisprudence of James Wilson," in *Scotland and America*, 193–208; John Fabian Witt, *Cosmopolitans and*

Patriots: Hidden Histories of American Law (Cambridge, MA: Harvard University Press, 2007), 15–82.

66. Wilson, *Works*, vol. 1, 81–82, 103–103, 216, 221–222. Wilson was careful to add that Blackstone himself was no "votary of despotick powers" and that Locke was no "friend to infidelity," but their ideas had lives of their own. (103–104). On Wilson's association of philosophical skepticism with undemocratic rule, see Stimson, "'Jury of the Country,'" 199.

67. Wilson, *Works*, vol. 1, 85, 90, 199.

68. Ibid., 143, 200, 202, 216–218.

69. Ibid., 136, 141, 143.

70. Ibid., 142, 306–308.

71. Ferguson, *Law and Letters*, 24–28.

72. Some sense of the working relationship between academic moralists and practicing lawyers can be gathered from the writings of moral philosophers such as Jasper Adams, a Massachusetts native and graduate of Brown University who served as president of the College of Charleston in South Carolina and attempted to help lawyers shed their reputation for hypocrisy and chicanery. Jasper Adams, *Elements of Moral Philosophy* (Cambridge, MA: Fulsom, Wells and Thurston, 1837).

73. Wilson made this rhetorical move in his inaugural lecture, and it was repeated in countless others across the nineteenth century. See, e.g., John W. Edmonds, "An Address to Law Students" (New York: Wm. C. Bryant, 1864), 9; George Sharswood, *Lectures Introductory to the Study of the Law* (Philadelphia: T. & J. W. Johnson & Co., 1870), 74.

74. An especially telling indication of what every aspiring lawyer was expected to read may be gleaned from David Hoffman's widely followed *Course of Study* (1817), an annotated syllabus organizing recommended texts in hierarchical order. Ranking at the very top of this list was the subject of "moral and political philosophy"; see David Hoffman, *A Course of Legal Study: Respectfully Addressed to Students of Law in the United States* (Baltimore: Coale & Maxwell, 1819), 32–38. Ferguson's *Law and Letters* describes it as a "standard manual of its kind well into the 1830s" (29); see also Howard Schweber, "The 'Science' of Legal Science: The Model of the Natural Sciences in Nineteenth-Century American Legal Education," *Law and History Review* 17 (1999): 421, 438.

75. Howe, *Making of the American Self*, 264. This rendering of the political divisions within the professions is drawn from Robert W. Gordon, "Legal Thought and Legal Practice in the Age of American Enterprise, 1870–1920," in *Professions and Professional Ideologies in America*, ed. Gerald L. Geison (Chapel Hill: University of North Carolina Press, 1983), 82–87. For evidence of the general influence of Common Sense realism in the profession, see Conrad, "Polite Foundation," 359–388; Ferguson, *Law and Letters*, 186–190; Schweber, "'Science' of Legal Science," 442–455; Stimson, "'Jury of the Country,'" 193–208; R. Kent Newmyer, "Harvard Law School, New England Legal Culture, and the Antebellum Origins of American Jurisprudence," *Journal of American History* 74 (1987): 826–827; Mark Warren Bailey, "Early Legal Education in the United States: Natural Law Theory and Law as a Moral Science," *Journal of Legal Education* 48 (1998): 311–328; Peter Charles Hoffer, "Principled Discretion: Concealment, Conscience, and Chancellors," *Yale Journal of Law and the Humanities* 3 (1991): 53–82. For a

study pointing to the continuing influence of this intellectual tradition in the late nineteenth century, see Mark Warren Bailey, *Guardians of the Moral Order: The Legal Philosophy of the Supreme Court, 1860–1910* (Dekalb: Northern Illinois University Press, 2004).

76. See, e.g., Mayes, "Address," 137; Nathaniel Chipman, *Principles of Government: A Treatise on Free Institutions, Including the Constitution of the United States* (Burlington, VT: E. Smith, 1833), 1–113; David Hoffman, *Legal Outlines: Being the Substance of a Course of Lectures Now Delivering in the University of Maryland* (Baltimore: Edward J. Coale, 1829), 14, 33.

77. Hoffman, *Legal Outlines*, 9–101. See also Chipman, *Principles of Government*, 9–55; Henry St. George Tucker, *A Few Lectures on Natural Law* (Charlottesville, VA: J. Alexander, 1844), 6–8, 15; James Kent, *A Lecture, Introductory to a Course of Law Lectures in Columbia College* (New York: Clayton and Van Norden, 1824), 9; Daniel Mayes, "An Address to the Students of Law in Transylvania University," in *The Gladsome Light of Jurisprudence: Learning the Law in England and the United States in the 18th and 19th Centuries*, ed. Michael H. Hoeflich (New York: Greenwood Press, 1988), 148, 149.

78. Timothy Walker, *Introduction to American Law* (Philadelphia: P. H. Nicklin & T. Johnson, 1837), 202–203. A revised second edition appeared in 1846; a third was published after his death in 1856, and it went through nine more editions, the last appearing in 1905.

79. Ibid., 222, 651; Timothy Walker, "The Reform Spirit of the Day. An Oration before the Phi Beta Kappa Society of Harvard University" (Boston and Cambridge: James Munroe and Company, 1850), 5–38. The strains in Walker's thought reflect "the uneasy union of theological liberalism and social conservatism," as Jeffrey Sklansky describes the broader cultural context in *The Soul's Economy*, 33–72.

80. Walker, *Introduction*, 163, 165, 650.

81. See, e.g., John Bouvier, *Institutes of American Law*, 2nd ed. (Philadelphia, Robert E. Peterson & Co., 1854), vol. 1, 71; Thomas W. Clerke, *Rudiments of American Law and Practice: On the Plan of Blackstone* (New York: Gould, Banks, & Co., 1842), 119, 135, 176, 191, 327, 345.

82. Meranze, *Laboratories of Virtue*, 253–292; Wiener, *Reconstructing the Criminal*, 146–149.

Chapter 2: The Medical Jurisprudence of Insanity

1. Philadelphia surgeon Philip Syng Physick served on the medical school faculty; Deborah C. Brunton, "The Edinburgh and Philadelphia Medical Schools," in *Scotland and America in the Age of the Enlightenment*, ed. Richard B. Sher and Jeremy Smitten (Edinburgh: Edinburgh University Press, 1990), 242, 252.

2. Benjamin Rush, "On the Study of Medical Jurisprudence," in *Sixteen Introductory Lectures* (Philadelphia: Bradford & Innskeep, 1811), 363, 380–381, 385–386, 392–393.

3. Donald J. D'Elia, "Benjamin Rush: Philosopher of the American Revolution," *Transactions of the American Philosophical Society* 64 (1974): 77; Benjamin Rush, *Medical Inquiries and Observations, upon the Diseases of the Mind* (Philadelphia: Kimbler & Richardson, 1812), v, 264, 367. The work went through

five editions by 1835; Norman Dain, *Concepts of Insanity in the United States, 1789–1865* (New Brunswick, NJ: Rutgers University Press, 1964), 22.

4. The most comprehensive treatment is James Mohr, *Doctors and the Law: Medical Jurisprudence in Nineteenth-Century America* (New York: Oxford University Press, 1993). Other discussions, which emphasize intra- as well as interprofessional conflicts, include Charles E. Rosenberg, *The Trial of the Assassin Guiteau: Psychiatry and Law in the Gilded Age* (Chicago: University of Chicago Press, 1968); David Brion Davis, *Homicide in American Fiction, 1798–1860* (Ithaca, NY: Cornell University Press, 1957), 59–83; Craig Haney, "Criminal Justice and the Nineteenth-Century Paradigm: The Triumph of Psychological Individualism in the 'Formative Era,'" *Law and Human Behavior* 6 (1982): 191–235; Janet A. Tighe, "A Question of Responsibility: The Development of Forensic Psychiatry, 1838–1940" (PhD diss., University of Pennsylvania, 1983). On English and Continental medico-legal discourse, see Roger Smith, *Trial by Medicine: Insanity and Responsibility in Victorian Trials* (Edinburgh: Edinburgh University Press, 1981); Joel Eigen, *Witnessing Insanity: Madness and Mad-Doctors in the English Court* (New Haven, CT: Yale University Press, 1995); Ruth Harris, *Murders and Madness: Medicine, Law, and Society in the Fin de Siècle* (New York: Oxford University Press, 1989); Jan E. Goldstein, *Console and Classify: The French Psychiatric Profession in the Nineteenth Century* (Chicago: University of Chicago Press, 1989); Martin J. Wiener, *Reconstructing the Criminal: Culture, Law, and Policy in England, 1830–1914* (New York: Cambridge University Press, 1990).

5. See David J. Rothman, *The Discovery of the Asylum: Social Order and Disorder in the New Republic* (Boston: Little, Brown, 1971), chaps. 5 and 6. In line with the work of Michel Foucault and Michael Ignatieff, Rothman portrayed the architects of these institutions as chiefly concerned with imposing "social control" upon an unruly populace. For valuable correctives, see Nancy Tomes, *A Generous Confidence: Thomas Story Kirkbride and the Art of Asylum-Keeping, 1840–1883* (New York: Cambridge University Press, 1984); Gerald N. Grob, *Mental Institutions in America: Social Policy to 1875* (New York: Free Press, 1973); Andrew Scull, *Social Order/Mental Disorder: Anglo-American Psychiatry in Historical Perspective* (Los Angeles: University of California Press, 1989); Richard Wightman Fox, *So Far Disordered in Mind: Insanity in California, 1870–1930* (Berkeley: University of California Press, 1978); Adam Hirsch, *The Rise of the Penitentiary: Prisons and Punishment in Early America* (New Haven, CT: Yale University Press, 1992); Mark Colvin, *Penitentiaries, Reformatories, and Chain Gangs: Social Theory and the History of Punishment in Nineteenth-Century America* (New York: St. Martin's Press, 1997); Michael Meranze, *Laboratories of Virtue: Punishment, Revolution, and Authority in Philadelphia, 1760–1835* (Chapel Hill: University of North Carolina Press, 1996); Benjamin Reiss, *Theaters of Madness: Insane Asylums and Nineteenth-Century American Culture* (Chicago: University of Chicago Press, 2008). On the inattention to the interface between law and "the disciplines" in the work of Foucault and those he has influenced, see Jan E. Goldstein, "Framing Discipline with Law: Problems and Promises of the Liberal State," *American Historical Review* 98 (April 1993): 364–375.

6. Samuel Finley, *The Madness of Mankind* (New York: Gaines, 1758); Benjamin Rush to John Adams, March 2, 1809, *Letters*, vol. 2, 996–997.

7. Benjamin Rush, *The Autobiography of Benjamin Rush. His "Travels through Life" together with his "Commonplace Book" for 1789–1813*, ed. George W. Corner (Princeton, NJ: Princeton University Press, 1948), 36–38; D'Elia, *Benjamin Rush*, 9–20.

8. Mary Ann Jimenez, *Changing Faces of Madness: Early American Attitudes and Treatment of the Insane* (Hanover, NH: University Press of New England). See also Gerald N. Grob, *The Mad among Us: A History of the Care of America's Mentally Ill* (New York: Free Press, 1994), 5–22; compare Albert Deutsch, *The Mentally Ill in America: A History of Their Care and Treatment from Colonial Times* (New York: Columbia University Press, 1946, 1–113; J. K. Hall and Gregory Zilboorg, eds., *One Hundred Years of American Psychiatry* (New York: Columbia University Press, 1944).

9. Leading accounts framed in terms of medicalization and/or secularization include Michel Foucault, *History of Madness*, trans. Jonathan Murphy (London: Routledge, 2006); Klaus Doerner, *Madmen and the Bourgeoisie: A Social History of Insanity and Psychiatry*, trans. J. Neugroschel and J. Steinberg (1969; repr., Oxford: Oxford University Press, 1981); Michael MacDonald, "Religion, Social Change, and Psychological Healing in England, 1600–1800," in *Sociability and Society in Eighteenth-Century Scotland*, ed. John Dwyer and Richard B. Sher (Edinburgh: Mercat Press, 1993), 194–209. For critical appraisals and revisions, see Roy Porter, *Mind Forg'd Manacles: A History of Madness in England from the Restoration to the Regency* (Cambridge, MA: Harvard University Press, 1987); Eigen, *Witnessing Insanity*; Robert A. Houston, *Madness and Society in Eighteenth-Century Scotland* (Oxford: Oxford University Press, 2000); Jonathan Andrews and Andrew Scull, *Undertaker of the Mind: John Munro and Mad-Doctoring in Eighteenth-Century England* (Berkeley: University of California Press, 2001); Jeremy Schmidt, *Melancholy and the Care of the Soul: Religion, Moral Philosophy and Madness in Early Modern England* (Aldershot: Ashgate, 2007); Angus Gowland, "The Problem of Early Modern Melancholy," *Past & Present* 191 (2006): 77–120; William L. Parry-Jones, *The Trade in Lunacy: A Study of Private Madhouses in England in the Eighteenth and Nineteenth Centuries* (London: Routledge; Toronto: Toronto University Press, 1972).

10. See Akihito Suzuki, "Anti-Lockean Enlightenment: Mind and Body in Early Eighteenth-Century English Medicine," in *Medicine in the Enlightenment* (Amsterdam: Rodopi, 1995), 336–359; Theodore M. Brown, "Descartes, Dualism, and Psychosomatic Medicine," in *The Anatomy of Madness*, ed. W. F. Bynum, Roy Porter, and M. Shepherd (London: Tavistock, 1985), vol. 1, 40–62. See also Jonathan Andrews and Andrew Scull, *Undertaker of the Mind: John Munro and Mad-Doctoring in Eighteenth-Century England* (Berkeley: University of California Press, 2001), 75–226; Michael MacDonald, "Insanity and the Realities of History in Early Modern England," *Psychological Medicine* 11 (1981): 11–25; Porter, *Mind Forg'd Manacles*, chap. 2; Houston, *Madness and Society*, esp. chaps. 6 and 7; Michael Heyd, *"Be Sober and Reasonable": The Critique of Enthusiasm in the Seventeenth and Early Eighteenth Centuries* (Leiden: E. J. Brill, 1995). On France, see Jan Goldstein, "Enthusiasm or Imagination? Eighteenth-Century Smear Words in Comparative National Context," in *Enthusiasm and Enlightenment in Europe, 1650–1850*, ed. Lawrence E. Klein and Anthony J. La Vopa (San Marino, CA: Huntington Library Press, 1998), 29–50.

11. Roy Porter, *Madmen: A Social History of Madhouses, Mad Doctors, and Lunatics* (Stroud: Tempus, 2001), 89–116; Akihito Suzuki, "Mind and Its Disease in Enlightenment British Medicine," (PhD thesis, University of London, 1992), 122–126. Hypochondria and hysteria acquired new salience as independent disease entities in Georgian England, though these nervous disorders were not cast in strongly gendered terms until the nineteenth century. See Mark S. Micale, *Hysterical Men: The Hidden History of Nervous Illness* (Cambridge, MA: Harvard University Press, 2008). On the cultural influence of these theories, see G. S. Rousseau, "Science Books and Their Readers in the Eighteenth Century," in *Books and Their Readers in Eighteenth-Century England*, ed. Isabel Rivers (Leicester: Leicester University Press, 1982), 197–237; Roy Porter, "Science, Provincial Culture and Public Opinion in Enlightenment England," *British Journal for Eighteenth-Century Studies* 3 (1980): 20–46. The circulation of this literature in colonial America is chronicled in Sarah Knott, *Sensibility and the American Revolution* (Chapel Hill: University of North Carolina Press, 2009), 69–107.

12. William Cullen, *First Lines of the Practice of Physic* (Edinburgh: C. Elliott, 1789), 109–123; William Cullen, *The Works of William Cullen, M.D.* (Edinburgh: Blackwood, 1827), 144–145. See John P. Wright, "Metaphysics and Physiology: Mind, Body and the Animal Economy in 18th-Century Scotland," in *Studies in the Philosophy of the Scottish Enlightenment*, ed. M. A. Stewart (Oxford: Oxford University Press, 1990), 251–301; Porter, *Madmen*, 180–187; Suzuki, "Mind and Its Disease," 273–277, 293–310; Christopher J. Lawrence, *Medicine as Culture: Edinburgh and the Scottish Enlightenment* (London: University of London Press, 1984), 312–416; Akihito Suzuki, "Dualism and the Transformation of Psychiatric Language," *History of Science* 33, no. 102, pt. 4 (1995): 417–447; W. F. Bynum, "Cullen and the Nervous System," in *William Cullen and the Eighteenth Century Medical World*, ed. A. Doig et al. (Edinburgh: Royal College of Physicians and Surgeons, 1991), 152–162; George Rousseau, "Nerves, Spirits, and Fibres: Towards Defining the Origins of Sensibility," in *Studies in the Eighteenth Century III*, ed. R. F. Brissenden and J. C. Eade (Toronto: Toronto University Press, 1976), 137–157; Christopher Lawrence, "The Nervous System and Society in the Scottish Enlightenment," in *Natural Order: Historical Studies of Scientific Culture*, ed. Barry Barnes and Steven Shapin (Beverly Hills, CA: Sage Publications, 1979), 19–40.

13. Suzuki, "Dualism"; Porter, *Madmen*, 172–227; Andrew Scull, *The Most Solitary of Afflictions: Madness and Society in Britain, 1700–1900* (New Haven, CT: Yale University Press, 1993), 46–110; Jan Goldstein, "Psychiatry," in *Companion Encyclopedia of the History of Medicine*, ed. W. F. Bynum and Roy Porter (London: Routledge, 1992), vol. 2, 1350–1372, 1350–1363; Dora B. Weiner, "Mind and Body in the Clinic: Philippe Pinel, Alexander Crichton, Dominique Esquirol, and the Birth of Psychiatry," in *Languages of the Psyche: Mind and Body in Enlightenment Thought*, ed. G. S. Rousseau (Berkeley: University of California Press, 1990) 331–390;

14. D'Elia, "Benjamin Rush, Philosopher," 20–51; Isaac Kramnick, *Republicanism and Bourgeois Radicalism: Political Ideology in Late-Eighteenth-Century England and America* (Ithaca: Cornell University Press, 1990), 93 (quoting James Burgh); Rush, *Autobiography*, 46.

15. Rush, *Autobiography*, 46; Robert H. Abzug, *Cosmos Crumbling: American Reform and the Religious Imagination* (New York: Oxford University Press, 1994), 11–29; Michael Meranze, "Introduction to Benjamin Rush," in *Essays: Literary, Moral, and Philosophical*, ed. Michael Meranze (Schenectady, NY: Union College Press, 1988), i–xxxi.

16. Benjamin Rush to Charles Lee, October 24, 1779, *Letters*, vol. 1, 243–244, 244; Benjamin Rush, "Address to the People of the United States," *The American Museum* 1 (January 1787), 8–11, 9; Benjamin Rush, "On the Mode of Education Proper in a Republic," in *Essays*, ed. Meranze, 7–9; see also Abzug, *Cosmos Crumbling*, 18–29; Noll, *America's God*, 64-65.

17. Benjamin Rush, *Benjamin Rush's Lectures on the Mind*, ed. Eric T. Carlson, Jeffrey L. Wollock, and Patricia S. Noel (Philadelphia: American Philosophical Society, 1981), 403–435, 519–520, 553; Benjamin Rush, "Thoughts on Common Sense," in *Essays*, 146–150. See generally Donald J. D'Elia, "Benjamin Rush, David Hartley, and the Revolutionary Uses of Psychology," *Proceedings of the American Philosophical Society* 114 (1970): 109–118; Sophia Rosenfeld, *Common Sense: A Political History* (Cambridge, MA: Harvard University Press, 2011), 150–151; Robert Ferguson, "The Commonalities of Common Sense," *William and Mary Quarterly* 57 (2000): 465–504; Meranze, "Introduction."

18. Rush, *Lectures on the Mind*, 525–529.

19. Benjamin Rush, *An Oration, Delivered before the American Philosophical Society, Held in Philadelphia on the 27th of February, 1786: Containing an Enquiry into the Influence of Physical Causes upon the Moral Faculty* (Philadelphia: Charles Cist, 1786); D'Elia, "Benjamin Rush, Philosopher," 74; Rush, *Diseases of the Mind*, 365; see also Eric T. Carlson, "Benjamin Rush and Mental Health," *Annals of the New York Academy of Sciences* 291 (1977): 95–96; John M. Kloos Jr., *A Sense of Deity: The Republican Spirituality of Dr. Benjamin Rush* (Chicago: Carlson Publishing, 1991), 76–77.

20. Rush, *Oration*, 1; Rush, *Diseases of the Mind*, 242.

21. Rush, *Oration*, 4–12.

22. Francis Hopkinson, "Some Thoughts on the Diseases of the Mind; with a Scheme for Purging the Moral Faculties of the Good People of Pennsylvania; Quite New and Very Philosophical," *American Museum* 4 (1788), 328.

23. Rush, "Address"; Benjamin Rush to John Redman Coxe, 5 September 1810, in *Letters*, vol. 2 1058–1060. See also Meranze, "Introduction," xiv, xvii–xxv; Fliegelman, *Declaring Independence*, 138–140.

24. On the controversy surrounding the statistics of insanity, which encompassed questions about the relative "liability" of men versus women, blacks versus whites, and Europeans versus Americans to the disease, see Gerald Grob, *Edward Jarvis and the Medical World of Nineteenth-Century America* (Knoxville: University of Tennessee Press, 1978), 70–74. Perceptions that insanity was on the rise and positively correlated with civilization are traced in Rothman, *Discovery of the Asylum*, 109–129. The problematic nature of the sources from which estimates of an increase are drawn is discussed by Andrew Scull in "Was Insanity Increasing?" in *Social Order/Mental Disorder Anglo-American Psychiatry in Historical Perspective* (Berkeley: University of California Press, 1989), 239–249.

25. Rush, "Medical Jurisprudence," 393; Rush, *Diseases of the Mind*, 66, 262, 264; see also Rush, *Lectures on the Mind*, 426–431. See generally Mohr, *Doctors*

and the Law, 7–8, 60–62. In this project, Rush drew not only on his experiences treating insane patients in a special ward of the Pennsylvania Hospital, but also on the researches of such pioneering British physicians as Franz Joseph Gall, J. G. Spurzheim, and George Combe, as well as their French counterparts Phillippe Pinel, Jean-Etienne-Dominique Esquirol, and Etienne-Jean Georget; see Eigen, *Witnessing Insanity*, 68–76.

26. Rush, *Diseases of the Mind*, 235.

27. Ibid., 360.

28. Alexander Crichton, *An Inquiry into the Nature and Origin of Mental Derangement* (London: T. Cadell and W. Davies, 1798), vol. 1, xxvii; Phillippe Pinel, *A Treatise on Insanity* (Sheffield, England: W. Todd, 1806), 51; Rush, *Sixteen Introductory Lectures*, 363–395; John Haslam, *Medical Jurisprudence as it Relates to Insanity, According to the Law of England*, in *Tracts on Medical Jurisprudence*, ed. Thomas Cooper (Philadelphia: James Webster, 1819), 291; John Conolly, *An Inquiry Concerning the Indications of Insanity* (London: J. Taylor, 1830), 39–40, 68–69, 92; Isaac Ray, "Criminal Law of Insanity," *American Jurist and Law Magazine* 14 (1835): 259; Jimenez, *Changing Faces of Madness*, 28–29, 65–79; Dain, *Concepts of Insanity*, 3–27; Arthur E. Fink, *Causes of Crime: Biological Theories in the United States, 1800–1915* (Philadelphia: Pennsylvania University Press, 1938), 1–75.

29. John Haslam, *Medical Jurisprudence, as It Relates to Insanity, According to the Law of England* (London: n.p., 1817), iii; Crichton, *Mental Derangement*; Pinel, *Treatise on Insanity*; Haslam, *Medical Jurisprudence*, cclxxxiv, 352; Rush, *Sixteen Introductory Lectures*, 363–395; Conolly, *Indications of Insanity*, 2 vols.; Ray, "Criminal Law of Insanity," 253; Theodric Romeyn Beck, *Elements of Medical Jurisprudence* (Albany: Websters and Skinners, 1823), vol. 1, 372–377.

30. Beck, *Elements of Medical Jurisprudence*, vol. 1, 372–377; Conolly, *Indications of Insanity*, vol. 1, 8, 59, 171; Haslam, *Medical Jurisprudence*, 288–293, 352.

31. These words were originally spoken by French advocate Henri François D'Aguesseau before Parliament in connection with a contested will. For legal treatises excerpting and glossing his speech, see Anthony Highmore, *A Treatise on the Law of Idiocy and Lunacy* (London: J. Butterworth, 1807), 14; George Dale Collinson, *A Treatise on the Law Concerning Idiots, Lunatics, and Other Persons Non Compotes Mentis* (London: W. Reed, 1812), 35.

32. Haslam, *Medical Jurisprudence*, 291–293; Beck, *Elements of Medical Jurisprudence*, vol. 1, 377. See also J. A. Paris and J. S. M. Fonblanque, *Medical Jurisprudence* (London: W. Phillips, 1823), vol. 1, 315–331. Medical experts might also find that an eccentric person in question was sane; see Joel Eigen, "Lesion of the Will: Medical Resolve and Criminal Responsibility in Victorian Insanity Trials," *Law & Society Review* 33 (1999): 425–460, 432.

33. Haslam, *Medical Jurisprudence*, 294–295, 299–300.

34. On the struggles of medical writers in this period to distinguish normal from pathological manifestations of passion, see Dain, *Concepts of Insanity*, 9; Jan Goldstein, *Console and Classify: The French Psychiatric Profession in the Nineteenth Century* (Cambridge: Cambridge University Press, 1987), 177.

35. Beck, *Elements of Medical Jurisprudence*, vol. 1, 342; see also Eigen, *Witnessing Insanity*, 73–76; Goldstein, *Console and Classify*, 155–158.

36. See Theodric Romeyn Beck and John B. Beck, *Elements of Medical Jurisprudence*, 6th ed. (Philadelphia: Thomas, Coperthwaite, 1838), vol. 1, 563–565; Isaac Ray, *A Treatise on the Medical Jurisprudence of Insanity* (Boston: Charles C. Little and James Brown, 1838), 168–234. James Cowles Prichard, *On the Different Forms of Insanity in Relation to Jurisprudence* (London: Hippolyte BailliÏre, 1842), 30–63. See also H. F. Augstein, *James Cowles Prichard's Anthropology: Remaking the Science of Man in Early Nineteenth-Century Britain* (Amsterdam: Rodopi, 1999).

37. Compare Alfred Swaine Taylor, *Medical Jurisprudence of Insanity*, ed. R. Egglesfield Griffith (Philadelphia: Lea and Blanchard, 1845), 500, 514–518, and Beck and Beck, *Elements of Medical Jurisprudence*, vol. 1, 563–565, 614–626, with Ray, *Medical Jurisprudence of Insanity*, 192, and Prichard, *Forms of Insanity*, 63–67.

38. Ray, *Medical Jurisprudence of Insanity*, vii, 256, 234; G. T. C., "Criminal Law of Insanity," *American Jurist & Law Magazine* 15 (1836): 83. Ray's treatise went through four editions before his death in 1880. Historians have tended to take the words of Ray's detractors at face value, carrying forward the mistaken impression that the doctor "accepted a view of human psychology that was deterministic." John Starrett Hughes, *In the Law's Darkness: Isaac Ray and the Medical Jurisprudence of Insanity in Nineteenth-Century America* (Dobb's Ferry, NY: Oceana Publications, 1986), 82.

39. Ray, *Medical Jurisprudence of Insanity*, 66, 97–98, 235.

40. Ibid., 19–20, 24, 35, 101, 184.

41. Ibid., 23, 47, 64, 142–145.

42. Eigen, *Witnessing Insanity*, 79–80; Alison Winter, *Mesmerized: The Powers of Mind in Victorian Britain* (Chicago: University of Chicago Press, 1998), 46; Smith, *Trial by Medicine*, 12–66; Hughes, *Law's Darkness*, 50–51.

43. Cooper was educated in England in the classics, medicine, and the natural sciences before he became a barrister. He immigrated to America in 1793, where he became a Jeffersonian judge and held academic posts in physical science. Cooper is also credited with founding South Carolina's first insane asylum and serving as chief editor of the state's statutes. See Mohr, *Doctors and the Law*, 9, 30; Merle Curti, *Human Nature in American Thought* (Madison: University of Wisconsin Press, 1980), 92. Cooper applied his study of the mind to the proslavery cause; while stopping short of claiming "the blacks are a distinct species," he maintained they were "an inferior variety of the human species; and not capable of the same improvement as the whites." See Dr. Thomas Cooper to Sen. Mahlon Dickerson, 1826, in Curti, *Human Nature*, 173.

44. British works that were reprinted in the United States included Samuel Farr's *Elements of Medical Jurisprudence* (1787); William Dease's *Remarks on Medical Jurisprudence* (n.d.); George Edward Male's *Epitome of Juridical or Forensic Medicine for the Use of Medical Men, Coroners, and Barristers* (n.d.); and John Haslam's *Medical Jurisprudence as It Relates to Insanity* (1817).

45. The first edition of Shelford's work was published in London in 1833, but an American edition appeared in the same year. Chitty's had two American editions in 1835 and 1836. There was no American edition of Collinson's *Treatise*, but it was frequently cited by American judges, lawyers, and jurists during the first half of the century. Chitty stood out among the three because he had medical training before taking up the law.

46. For typical renderings of this maxim, *furiosus furore solum punitur*, see Highmore, *Law of Idiocy and Lunacy*, 196; Asa Kinne, *The Most Important Parts of Blackstone's Commentaries: Reduced to Questions and Answers*, 2nd ed. (New York: W. E. Dean, 1839), 187–262, referencing William Blackstone's chapter, "Of the Persons Capable of Committing Crimes," in the fourth volume of his *Commentaries on the Laws of England*. .

47. Collinson, *Idiots, Lunatics, and Other Persons*, 6–36, 75–85.

48. Leonard Shelford, *A Practical Treatise on the Law Concerning Lunatics, Idiots, and Persons of Unsound Mind* (Philadelphia: J. S. Littell, 1833), xxi–lix, 1–5; Joseph Chitty, *A Practical Treatise on Medical Jurisprudence*, 2nd Am. ed. (Philadelphia: Carey, Lea, and Blanchard, 1836), 323–367.

49. Shelford, *Lunatics, Idiots, and Persons of Unsound Mind*, xxxii–xxxvi, xliv, 46–47. Shelford registered some hesitancy about the idea of moral insanity and suggested that some sort of intellectual impairment was likely involved in every purported case. He did not indicate whether "moral" causes had underlying physical ones or were original, in and of themselves.

50. Chitty, *Practical Treatise on Medical Jurisprudence*, 344–345, 311–320, 323–324, 344–357. Chitty also seemed persuaded by a slippery slope argument, suggesting that medical standards of mental health might warrant putting "half the world" in straightjackets (339). Although he never directly addressed physicians' complaints about the different rules of responsibility applied in civil and criminal cases, he appeared satisfied with the application of a lower threshold of capacity in criminal law (351–362).

51. Ibid., 51.

52. Francis Wharton and Moreton Stillé, *A Treatise on Medical Jurisprudence* (Philadelphia: Kay and Brother, 1855), iii, ix, xi. Stillé died shortly before the publication of the first edition and Wharton indicates in the preface that while they collaborated closely on the project as a whole, it was he, rather than the doctor, who had drafted the sections on mental unsoundness as a matter of law and psychology. Wharton also authored these portions of the three subsequent editions published during his lifetime, in 1860, 1873, and 1882. For discussions of the historical significance of Wharton's work, see Janet A. Tighe, "Francis Wharton and the Insanity Defense: The Origins of a Reform Tradition" *American Journal of Legal History* 27 (1983): 223–253; Stephen A. Siegel, "Francis Wharton's Orthodoxy: God, Historical Jurisprudence, and Classical Legal Thought," *American Journal of Legal History* 46 (2004): 422–446; David M. Rabban, *Law's History: American Legal Thought and the Transatlantic Turn to History* (Cambridge: Cambridge University Press, 2014), 1–21, 364–367, 514–517.

53. Amos Dean, *Principles of Medical Jurisprudence Designed for the Professions of Law and Medicine* (Albany, NY: Gould, Banks and Gould, 1850), 464, 530–554, 575–579, 585–590.

54. Wharton and Stillé, *Treatise on Medical Jurisprudence*, 17–29, 35–47, 86, 137, 142–149, 215–221. Francis Wharton, *Wharton and Stillé's Medical Jurisprudence*, 3rd ed. (Philadelphia: Kay and Brother, 1873), 749–750, 764–771. See also Tighe, "A Question of Responsibility," 169–172; Isaac Ray, "Review of Wharton's Monograph on Mental Unsoundness," *American Journal of Insanity* 12 (January 1856): 285–292.

55. John P. Gray, "Moral Insanity," *American Journal of Insanity* 14 (April 1858): 311–322. See also D. Meredith Reese, "Report on Moral Insanity in Its Relation to Medical Jurisprudence," *Transactions of the American Medical Association* 11 (1858): 723–746 (opposing the doctrine; dissenting from AMA majority); compare C. B. Coventry, "Report on Medical Jurisprudence of Insanity," *Transactions of the American Medical Association* 11 (1858): 473–524 (AMA majority view). On the moral insanity controversy, see Hughes, *Law's Darkness*, 77–96; Gary S. Belkin, "Moral Insanity, Science, and Religion in Nineteenth-Century America: The Gray-Ray Debate," *History of Psychiatry* 7 (1996): 591–613; Robert J. Waldinger, "Sleep of Reason: John P. Gray and the Challenge of Moral Insanity," *Journal of the History of Medicine and Allied Sciences* 34 (1979): 163–179; S. P. Fullinwider, "Insanity as Loss of Self: The Moral Insanity Controversy Revisited," *Bulletin of the History of Medicine* 49 (1975): 87–101; Norman Dain and Eric T. Carlson, "Moral Insanity in the United States, 1835–1866," *American Journal of Psychiatry* 118 (1962): 795–800; Nicole Rafter, "The Unrepentant Horse-Slasher: Moral Insanity and the Origins of Criminological Thought," *Criminology* 42 (2004): 979–1008; Heidi Rimke and Alan Hunt, "From Sinners to Degenerates: The Medicalization of Morality in the 19th Century," *History of the Human Sciences* 15 (2002): 59–88. For more on Gray's influence and the fate of the doctrine of moral insanity in postbellum America, see Rosenberg, *Trial of the Assassin Guiteau*, 68–74; on the controversy as it played out in the courtrooms of Victorian England, see Smith, *Trial by Medicine*, 113–123.

56. John Elwell, *A Medico-Legal Treatise on Malpractice and Medical Evidence: Comprising the Elements of Medical Jurisprudence* (New York: J. S. Voorhies, 1860), i, 11, 355, 402. Elwell was professor of medical jurisprudence in the Ohio State and Union Law College and in the medical department of Western Reserve University. He became a more outspoken critic of the doctrine of moral insanity over time, especially in the wake of the trial of President Garfield's assassin, Charles Guiteau; by that time, Elwell appeared to have adopted a rationale for criminal punishment based entirely on the society's right to defend itself. See J. J. Elwell et al., "The Moral Responsibility of the Insane," *North American Review* 302 (1882): 1–11.

57. Forbes Winslow, quoted in Elwell, *Medico-Legal Treatise*, 338–353.

58. Elwell, *Medico-Legal Treatise*, 360, 404. Despite this apparent absolutism, Elwell was at least willing to entertain the concept of graduated punishment (ibid., 409).

59. Ibid., 404–405.

Part II: The Mind in Issue

1. Jonathan Crary, *Techniques of the Observer: On Vision and Modernity in the Nineteenth Century* (Cambridge: MIT Press, 1990); Laura Burd Schiavo, "From Phantom Image to Perfect Vision: Physiological Optics, Commercial Photography, and the Popularization of the Stereoscope," in *New Media, 1740–1915*, ed. Lisa Gitelman and Geoffrey B. Pingree (Cambridge, MA: MIT Press, 2003), 113; Robert J. Silverman, "The Stereoscope and Photographic Depiction in the 19th Century," *Technology and Culture* 34 (1993): 729 (quoting the British physicist

Sir Charles Wheatstone). See generally Lorraine Daston and Peter Galison, *Objectivity* (New York: Zone Books, 2007).

2. "The Stereoscope," *Godey's Lady Book and Ladies' American Magazine* 45 (October 1852); 340–343, 342; Silverman, "Stereoscope," 736; Schaivo, "Phantom Image," 123, 127–129, 135; Alan Trachtenberg, *Reading American Photographs* (New York: Macmillan Co., 1990), 16–20; Miles Orvell, *The Real Thing: Imitation and Authenticity in American Culture, 1880–1940* (Chapel Hill: University of North Carolina Press, 1989), 36, 73, 78. On Barnum's promotional strategies and his creation and sale of stereographs of historical scenes, see James Cook, *The Arts of Deception: Playing with Fraud in the Age of Barnum* (Cambridge: Harvard University Press, 2001), esp. 1–29. On the emergence of this middle-class consumer culture and its broader socio-economic ramifications, see David Jaffee, *The New Nation of Goods: Artisans, Consumers, and Commodities in Early America, 1790–1860* (Philadelphia: University of Pennsylvania Press, 2010).

3. Oliver Wendell Holmes, "The Stereoscope and the Stereograph," *The Atlantic Monthly* 3 (June 1859): 738–749, 742; Oliver Wendell Holmes, "Sun-Painting and Sun-Sculpture," *The Atlantic Monthly* 8 (July 1861): 13–29, 15, 16, 18, 23; see also Oliver Wendell Holmes, "Doings of the Sunbeam," *The Atlantic Monthly* 12 (July 1863): 1–16. In exploring the cultural significance of Holmes's invention of and writing about what came to be known as the "American stereoscope," Miles Orvell notes that he freely gave away the rights to his design for a mass-produced instrument, "so as to encourage the popular enjoyment of photography," and takes him to epitomize the Victorian fascination with this new medium, "one moment celebrating its capacity for a seemingly literal imitation of reality and the next its use as a vehicle for fantasy and illusion," often doing so "without any sense of contradiction." Orvell, *Real Thing*, 75–77. See generally Peter Gibian, *Oliver Wendell Holmes and the Culture of Conversation* (Cambridge: Cambridge University Press, 2001). For a historical exploration of how this kind of visual evidence was treated in the nineteenth-century American courtroom, see Jennifer L. Mnookin, "The Image of Truth: Photographic Evidence and the Power of Analogy," *Yale Journal of Law and the Humanities* 10 (1998): 1–74.

4. I. R. [Isaac Ray], "Review," *American Journal of Insanity* 12 (January 1856): 285–292; Francis Wharton, *Wharton and Stillé's Medical Jurisprudence*, 3rd ed. (Philadelphia: Kay and Brother, 1873), vol. 1, xii–xiii.

5. Wharton, *Medical Jurisprudence* (1873), 299; Janet A. Tighe, "A Question of Responsibility: The Development of Forensic Psychiatry, 1838–1940" (PhD diss., University of Pennsylvania, 1983), 63. On the emergence of the adversarial trial and the problem of partisan expert testimony as it played out across the nineteenth century, see especially Tal Golan, *Laws of Men and Laws of Nature: The History of Scientific Expert Testimony in England and America* (Cambridge: Harvard University Press, 2004), chaps. 1–3.

6. I address this cultural ferment in greater detail in Susanna L. Blumenthal, "The Default Legal Person," *UCLA Law Review* 54 (2007): 1179–1203. See also James Mohr, *Doctors and the Law: Medical Jurisprudence in Nineteenth–Century America* (New York: Oxford University Press, 1993), 164–172.

7. Golan, *Laws of Men*, 108; Stephanie P. Browner, *Profound Science and Elegant Literature: Imagining Doctors in Nineteenth–Century* America (Philadelphia:

University of Pennsylvania Press, 2013), 134; Tighe, "A Question of Responsibility," 77–125, 181–226; Mohr, *Doctors and the Law*, 173–179.

8. John Ordronaux, *Commentaries on the Lunacy Laws of New York* (Albany, NY: J. D. Parsons, Jr., Law Publisher, 1878), xxv–xxvi. Importantly, the legal inquiry Ordronaux described did not reduce to a consideration of the transaction instead of the individual as legal realists like Milton Green have suggested. See Milton D. Green, "Proof of Mental Incompetency and the Unexpressed Major Premise," *Yale Law Journal* 53 (1994): 271–311.

9. John Ordronaux, "History and Philosophy of Medical Jurisprudence," *American Journal of Insanity* 25 (1868): 192–193, 196; Ordronaux, *Commentaries*, 192–193, 355; Ordronaux, "Moral Insanity," *American Journal of Insanity* 29 (January 1873): 317.

10. Mohr, *Doctors and the Law*, 174–175.

11. For a penetrating set of studies on the historical relationship between selfhood and criminal responsibility in England, ranging from the eighteenth century to the late twentieth century, see Nicola Lacey, "Responsibility and Modernity in Criminal Law," *Journal of Political Philosophy* 9 (2001): 249–77; Lacey, "In Search of the Responsible Subject: History, Philosophy and Criminal Law Theory," *Modern Law Review* 64 (2001): 350–371; Lacey, *Women, Crime and Character: From Moll Flanders to Tess of the d'Urbervilles* (Oxford University Press 2008) (The Clarendon Law Lectures). For general insights into the question of self-consciousness in European and American thought, see Charles Taylor, *Sources of the Self: The Making of the Modern Identity* (Cambridge: Cambridge University Press, 1989); J. B. Schneewind, *The Invention of Autonomy: A History of Modern Moral Philosophy* (Cambridge University Press, 1998); Jerrold Siegel, *The Idea of the Self: Thought and Experience in Western Europe Since the Seventeenth Century* (Cambridge: Cambridge University Press, 2005).

12. Golan, *Laws of Men*, 112. On the narrowing of the scope of scientific inquiry, see the classic essay by David A. Hollinger, "The Knower and the Artificer," *American Quarterly* 39 (1987): 37–55. This dichotomy has been criticized as overdrawn in more recent work showing that many academics and professionals on the borders between the natural sciences and social questions tried to finesse the epistemological problem. See Harvey J. Graff, *Undisciplining Knowledge: Interdisciplinarity in the Twentieth Century* (Baltimore: Johns Hopkins University Press, 2015), chap. 1. On the new determinisms and the threats they posed to conventional notions of human agency and responsibility see Thomas L. Haskell, *The Emergence of Professional Social Science* (Urbana: University of Illinois Press, 1977); Martin J. Wiener, *Reconstructing the Criminal* (New York: Cambridge University Press, 1990); Lorraine Daston, "British Responses to Psycho-Physiology, 1860-1900," *Isis* 69 (1979); 192–208. The emergence of a new form of scientific objectivity linked to a fear of the "subjective self" is elaborated most fully in Daston and Galison, *Objectivity*. As has been shown by scholars of French and English history, subjectivity posed problems well before the end of the nineteenth century though it did not provoke a decisive shift in legal thinking until the 1890s in the United States or Western Europe. See Crary, *Techniques of the Observer* and Jan Goldstein "The Advent of Psychological Modernism," in *Modernist Impulses in the Human Sciences, 1870-1930* (Baltimore: Johns Hopkins University Press, 1994), 190–209.

13. Wiener, *Reconstructing the Criminal*, 170 (quoting Henry Sidgwick); "Slave or Master," *The Century Magazine* 25 (April 1883): 953. See generally T. J. Jackson Lears, *No Place of Grace: Antimodernism and the Transformation of American Culture, 1880-1920* (Chicago: University of Chicago Press, 1981), 4–58. On the perplexities concerning legal personhood in this era, as expressed in literature as well as law, see especially Howard Horwitz, *By the Law of Nature: Form and Value in Nineteenth-Century America* (New York: Oxford University Press, 1991); Colin Dayan, *The Law is a White Dog: How Legal Rituals Made and Unmake Persons* (Princeton, NJ: Princeton University Press, 2011); Jeannine Marie DeLombard, *In the Shadows of the Gallows:Race, Crime, and American Civil Identity* (Pennsylvania: University of Pennsylvania Press, 2012).

14. Ordronaux, "Moral Insanity," 330; Ordronaux, "History and Philosophy of Insanity," 204–205.

15. John Ordronaux, Valedictory Address delivered before the Graduated Class of the National Medical College, March 6, 1867, excerpted in the *American Journal of Insanity* 25 (January 1869): 380–383. This character ideal was projected in late nineteenth-century success manuals as a means of survival in an industrial age. See Judy Hilkey, *Character Is Capital: Success Manuals and Manhood in Gilded Age America* (Chapel Hill: University of North Carolina Press, 1997).

16. John Ordronaux, "Is Habitual Drunkenness a Disease?" *American Journal of Insanity* 30 (1874): 430–443, 430-433. 442–443.

17. Ordronaux, "Medical Jurisprudence," 190.

18. The analysis offered in the chapters that form Part 2 is based upon over 800 published (usually appellate) opinions. Many of these cases were identified in the same way a nineteenth-century lawyer might have investigated the matter: by mining the notes of leading works on the medical jurisprudence of insanity as well as legal treatises devoted to discrete doctrinal areas. But I also drew from the databases of cases found on Westlaw and Lexis as well as various online archives of newspapers and periodical literature. In addition, I read virtually all the articles collected on HeinOnline relating to civil capacity as well as selected others from medical and medico-legal publications, which contained surveys of the leading cases that I could check against the treatise literature as I worked to reconstruct the main lines of doctrinal development over the course of the century. Finally, I surveyed the libraries of law schools and universities as well as the holdings at the New York Bar Association Library for published trial transcripts and related pamphlet material.

19. Michael Zakim, "Free Soil, Free Labor, and Free Markets," in *Contested Democracy: Freedom, Race, and Power in American History* (New York: Columbia University Press, 2007), 97, 104; Jeffrey Sklansky, "The Elusive Sovereign: New Intellectual and Social Histories of Capitalism," *Modern Intellectual History* 9 (2012): 240; see also Amy Dru Stanley, *From Bondage to Contract: Wage Labor, Marriage, and the Market in the Age of Slave Emancipation* (Cambridge: Cambridge University Press, 1998); Thomas Augst, *The Clerk's Tale: Young Men and Moral Life in Nineteenth-Century America* (Chicago: University of Chicago Press, 2003); Edward Balleisen, *Navigating Failure: Bankruptcy and Commercial Society in Antebellum America* (Chapel Hill: University of North Carolina Press, 2001); Brian Luskey, *On the Make: Clerks and the Quest for Capital in Nineteenth-Century America* (New York:

New York University Press, 2010); Scott A. Sandage, *Born Losers: A History of Failure in America* (Cambridge, MA: Harvard University Press, 2005).

20. Robert B. Warden, *A Familiar Forensic View of Man and Law* (Columbus, OH: Follett, Foster, and Co., 1859), 135, 145, 534.

21. Norma Basch, *Framing American Divorce: From the Revolutionary Generation to the Victorians* (Berkeley: University of California Press, 1999), 151; *The Parish Will Case in the Court of Appeals: The Statement of Facts, and of the Opinion of the Court* (New York: D. Appleton and Company, 1862), 461–463; see also Daniel A. Cohen, *Pillars of Salt, Monuments of Grace: New England Crime Literature and the Origins of American Popular Culture, 1674–1860* (New York: Oxford University Press, 1993), 251, which contends that narratives of criminal trials in this period "suggested an epistemology that was well suited to a legalistic, romantic, and pluralistic culture," and Karen Halttunen, *Murder Most Foul: The Killer and the American Gothic Imagination* (Cambridge, MA: Harvard University Press, 2000), 3, which similarly argues that crime narratives were presented in this period as mysteries, using "incomplete, fragmented, and chronologically confused narratives" that were designed "to impress upon readers the impossibility of achieving a full knowledge of the crime."

22. *The Parish Will Case in the Court of Appeals,* 461–463; Norma Basch, *Framing American Divorce: From the Revolutionary Generation to the Victorians* (Berkeley: University of California Press, 1999), 151, 160. It is exceedingly difficult to generalize about outcomes because a substantial number of cases settled before they reached a court of last resort, often leaving no indication of how the matter played out. Moreover, given the fact-intensive nature of these proceedings and how much is left out of the published opinions, it is not easy to say why a particular petition was granted or refused, nor can we speak with great confidence about judicial trends toward more "liberal" or "conservative" rulings.

23. John Charles Bucknill, *Unsoundness of Mind in Relation to Criminal Acts* (London: Samuel Highley, 1854), 125. This frequently quoted passage was most often attributed to an unnamed writer in the London Times who was quoted in Bucknill's prizewinning work on lunacy.

24. Michael Zakim, "Creating a Democracy of Common Men," in *A Companion to the Era of Andrew Jackson*, ed. Sean Patrick Adams (Malden, MA; Wiley-Blackwell, 2013), 170-193." This approach is distinguishable from the "bastard pragmatism" described by James Willard Hurst, which essentially underwrote a short-sighted utilitarianism, as well as from the philosophical movement that became known as Pragmatism. See James Willard Hurst, *Law and Economic Growth,* 34–37 (Madison: University of Wisconsin Press, 1964); James T. Kloppenberg, *Uncertain Victory: Social Democracy and Progressivism in European and American Thought,* 1870–1920 (New York: Oxford University Press, 1986).

25. Daniel Clark, "Medical Evidence in Courts of Law," *The Canada Lancet* 11 (1878), 97–106, 104; Clark, "Medical Evidence in Courts of Law," *The Canadian Journal of Medical Science* 4 (1879): 23–27.

Chapter 3: Unnatural Dispositions

1. Johnson v. Moore's Heirs, 11 Ky. (1 Litt.) 371, 371–372 (1822).
2. Ibid., 372, 374.

3. Ibid., 373, 377, 378, 384, 387–388.

4. "Last Wills—Unsound Mind and Memory," *American Journal of Insanity* 25 (1868): 213–225, 234; James C. Mohr, "The Paradoxical Advance and Embattled Retreat of the 'Unsound Mind': Evidence of Insanity and the Adjudication of Wills in Nineteenth-Century America," *Historical Reflections/Reflexions Historiques* 24 (1998): 428–434; Karen Halttunen, "Early American Murder Narratives: The Birth of Horror," in *The Power of Culture: Critical Essays in American History*, ed. Richard Wightman Fox and T. J. Jackson Lears (Chicago: University of Chicago Press, 1993), 80.

5. See, e.g., Clapp v. Fullerton, 34 N.Y. 190, 197 (1866); Boardman v. Woodman, 47 N.H. 120, 139 (1865); Sears v. Shafer, 1 Barb. 408, 411 (1847), quoting Leonard Shelford's *A Practical Treatise on the Law Concerning Lunatics, Idiots, and Persons of Unsound Mind*; repr. Philadelphia: J. S. Littell, 1833), 170. See generally James L. Huston, *Securing the Fruits of Labor: The American Concept of Wealth Distribution, 1765–1900* (Baton Rouge: Louisiana State University Press, 1998).

6. Johnson, 11 Ky. at 387; Isaac F. Redfield, *The Law of Wills, Embracing Also, The Jurisprudence of Insanity . . .* (Boston: Little, Brown and Company, 1964), vol. 1, 1; J. T. M., "Isaac F. Redfield," *American Law Register* 24 (1876): 257–263, 257.

7. See Melanie B. Leslie, "The Myth of Testamentary Freedom," *Arizona Law Review* 38 (1996): 235–290; Ray D. Madoff, "Unmasking Undue Influence," *Minnesota Law Review* 81 (1997): 571–630. Jane B. Baron, "Empathy, Subjectivity, and Testamentary Capacity," *San Diego Law Review* 24 (1987): 1043–1080, suggests that courts try to account for individual subjectivity but fall short of this goal. In many ways, these lines of argument are reminiscent of earlier ones advanced by Legal Realists. See especially Milton D. Green, "Proof of Mental Incompetency and the Unexpressed Major Premise," *Yale Law Journal* 53 (1944): 271–311; Green, "The Operative Effect of Mental Incompetency on Agreements and Wills," *Texas Law Review* 21 (1943): 554–589, 580–588; compare John H. Langbein, "Living Probate: The Conservatorship Model," *Michigan Law Review* 77 (1978): 64–68 (pointing to rules and practices internal to the American legal system to account for the "widespread" perception [in the absence of "comparative data directly on point"] that capacity litigation "occurs more frequently in the United States than on the Continent or in England" and further noting that "the odor of the strike suit hangs heavily over this field").

8. Lawrence M. Friedman, *Dead Hands: A Social History of Wills, Trusts, and Inheritance Law* (Stanford, CA: Stanford University Press, 2009), 92, presents will contests as reflections of conventional moral standards but finds judges generally resistant to claims of incapacity and undue influence, invalidating wills on these bases "sporadically, and somewhat irrationally" (96). Mohr, "Paradoxical Advance," also figures the law in a reactive posture, though he suggests that judges grew more tolerant of eccentric testators as they perceived the social order to be stabilizing toward the end of the century (434–435).

9. Yvonne Pitts, *Family, Law, and Inheritance in America: A Social and Legal History of Nineteenth-Century Kentucky* (Cambridge: Cambridge University Press, 2013); Bernie D. Jones, *Fathers of Conscience: Mixed-Race Inheritance in the Antebellum South* (Athens: University of Georgia Press, 2009). These accounts build

upon Adrienne Davis, "The Private Law of Race and Sex: An Antebellum Perspective," *Stanford Law Review* 51 (1999): 221–288, which considers appellate court records. For a study of will contests in the law and literature of Victorian and Edwardian England, see Cathrine O. Frank, *Law, Literature, and the Transmission of Culture in England, 1837-1925* (Burlington, VT: Ashgate, 2010).

10. American cultural historians have most fully analyzed the liberal response to this problem within the context of the criminal law. See Daniel A. Cohen, *Pillars of Salt, Monuments of Grace: New England Crime Literature and the Origins of American Popular Culture, 1674–1860* (New York: Oxford University Press, 1993); David Brion Davis, *Homicide in American Fiction, 1798–1860* (Ithaca, NY: Cornell University Press, 1957); Karen Halttunen, *Murder Most Foul: The Killer and the American Gothic Imagination* (Cambridge, MA: Harvard University Press, 1998). For explorations of similar developments in English law and culture, see Martin J. Wiener, *Reconstructing the Criminal: Culture, Law and Policy in England, 1830–1914* (Cambridge: Cambridge University Press, 1994); Lisa Rodensky, *The Crime in Mind: Criminal Responsibility and the Victorian Novel* (New York: Oxford University Press, 2003); Nicola Lacey, *Women, Crime and Character: From Moll Flanders to Tess of the d'Urbervilles* (Oxford University Press 2008) (The Clarendon Law Lectures). Scholars of law tend to address this problem under the rubric of determinism. For an overview, see Richard C. Boldt, "The Construction of Responsibility in the Criminal Law," *University of Pennsylvania Law Review* 140 (1992): 2246–2250.

11. Edward Champlin, *Final Judgments: Duty and Emotion in Roman Wills, 200 B.C.–A.D. 250* (Berkeley: University of California Press, 1991); Michael M. Sheehan, *The Will in Medieval England* (Toronto: Pontifical Institute of Mediaeval Studies, 1963), 107–230; Henry Swinburne, *A Treatise of Testaments and Last Wills* (London: Henry Lintot/S. Birt; D. Brown; and J. Shuckburgh, 1743), 12, 73–118. For a similar classification scheme, see John Godolphin, *The Orphans Legacy*, 2nd ed. (London: Wilkinson 1677), 21–38.

12. Swinburne, *Testaments and Last Wills*, 131, 153, 154; William Blackstone, *Commentaries on the Laws of England* (Chicago: University of Chicago Press, 1979), 373–374.

13. Stanley N. Katz, "Republicanism and the Law of Inheritance in the American Revolutionary Era," *Michigan Law Review* 76 (1977): 14; John V. Orth, "After the Revolution: The 'Reform' of the Law of Inheritance," *Law and History Review* 10 (Spring 1992): 33–44; Gregory S. Alexander, *Commodity & Propriety: Competing Visions of Property in American Legal Thought, 1776–1970* (Chicago: University of Chicago Press, 1997), 37–38; Holly Brewer, *By Birth or Consent: Children, Law, & the Anglo-American Revolution in Authority* (Chapel Hill: University of North Carolina Press, 2005), 36–39; Stuart Banner, *American Property: A History of How, Why, and What We Own* (Cambridge, MA: Harvard University Press, 2011), 13–16. Huston, *Securing the Fruits of Labor*, 46–50. For an illuminating sociological study of postrevolutionary American institutions and practices in transatlantic perspective, see Jens Beckert, *Inherited Wealth*, trans. Thomas Dunlap (Princeton, NJ: Princeton University Press, 2008 [original German edition, Frankfurt/Main, Germany: Campus Verlag, 2004]).

14. Joel Barlow, "Advice to the Privileged Orders in the Several States of Europe. Resulting from the Necessity and Propriety of a General Revolution in the

Principles of Government," in *The Political Writings of Joel Barlow* (New York: Mott and Lyon, 1796), 29–30; Benjamin Rush, *An Enquiry into the Natural History of Medicine among the Indians in North America* (1774), reprinted in *Medical Inquiries and Observations* (Philadelphia: Prichard and Hall, 1789), 54. Rush to Enos Hitchcock, 24 April 1789, in *Letters of Benjamin Rush*, vol. 1, 511.

15. Orth, "After the Revolution," 39–40, notes that other Southern legislatures followed a course similar to that taken in Virginia in this period, though with respect to the institution of entail they were really uprooting colonial laws passed by indigenous assemblies rather than the law then in force in metropolitan England. Once these changes were implemented, he further observes, "the reformers' zeal waned"; they looked primarily to "social custom, individualism, and democratic mores . . . to prevent the emergence of a native landed aristocracy in the new republic." On the hierarchies of age, gender, and race sustained by way of the law of succession, see Brewer, *By Birth or Consent*, 37–39; Pitts, *Family, Law, and Inheritance in America*; Jones, *Fathers of Conscience*; Thomas D. Morris, *Southern Slavery and the Law, 1619–1860* (Chapel Hill: University of North Carolina Press, 1996), 81–101.

16. Timothy Walker, *Introduction to American Law: Designed as a First Book for Students* (Philadelphia: P. H. Nicklin and T. Johnson, 1837), 339; James Kent, *Commentaries on American Law* (New York: O. Halsted, 1830), vol. 4, 489–490; David Hoffman, *Legal Outlines: Being the Substance of the First Title of a Course of Lectures now delivering in the University of Maryland* (Baltimore: Joseph Neal, 1836), 121, 139, 140–141, 143; Orth, "After the Revolution," 33.

17. Judges and jurists noted that most states' statute of wills affirmatively required that the testator be of sound mind, whereas the English version originally allowed all persons to make a will and it was only subsequently amended to introduce exceptions. See, e.g, Crowninshield v. Crowninshield, 2 Gray 524, 68 Mass. 524, 532 (observing the difference between the English and the Massachusetts statute of wills and further opining that "there are strong reasons why the same presumption as to sanity should not attach to wills as to deeds and ordinary contracts. Wills are supposed to be made *in extremis*. In point of fact, a large proportion of them are made when the mind is to some extent enfeebled by sickness or old age."); but see Redfield, *The Law of Wills*, vol. 1, 30–51, criticizing the "modern" rule announced in *Crowninshield* and defended by other commentators.

18. Chancellor James Kent's influential decision in Van Alst v. Hunter, 5 Johns. Ch. 148, 159–160 (N.Y. Ch. 1821) provides an illustrative example of the balancing act judges typically had to perform. See generally Susanna L. Blumenthal, "The Default Legal Person," *UCLA Law Review* 54 (2007): 1206–1215.

19. In re Violet's Will and Testament, 4 Ky. (1 Bibb) 617, 617–618 (1809); Heister v. Lynch, 1 Yeates 108, 114 (Pa. 1792); Spencer v. Moore, 8 Va. (4 Call) 423, 427–28 (1798); Tomkins v. Tomkins, 17 S.C.L. (1 Bail.) 92, 96 (1828); Den ex dem. Merritt v. Johnson, 5 N.J.L. 454, 455 (Sup. Ct. 1819); Stevens v. Vancleve, 23 F. Cas. 35, 38 (C.C.D.N.J. 1822) (No. 13,412); Harrison v. Rowan, 11 F. Cas. 658, 660–61 (C.C.D.N.J. 1820) (No. 6,141); In re Cochran's Will & Testament, 6 Ky. (3 Bibb) 491, 493–94 (1814); Lide v. Lide, 4 S.C.L. (2 Brev.) 403, 405 (Const. Ct. 1810).

20. Joel Peter Eigen, "Lesion of the Will: Medical Resolve and Criminal Responsibility in Victorian Insanity Trials," *Law & Society Review* 33 (1999): 433.

21. Benjamin Rush, "On the Study of Medical Jurisprudence," in *Sixteen Introductory Lectures* (Philadelphia: Bradford and Innskeep, 1811), 363, 391.

22. Greenwood v. Greenwood 3 Curt. (App.) i, 163 Eng. Rep. 930, 939 (K.B.) (1790). After further proceedings, the parties reached an out-of-court settlement. The volume of law reports in which this case appears (as an appendix) was published in 1844–1845. Long before this, it gained wide notoriety after it received mention in Lord Erskine's speech in Hadfield (1800); it is worth adding that Erskine was the proponent's attorney in *Greenwood* and Kenyon presided over the trial in *Hadfield.* From this date forward, *Greenwood* was commonly invoked in legal arguments and judicial decisions on both sides of the Atlantic and excerpted in significant part in treatises as well. Ray's 1838 treatise on medical jurisprudence, for instance, drew what he knew of the case from an appendix to the 1826 English edition of Robert Joseph Pothier's treatise on contracts, and Beck's 1823 treatise from Cooper's reprinting of Erskine's speech in his collection of reprinted medical jurisprudence texts, published in 1819. See Robert Joseph Pothier, *A Treatise on the Law of Obligations, or Contracts: Translated from the French, with an Introduction, Appendix, and Notes, Illustrative of the . . .* (Philadelphia: R.H. Small, 1826), vol. 2, appendix, 28; Thomas Cooper, *Tracts on Medical Jurisprudence: Including Farr's Elements of Medical Jurisprudence, Dease's Remarks on Medical Jurisprudence, Male's Epitome of Juridical or Forensic Medicine, and Haslam's Treatise on Insanity: With a Preface, Notes, and a Digest of the Law Relating to Insanity and Nuisance . . .* (Philadelphia: James Webster, 1819), 387, 395.

23. Dew v. Clark (1826) 3 Add. 79, 162 Eng. Rep. 410, 420, 425–426, 428, 432, 452 (Prerog. Ct.); Dew v. Clark (1822) 1 Add. 279, 162 Eng. Rep. 98, 98 (Prerog. Ct.). A version of the decision that was "edited, by permission, from the judge's reports" was published by John Haggard and often cited instead of the official law report. See John Haggard, ed., *A Report of the Judgment in Dew v. Clark and Clark* (London: A. Strahan/Joseph Butterworth and Son, 1826).

24. *Dew,* 162 Eng. Rep., 412–414, 455; *Dew,* 162 Eng. Rep., 99–100; Haggard, ed., *Report,* 7. See also Waring v. Waring (1848) 6 Moore 341, 13 Eng. Rep. 715, 720 (P.C.) (quoting a version of the opinion in *Dew* that had been corrected by Nicholl).

25. *Dew,* 162 Eng. Rep., 453–455; Haggard, ed., *Report,* 99.

26. Although *Dew* was the decision of an English ecclesiastical court, acting without a jury as it decided questions of fact as well as law, it was regularly cited and deemed applicable in common law courts. See, e.g., Boyd v. Eby, 8 Watts 66, 71 (Pa. 1839).

27. Heirs at Law of Lee v. Ex'r of Lee, 15 S.C.L. (4 McCord) 183, 184–185, 196–197 (1827), quoting Lee's will.

28. Ibid., 185–186, 188–189, 195.

29. Ibid., 190–191, 193. The proponents' argument was based upon an array of English precedents, among which was *Greenwood v. Greenword.*

30. *Lee,* 15 S.C.L. (4 McCord), 192–196. The South Carolina legislature distributed the state's portion of the Lee estate to his heirs at law by way of a special act in 1829, though it had been depleted by the litigation. In contrast, Tennessee sold its portion and used the proceeds to fund public education. See

Ernest Rigney, "The Contentious Will of Mason Lee: A Clarification of South Carolina's Leading Case Regarding Testamentary Capacity," *Journal of Southern History* 20 (2012): 70.

31. See Kinne v. Kinne, 9 Conn. 101, 102–104, 106 (1831) (singularity, old age, and ill temper); Duffield v. Robeson, 2 Del. (2 Harr.) 375, 383–384 (Super. Ct. 1838) (intoxication); George Weir's Will, 39 Ky. (9 Dana) 434, 440–445 (1840) (singularity); Elliott's Will, 25 Ky. (2 J. J. Marsh) 340, 342 (1829) (old age); Brooks v. Barrett, 24 Mass. (7 Pick.) 94, 96–97 (1828) (old age); Lowe v. Williamson, 2 N.J. Eq. 82, 85 (Prerog. Ct. 1838) (intemperance); Whitenack v. Stryker, 2 N.J. Eq. 8, 26–28 (Prerog. Ct. 1838) (singularity); Kachline v. Clark, 4 Whart. 316, 319 (Pa. 1839) (intoxication).

32. Beck, *Medical Jurisprudence* (1838), 656–661, commended Breckinridge's petition as "well worthy of perusal," though he remained neutral on the merits of the case. He noted that the petition's "main object is to show that what by many are deemed *delusions of the head,* may originate from *depravity of the heart,*" adding that it had been overruled by the court.

33. See Townshend v. Townshend, 7 Gill 10, 27 (Md. 1848) (referencing the evidentiary rule allowing physicians to offer opinions as to the testator's sanity); Hathorn v. King, 8 Mass. 371, 371–372 (1811) (same where medical opinion based upon personal observation of the testator); see also Harrison v. Rowan, 11 F. Cas. 658, 661 (C.C.D.N.J. 1820) (No. 6,141) (allowing same where based upon the testimony of other witnesses); Potts v. House, 6 Ga. 324, 335 (1849) (same); compare Brock v. Luckett's Ex'rs, 5 Miss. (4 Howard) 459, 478–479, 482 (1840) (allowing a physician to testify on the basis of the testimony of other witnesses but according greater weight to opinions of subscribing witnesses). Under traditional common law rules, only subscribing witnesses had been allowed to offer opinions as to the testator's sanity. See, e.g., Poole v. Richardson, 3 Mass. (2 Tyng) 330, 330 (1807).

34. Ware v. Ware, 8 Me. 42, 57 (1831).

35. *Boyd,* 8 Watts, 66–68, 70.

36. Ibid., 71–73.

37. No doubt many litigants filed suits in order to force settlements, which are harder to trace through the surviving sources. See John H. Langbein, "Will Contests," *Yale Law Journal* 103 (1994): 2043.

38. See Kinne v. Kinne, 9 Conn. 102 (1831); In re Singleton's Will, 38 Ky. (8 Dana) 315 (1839); Lowe v. Williamson, 2 N.J. Eq. 82 (Prerog. Ct. 1838); Whitenack v. Stryker, 2 N.J. Eq. 8 (Prerog. Ct. 1838); Kachline v. Clarke, 4 Whart. 316 (Pa. 1839).

39. Duffield v. Robeson, 2 Del. (2 Harr.) 375, 378–379 (Super. Ct. 1838); see also Kinne v. Kinne, 102, 106 (will admitted to probate, only to be set aside by the jury, whose verdict was in turn set aside by the appellate court, which ordered a new trial); Martin v. Teague, 29 S.C.L. (2 Speers) 260, 260–261, 268 (1843) (same); Davis v. Calvert, 5 G. & J. 269, 281, 313 (Md. 1833) (jury verdict in favor of a will set aside by the appellate court, which ordered a new trial); Gass' Heirs v. Gass' Ex'rs, 22 Tenn. (3 Hum.) 278, 281, 287 (1842) (same); *Whitenack,* 2 N.J. Eq., 29 (verdict against a will set aside on appeal); Kachline v. Clarke, 316–320 (same); *Singleton,* 38 Ky. (8 Dana), 315–319, 331, 333 (jury verdict reversed by appellate court with concurring and dissenting opinions).

40. *Whitenack*, 2 N.J. Eq. at 26.

41. *Singleton*, 38 Ky. (8 Dana), 341 (dissenting opinion).

42. Stewart's Executor v. Lispenard, 26 Wend. 255, 300–304 (N.Y. 1841) (internal quotation marks omitted). The vehemence with which he defended the will in this case stemmed in no small part from the fact that Verplanck believed liberty of testation was a natural right.

43. See Thompson v. Thompson, 21 Barb. 107, 115–117 (N.Y. Gen. Term 1855) (Clerke, J., dissenting) (questioning the authority and wisdom of *Lispenard*); Newhouse v. Godwin, 17 Barb. 236, 257 (N.Y. Gen. Term 1853) (questioning whether "the principle" stated in *Lispenard* "has not been extended further than good policy requires"); Ex'r of Converse v. Converse, 21 Vt. 168, 170 (1849) was the leading case on this point; see Redfield, *Law of Wills*, vol. 1, 129–131 and n45. The only other jurisdiction to follow the rule in *Lispenard* was Georgia; see Potts v. House, 6 Ga. 324, 352–353 (1849). *Lispenard* was effectively overruled by New York's highest court in the celebrated *Parish Will Case*; Delafield v. Parish, 25 N.Y. 9 (1862). See also Francis Wharton, *Wharton and Stillé's Medical Jurisprudence*, 3rd ed. (Philadelphia: Kay and Brother, 1873), vol. 1, 27–38.

44. See Thomas Jarman, *A Treatise on Wills*, 1st Am. ed. (Boston: Charles C. Little and James Brown, 1845), vol. 1, 27d–e27n1; Alfred S. Taylor, *Medical Jurisprudence* (Philadelphia: Lea & Blanchard, 1845), 510–511.

45. *Lispenard*, 26 Wend., 305, 313–314.

46. For a particularly clear explanation of this problem, see Woodbury v. Obear, 73 Mass. (7 Gray) 467, 471 (1856) (Shaw, C. J.).

47. Francis Wharton and Moreton Stillé, *A Treatise on Medical Jurisprudence* (Philadelphia: Kay and Brother, 1855), 215–221, excerpting large portions of Reverend Barlow's sermon "On Man's Power over Himself to Prevent or Control Insanity," which was circulated widely in pamphlet form and reprinted in full in the *American Journal of Insanity*. See "On Man's Power over Himself to Prevent or Control Insanity," *American Journal of Insanity* 1 (April 1845): 289–319.

48. Leonard Shelford, *A Practical Treatise on the Law Concerning Lunatics, Idiots, and Persons of Unsound Mind* (London, 1833; repr. Philadelphia: J. S. Littell, 1833), xxvii–xxxvi (quoting Byron). In the apt phrasing of David Brion Davis, they were "successful rebels slightly frightened by their own freedom." As he goes on to observe, "Even the most optimistic exponent of man's goodness" in antebellum America could not help but notice all sorts of worrying signs: "A mobile and dispersed population, the presence of slaves within the country and of savages inside and beyond the frontiers, the opportunities for successful crime and fraud all contributed to the uncertainty of moral values." Davis, *Homicide in American Fiction*, 13.

49. Jon Butler, *Awash in a Sea of Faith: Christianizing the American People* (Cambridge, MA: Harvard University Press, 1991), 2, 225–256.

50. The history of enslavement and abolition in Delaware is relevant to this contest. Delaware was one of those states in which slave labor in agriculture became unprofitable and Quakers advocated manumission and abolition. But poor whites feared competition from free blacks, and white elites sought to secure property rights. Wills manumitting slaves were contested in court. As the majority of the state's black residents became free (79 percent were free by 1810) the legislature passed stringent "black codes" to control them. The position of

free blacks was as hotly contested within and outside of the courts. Delaware never passed a gradual emancipation law. See William H. Williams, *Slavery and Freedom in Delaware, 1639–1865* (Wilmington, DE: Scholarly Resources, 1996).

51. Chandler v. Ferris, 1 Del. (1 Harr.) 454–455, 458, 461–564 (Super. Ct. 1834).

52. *George Weir's Will*, 39 Ky. (9 Dana) 434, 439 (1840) (emphasis omitted). These were the words of a Dr. Blackburn, who was described as "a neighbor and intimate friend."

53. Ibid., 440–441, 445.

54. Stackhouse v. Horton, 15 N.J. Eq. 202, 208 (Prerog. Ct. 1854); Dorsey v. Warfield, 7 Md. 65, 74 (1854); Gass' Heirs v. Gass' Ex'rs, 278, 284 (1842).

55. Woodbury v. Obear, 467, 470 (1856) (Shaw, C. J.).

56. Beyond the early Kentucky case of Johnson v. Moore's Heirs, 11 Ky. (1 Litt.) 371 (1822), a survey of appellate law reports reveals only two other decisions setting aside a will that benefited a slave concubine or her children, the one operating to disinherit the testator's legitimate children and the other benefiting a child the testator was allegedly defrauded into believing was his. See Denton v. Franklin, 48 Ky. (9 B. Mon.) 28 (1848); Davis v. Calvert, 5 G. & J. 269 (Md. 1833).

57. Farr v. Thompson, 25 S.C.L. (Chev.) 37, 38, 40–41 (1839); Thompson v. Farr, 28 S.C.L. (1 Speers) 93, 97 (1842).

58. *Thompson*, 28 S.C.L. (1 Speers) 101, 109; Farr v. O'Neall, 30 S.C.L. (1 Rich.) 80, 83–84 (1844). Formally, the court's order was for a new trial, but there is no evidence of further litigation of the will in the surviving records. Other records concerning Farr's estate suggest that some sort of settlement was reached between the parties.

59. Potts v. House, 6 Ga. 324, 360 (1849); Jolliffe v. Fanning 44 S.C.L. 186, 192, 199 (1856); see also Pool v. Pool's Heirs, 35 Ala. 12 (1859) (upholding meretricious will benefiting slave mistress). For further discussion of these cases as well as others following the same lines, see Davis, *Private Law of Race and Sex*, 250–269; Jones, *Fathers of Conscience*, 32–42; Pitts, *Family, Law and Inheritance in America*, 62–83 (suggesting how testimony of a slave mistress's control over her master "allowed juries and the testifying witnesses to condemn testators or beneficiaries' behavior" by deploying mythical notions about Southern families "embedded in law . . . that structured dominant social values"). On the legal regulation of interracial relationships, see Joshua D. Rothman, *Notorious in the Neighborhood: Sex and Families across the Color Line in Virginia, 1787–1861* (Chapel Hill: University of North Carolina Press, 2003); Rachel Moran, *Interracial Intimacy: The Regulation of Race and Romance* (Chicago: University of Chicago Press, 2001); Werner Sollors, ed., *Interracialism: Black-White Intermarriage in American History, Literature, and Law* (New York: Oxford University Press, 2000); Martha Hodes, ed., *Sex, Love, Race: Crossing Boundaries in North American History* (New York: New York University Press, 1999).

60. Dunlap v. Robinson, 28 Ala. 100, 105, 107 (1850). See also Howell v. Troutman, 53 N.C. 304 (1860).

61. Isaac Ray, *A Treatise on the Medical Jurisprudence of Insanity*, 3rd ed., 37–38, 237 (1853). For the landmark Supreme Court decision, see Gibbons v. Ogden, 22 U.S. (9 Wheat.) 1 (1824).

62. Trumbull v. Gibbons, 22 N.J.L. 117, 125–126, 128, 136, 144–145, 150 (Sup. Ct. 1849).

63. Ibid., 128.
64. Ibid., 134, 137–138, 159.
65. Ibid., 138–140.
66. Ibid., 151, 153, 155–157.
67. The most authoritative rejection of moral insanity came in Frere v. Peacocke (1846) 1 Rob. Ecc. 442, 163 Eng. Rep. 1095 (Prerog. Ct.), which held that "moral perversion of the feelings, unaccompanied with delusion," did not constitute "unsoundness of mind, so as to render an act performed per se invalid" (ibid., 1097, 1100).
68. *Waring*, 13 Eng. Rep., 718–721 (P.C.). English courts later rejected the *Waring* rule. See, e.g., Smee v. Smee (1879) 5 P.D. 84, 90–91 (Prob. Ct.); Boughton v. Knight (1873) 3 L.R.P. & D. 64, 73–76 (Prob. Ct.); Banks v. Goodfellow (1870) 5 L.R.Q.B. 549, 559–572.
69. Wharton, *Medical Jurisprudence* (1855), 20–29; Dunham's Appeal, 27 Conn. 192, 205 (1858); See also Amos Dean, "Unsolved Problems of the Law, as Embraced in Mental Alienation," *American Law Register*, n.s., 1 (July 1862): 521 (declaring that "no court in this country" had accepted this formulation of the *Waring* rule).
70. Dunham's Appeal, 205 (1858).
71. Ibid., 201–202, 205.
72. McClintock v. Curd, 32 Mo. 411, 420 (1862); Beaubien v. Cicotte, 12 Mich. 459, 502 (1864).
73. Means v. Means, 36 S.C.L. (5 Strob.) 167, 191 (1850).

Chapter 4: The Eccentricity of the Will

1. His sisters were separately represented and they claimed that the will had been expressly or impliedly revoked, meaning that Parish died intestate. They were unsuccessful at every stage of the litigation. Delafield v. Parish, 1 Redf. Surr 1, 51-75, 103-111, 128-129 (N.Y. Sur. 1857); 16 Abb. Pr. 397, 42 Barb. 274, 278–279 (N.Y. Sup. Gen. Term. 1858) (Davies, P. J.); Delafield v. Parish, 1 Redf. Surr. 130, 25 N.Y. 9, 98-100 (1862).
2. *The Parish Will Case in the Court of Appeals: The Statement of Facts, and the Opinion of the Court* (New York: D. Appleton and Company, 1862), 30, 226, 623.
3. "The Parish Will Case," *New York Times*, Nov. 23, 1857; *Medical Opinions upon the Mental Competency of Mr. Parish* (New York: John F. Trow, 1857) (quoting from Watson, Ray, and Bell), 350, 387, 465.
4. *Delafield*, 25 N.Y., 16-121. The conclusion of the majority opinion was that the testator's mental life came to an end for all intents and purposes at the time of the apoplectic attack: "He then ceased to be Henry Parish and was no longer an accountable being" (48).
5. Ibid., 109.
6. *Evening Post*, Sept. 19, 1862, vol. 61, p. 3 (advertisement).
7. See, e.g., "The Parish Will Case," *American Journal of Insanity* 19 (October 1862): 210–227, which suggests New York had lagged behind most states in holding to *Lispenard*, the author pronouncing it to be "gratifying to know it has been overruled," though he went on to express doubts about "whether any

rules can be given" that could guide cases, each one needing to be taken on its own facts (223–224).

8. Isaac Redfield, *Law of Wills: Embracing Also, the Jurisprudence of Insanity . . .* (Boston: Little Brown, 1864), 104, 155.

9. "Bibliographical," *American Journal of Insanity* 22 (April 1866): 551–553 (quoting Dr. Andrew McFarland as recorded in the Biennial Report of the Illinois State Hospital for the Insane).

10. "Bibliographical," *American Journal of Insanity* 21 (April 1865): 522–523 (review of Redfield's *Law of Wills* attributed to Isaac Ray).

11. Ibid, 525, 526–527, 531. See also "Review," *Law Magazine and Law Review*, 3rd ser., 18 (1864–1865): 353–358.

12. John Ordronaux, "History and Philosophy of Medical Jurisprudence," *American Journal of Insanity* 25 (October 1868): 200.

13. Ibid., 192; John Ordronaux, *Commentaries on the Lunacy Laws of New York: And on the Judicial Aspects of Insanity at Common Law and in Equity* (Albany, NY: J. D. Parsons, Jr., Law Publisher 1878), 355–356.

14. Ordronaux, "History," 190; John Ordronaux, "Moral Insanity," *American Journal of Insanity* 29 (1873): 314–315.

15. Francis Wharton, *Wharton and Stillé's Medical Jurisprudence*, 3rd ed. (Philadelphia: Kay and Brother, 1873), vol. 1, 295–296, 324–325.

16. La Bau v. Vanderbilt, 3 Red. Sur. Ct. 384, 426 (N.Y. Sur. Ct. 1879); Hardy v. Merrill, 56 N.H. 227, 245 (1875); United States v. McGlue, 26 F. Cas. 1093, 1095 (C.C.D. Mass. 1851) (No. 15,679). See also Henry F. Buswell, *The Law of Insanity* (Boston: Little, Brown, 1885), vi (extending the reasoning of McGlue, a criminal case, to the civil sphere); S. V. Clevenger, *Medical Jurisprudence of Insanity or Forensic Psychiatry*, 2 vols. (Rochester, NY: Lawyers' Co-operative Publishing, 1898), 10 (contending that the law seeks practical rules, rather than medical definitions, when dealing with the question of insanity).

17. This approach did not provide much by the way of conceptual order, as can be seen in Redfield's similar way of dealing with the problem of definition at the outset of a section on "Insanity From Disease—Lunacy": "The symptoms of insanity are quite incapable of description or classification. It is sometimes very obvious, and at others exhibits itself in modes and forms so subtle, as to almost elude the observation of the most wary and experienced." Redfield, *Law of Wills*, 67.

18. Amos Dean, "Unsolved Problems of the Law, as Embraced in Mental Alienation, *American Law Register*, n.s., 1 (July 1862): 513, 514; Dean, "Unsolved Problems of the Law, as Embraced in Mental Alienation, No. 2," *American Law Register*, n.s., 1 (August 1862): 593.

19. The *American Journal of Insanity* alone contains numerous allusions to "Dryden's couplet." See, e.g., Andrew McFarland, "Minor Mental Maladies," *American Journal of Insanity* 20 (July 1863): 10–26, in which this asylum superintendent notes, "The 'thin partitions,' recognized in Dryden's couplet, fade away almost entirely in regard to a great number of cases of mental impairment, creating a border territory, on the domain of which reason or madness may be supposed to hold sway, much according to the caprice in opinion of whoever may, for the time being, pass judgment thereupon" (11).

20. Gerald Grob, *Mental Illness and American Society, 1875–1940* (Princeton, NJ: Princeton University Press, 1983), 37–38; Hendrik Hartog, "Mrs. Packard on

Dependency," *Yale Journal of Law and the Humanities* 1 (1989): 79–103; Bonnie Bluestein, "'A Hollow Square of Psychological Science': American Neurologists and Psychiatrists in Conflict," in *Madhouses, Mad-Doctors and Madmen*, ed. Andrew Scull (Philadelphia: University of Pennsylvania Press, 1981), 241–270.

21. Redfield, *Law of Wills*, 69, 71–72. Yet in a footnote he added: "But we have known some marked cases of confirmed insanity, where the patient held such control of voluntary action, both of mind and body, as not to disclose any symptom of derangement to strangers" (72n).

22. Ibid., 82–84. His position on religious delusions was also revealing of the limits he placed upon sanity. For while he generally agreed with English and American decisions upholding the wills of testators who held eccentric beliefs about speculative matters, he also considered a belief in "modern spiritualism" to be an entirely acceptable basis for impeaching the testimony of a witness or disqualifying him or her from testifying altogether. Ibid., 79–80n9. Redfield's long and impassioned commentary on this matter in his 1874 *Leading Cases* was inspired by an 1870 will contest in Maine where the court admitted testimony going to show that the testatrix was not only insane on account of her belief in spiritualism but also unduly influenced by her dearly departed husband. Admitting evidence of spiritual influences into the courtroom seemed to Redfield like an invitation to reenact the disastrous Salem witchcraft trials. Isaac F. Redfield, *Leading American Cases and Notes upon the Law of Wills* (Boston: Little, Brown, and Company, 1874), 365–390.

23. [Holmes], Book Notices, *American Law Review* 1 (April 1867): 544–545 (reviewing Redfield's edited volume of Story's *Commentaries on Equity Jurisprudence*). For a discussion of this review suggesting that the younger generation tended to separate law from morality, see William P. LaPiana, *Logic and Experience: The Origin of Modern American Legal Education* (New York: Oxford University Press, 1994), 118.

24. Boardman v. Woodman, 47 N.H. 120, 127, 139 (1866), overruled in part by Hardy v. Merrill, 56 N.H. 227 (1875). In addition to citing Trumbull v. Gibbons and Frere v. Peacocke in support of the court's ruling as to moral insanity, Judge Sargent relied on a contemporary survey in the *American Law Register* produced by a law student: Edmund Wetmore, "Mental Unsoundness as Affecting Testamentary Capacity," *American Law Register*, n.s., 3 (November 1863): 6: "Partial moral insanity, in the same manner as general moral insanity, is not of itself sufficient to render a will invalid, if without cognate mental delusions." Sargent may also have been familiar with Dr. J. Parigot's remarks on Wetmore's essay, "Mental Unsoundness as Affecting Testamentary Capacity," *American Law Register*, n.s., 3 (May 1864): 385–398, conceding that "the term moral insanity is in opposition with the real nature of the disease, and a riddle conveying false notions to the jurist and the physician" but nonetheless insisting upon the existence of non-intellectual disorders, which the doctor cast as forms of "Diastrephia" and maintained ought to be regarded as legally disabling. (390, 394)

25. *Boardman*, 47 N.H., 139.

26. See Louis E. Reik, "The Doe-Ray Correspondence: A Pioneer Collaboration in the Jurisprudence of Mental Disease," *Yale Law Journal* 63 (1953): 183–196; John Reid, "Understanding the New Hampshire Doctrine of Criminal Responsibility," *Yale Law Journal* 69 (1960): 367–420; Reid, *Chief Justice: The*

Judicial World of Charles Doe (Cambridge, MA: Harvard University Press, 1967), 109–121; John Starrett Hughes, *In the Law's Darkness: Isaac Ray and the Medical Jurisprudence of Insanity in Nineteenth-Century America* (New York: Oceana Publications, 1986), 97–113; Tighe, "Question of Responsibility," 32–36, 85–93.

27. *Boardman*, 47 N.H., 150 (Doe, J., dissenting). Doe likened the judicial tests of insanity to Lord Hale's infamous instruction to jurors that the existence of witches was an established fact.

28. Ibid., 148–150 (Doe, J., dissenting). The full instruction that Doe said ought to have been given to the jury was: "The question of whether Miss Blydenburgh had a mental disease was a question of fact for the jury, and not a question of law for the court. Whether delusion is a symptom, or a test, of any mental disease, was also a question of fact, and the instructions given to the jury were erroneous in assuming it to be a question of law. The jury should have been instructed that if the writing propounded in the probate court was the offspring of mental disease, the verdict should be that Miss Blydenburgh was not of sound mind" (147–148).

29. See State v. Pike, 49 N.H. 399 (1869) (Perley, J.); accord, State v. Jones, 50 N. H. 369, 381–398 (1871) (Ladd, J., affirming jury instructions given by Perley). Chief Justice Ira Perley's instruction in *Pike* stated the test most succinctly: "The legal principle however much it may formerly have been obscured by pathological darkness and confusion of law and fact, is, that a product of mental disease is not a contract, a will, or a crime." *Pike*, 44 N.H., 438). See also Reid, "New Hampshire Doctrine," indicating that Judge Doe convinced Chief Justice Perley to charge the jury in *Pike* "along the lines suggested in the *Boardman* dissent" (376–377).

30. The New Hampshire rule announced in *Pike* and elaborated in *Jones* sparked debate and reconsideration of the M'Naughten test in many other jurisdictions. See Charles E. Rosenberg, *The Trial of the Assassin Guiteau: Psychiatry and Law in the Gilded Age* (Chicago: University of Chicago Press, 1968), 103–104. It also prompted more far-reaching reconsideration of judicial tests of insanity in civil cases. See Wharton, *Medical Jurisprudence* (1873), 762–763; Buswell, *Law of Insanity*, 174–176; Clevenger, *Medical Jurisprudence*, 160–162.

31. Jamison v. Jamison's Will, 8 Del. (3 Houst.) 108, 119, 120 (Super. Ct. 1865); Gardner v. Lamback, 47 Ga. 133, 192 (1872); Francis Wharton, *Wharton and Stillé's Medical Jurisprudence*, 4th ed. (Philadelphia: Kay & Bro., 1882), vol. 1, 237; see also Carpenter v. Calvert, 83 Ill. 62, 70–71 (1876) (finding error in the trial court instruction insofar as it gave greater weight to a physician's opinion of the testator's mental capacity and suggesting that this expert's opinion be placed on equal footing with those of "other men of good, common sense"); Fraser v. Jennison, 42 Mich. 206, 219, 227–236 (1879) (Cooley, J.) (complaining about misleading expert testimony, which served only to "bring jurors and the public to a conviction that . . . one person is as sane as another, and not even a thin appreciable partition divides reason from madness" and affirming a lower court ruling that limited the number of medical experts who could testify on behalf of the contestants). For other manifestations of judicial impatience with medical experts and broader public skepticism as well, see James Mohr, *Doctors and the Law; Medical Jurisprudence in Nineteenth-Century America* (New York: Oxford University Press, 1993), chap. 12.

32. American Seaman's Friend Soc'y v. Hopper, 33 N.Y. 619, 621, 634, 638 (1865). The drafting lawyer was named as one of the executors, and one of the charitable societies named as a beneficiary was administered by his wife. The nurse was to receive a bequest of $200.

33. Ibid., 623, 627, 629.

34. Ibid., 622–623, 631.

35. American Seaman's Friend Soc'y v. Hopper, 43 Barb. 625, 625, 627 (N.Y. Gen. Term 1864). One of the three judges (Sutherland) dissented, considering the evidence "very conflicting" and thus deeming it "a peculiarly proper case for awarding . . . a feigned issue to try the question of competency" (628).

36. *Hopper*, 33 N.Y., 623–624, 637, 628, 633–637.

37. Ibid., 624; William Alexander Hammond, *Insanity in Its Medical Relations: Opinion Relative to the Testamentary Capacity of the Late James C. Johnston of Chowan County, North Carolina*, 2nd ed. (New York: Baker, Voohis, 1867), 81 (quoting the jury charge in the case).

38. In re Forman's Will, 54 Barb. 274, 278–279, 294–295 (N.Y. Gen. Term 1869)(citing *Hopper*). For other cases citing *Hopper* in the course of upholding a will, see In re White's Will, 5 N.Y.S. 295, 299 (Gen. Term 1889); and In re Keeler's Will, 3 N.Y.S. 629, 631 (Gen. Term 1889).

39. This seems to be a quote from the novelist Susanna Rowson's *Charlotte Temple* (1791; first American edition, 1794); it is also close to lines from *Hamlet*, act 1, scene 5, line 6, uttered by the protagonist about his mother.

40. *Forman's Will*, 54 Barb., 295.

41. Chafin Will Case, 32 Wis. 557, 560–562 (1873).

42. Ibid., 565–568.

43. Less commonly, courts viewed consistently perverse behavior as a sign of "habitual insanity." See, e.g., In re Stewart, 22 N.W. 392, 393 (Wis. 1885) ("This shows . . . how long and entirely the testatrix had become subject to the insane delusion which controlled her action [until her] death").

44. Tyler v. Gardiner, 35 N.Y. 559, 613 (1866); Pierce v. Pierce, 38 Mich. 412, 420–421 (1878); Hutchinson v. Hutchinson, 38 N.E. 926, 927 (Ill. 1894); In re Jones' Will, 25 N.Y.S. 109, 113 (Sur. Ct. 1893); Bush v. Lisle, 12 S.W. 762, 762 (Ky. 1889).

45. See Hoerth v. Zable, 17 S.W. 360, 361 (Ky. 1891) (will upheld); McFadin v. Catron, 25 S.W. 506, 511 (Mo. 1894) (same); In re Clark's Will, 25 N.Y.S. 712, 714 (Sur. Ct. 1893) (same); Potter v. Jones, 25 P. 769, 773 (Or. 1891) (same); Hubbard v. Hubbard, 7 Or. 42, 46 (1879) (same); In re Stickney's Will, 80 N.W. 921, 925 (Wis. 1899) (same).

46. See Robinson v. Adams, 62 Me. 369, 374–375, 384 (1870); Bonard's Will, 16 Abb. Pr. (n.s.) 128, 182–189 (N.Y. Sur. Ct. 1872); In re Will of Storey, 20 Ill. App. 183, 197 (1886); Otto v. Doty, 15 N.W. 578, 579 (Iowa 1883); Schildnecht v. Rompf's Ex'x, 4 S.W. 235, 237 (Ky. 1887); Brown v. Ward, 53 Md. 376, 395–396 (1880); Hegney v. Head, 29 S.W. 587, 589–590 (Mo. 1895); McClary v. Stull, 62 N.W. 501, 505 (Neb. 1895); Middleditch v. Williams, 17 A. 826, 829–831 (N.J. 1889); Gen. Convention of the New Jerusalem Church v. Crocker, 7 Ohio C.C. 327, 336–337 (Cir. Ct. 1893); In re Trich's Will, 30 A. 1053, 1057–1058 (Pa. 1895); In re Will of Smith, 8 N.W. 616, 620–621 (Wis. 1881). However, Am. Bible Soc'y v. Price, 5 N.E. 126, 134 (Ill. 1886) invalidated the will of a testator who donated most of his estate to religious organizations.

47. Mayo v. Jones, 78 N.C. 402, 402, 406 (1878); In re Jones' Will, 25 N.Y.S. 109, 113 (Sur. Ct. 1893); In re Wilson's Estate, 49 P. 172, 175–176 (Cal. 1897); Ross v. Weaver, 11 Ky. Op. 131, 131 (1881); Sunderland v. Hood, 84 Mo. 293, 296 (1884); Arnault v. Arnault, 31 A. 606, 607 (N.J. Prerog. Ct. 1895); In re Mondorf's Will, 18 N.E. 256, 256–257 (N.Y. 1888); In re Hamilton's Will, 62 N.Y.S. 820, 822–823 (Sur. Ct. 1899); Monroe v. Barclay, 17 Ohio St. 302, 303, 317–319 (1867); Carter v. Dixon, 69 Ga. 82, 91 (1882).

48. John Hutton Balfour Browne, *The Medical Jurisprudence of Insanity*, (San Francisco: S. Whitney, 1875), 117.

49. *La Bau,* 3 Red. Sur. Ct., 384, 423–424.

50. "New York Gossip . . . Com. Vanderbilt's Will," *Chicago Daily Tribune*, June 4, 1876, p. 13; "Commodore Vanderbilt's Will," *Daily Rocky Mountain News*, June 10, 1876, col. C; "Vanderbilt. The Stock-Jobbers again Speculate on the Old Man's Physical Weakness," *Chicago Daily Tribune*, Oct. 17, 1876, p. 7; "The 'Vanderbilt Guard.' Something about the Squad of Benevolent Reporters Who Surround the Sick Commodore's Mansion," *Daily Evening Bulletin*, Nov. 24, 1876, col. G (reprinted from the *New York Tribune*); "Cornelius Vanderbilt," *Milwaukee Daily Sentinel*, Jan. 6, 1877, issue 6, col. C.

51. "Vanderbilt," *Chicago Daily Tribune*, Jan. 5, 1877. For additional examples, see "Vanderbilt's Millions: The Relations Said to Be Quarreling over the Will—A Contest Not Improbable," *St. Louis Globe-Democrat*, Jan. 10, 1877; "Commodore Vanderbilt's Will—Prospect of a Family Contest," *Boston Daily Advertiser*, Jan. 10, 1877, issue 9, col. H.

52. "Of Course. Vanderbilt's Will to Be Contested," *Davenport Democrat*, Jan. 11, 1877, p. 2; [No title], *St. Louis Globe-Democrat*, Feb. 25, 1877, p. 4, issue 281, col. A; "Battle of the Heirs," *St. Louis Globe-Democrat*, July 4, 1875; "The Vanderbilt Will Contest," *Daily Rocky Mountain News*, March 3, 1877, col. C (reprinted from *New York Tribune*); "The Misfortune of Being Too Rich," *Daily Evening Bulletin*, July 13, 1877; "Big Wills," *St. Louis Globe-Democrat*, July 9, 1878.

53. "Vanderbiltiana," *Puck*, Sept. 25, 1878, p. 3; T. J. Stiles, *The First Tycoon: The Epic Life of Cornelius Vanderbilt* (New York: Alfred A. Knopf, 2009), 563; "The House of Vanderbilt," *New York Times* Nov. 13, 1877; "The Commodore's Money," *New York Times*, Nov. 14, 1877; "The Vanderbilt Will," *New York Herald*, Nov. 13, 1877 [NYPL file]; "Scott Lord on Vanderbilt," *The Sun*, Nov. 13, 1877 [NYPL file]; "Vanderbilt's Will," *New York Herald*, Nov. 14, 1877 [NYPL file]; "The Great Will Contest," Nov. 14, 1877 [NYPL file]; "The Vanderbilt Will," *The World*, Nov. 14, 1877 [NYPL file].

54. "The House of Vanderbilt," *New York Times*, Nov. 13, 1877; "Vanderbilt's Physicians," *New-York Daily Tribune*, Nov. 15, 1877 [NYPLfile]; "The Fight for a Million," *New York Times*, Nov. 17, 1877; "The Vanderbilt Fight," *The World*, Nov. 17, 1877 [NYPL file]; "Vanderbilt's Infirmities," *New York Herald*, Nov. 17, 1877 [NYPL file]; "The Vanderbilt Will Case," *New York Times*, June 26, 1878.

55. "The Commodore's Money," *New York Times*, Nov. 14, 1877; "The Vanderbilt Contest," *New York Times*, Nov. 15, 1877; "The Fight for a Million," *New York Times*, Nov. 17, 1877; "Vanderbilt's Millions," *New York Times*, Dec. 5, 1877; "Vanderbilt's Physicians," *New-York Daily Tribune*, Nov. 15, 1877 [NYPL file]; "The Commodore Dissected. Painful Diseases That Immense Wealth Could Not Cure," *The Sun*, Nov. 17, 1877 [NYPL file]; "Vanderbilt's Struggle with Disease,"

Daily Evening Bulletin, Nov. 27, 1877, issue 44, col. D; "The Sick Commodore," *The World*, Dec. 5, 1877; "The Fight for Millions," *The Sun*, Dec. 5, 1877 [NYPL file].

56. "Vanderbilt's Millions," *New York Times*, Dec. 5, 1877; Vanderbilt's Doctors," *New-York Daily Tribune*, Dec. 5, 1877 [NYPL file]; "The Fight for Millions," *The Sun*, Dec. 5, 1877 [NYPL file]; "The Will of Vanderbilt," *New York Times*, Dec. 8, 1877; "The Great Will Contest," *The Sun*, Dec. 8, 1877 [NYPL file]. The most scandalous allegations about their relationship with Vanderbilt was that they exchanged sexual favors for stock tips and made a fortune—which they then used to fund their radical feminist newspaper, *The Revolution*. For a fuller treatment of the ways Woodhull and Claflin figured in Vanderbilt's life and the postmortem trial of his will, see Stiles, *The First Tycoon*, 484–485, 502–505, 555–556, 688–689n107.

57. "The Vanderbilt Will Case," *New York Times*, June 26, 1878; "The Vanderbilt Contest," *New York Times*, June 27, 1878; "The Vanderbilt Will Contest," *New York Times*, June 28, 1878; "The Vanderbilt Will Contest," July 4, 1878; "Fighting for Millions," *New York Times*, Sept. 25, 1878; "The Vanderbilt Will Case," *New York Times*, Sept. 26, 1878; "Mrs. La Bau's Case Closed," *New York Times*, Nov. 13, 1878.

58. "The Vanderbilt Will Case," *New York Times*, Nov. 20, 1878, Nov. 21, 1878, and Nov. 23, 1878.

59. "The Vanderbilt Will Case," *New York Times*, Feb. 5, 1879; "The Vanderbilt Will Case," *New York Times*, Feb. 6, 1879; "The Vanderbilt Will Case," *New York Times*, Feb. 8, 1879; "Some Talks with the Commodore," *New York Times*, Feb. 10, 1879; "The Vanderbilt Will Case," *New York Times*, Feb. 12, 1879; "Vanderbilt's Sanity," *St. Louis Globe-Democrat*, Feb. 13, 1879; "The Vanderbilt Will Contest," *New York Times*, Feb. 15, 1879; "The Vanderbilt Will Case," *New York Times*, Feb. 19, 1879; "The Vanderbilt Will Contest," *New York Times*, Feb. 20, 1879; "Vanderbilt's War with Erie," *New York Times*, Feb. 22, 1879; "The Vanderbilt Will Case," *New York Times*, Feb. 26, 1879; "An Expert on Insanity," *New York Times*, Feb. 27, 1879.

60. "Ended after Many Days," *New York Times*, March 5, 1879; "Curiosities of the Vanderbilt Will Case," *Baltimore Sun*, March 7, 1879, p. 1; "The Vanderbilt Will Case," *Daily Evening Bulletin*, Mar. 17, 1879, issue 145, col. F.

61. *La Bau*, 3 Red. Sur. Ct., 384, 422–444.

62. Ibid., 423–425.

63. Ibid., 430–443.

64. Ibid., 443–444.

65. "Vanderbiltiana," *Puck*, Sept. 25, 1878, p. 3; "Vanderbilt and His Railroad," *Boston Daily Advertiser*, Jan. 6, 1877, issue 6, col. B.; Irenaeus, "Three Rich Men's Wills," *New York Observer and Chronicle*, Jan. 18, 1877; "Highways Not Personal Chattels," *Galveston Daily News*, Mar. 22, 1877, issue 311, col. A; "The Vanderbilt Skeleton," *Daily Evening Bulletin*, Mar. 5, 1879. William figured himself as yielding to the "growing public opinion" arrayed "against one-man power" in a November 1879 interview granted after selling his controlling interest in New York Central Railroad. "State of Trade," *Daily Inter Ocean*, Nov. 27, 1879, p. 5, issue 203, col. C.; cf. "The Ambition of Rich Men," *Daily Evening Bulletin*, Nov. 28, 1882.

66. *Chicago Daily Tribune*, June 3, 1882, p. 4; "Gossip from Gotham," *Daily Evening Bulletin* (San Francisco), June 12, 1882, issue 56, col. A. On the pronounced ambivalence with which the public regarded the exploits of Vanderbilt and his way to wealth, see Steve Fraser, *Every Man a Speculator: A History of Wall Street in American Life* (New York: HarperCollins, 2005), 94–105, 124–135, 138, 252–253.

67. "Battle of the Heirs," *St. Louis Globe Democrat*, July 4, 1875; "Our New York Letter," *Independent Statesmen*, June 7, 1877; "The Vanderbilt Will," *Chicago Daily Tribune*, Dec. 21, 1877; "The Curse of Dying Rich," *Sunday Times and Messenger*, Dec. 23, 1877 [NYPL file]; "Have Fathers Any Rights Which Sons Are Bound to Respect?" *The Sun*, Jan. 23, 1878; "Legal, but Not Wise," *The Sun*, Apr. 14, 1878; "Dare the Rich Die?" *Daily Arkansas Gazette*, Nov. 12, 1878. The justice of the criticism of profiteering lawyers is suggested by a striking admission in the *Albany Law Journal*, as the storm that coalesced into the Vanderbilt will contest was brewing: "While it would be well if the last will of a competent testator could be carried out without opposition or interference on the part of the descendants of such testator, we cannot forget that if it were not for sickness physicians would starve, and if it were not for litigation the judicial office would be a sinecure." *Albany Law Journal* 15 (1877): 174.

68. "Wealth and Insanity," *St. Louis Daily Globe Democrat*, Jan. 29, 1878, p. 4; "A Mad World, My Masters!" *New York Tribune*, Feb. 1, 1878, p. 4; "The Drawbacks of Riches," *New York Times*, Nov. 9, 1878; "Millionaires Miseries," *Puck*, Mar. 5, 1879; "The Great Will Case," *New York Times*, Mar. 6, 1879, p. 4; "Current Topics," *Albany Law Journal*, 19 (1879): 245-246; "Richardson's Millions," *Denver Evening Post*, Oct. 15, 1897, p. 4.

69. Smith v. Smith, 25 A. 11, 12 (N.J. Prerog. Ct. 1891); Smith v. Smith, 19 A. 255, 255–257 (N.J. 1890).

70. *Smith*, 25 A., 13–14.

71. Ibid.

72. Ibid., 14.

73. Ibid., 12, 16.

74. Ibid., 17–18.

75. Ibid., 19 (quoting Trumbull v. Gibbons. Yet what the law gave in this 1891 proceeding it took away in 1897. In construing the meaning of Hezekiah's will, state courts ruled that the trust it set up was too vague and indefinite to be executed. Smith v. Smith, 32 A. 1069, 1072 (N.J. Ch. 1895), aff'd, 41 A. 1116, 1116 (N.J. 1897). The court based its decision on a strained interpretation of the applicable statutes and precedents, indicating that judges had other means of policing testamentary dispositions that strayed too far from communal standards of justice. With this ruling, Hezekiah's property descended to his heirs at law, though it came too late for Eveline, who died just before it was handed down.

76. Paul Jerome Croce, *Science and Religion in the Era of William James: The Eclipse of Certainty, 1820–1880* (Chapel Hill: University of North Carolina Press, 1995), 87, 219; McMasters v. Blair, 29 Pa. 298, 304 (1857); see also Wood v. Sawyer, 61 N.C. (Phil.) 251, 275 (1867); Smith v. Harrison, 49 Tenn. (2 Heisk.) 230, 247 (1871).

77. Wharton, *Medical Jurisprudence*, (1882), vol. 1, 85n1; Mullins v. Cottrell, 41 Miss. 291, 315 (1866) (quoting the 1838 English case Morgan v. Boys); see

also Denson v. Beazley, 34 Tex. 191, 201 (1870) (same). The fascination with eccentric wills was manifest in popular culture as well. See John Proffatt, *The Curiosities and Law of Wills* (San Francisco: Sumner Whitney, 1876); William Tegg, *Wills of Their Own: Curious, Eccentric, and Benevolent* (London: William Tegg, 1876).

78. See Fraser v. Jennison, 3 N.W. 882, 900 (Mich. 1879) (collecting cases).

79. In re Will of Blakely, 4 N.W. 337, 340 (Wis. 1880); see also Probate of Will of Jackman, 26 Wis. 104, 116–117 (1870); but see Probate of Will of Jackman, 141–142 (Paine, J., dissenting) (peeking behind the "sacred veil" of the "conjugal relation" and finding that the testator's wife had subverted his will). Judges struggled to reconcile the conflicting testimony so as to avoid the imputation of perjury, see, e.g., La Bau v. Vanderbilt, 424 (lamenting the efforts of children to "magnify [their father's] eccentricities into dementia; his social foibles into immorality; his business differences into dishonesty and treachery; and to ascribe his diseases to obscene practices"); Fairchild v. Bascomb, 35 Vt. 398, 410 (1862) (finding it "somewhat difficult to believe that the same woman, at periods of time near to each other, when talking upon the same subject,—her property,—and that the subject on which she is alleged to have been insane, should have talked to one set of witnesses rationally and to the other wildly and insanely"). See generally William Henry Loyd Jr., "Unjust and Unnatural Wills," *American Law Register and Review* 43 (1895): 247–257, which surveys the decisional law, estimates that few of the "hundreds" of capacity challenges brought every year in the United States are successful, and opines that "this is as it should be, for in most instances they are undertaken through personal animosity or in hope of extorting a compromise from the beneficiaries under the will" (251, 257).

80. William James, "Pragmatism: The Present Dilemma in Philosophy," in *Pragmatism and Other Writings*, ed. Giles Gunn (London: Penguin Books, 2000), 7, 15.

81. Wharton, *Medical Jurisprudence,* 4th ed., vol. 1, 334.

Chapter 5: Speculative Mania in the Age of Contract

1. Beals v. See, 10 Pa. 56, 56–57 (1848).

2. Ibid., 60–61.

3. Adam Smith, *An Inquiry into the Nature and Causes of the Wealth of Nations* (New York: P. F. Collier and Sons, 1909), 15, 120–121. The accelerated pace of economic and social change was commonly said to be mentally destabilizing; commentators registered concern as well as wonder as they contemplated the "crazing, unobservant, lightening-like speed" of everyday life as well as the "general fermentation and excitement of matter and of mind" that imperiled "our great political and civil institutions and the social and moral principles upon which they depend for their existence and perpetuity." Michael Zakim and Gary J. Kornblith, "Introduction: An American Revolutionary Tradition," in Michael Zakim and Gary John Kornblith, eds., *Capitalism Takes Command: The Social Transformation of Nineteenth-Century America* (Chicago: University of Chicago Press, 2012), 2 (quoting from an 1843 memoir).

4. See, e.g., "Money-Making Mania," *American Journal of Insanity* (April 1863) 19; 327–343. On American ambivalence toward speculation, see Jennifer

J. Baker, *Securing the Commonwealth: Debt, Speculation, and Writing in the Making of Early America* (Baltimore: Johns Hopkins University Press, 2005); Edward Balleisen, *Navigating Failure: Bankruptcy and Commercial Society in Antebellum America* (Chapel Hill: University of North Carolina Press, 2001), 52–54. 188; Stuart Banner, *Anglo-American Securities Regulation: Cultural and Political Roots* (Cambridge: Cambridge University Press, 1998), esp. chap. 6; Ann Fabian, *Card Sharps, Dream Books, & Bucket Shops: Gambling in Nineteenth-Century America* (London: Routledge, 1999); Steve Fraser, *Every Man a Speculator: A History of Wall Street in American Life* (New York: HarperCollins, 2005); Jane Kamensky, *The Exchange Artist: A Tale of High-Flying Speculation and America's First Banking Collapse* (New York: Viking, 2008); Roy Kreitner, *Calculating Promises: The Emergence of Modern American Contract Doctrine* (Stanford: Stanford University Press, 2007), esp. chaps. 5, 6, 7, and 8; Jackson Lears, *Something for Nothing: Luck in America* (New York: Viking, 2003); Bruce Mann, *A Republic of Debtors: Bankruptcy in the Age of American Independence* (Cambridge, MA: Harvard University Press, 2002), esp. chap. 6; Karen Ann Weyler, *Intricate Relations: Sexual and Economic Desire in American Fiction, 1789–1814* (Iowa City: Iowa University Press, 2004), chap. 3. For an account from one who was both perpetrator and victim of money-making schemes, see P. T. Barnum, *Humbugs of the World: An Account of Humbugs, Delusions, Impositions, Quackeries, Deceits and Deceivers Generally, in All Ages* (New York: Carleton, 1866), 195–232.

5. Benjamin Rush, *The Autobiography of Benjamin Rush. His "Travels through Life" together with his "Commonplace Book" for 1789–1813*, ed. George W. Corner (Princeton, NJ: Princeton University Press, 1948), 203–204, 237; Rush, *Medical Inquiries and Observations, upon the Diseases of the Mind* (Philadelphia: Kimbler & Richardson, 1812), 64, 66; Rush, *Medical Inquiries and Observations*, 2nd ed. (Philadelphia, J. Conrad & Co., 1794), vol. 1, 275; Rush, *Benjamin Rush's Lectures on the Mind*, ed. Eric T. Carlson, Jeffrey L. Wollock, and Patricia S. Noel (Philadelphia: American Philosophical Society, 1981), 166n1.

6. Mark Noll, "Introduction" and "Protestant Reasoning about Money and the Economy," in *God and Mammon: Protestants, Money, and the Market, 1790–1860*, ed. Mark Noll (Oxford: Oxford University Press, 2001), 3–29, 265–295; Stewart Davenport, *Friends of the Unrighteous Mammon: Northern Christians and Market Capitalism, 1815–1860* (Chicago: Chicago University Press, 2008), 151; William E. Channing, "An Address, Delivered Before the Mercantile Library, of Philadelphia (Philadelphia, J. Crissy, 1841), 29; Kamensky, *Exchange Artist*, 5; Michael Rogin, *Fathers and Children: Andrew Jackson and the Subjugation of the American Indian* (New York: Alfred A. Knopf, 1975), 214; Lydia Marie Child, *Letters from New York* (London: Richard Bentley, 1843). On the cultural strains occasioned by economic volatility, see Andrew Lawson, *Downwardly Mobile: The Changing Fortunes of American Realism* (Oxford: Oxford University Press, 2012); Jessica M. Lepler, *The Many Panics of 1837: People, Politics, and the Creation of a Transatlantic Financial Crisis* (New York: Cambridge University Press, 2013); Scott A. Sandage, *Born Losers: A History of Failure in America* (Cambridge, MA: Harvard University Press, 2005); Hildegard Hoeller, *From Gift to Commodity: Capitalism and Sacrifice in Nineteenth-Century American Fiction* (Lebanon, NH: University Press of New England, 2012); Susan Walsh, "'Arithmetic of Bedlam!': Markets and Manhood in Charles Reade's *Hard Cash*," *Nineteenth-Century Literature* 63,

(2008): 1–40; Jeffrey Sklansky, "William Leggett and the Melodrama of the Market," in *Capitalism Takes Command,* ed. Zakim and Kornblith, 199–221.

7. See, e.g., Edward Jarvis, "On the Comparative Liability of Males and Females to Insanity, and their Comparative Curability and Mortality when Insane," *American Journal of Insanity* 7 (October 1849): 142–171, which concludes that "man is more exposed to, is less frequently cured of, and falls more under the attacks of this class of diseases than women" (171). Though financial strains were regularly observed to impair the mental health of women as well, they tended to be comprehended under the more general designation of "domestic afflictions" or domestic "trouble" in asylum registers. See Gerald N. Grob, *The Mad Among Us,* 90 (Cambridge, MA: Harvard University Press, 1994); David Rothman, *The Discovery of the Asylum: Social Order and Disorder in the New Republic* (Boston: Little, Brown, 1971), 109–122, 125–129. On the causation of insanity in psychiatric theory, see Norman Dain, *Concepts of Insanity in the United States, 1789–1865* (New Brunswick, NJ: Rutgers University Press, 1964), 84–113.

8. Edward Jarvis, "Causes of Insanity," *Boston Medical and Surgical Journal* 45 (November 1851): 303–305; Isaac Ray, "Report of the Superintendent for the Year 1853," in *Reports of the Trustees and Superintendent of the Butler Hospital, Presented to the Corporation, at their Annual Meeting* (Providence: Knowles, Anthony & Co., 1853), 29. See also Rothman, *Discovery of the Asylum;,* 110–119; Grob, *Mental Institutions in America,* 155–158; Benjamin Reiss, *Theaters of Madness: Insane Asylums and Nineteenth-Century American Culture* (Chicago: University of Chicago Press, 2008), 7–9, 85–86, 96, 125; Balleisen, *Navigating Failure,* 14.

9. James Willard Hurst, *Law and the Conditions of Freedom in the Nineteenth-Century United States* (Madison: University of Wisconsin Press, 1956), 6.

10. The accounts offered in this chapter and the next are based upon over three hundred appellate cases involving disputed contracts and deeds, as well as the underlying trial transcripts in over a dozen cases. Although these suits did not tend to involve the same sorts of theatrics and newspaper coverage as will contests, they could be every bit as ugly and drawn out, particularly when they involved instruments that were used as will substitutes.

11. Zakim and Kornblith, "Introduction," 3. On the reconfiguration of social relations in an expanding market society, see, e.g., Toby Ditz, "Shipwreck; or, Masculinity Imperiled: Mercantile Representations of Failure and the Gendered Self in Eighteenth-Century Philadelphia," *Journal of American History* 81 (June 1994): 51–80; Jeanne Boydston, *Home and Work: Housework, Wages, and the Ideology of Labor in the Early Republic* (Oxford: Oxford University Press, 1990); Christopher Tomlins, "Subordination, Authority, Law: Subjects in Labor History," *International Labor and Working Class History* 47 (Spring 1995): 56–90; Amy Dru Stanley, "Slave Breeding and Free Love," in *Capitalism Takes Command,* ed. Zakim and Kornblith, 119–144; Stanley, *From Bondage to Contract: Wage Labor, Marriage, and the Market in the Age of Slave Emancipation* (Cambridge: Cambridge University Press, 1998), 1–59.

12. Daniel Vickers, "Competency and Competition: Economic Culture in Early America," *William and Mary Quarterly* 47 (1990): 28; see also Anne S. Lombard, *Making Manhood: Growing Up Male in Colonial New England* (Cambridge, MA: Harvard University Press, 2003), 4–7; Jeffrey Sklansky, *The Soul's Economy:*

Market Society and Selfhood in American Thought, 1820–1920 (Chapel Hill: University of North Carolina Press, 2002), 23–24. On the competency and the capacity of minors to contract in postrevolutionary America, see Holly Brewer, *By Birth or Consent: Children, Law, and the Anglo-American Revolution in Authority* (Chapel Hill: University of North Carolina Press, 2005), 267–271.

13. Noah Webster, *An American Dictionary of the English Language,* 3rd ed. (New York: S. Converse, 1830), 168; George Crabb, *English Synonymes Explained in Alphabetical Order: With Copious Illustrations and Examples,* 3rd rev. and corr. London ed. (New York: J. & J. Harper, 1826), 193–194; [William Rathbone Greg], *The Living Age* 42, (Sept. 16, 1854): 546–576, 553. On the views expressed by ministers and moralists, see Davenport, *Friends of the Unrighteous Mammon,* esp. chap. 14. On the tension-ridden concept of competition and its shaping effects on economic policy in the United States, see Morton J. Horwitz, *The Transformation of American Law, 1780–1860* (Cambridge, MA: Harvard University Press, 1977), 109–139; Stanley I. Kutler, *Privilege and Creative Destruction: The Charles River Bridge Case* (New York: W. W. Norton, 1978); Herbert Hovenkamp, *Enterprise and American Law, 1836–1937* (Cambridge, MA: Harvard University Press, 1991); Jonathan Levy, *Freaks of Fortune: The Emerging World of Capitalism and Risk in America* (Cambridge, MA: Harvard University Press, 2012), esp. chap. 8; Rudolph J. R. Peritz, *Competition Policy in America 1888-1992: History, Rhetoric, Law* (Oxford: Oxford University Press, 1996), 3–58; Mary S. Morgan, "Competing Notions of 'Competition' in Late Nineteenth-Century American Economics," *History of Political Economy* 25 (1993): 563–604.

14. Charles Sellers, *The Market Revolution: Jacksonian America, 1815–1846* (Oxford: Oxford University Press, 1991), 47–55; see also Horwitz, *Transformation,* chap. 5; William E. Nelson, *Americanization of the Common Law: The Impact of Legal Change on Massachusetts Society* (Cambridge, MA: Harvard University Press, 1975), 117–118; Lawrence Friedman, *History of American Law,* 3rd ed. (New York: Simon and Schuster, 2005), esp. chap. 3; Hurst, *Law and the Conditions of Freedom*; Craig Haney, "Criminal Justice and the Nineteenth-Century Paradigm: The Triumph of Psychological Individualism in the 'Formative Era,'" *Law and Human Behavior* 6 (1982): 191–235. Thomas L. Haskell provides a suggestive reformulation of the historical interrelationships between individualism, formalism, and capitalism in "Persons as Uncaused Causes: John Stuart Mill, the Spirit of Capitalism, and the 'Invention' of Formalism," in *The Culture of the Market,* ed. Thomas L. Haskell and Richard F. Teichgraeber III (Cambridge: Cambridge University Press, 1993), 493–502.

15. Horwitz, *Transformation,* 183; Among the many works that have explored the role of law in sustaining hierarchies based on gender, race, class, age, and ability (mental and physical), the account offered here draws in particular on Christopher Tomlins, *Law, Labor and Ideology in the Early American Republic* (Cambridge: Cambridge University Press, 1993); Nancy Isenberg, Sex and Citizenship in Antebellum America (Chapel Hill: University of North Carolina Press, 1998); Elizabeth B. Clark, "Matrimonial Bonds: Slavery and Divorce in Nineteenth-Century America," *Law and History Review* 8 (1990): 25–54; Siegel, "Home as Work: The First Woman's Rights Claims Concerning Wives' Household Labor, 1850–1880," *Yale Law Journal* 103 (1994): 1073–1217; Siegel, "'The Rule of Love': Wife Beating as Prerogative and Privacy," *Yale Law Journal* 105

(1996): 2117–2206; Stanley, *Bondage to Contract*; Barbara Young Welke, *Law and the Borders of Belonging in the Long Nineteenth Century United States* (Cambridge: Cambridge University Press, 2010).

16. Another frequently cited example is Hurst, *Law and the Conditions of Freedom*, 12, based on the ruling in Printing and Numerical Registering Co. v. Sampson, 1874–1875 L.R. 19 Eq. 462 (1875). For a corrective to this line of scholarship, documenting the extent to which judges were animated by a "jurisprudence of the heart," see Peter Karsten, *Heart versus Head: Judge-Made Law in Nineteenth-Century America* (Chapel Hill: University of North Carolina Press, 1997).

17. While distinguishing moral from legal obligations, some jurists nonetheless conceived of the law as a means of enforcing "all the moral and social duties, so far as human tribunals are competent." Daniel Chipman, *An Essay on the Law of Contracts for the Payment of Specifick Articles* (Middlebury, VT: Copeland, 1822) 81–82, 179; see also William W. Story, *A Treatise on the Law of Contracts Not under Seal*, 2nd ed. (Boston: Little, Brown, 1847), 4–5.

18. Theophilus Parsons, *The Law of Contracts* (Boston: Little, Brown, 1853), vol. 1, 3–5.

19. See, e.g., Lawrence M. Friedman, *Contract Law in America* (Madison: University of Wisconsin Press, 1965), 55–57, treating questions of capacity as external to the realm of "'pure' contract doctrine," which is "blind to the details of subject matter and person" and William M. Wiecek, *The Lost World of Classical Legal Thought: Law and Ideology in America, 1886–1937* (New York: Oxford University Press, 1998), 103, suggesting that the law of the classical era supported "a regime of the utmost contractual freedom" as it assumed "parties of full age were competent to enter into contracts" and "recognized only objective manifestations of the parties' assent"; and compare with Milton D. Green, "The Operative Effect of Mental Incompetency on Agreements and Wills," *Texas Law Review* 21 (1943): 557–580; and Green, "Proof of Mental Incompetency and the Unexpressed Major Premise," *Yale Law Journal* 53 (1944): 275, attending to contracts cases raising questions of mental incompetency but contending that courts have been evolving toward "an inarticulate standard calculated to judge the transaction and not the individual" (275).

20. James Kent, *Commentaries on American Law*, 2nd ed. (New York: O. Halsted, 1832), vol. 2, 450; John Powell, *An Essay upon the Law of Contracts and Agreements*, 2nd ed. (Walpole: Thomas and Thomas 1809), vol. 1, 9–10, 93; Joseph Chitty, *A Practical Treatise on the Law of Contracts and upon the Usual Defences to Action Thereon* (London: S. Sweet, 1834), 107–108; see also Story, *Law of Contracts*, 13.

21. See, e.g., Story, *Law of Contracts*, 13–51; John Newland, *A Treatise on Contracts within the Jurisdiction of Courts of Equity* (Philadelphia: Benjamin Warner, 1821), 1–33; Chitty, *Law of Contracts*, 107–170.

22. The treatise went through six editions during Parsons's lifetime: 1853, 1855–1857, 1857, 1860, 1864–1866, and 1873. A seventh edition by William V. Kellen was published in 1883, a year after Parsons's death, an eighth by Samuel Williston in 1893, and a ninth by John M. Gould in 1904. Compare Parsons, *Law of Contracts*, vol. 1, 9–10 with Parsons, *Law of Contracts*, 6th ed. (Boston: Little, Brown, and Co., 1873), vol. 1, 9–10, which removes "bankrupts

or insolvents" from the list but adds a new section on the law of insolvency to the treatise, and with Parsons, *Law of Contracts*, 7th ed. (Little, Brown, and Co., 1883), vol. 1, 9–10, which drops slaves from the list, although the chapter on this class of persons had been removed by the time of the 6th edition. The eighth and ninth editions, edited by Samuel Williston and John M. Gould, respectively, make no further alterations of this list.

23. Theophilus Parsons, *Law of Contracts*, 3rd ed. (Boston: Little, Brown, and Co., 1857), vol. 1, 295–296, 319–329; Parsons, *Law of Contracts*, 4th ed (Boston: Little, Brown, and Co., 1860), vol. 1, 329–330, 370–380; Parsons, *Law of Contracts*, 5th ed. (Boston: Little, Brown, and Co., 1864), vol. 1, 339–340, 370–380; Parsons, *Law of Contracts*, 6th ed., vol. 1, 373–374, 407–423; Parsons, *Law of Contracts*, 7th ed., vol. 1, 378–379, 412–432.

24. Parsons, *Law of Contracts*, 5th ed., vol. 1, 399–401, 406–407, 408–409. Significantly, this principle meant that a slave's agreement with his master to purchase his or her own freedom was legally unenforceable.

25. Parsons, *Law of Contracts*, 5th ed., 414–415. The chapter on slaves remained unaltered from the first through the fifth editions of the treatise.

26. Henry St. George Tucker, *Blackstone's Commentaries: With Notes of Reference to the Constitution and Laws, of the Federal Government of the United States, and of the Commonwealth of Virginia* (Philadelphia: William Young Birch, and Abraham Small, 1803), vol. 3, 291; Joseph Story, *Commentaries on Equity Jurisprudence*, vol. 1, 229; Isaac Ray, *Treatise on the Medical Jurisprudence of Insanity* (Boston: Charles C. Little and James Brown, 1838), 12–14; see also Nathan Dane, *A General Abridgment and Digest of American Law* (Boston: Cummings, Hilliard, 1823), vol. 2, 19; Thomas Cooper, *Tracts on Medical Jurisprudence* (Philadelphia: James Webster, 1819), 377; Leonard Shelford, *A Practical Treatise on the Law Concerning Lunatics, Idiots, and Persons of Unsound Mind* (London, 1833; repr. Philadelphia: J. S. Littell, 1833), 166–167. Among the leading American cases explicitly rejecting the English maxim were Webster v. Woodford, 3 Day 90 (Conn. 1808); Somes v. Skinner, 16 Mass. R. 348 (1820); Mitchell v. Kingman, (5 Pick.) 431 (1827); Rice v. Peet, 15 Johns. 503 (N.Y. 1818).

27. Jackson ex dem. Caldwell v. King, 4 Cow. 207, 218 (N.Y. 1825); Hale v. Hills, 8 Conn. 39, 43–44 (1830); Prather v. Naylor's Adm'r, 40 Ky. (1 B. Mon.) 244, 247–248 (1841); Dennett v. Dennett, 44 N.H. 531, 537–538 (1863).

28. Converse v. Converse, 21 Vt. 168, 170–171 (1849); see also Mann v. Betterly, 21 Vt. 325, 239 (1849); Frazer v. Frazer, 2 Del. Ch. 260, 263 (Ch. 1861); Hovey v. Chase, 52 Me. 304, 306 (1863); Somers v. Pumphrey, 24 Ind. 231, 245 (1865).

29. Osmond v. Fitzroy and Duke of Cleveland, 24 E.R. 997 (1731); compare Earl of Chesterfield v. Janssen, 28 E.R. 82, 2 Vesey Senior 125 (1751). For American cases following *Osmond*, see, e.g., *Webster*, 3 Day, 93 (Conn. 1808); Poston v. Balch, 69 Mo. 115, 122 (1878).

30. Baxter v. The Earl of Portsmouth, 108 E.R. 63 (1826); s.c. 172 E.R. 81, 83 (1826). On the context of this case, see Akihito Suzuki, *Madness at Home: The Psychiatrist, the Patient, and the Family in England, 1820–1860* (Berkeley: University of California Press, 2006), 12–38, 103–115.

31. See Huguenin v. Baseley, 14 Vesey 273 (1807); Parfitt v. Lawless, L.R. 2 Prob. & Div. 468 (1872), followed in, e.g., Bancroft v. Otis, 91 Ala. 279, 286–287

(1890); Smith v. Smith, 84 Kan. 242, 246–247 (1911). See generally John Davison Lawson, *The Principles of the American Law of Contracts at Law and in Equity* (St. Louis: F. H. Thomas, 1893), 276–282 (collecting cases).

32. The phrase appears to have been taken from the field of boxing, where it was said that "the weaker man may overcome the stronger, if he can keep him from closing" by holding him "at arm's end." Samuel Johnson, *A Dictionary of the English Language* (London: W. Strahan, 1755), vol. 1, 13.

33. Williams v. Williams, 63 Md. 371, 400 (1885) (quoting *Huguenin*); Craddock v. Cabiness, 31 Tenn. 474, 481–484 (1852); Gass v. Mason, 4 Sneed 497, 505–507 (Tenn. 1857); see also Buffalow v. Buffalow, 2 Dev. & Bat. Eq. 241, 252–254 (N.C. 1839); Todd v. Grove, 33 Md. 188, 190–204, 208 (1870); however, compare Pressley v. Kemp, 16 S.C. 334, 342–347 (1882); see generally Frederick Thomas White, *A Selection of Leading Cases in Equity* (Philadelphia: T. and J. W. Johnson, 1889), vol. 2, 659–679 (collecting cases and documenting the expansiveness of the equitable doctrine).

34. Story, *Commentaries on Equity Jurisprudence*, 221–228; Wilson v. Watts, 9 Md. 356, 386 (1856); see also Somers v. Pumphrey, 24 Ind. 231, 236–240, 244–248 (1865).

35. In so doing, they reasoned by analogy from cases involving infants, who were allowed to ratify or disaffirm their contracts upon reaching the age of majority, though it would prove considerably more difficult to establish whether a party's reason was restored than it was to mark the attainment of adulthood. For cases holding the contracts of the insane to be wholly void, see, e.g., Seaver v. Phelps, 28 Mass. (11 Pick.) 304, 306–307 (1831); Jenkins v. Jenkins' Heirs, 32 Ky. 72, 73, 2 Dana 102, 104 (1834); Cole v. Cole, 37 Tenn. (5 Sneed) 57, 59 (1857). For those holding them to be merely voidable, see, e.g., Allis v. Billings, 47 Mass. (6 Met.) 415, 418 (1843); Key's Lessee v. Davis, 1 Md. 32, 42 (1851); Wait v. Maxwell, 22 Mass. (5 Pick.) 217, 224 (1827); Jackson ex dem. Merritt v. Gumaer, 2 Cow. 552, 568 (N.Y. Sup. Ct. 1824).

36. See, e.g., *Seaver*, 28 Mass. (11 Pick.), 307.

37. See, e.g., Burke v. Allen, 29 N.H. 106, 115 (1854); Fay v. Burditt, 81 Ind. 433, 438–442 (1882); Northwestern Mut. Fire Ins. Co. v. Blankenship, 94 Ind. 535, 541–549 (1884).

38. Alston v. Boyd, 24 Tenn. (6 Hum.) 504, 505–508 (1846).

39. See Jerry v. Townshend, 9 Md. 145, 158 (1856); Bond v. Bond, 89 Mass. (7 Allen) 1, 8 (1863); Gillespie v. Shuliberrier, 50 N.C. (5 Jones) 161, 164 (1857).

40. Thornton v. Appleton, 29 Me. 298, 300–302 (1849). In the late nineteenth century, some courts moved even more decisively to bring the doctrine of delusion in cases involving *inter vivos* transactions in line with that applied in those involving wills, requiring that the instrument be the offspring of the diseased mind. See, e.g., Lewis v. Arbuckle, 85 Iowa 335, 52 N.W. 237, 239–240 (1892); Curtis v. Brownell, 42 Mich. 165, 170 (1879); Cutler v. Zollinger, 117 Mo. 92 22 S.W. 895, 897 (1893); Dewey v. Algire, 37 Neb. 6 55 N.W. 276, 278 (1893); Lozear v. Shields, 23 N.J. Eq. 509, 510–511 (1872); Wright v. Jackson, 59 Wis. 569 18 N.W. 486, 491 (1884); Ripley v. Babcock, 13 Wis. 425, 428–429 (1861).

41. Molton v. Camroux 154 Eng. Rep. 584, 590 (1848); aff'd 154 Eng. Rep. 1107, 1108 (1849). Although the principles governing this decision had

been regularly applied in courts of equity, *Molton* was regarded as the first English decision to declare them equally applicable in proceedings at law. See Samuel Williston, *The Law of Contracts* (New York: Baker, Voorhis, 1920), vol. 1, 494–495. For leading American cases adopting the *Molton* rule, see Behrens v. McKenzie, 23 Iowa 333 (1867); Young v. Stevens, 48 N.H. 133 (1868); Matthiessen v. McMahon's Administrator, 38 N.J.L. 536 (1876); Lancaster County National Bank v. Moore, 78 Pa. 407 (1875); Lincoln v. Buckmaster, 32 Vt. 652 (1860).

42. *Lincoln,* 32 Vt., 662–663, 665. See also Chew v. Bank of Balt., 14 Md. 299, 319 (1859), conceding there may be "no actual fault on the part of the bank" for the loss but deciding on grounds of "justice and expediency" that it is the party "who can best provide against it"; Curtis v. Brownell, 3 N.W. 936, 941 (Mich. 1879), ruling against the sane party who had adequate notice to place him on guard, though his conduct was not deemed "open to serious censure," the court concluding that "it is nearly as much his misfortune as his fault."

43. *Lincoln,* 32 Vt., 657–665. Importantly, questions of mental capacity did not simply reduce to determinations of fairness in a more objective sense and judges resisted any easy equation of sanity with the apparent rationality of the disputed instrument or transaction. See, e.g., Corbit v. Smith, 7 Clarke 60, 64–66 (Iowa 1858); see also Bishop, *Contracts,* 381.

44. For cases following *Lincoln,* see Wilder v. Weakley, 34 Ind. 181 (1870); Behrens v. McKenzie, 23 Iowa 333 (1867); Rusk v. Fenton, 77 Ky. (14 Bush) 490 (1879); Young v. Stevens, 48 N.H. 133 (1868); Yauger v. Skinner, 14 N.J. Eq. 389 (Ch. 1862); Mut. Life Ins. Co. of N.Y. v. Hunt, 79 N.Y. 541 (1880); Riggan v. Green, 80 N.C. 237 (1879); Lancaster County Nat'l Bank v. Moore, 78 Pa. 407 (1875); Sims v. McLure, 29 S.C. Eq. (8 Rich. Eq.) 286 (1856).

45. Cases adopting rules more favorable to the insane include Somers v. Pumphrey, 24 Ind. 231 (1865); Gibson v. Soper, 72 Mass. (6 Gray) 279 (1856); Hovey v. Hobson, 55 Me. 256 (1867); Rawdon v. Rawdon, 28 Ala. 565 (1856).

46. Hall v. Unger, 2 Abb. U.S. 508, 11 F. Cas. 261 (1867).

47. Ibid., 266.

48. Ibid., 267; Michael Grossberg, *Governing the Hearth: Law and the Family in Nineteenth-Century America* (Chapel Hill: University of North Carolina Press, 1985), xii; Dexter v. Hall, 15 Wall (82 U.S.) 9, 20 (1875).

49. *Hudson River Chronicle,* June 28, 1839; *The North American* (Philadelphia), June 28, 1839, p. 82, col. D; *New-York Spectator,* July 1, 1839, col. E.

50. Breasted v. Farmers' Loan and Trust Co., 4 Hill 73 (1843); Breasted v. Farmers' Loan and Trust Co., 8 N.Y. (4 Seld.) 299 (1853).

51. *Breasted* 8 N.Y. (94 Seld.), 309–310.

52. "A Novel Form of Insurance—'Maiden Assurance Companies.,'" *New York Times,* Oct. 15, 1868; "Life Insurance Illustrated," *New York Times,* Dec. 31, 1860 (reprinted from the *Wall Street Underwriter*); Sharon A. Murphy, *Investing in Life: Insurance in Antebellum America* (Baltimore: Johns Hopkins University Press, 2010), 125; The Mutual Benefit Life Insurance Company, Script Dividend, 1867; see also Zelizer, *Morals and Markets: The Development of Life Insurance in the United States* (New York: Columbia University Press, 1983); Viviana A. Zelizer, *Economic Lives: How Culture Shapes the Economy* (Princeton, NJ: Princeton University Press, 2011), 21. On history of risk and of risk management, see Lears,

Something for Nothing; Mann, *Republic of Debtors*; Balleisen, *Navigating Failure*; Levy, *Freaks of Fortune*.

53. See Michael MacDonald, "The Medicalization of Suicide in England: Laymen, Physicians, and Cultural Change, 1500–1870," *Milbank Quarterly* 67 (1989): 69–91; Richard Bell, *We Shall Be No More: Suicide and Self-Government in the Newly United States* (Cambridge, MA: Harvard University Press, 2012).

54. See "Suicide in Life Insurance—Sane or Insane," *Central Law Journal* 4 (1877): 51–53 (puzzling over why American companies trailed thirty years behind the English in inserting such a clause).

55. Bigelow v. Berkshire Life Ins. Co., 93 U.S. 284, 286 (1876). For subsequent affirmations of the point that there is nothing in the provision affecting public policy or morality, see, e.g., Latimer v. Sovereign Camp Woodmen of the World, 62 S.C. 145 (1901); Brunner v. Equitable Life Assur. Soc., 100 Ill. App. 22 (1902).

56. *Bigelow*, 93 U.S., 285, 287, 288.

57. Ibid., 287; Mallory v. Travelers' Ins. Co., 47 N.Y. (2 Sickels) 52, 54–55.

58. Mut. Benefit Life Ins. Co. v. Daviess' Ex'r, 87 Ky. 541, 9 S.W. 812, 816 (1888).

59. *Bigelow*, 93 U.S., 288.

60. De Gogorza v. Knickerbocker Life Insurance Company, 65 N.Y. 232, 237 (1875).

61. Ibid., 236–237, 241–242. For other jurisdictions following this ruling, see Chapman v. Rockford Ins. Co., 89 Wis. 572 (1895); Billings v. Accident Ins. Co., 64 Vt. 78 (1892); Scherar v. Prudential Ins. Co., 63 Neb. 530 (1902); Scarth v. Security Mut. L. Soc., 75 Iowa 346 (1888); Tritschler v. Keystone Mut. Benefit Ass'n, 180 Pa. St. 205 (1897); Keefer v. Pacific Mut. Life Ins. Co., 201 Pa. St. 448 (1902); Seitzinger v. Modern Woodmen of America, 204 Ill. 58 (1903); Moore v. Northwestern Mut. L. Ins. Co., 192 Mass. 468 (1906); Haynie v. The Knight Templars and Masons' Indemnity Co., 139 Mo. 416 (1897); Sparks v. Knights Templars & Masons L. Indemnity Co., 1 Mo. App. Rep. 334 (1897); Zimmerman v. Masonic Aid Ass'n of Dakota, 75 F. 236 (C.C.D. Neb. 1896); Union Central L. Ins. Co. v. Hollowell, 14 Ind. App. 611 (1896); Bachmeyer v. Mut. Reserve Fund Life Ass'n, 87 Wis. 328 (1894); Streeter v. Western Union Mut. Life & Acc. Soc'y, 65 Mich. 199 (1887); Kelley v. Mut. Life Ins. Co. of New York, 75 F. 637 (C.C.S.D. Iowa 1896). For a case providing an especially elaborate discussion of the distinction between suicide and accident, see Penfold v. Universal Life Ins. Co., 85 N.Y. 317 (1881).

62. *De Gogorza*, 65 N.Y., 243 (Earl, J., dissenting). For other jurisdictions anticipating or following this line of reasoning, see Pierce v. Traveler's Life Ins. Co., 34 Wis. 389 (1874); Keels v. Mut. Reserve Fund Life Ass'n., 29 Fed. 198 (C.C.D.S.C. 1886).

63. "Suicide and Life Insurance," *The Independent*, Nov. 22, 1883, p. 24.

64. Charles Burke Elliott, "Suicide – Effect upon a Life Insurance Policy," *Central Law Journal* 21 (1885): 378; see also John Wilder May, *The Law of Insurance*, 3rd rev. ed. (Boston: Little, Brown, 1891), vol. 1, 627, editorializing: "The prospect of providing for wife and family may in some states of mind be an irresistible motive, yet it is the very one the company wishes to exclude." For a medical opinion in line with this assessment, penned by an examining physician employed by an insurance company, see Brandreth Symonds, "The

Medical Jurisprudence of Life Insurance," in *A System of Legal Medicine*, ed. Allan McLane Hamilton and Lawrence Godkin (New York: E. B. Treat, 1894), vol. 1, 575–577.

65. Murphy, *Investing in Life*, 191; see also S. V. Clevenger, *Medical Jurisprudence of Insanity or Forensic Psychiatry* (Rochester, NY: Lawyer's Co-operative Publishing, 1898), vol. 1, 212 (observing that "business competition, probably more than anything else, is inducing abandonment of restricting clauses as to suicide on policies").

66. "Editorial Article 6," *Washington Post*, July 13, 1884, p. 4; W. H. Lawton, "Suicide and Life Insurance," *North American Review* 179 (1904): 700.

67. Murphy, *Investing in Life*, 145, 193–197.

68. Missouri did so in the 1880s; Colorado followed in 1903, North Dakota in 1905, and Texas in 1914. Georgia made suicide a defense by statute if intentionally perpetrated, although this defense could be waived by contract, unlike the antisuicide legislation pioneered by Missouri. The legality of the Missouri statute was tested and upheld in Whitfield v. Aetna Life Ins., 205 U.S. 489 (1895). See W. R. V., "Suicide as a Defense in Life Insurance," *Yale Law Journal* 30 (1921): 401, 402.

69. Ritter v. Mut. Life Ins. Co. of New York, 169 U.S. 139 (1898) Transcript of Record. File Date: 3/9/1896, p. 21. Term Year: 1897, U.S. Supreme Court Records and Briefs, 1832-1978.

70. Ibid., 53, 118, 121.

71. Ibid., 147, 151–152, 154. See also Hopkins v. Northwestern Life Assur. Co., 94 Fed. 729, 730–731 (C.C.E.D. Pa. 1899), extending the logic of *Ritter* to deny recovery to the wife and designated beneficiary of the insured.

72. Campbell v. Supreme Conclave, 66 N.J.L. 274, 278–280, 283–284 (1901). See also Lange v. Royal Highlanders, 75 Neb. 188, 203–204 (1907) (likewise criticizing the reasoning of *Ritter* and suggesting most state courts allow recovery, at least to third-party beneficiaries, in cases of sane suicide where the policy does not exclude coverage on this score); Patterson v. Natural Premium Life Ins. Co., 100 Wis. 118, 121–125 (1898) (refusing to apply *Ritter* where the policy had been assigned with the consent of the company to the children of the insured without deciding whether recovery would be allowed where the policy benefited the estate of the insured); Parker v. Des Moines Life Ass'n, 108 Ia. 117, 123 (1899) (allowing recovery where wife was beneficiary); Seiler v. Economic Life Ass'n of Clinton, 105 Ia. 87, 92–95 (1898) (holding that, as against a beneficiary, suicide is not a defense); Supreme Conclave v. Miles, 92 Md. 613, 626–628 (1901) (same); but see Mooney v. Ancient Order, 114 Ky. 950, 960 (1903) (following *Ritter*); Shipman v. Protected Home Circle, 174 N.Y. 398, 408 (1903) (same, in dicta). The U.S. Supreme Court significantly undercut *Ritter* in a series of cases culminating with Justice Oliver Wendell Holmes's decision in Northwestern Mut. Life Ins. Co. v. Johnson, effectively declaring the availability of the defense of suicide in insurance cases to be a matter of public policy left for the states to decide and suggesting that the true grounds of the decision in *Ritter* was the fact that the insured purchased insurance with the intent to commit suicide. 254 U.S. 96, 101 (1920).

73. The number of litigated cases involving suicide clauses across the nineteenth century cannot be precisely determined, given how many were settled

before reaching the court of last resort; the number of reported appellate cases approaches two hundred. However, it was not so much the volume of litigation as the "irreconcilable" nature of the judicial conflict that excited concern among members of the bench and bar, "the prospect of agreement" seemingly growing ever more unlikely as the century came to a close. Ward B. Coe, "The Suicide Clause in Life Policies," *Central Law Journal* 41 (1895): 272. For similar critical appraisals of the doctrinal landscape, see"Suicide and Life Insurance," *Albany Law Journal* 4 (1871): 53–56; "Insanity and Suicide," *The Independent*, June 9, 1881, p. 24; J. F. Kelly, "The Effect of Self-Destruction in Life Insurance," *American Law Journal* 1 (1884): 324–328; "Suicide of Insurance Policy-Holder," *Virginia Law Review* 13 (1889): 553–556; George Lawyer, "The Suicide Clause in Life Insurance Contracts," *Central Law Journal* 52 (1901): 107–111.

74. Morton Keller, "The Judicial System and the Law of Life Insurance, 1888–1910," *Business History Review* 35 (1961): 317–335, 335.

75. Here it is instructive to consider, by comparison, the figures of the (male) beggar, (female) prostitute, and (male) bankrupt, as drawn by legal professionals and reformers; the first was cast as a moral failure, the second as a victim of social and economic circumstances, and the third as suffering from the ill effects of market failure rather than his own character flaws. On beggars and prostitutes, see Stanley, *Bondage to Contract*, 98–137, 218–263; on bankrupts, see John Fabian Witt, "Narrating Bankruptcy/Narrating Risk," *Northwestern Law Review* 98 (2003): 303–334.

76. E. Anthony Rotundo, *American Manhood: Transformations in Masculinity from the Revolution to the Modern Era* (New York: Basic Books, 1993), 178–185; see also Michael Grossberg, "Institutionalizing Masculinity: The Law as a Masculine Profession," in *Meanings for Manhood: Constructions of Masculinity in Victorian America*, ed. Mark C. Carnes and Clyde Griffin (Chicago: University of Chicago Press, 1990), 133–151; Judy Hilkey, *Character Is Capital: Success Manuals and Manhood in Gilded Age America* (Chapel Hill: University of North Carolina Press, 1997), esp. chap. 7.

Chapter 6: The Consideration of Love

1. Conner v. Stanley, 65 Cal. 183, 184–186 (1884).
2. Conner v. Stanley, 72 Cal. 556, 559–560, 561, 562 (1887).
3. Ibid., 558–559.
4. All of these radical movements had sexual dimensions: Mormons practiced polygamy, Mesmerism put women's bodies under a man's control, Fourierists often espoused free love, and Socialism implied a community of women.
5. Frederic Rowland Marvin," *The Philosophy of Spiritualism and the Pathology and Treatment of Mediomania* (New York: Asa K. Butts and Co., 1879), 47. This account of Spiritualism draws particularly on Anne Braude, *Radical Spirits: Spiritualism and Women's Rights in Nineteenth-Century America* (Boston: Beacon Press, 1989); Molly McGarry, *Ghosts of Futures Past: Spiritualism and the Cultural Politics of Nineteenth-Century America* (Berkeley: University of California Press, 2008); R. Laurence Moore, *In Search of White Crows: Spiritualism, Parapsychology, and American Culture* (New York: Oxford University Press, 1977); Robert S. Cox, *Body and Soul: A Sympathetic History of American Spiritualism* (Charlottesville: University

of Virginia Press, 2003); John Lardas Modern, *Secularism in Antebellum America, with Reference to Ghosts, Protestant Subcultures, Machines, and their Metaphors; Featuring Discussions of Mass Media, Moby-Dick, Spirituality, Phrenology, Anthropology, Sing Sing State Penitentiary, and Sex with the New Motive Power* (Chicago: University of Chicago Press, 2011); Bret E. Carroll, *Spiritualism in Antebellum America* (Bloomington: Indiana University Press, 1997); Cathy Gutierrez, *Plato's Ghost: Spiritualism in the American Renaissance* (New York: Oxford University Press, 2009). For studies exploring the cultural significance of Spiritualism in Victorian England see Alex Owen, *The Darkened Room: Women, Power and Spiritualism in Late Victorian England* (London: Virago Press, 1989); Janet Oppenheim, *The Other World: Spiritualism and Psychical Research in England, 1850–1914* (Cambridge: Cambridge University Press, 1985). On the social purity movement, see John D'Emilio and Estelle B. Freedman, *Intimate Matters: A History of Sexuality in America*, 3rd ed. (Chicago: University of Chicago Press, 2012).

6. Nathaniel Hawthorne, *The Blithedale Romance: An Authoritative Text, Backgrounds and Sources, Criticism*, ed. Seymour Lee Gross and Rosalie Murphy (New York: Norton, 1978). On the novel's relationship to Brook Farm, the utopian community established by Transcendentalists in 1841 that adopted Fourier's ideas in 1844 and dissolved in 1847, see Sterling F. Delano, *Brook Farm: The Dark Side of Utopia* (Cambridge, MA: Belknap Press, 2004); Carl Guarneri, *The Utopian Alternative: Fourierism in Nineteenth-Century America* (Ithaca, NY: Cornell University Press, 1991); Anne C. Rose, *Transcendentalism as a Social Movement, 1830-1850* (New Haven, CT: Yale University Press, 1981). Hawthorne lived there from the spring through the fall of 1841 and frequently visited his friends there after he had gone back to Concord.

7. William Herbert Page, *The Law of Contracts* (Cincinnati: The W. H. Anderson Co., 1905), vol. 1, 399; Bancroft v. Otis, 91 Ala. 279, 289 (1890).

8. Reva Siegel, "'The Rule of Love': Wife Beating as Prerogative and Privacy," *Yale Law Journal* 105 (1996): 2146, 2147n112; Michael Grossberg, *Governing the Hearth: Law and the Family in Nineteenth-Century America* (Chapel Hill: University of North Carolina Press, 1985), 291; Joel Prentiss Bishop, *Commentaries on the Law of Marriage and Divorce* (Boston: Little, Brown & Co., 1852), 25; Matthew J. Lindsay, "Reproducing a Fit Citizenry: Dependency, Eugenics, and the Law of Marriage in the United States, 1860-1920," *Law & Social Inquiry* 23 (1998: 544); Ditson v. Ditson, 4 R.I. 87, 101 (1856).

9. Hamaker v. Hamaker, 18 Ill. 137, 137, 139 (1856).

10. The statute in question provided that "in addition to the causes hereinbefore provided for divorces from the bonds of matrimony, courts of chancery in this state shall have full power and authority to hear and determine all causes for divorce not provided for by any law of this state." In a previous ruling, the Illinois Supreme Court had held that this provision did not "confer upon courts an unlimited discretion to grant divorces in all cases where they may deem it expedient or advisable." Birkby v. Solomons, 15 Ill. 120, 121–122 (1853).

11. *Hamaker*, 18 Ill., 140–141.

12. Nancy F. Cott, *Public Vows: A History of Marriage and the Nation* (Cambridge, MA: Harvard University Press, 2000), 11, emphasizes the power of "the marital metaphor" in early republican political discourse, which displaced the parent-child relationship as a means of modeling good government because it

was "a freely chosen structure of authority and obligation." Norma Basch, *Framing American Divorce: From the Revolutionary Generation to the Victorians* (Berkeley: University of California Press, 1999), 21–27; Hendrik Hartog, *Man and Wife in America: A History* (Cambridge, MA: Harvard University Press, 2000), 93–96. See generally Richard H. Chused, *Private Acts in Public Places: A Social History of Divorce in the Formative Era of American Family Law* (Philadelphia: University of Pennsylvania Press, 1994); Mark E. Kann, *Taming the Passion for the Public Good: Policing Sex in the Early Republic* (New York: New York University Press, 2013); Grossberg, *Governing the Hearth*, 3–30.

13. Cott, *Public Vows*, 11.

14. John Ordronaux, *Commentaries on the Lunacy Laws of New York* (Albany, NY: J. D. Parsons, Jr., Law Publisher, 1878). This was in contrast to the "dark ages," when marriage was held to be so "sacred" and "mysterious" that even the marriage of an idiot was held to be binding. Bishop, *Law of Marriage and Divorce*, vol. 1, 139–140.

15. Ibid, 76.

16. See, e.g., Joseph Story, *Commentaries of the Conflict of Laws* (Boston: Hilliard, Gray, 1834), 168, maintaining that "Marriage is not to be treated as a mere contract between the parties, subject, as to its continuance, dissolution, and effects, to their mere pleasure and intentions. But it is treated as a civil institution, the most interesting and important in its nature of any in society"; and Cole v. Cole, 37 Tenn. (5 Sneed) 57, 59–60 (1857), holding that the marriage stood or fell "by the usual tests applicable to contracts" but also stated that "every consideration of policy and humanity admonishes us that a contract so essentially connected with the peace and happiness of individuals and families, and the well-being of society, should not be annulled" unless the incapacity was "clearly made out." Cott, *Public Vows*, 47, observes that even as they worked to modernize the rules, lawmakers continued to think of the marital relation as governed in a more basic sense by God or natural law. Basch, Framing American Divorce, 21–28, emphasizes that "the wholesale legitimation of divorce" in the early republic amounted to a radical departure from English law, particularly in "its gender-neutral approach to fault, in the completeness of its dissolutions, and in the access it afforded litigants." But she further notes the reluctance of postrevolutionary Americans to embrace a "thoroughly contractual" model of marriage and their struggle to provide for the dissolution of unions "that had been so seriously violated as to destroy the ends of marriage . . . without at the same time destroying marriage itself"; see also Hartog, Man and Wife, 70–86, which illustrates the strained relationship between "the sanctity of marriage" and "the sanctity of contract."

17. See Bishop, *Law of Marriage and Divorce*, vol. 1, 37; Henry Folsom Page, *A View of the Law Relative to the Subject of Divorce, in Ohio, Indiana and Michigan* (Columbus: J. H. Riley & Co., 1850), 183. Statutes in some states blurred the distinction between suits for nullity and those for divorce, most notably in providing that a sentence of nullity made the marriage void only from the date of the suit forward. Bishop, *Law of Marriage and Divorce*, vol. 1, 49, sharply criticized this provision.

18. Basch, *Framing American Divorce*, 38–40; see also Ariela R. Dubler, "Governing through Contract: Common Law Marriage in the Nineteenth Century," *Yale Law Journal* 107 (1998): 1885–1920; Dubler, "Wifely Behavior: A Legal History of Acting Married," *Columbia Law Review* 100 (2000): 957–1021.

19. Hartog, *Man and Wife*, 71; William H. Cord, *A Treatise on the Legal and Equitable Rights of Married Women: As Well in Respect to their Property and Persons as to their Children*, 2nd ed. (Philadelphia: Kay and Brother, 1885), vol. 1, 22–25, reiterating and glossing Justice's Story's 1819 concurring opinion in the *Dartmouth College* case; but see Bishop, *Law of Marriage and Divorce*, vol. 1, 628–629, 636, insisting that Story's "more mature opinion is shown to have been the other way." See generally Hartog, *Man and Wife*, 71–72, 330n18.

20. Basch, *Framing American Divorce*, 16, 64; Benton v. Benton, 1 Day, 111, 113 (Conn. 1803); see also Sullivan v. Sullivan, 2 Hagg. C.R. 238 (1818); Lewis v. Lewis, 44 Minn. 124 (1890). But Tapping Reeve, *The Law of Baron and Femme*, 2nd ed. (New York: Banks, Gould, 1846), 206, read "fraudulent contract" to provide a broader basis for granting divorces than allowed by *Benton*. See also Bishop, *Law of Marriage and Divorce*, vol. 1, 79–80. Sexual virtue was a much touchier subject, though the definition of fraud was narrowly drawn here as well; see Bishop, *Law of Marriage and Divorce*, vol. 1, 81–83.

21. Ariela J. Gross, *Double Character: Slavery and Mastery in the Antebellum Southern Courtroom* (Princeton, NJ: Princeton University Press, 2000), chap. 5 discusses warranty cases that involved slaves alleged to be unsound of mind, body, or both.

22. Bishop, *Law of Marriage and Divorce*, vol. 1, 76–78.

23. Jenkins v. Jenkins' Heirs, 2 Dana 102, 104 (1834).

24. "Report of the Select Committee, To which was referred House bill No. 73, to divorce Horace P. Dunbar from his wife Mary Ann Dunbar," *Journal of the House of Representatives of the State of Ohio* (Columbus: Chas. Scott's Steam Press, Jan. 12, 1848), vol. 46, 34. Though the rest of the members of Ohio's General Assembly may have agreed with this assessment, the case got tangled up in the constitutional politics of legislative divorces, and the husband's bill was ultimately voted down because of widespread uncertainty and turmoil both within and beyond this state about whether and when such discretion could be exercised by legislators or delegated to courts without destroying all that was valuable about marriage (ibid., 340–345; quoting Story's concurrence in the *Dartmouth College* case); *Journal of the Senate of the State of Ohio* (Columbus: Chas. Scott's Steam Press, February 5, 1828), 455–456; David M. Gold, *Democracy in Session: A History of the Ohio Assembly* (Athens: Ohio University Press, 2009), 216. See generally Basch, *Framing American Divorce*, 43–44, 65–66.

25. Page, *Law Relative to the Subject of Divorce*, 185–186n3. For a newspaper critique of the proposed New York bill, representing it to be against the moral sense of the community, see "Insanity a Cause of Divorce," *The Weekly Herald*, March 17, 1849, issue 11, col. A.

26. Page, Law Relative to the Subject of Divorce, 186n3; Bishop, *Law of Marriage and Divorce*, vol. 1, 224–225. See also Joel Prentiss Bishop, *Commentaries on the Law of Marriage and Divorce*, 6th rev. ed. (Boston: Little, Brown, 1881), 109n3.

27. Isaac Ray, *A Treatise on the Medical Jurisprudence of Insanity*, 2nd ed. (Boston: William D. Ticknor and Co., 1844), 234–235.

28. See Linda Gordon, *The Moral Property of Women: The History of Birth Control Politics in America* (Champaign: University of Illinois Press, 2004), chap. 4.

29. Because the rules for those seeking an annulment were incorporated into state statutes concerning divorce, a claim of incapacity was often formally

brought as a ground for divorce, though these statutes clearly indicated that insanity subsequent to marriage was not a cause of divorce and some provided that a decree of nullity would not operate to bastardize children born of the union. See, e.g., Middleborough v. Rochester, 12 Mass. 363 (1815); Concord v. Rumney, 45 N.H. 423 (1860); Clement v. Mattison, 3 Rich. 92 (1846); Reading v. Ludlow, 43 Vt. 628 (Vt. 1871); Bell v. Bennett, 73 Ga. 784 (1884); Nonnemacher v. Nonnemacher, 159 Pa. 634 (1894). On the importance of a judicial decree of nullity, as "equally conducive to good order and decorum and to the peace and conscience of the party," see James Kent, *Commentaries on American Law* (New York: O. Halsted, 1827), vol. 2, 76, quoting his own ruling in Wightman v. Wightman, 4 Johns. Ch. 343, 345 (N.Y. Ch. 1820); see also Waymire v. Jetmore, 22 Ohio St. 271 (1872). Though there was technically no union to put asunder on this understanding, some courts held that a lunatic's contract could be ratified, i.e., "made good by subsequent conduct," without the need for a new ceremony. See, e.g., Cole v. Cole, 37 Tenn. (5 Sneed) 57 (Tenn. 1857); Castor v. Davis, 120 Ind. 231 (1889); Lewis v. Lewis, 44 Minn. 124 (1890); Prine v. Prine, 36 Fla. 676 (1895). Others refused to entertain a capacity challenge after the death of one or both of the parties, effectively fixing their status as husband and wife ever after regarding them as if they had been lawfully wed. See, e.g., Goshen v. Richmond, 4 Allen 458 (1862); Wiser v. Lockwood, 42 Vt. 720 (1870).

30. Ray, *Medical Jurisprudence of Insanity*, 1844, 2nd ed., 235–236.

31. Basch, *Framing American Divorce*, 3. This understanding of the foundational importance of the marriage contract continued to shape judicial thinking well into the twentieth century. For one such expression, see Wiley v. Wiley, 75 Ind. App. 456 123 N.E. 252 (1919): "When we reflect upon the nature of marriage and contemplate its importance in the development of the race, we realize the necessity of cherishing so precious an institution and of maintaining its essential characteristics. It is the foundation of the home and the origin of those family ties without which we would cease to be human. It is the source of those motives which prompt us to provide care and comfort for childhood and old age, and to plan and toil and sacrifice for the welfare of future generations . . . . By declaring the ceremonial marriage of an insane person void, the law frustrates the unscrupulous by blasting the hope of pecuniary gain" (256).

32. Cases that set the capacity for marriage at the same level as that for other civil contracts include Anonymous, 21 Mass. (4 Pick.) 32 (1826); Ex parte Glen, 4 S.C. Eq. 546, 549 (1816); Kern v. Kern, 51 N.J. 574 (1893); Inhabitants of St. George v. Biddleford, 76 Me. 593 (1885); Atkinson v. Medford, 46 Me. 510 (1859); Lewis v. Lewis, 44 Minn. 124 (1890).

33. Elzey v. Elzey, 1 Houst. 308 (Del. 1857); Gillett v. Gillett, 78 Mich. 184 (1889); Joel Prentiss Bishop, *New Commentaries on Marriage, Divorce, and Separation* (Chicago: T. H. Flood, 1891), vol. 1, 257–259.

34. For especially notable cases combining claims of incapacity with fraud and undue influence to invalidate wills as well as marriages, see Orchardson v. Cofield, 171 Ill. 14 (1897); Christy v. Clarke, 45 Barb. 529 (N.Y. 1866). Courts visibly struggled to determine who among the litigants were proceeding in earnest; they sometimes betrayed suspicions that there was perjured testimony on both sides of a given case. See, e.g., *Clement*, 37 S.C.L., 96.

35. Bishop, *Marriage, Divorce, and Separation*, vol. 1, 252–280, 537–538, 625–626, 656, 732–733, 742; "Insanity as a Ground of Divorce," *American Journal of Insanity* 39 (1882): 213–227.

36. See, e.g., Pyott v. Pyott, 90 Ill. App. 210 (1899); Buchanan v. Buchanan, 103 Ga. 90 (1897).

37. Johnson v. Kincade, 37 N.C. 470, 471, 473, 474, 477 (1843).

38. Crump v. Morgan, 38 N.C. 91, 92, 93–94, 95 (1843). For a case of virtual abduction involving an extremely imbecilic woman taken across state lines to be married without the knowledge or consent of her family, see True v. Ranney, 1 Fost. 52 (N.H. 1850). Judges took an especially dim view of gold-digging women who preyed on imbecilic men. See, e.g., Foster v. Means, 17 S.C. Eq. 569 (1844); Goodhart v. Speer, 7 Ohio C.D. 47 (1893); Hides v. Hides, 65 How. Pr. 17. (N.Y. 1883); Thayer v. Thayer, 9 R.I. 377 (1869); but see, e.g., Baughman v. Baughman, 32 Kan. 538, 4 P. 1003, 1005–1006 (1884), ordering a new trial due to erroneous rulings barring the putative wife's own testimony as to her alleged husband's mental state and excluding affectionate letters he wrote to her; such evidence was deemed competent not only as to his capacity to marry but also concerning the existence of fraud or imposition on her part.

39. *Crump*, 38 N.C., 100; Bates v. Meade, 174 Ky. 545, 192 S. W. 666, 669, 670 (1917); see also Park v. Barron, 20 Ga. 702 (1856); Brown v. Westbrook, 27 Ga. 102 (1859). On the changes in bastardy law, see Michael Grossberg, "Crossing Boundaries: Nineteenth-Century Domestic Relations Law and the Merger of Family and Legal History," *American Bar Foundation Research Journal* 10 (1985): 799–847, 835–847; Grossberg, *Governing the Hearth*, chap. 6.

40. *Brown*, 27 Ga., 103, 105.

41. Ibid., 107, 108. With a flair for the dramatic and an inclination to reach for biblical parallels, Lumpkin elaborated what he felt bound to do in this case as a self-appointed representative of "the genius and gallantry of the men of Georgia": "I care not what forum the lunatic, by his guardian, appeals; nor what form of proceeding he adopts; a jury in Georgia will never be found who will pronounce a woman, whose conduct is unimpeached, a fornicatress, and her babe a bastard. And yet this result is inevitable under a sentence of nullity" (108).

42. Ibid., 111, 112. Similar doctrinal difficulties were presented where the sane spouse was the one who initiated the suit, as in Powell v. Powell, 18 Kan. 371 (1877).

43. Smith v. Smith, 47 Miss. 211, 211 (1872).

44. Rawdon v. Rawdon, 28 Ala. 565, 566, 568 (1856). Forman v. Forman, 24 N.Y.S. 917, 917–918 (1893), concluded that a sane spouse who fails to bring a suit for nullity "within a reasonable time" after discovering the insanity and "continues to cohabitat with the alleged lunatic, and has two children by him" could be taken to prove one of two things: "(1) That the party was not insane at the time; (2) or that the other party has elected to treat the contract as a valid and subsisting one." The more the facts of the case seemed to reveal incompatibility rather than incapacity, the less inclined a court was to grant a divorce petition. See, e.g., Slais v. Slais, 9 Mo. App. 96 (1880); Secor v. Secor, 1 MacArth. 630 (D.C. Sup. 1874); compare Keyes v. Keyes, 2 Fost. 553 (1851); Champline v.

Stone, 77 Mo. App. 523 (1898). For a fascinating discussion of the broader cultural implications of the *Rawdon* case, see Loren Schweninger, *Families in Crisis in the Old South: Divorce, Slavery, and the Law* (Chapel Hill: University of North Carolina Press, 2012), ch. 3, though it relies on local court records and other sources in finding Lydia was successful in obtaining a divorce without attending to the subsequent ruling of the Alabama Supreme Court, which affirmed the decree of the chancellor, who had found the marriage valid on grounds that it had been contracted in a lucid interval. See *Rawdon*, 28 Ala., 566.

45. Tiffany v. Tiffany, 84 Iowa 122, 50 N.W. 554, 554, 555 (1891). For other cases articulating similarly high expectations of husbands, see, e.g., Pile v. Pile, 15 Ky. L. Rpter 88 (1893); Franklin v. Franklin, 53 Kan. 143 (1895).

46. The desertion and cruelty cases that were most likely to yield divorces were those involving almost preposterously "good wives." See, e.g., Avery v. Avery, 33 Kan. 1 (1885); Barber v. Barber, 74 Iowa 301 (1888); Douglass v. Douglass, 31 Iowa 421 (1871). The cases that caused the most difficulty involved plaintiffs who were alleged to be insanely jealous and unduly suspicious that their spouse was cheating, prone to inflict wounds on themselves that they attributed to their spouse, or otherwise imagined forms of wrongdoing that never took place. Judicial decisions in such cases were especially tortured and quite lengthy productions; see, e.g., Duvale v. Duvale, 34 A. 888 (N.J. Eq. 1896).

47. See Broadstreet v. Broadstreet, 7 Mass 474 (1811).

48. Matchin v. Matchin, 6 Pa. St. (Barr.) 332, 336–337 (Pa. Sup. Ct. 1847).

49. Nichols v. Nichols, 31 Vt. 328, 329, 330, 331–332 (1858); see also Wray v. Wray, 19 Ala. 522 (1851).

50. Ordronaux, *Commentaries*, 336–342. The hardening of hereditarian ideas toward the turn of the twentieth century raised the stakes of these suits. The clearest evidence of this intensification of concern was at the legislative level, as reformers campaigned for new measures empowering the state to police the processes of social and biological reproduction. Yet even then, only *incurable* insanity was recognized as a cause of divorce, and the sane spouse had to provide support and care in the form of alimony. In a number of states, legislation along these lines was passed and then quickly repealed, apparently because one or two lawsuits proved it to be a bad idea. With these quite limited exceptions, the fault paradigm remained in place, which meant that insanity was not recognized as a cause for divorce. At the turn of the twentieth century, Clevenger reported that Arkansas, Kentucky, and Washington had such statutes on the books. S. V. Clevenger, *Medical Jurisprudence of Insanity or Forensic Psychiatry* (Rochester, NY: Lawyer's Co-operative Publishing, 1898), 391–392. For cases decided under these provisions, see, e.g., Newcomb's Ex'rs v. Newcomb, 76 Ky. (13 Bush) 544 (1877); Hickman v. Hickman, 1 Wash. 257 (1890).

51. C. A. Hereshoff Bartlett, "The Problem of Marriage and Divorce," *Law Magazine and Review: A Quarterly Review of Jurisprudence* 36 (1910), 6–7.

52. Harding v. Wheaton, 2 Mason 378, 11. F. Cas. 491, 493, 495 (1821).

53. Harding v. Handy, 24 U.S. 103, 123, 125 (1826); *Harding*, 11 F. Cas., 493, 495-496.

54. See, e.g., Haydock's Ex'rs v. Haydock, 33 N.J. Eq. 494 (1881); Guild v. Warne, 149 Ill. 105 (1893).

55. *Harding*, 11 F. Cas., 495; *Harding*, 24 U.S., 124.
56. *Harding*, 24 U.S., 123; *Harding*, 11 F. Cas., 493.
57. Nineteenth-century American courts commonly spoke of the family as "the sort of relation that excludes the inference that the parties were dealing on the footing of contract." Charles Fisk Beach, Jr., *A Treatise on the Modern Law of Contracts* (Indianapolis, Bowen-Merrill Co., 1896), vol. 1, 49–50n1. See also James v. Gillen, 3 Ind. App. 472, 30 N.E. 7 (1892): "It is the policy of the law to inculcate harmony, confidence, and affection in the domestic relation, and this can better be accomplished by permitting the sense of filial regard in a large measure to regulate the hearthstone economy, than by reducing it to a mercenary basis by applying the rules relating to master and servant. The doctrine applies with peculiar force to parent and child, and those occupying that relation by arrangement or adoption, and continues as long as the relation exists, regardless of the age of the parties" (9).
58. Hendrik Hartog, *Someday All This Will Be Yours: A History of Inheritance and Old Age* (Cambridge, MA: Harvard University Press, 2012), 209. See also Lawrence M. Friedman, *Contract Law in America* (Madison: University of Wisconsin Press, 1965), 28–30.
59. Friedman, *Contract Law in America*, 29–30, suggests greater clarity about the boundary between the family and the market in nineteenth-century America than I have found.
60. See, e.g, Robinson v. Allbee, 4 Ohio C.D. 185 (1894); Wiley v. Ewalt, 66 Ill. 26 (1872); Glocke v. Glocke, 113 Wis. 303 (1902).
61. *Whelan*, 3 Cow., 537; This was likely no coincidence, since scholars have suggested that the Declaration of Independence was modeled after bills in equity. See Basch, *Framing American Divorce*, 28.
62. Walton v. Northington, 5 Sneed (TN) 282, 283 (1857); Nace v. Boyer, 30 Pa. 99, 100 (1858); Whitehorn v. Hines, 15 Va. (1 Munf.) 557, 558 (1810).
63. Gass v. Mason, 4 Sneed 497, 500 (Tenn. 1857); see also Whitehorn v. Hines, 1 Munf. 537 (Va. 1810); *Whelan,* 3 Cow., 537; Craddock v. Cabiness, 31 Tenn. 474 (1852); Tracey v. Sacket, 1 Ohio St. 54 (1852); Walton v. Northington, 5 Sneed 282 (Tenn. 1857); *Nace*, 30 Pa., 99; Highberger v. Stiffler, 21 Md. 338 (1864); Jacox v. Jacox, 40 Mich. 473 (1879); Willemin v. Dunn, 93 Ill. 511 (1879); McDaniel v. McCoy, 68 Mich. 332 (1888); Britton v. Britton, 23 Pa. C.C. 89 (Pa. Com. Pl. 1899); Farnsworth v. Noffsinger, 46 W. Va. 410 (1899).
64. *Nace*, 30 Pa., 111–112, 113; Alcorn v. Alcorn, 76 Miss. 907, 25 So. 877, 878 (1899); Pennington v. Stanton, 125 Mo. 658, 28 S.W. 1067, 1069 (1894); Maxham v. Stewart, 133 Wis. 525, 113 N.W. 972, 972 (1907).
65. Historians have argued that the nineteenth century was marked by "an intensification of anxiety about the aging process and hostility toward the aged." Jesse F. Ballenger, *Self, Senility, and Alzheimer's Disease in Modern America* (Baltimore: Johns Hopkins University Press, 2006), 14; see also W. Andrew Achenbaum, *Old Age in the New Land* (Baltimore: Johns Hopkins University Press, 1978); Carole Haber, *Beyond Sixty-Five: The Dilemma of Old Age in America's Past* (Cambridge: Cambridge University Press, 1983); Thomas Cole, *The Journey of Life: A Cultural History of Aging in America* (New York: Cambridge University Press, 1993); Carole

Haber and Brian Gratton, *Old Age and the Search for Security: An American Social History* (Bloomington: Indiana University Press, 1994); David Hackett Fischer, *Growing Old in America* (New York: Oxford University Press, 1977).

66. *Whelan*, 3 Cow., 552.

67. Ibid., 554, 572, 577, 587. For similar rulings in the latter half of the century, see, e.g., *Jacox*, 40 Mich., 473 (1879); Brand v. Brand, 39 How. Pr. 193 (1870).

68. *Nace*, 30 Pa., 103, 106, 111, 113.

69. Quantitative studies of residence patterns suggest that elderly women were far less likely than their male counterparts to remain heads of household after the loss of a spouse; Haber and Gratton, *Search for Security*, 29; Steven Ruggles, "Living Arrangements of the Elderly in America: 1880–1980," in *Aging and Generational Relations over the Life Course: A Historical and Cross-Cultural Perspective*, ed. Tamara K. Hareven (Berlin: de Gruyter, 1996), 254–271.

70. Such assumptions were also commonly voiced by witnesses. See, e.g., Millican v. Millican, 24 Tex. 426, (1859), in which one woman was represented as describing another "as being capable of managing any business; but this is qualified, to mean the ordinary business of her sex, for she declares, that women are not as capable of men to transact such business, as that of administering an estate" (432).

71. But see Saufley v. Jackson, 16 Tex. 579 (1856), in which the court observed that the petition contained "'much foul allegation'" that was extraneous, but emphasized this was not meant as a criticism of the lawyer who drafted the document, "because we are well aware how very difficult it is for counsel at all times to restrain and control a party in the construction of the petition, and particularly a female client. To them it often appears important to allege matter immaterial, and that, too, in their own strong language" (579).

72. Revels v. Revels, 64 S.C. 256, 42 S.E. 111 (1902).

73. Ibid., 115, 116 (quoting Shakespeare's *King Lear*).

74. Ibid., 113, 114, 115, 117, 118, 119; see also Storms v. Peer, 52 A. 705 (N.J. Eq. 1902); Soper v. Cisco, 85 N.J. Eq. 165 (1915).

75. For an intriguing indicator of such behavior, see Steven Ruggles, "Intergenerational Coresidence and Family Transitions in the United States, 1850–1880," *Journal of Marriage and Family* 73, (2011): 138–148, noting that "The 1880 [census] instructions caution enumerators that respondents 'are disposed to conceal, or even deny, the existence of such infirmities'" (142).

76. Burt v. Quisenberry, 132 Ill, 385, 399 (1890); *Saufley*, 16 Tex., 581; see also *Millican*, 24 Tex., 426; Mott v. Mott, 49 N.J. Eq. 192 (1891); Oliphant v. Liveridge, 142 Ill. 160 (1892); Yeakel v. McAtlee, 156 Pa. 600 (1893); Clark v. Clark, 174 Pa. 309 (1896); Slayback v. Witt, 151 Ind. 376 (1898). See generally John Norton Pomeroy, *A Treatise in Equity Jurisprudence* (San Francisco: Bancroft-Whitney, 1905), vol. 2, 962; Melville Madison Bigelow, *A Treatise on the Law of Fraud on Its Civil Side* (Boston: Little, Brown, 1888), 357.

77. *Otis*, 91 Ala., 289; Malone v. Kelley, 54 Ala. 532, 539 (1875); Waddell v. Lanier, 62 Ala. 347, 351–352 (1878); see also Soberanes v. Soberanes, 97 Cal. 140 (1893); Highberger v. Stiffler, 21 Md. 338 (1864); Mott v. Mott, 49 N.J. Eq. 192 (1891).

Chapter 7: The Responsible Originator

1. Williams v. Hays, 157 N.Y. 541, 541–546; (1899); William B. Hornblower, "Insanity and the Law of Negligence," *Columbia Law Review*, 5 (April 1905): 278, 285–286.

2. Hornblower, "Insanity and the Law of Negligence," 286 (quoting from the jury charge); Williams v. Hays, 143 N.Y. 442, 446 (1894). At least one other appellate case exists concerning the wreck of the *Sheldon*: Hutchins v. Ford, 82 Me. 364 (1890). This case involved another set of co-owners whose policy covered the barratry—willful wrongdoing injuring owners—of the mariners but not the master. The court considered the stranding of the vessel, which was a peril insured against, to be compensable even if caused by the negligence of the master or crew, which the judges took to encompass insanity and intoxication where it rendered the master incapable of intentionally designing to strand the vessel.

3. As a matter of contract law, it appears clear that the owners of the ship (including Hays) would have been answerable for a breach of contract even if it had been caused by the insanity of the master, for the owners were liable for the nonperformance of their agents regardless of any supervening mental disabilities; see Higginson v. Weld, 80 Mass. 165 (1859). This idea was later rationalized on the basis of a distinction between "objective and subjective impossibility"; a promisor could be released from liability only where performance was objectively impossible, in the sense of being something impossible for anyone to do, not just the promisor personally. See Oklahoma Gas and Elec. Co. v. Pinkerton's Inc., 742 P. 2d 546, 548 (1986).

4. Thomas M. Cooley, *Treatise on the Law of Torts: Or the Wrongs Which Arise Independent of Contract* (Chicago: Callaghan and Co., 1879), 99–100; Francis Wharton, *A Treatise on the Law of Negligence* (Philadelphia: Kay and Brother, 1874), 92; Joel Prentiss Bishop, *Commentaries on Non-Contract Law* (Chicago, IL: T. H. Flood & Co., 1889), 223. General treatises on civil actions offered conflicting perspectives on the liability of the insane for their civil wrongs. Compare Francis Hilliard, *The Elements of Law; Being a Comprehensive Summary of American Civil Jurisprudence* (Boston: Hilliard, Gray, and Co., 1835), 234; and Rowland Jay Browne, *A Practical Treatise on Actions at Law* (London, 1843; repr., Philadelphia: John S. Littell, 1844), 87, holding the insane responsible for their non-intentional civil wrongs, with Theodore Sedgwick, *A Treatise on the Measure of Damages*, 2nd ed. (New York: John S. Voorhies, 1852), 455–456, arguing against the liability of a lunatic who is not "competent to foresee and guard against the consequences of his conduct" and treating the torts of the insane as "inevitable accidents." Treatises specifically devoted to torts or negligence continued to manifest this split, though both sides admitted insanity as a defense in cases involving intentional torts. Compare Francis Hilliard, *The Law of Torts or Private Wrongs* (Boston: Little, Brown and Co., 1859), vol. 1, 244; and Thomas G. Shearman and Amasa A. Redfield, *A Treatise on the Law of Negligence* (New York: Baker, Voorhis, 1869) 55–56, 63, maintaining that insanity was material only where intent was an element with "Bishop, Non-Contract Law, 223–225, 227–228, conceiving of insanity as "an act of God" that may "excuse an injurious doing" and Wharton, *Negligence*, 92–93, 829–832, maintaining that "a person destitute of reason" cannot be held liable for negligence or an intentional tort but excluding moral insanity from the class of mental illnesses "conferring irresponsibility."

5. The insurer paid the policyholders $916.98 in compensation. Hays argued that his success in the first suit barred this negligence action, but the court disagreed. Williams v. Hays, 17 N.Y. Civ. Proc. R. 97, 53 Hun. 630, 23 N.Y. St. Rep. 489, 5 N.Y.S. 666 (1889); 64 Hun. 202, 46 N.Y. St. Rep. 100, 19 N.Y.S. 61 (1892), rev'd on other grounds, 143 N.Y. (98 Sickels) 442, 38 N.E. 449 (1894).

6. The court held that because Hays was a part-owner and the master in command at the time of the loss, he could not claim a loss arising from barratry. Hays v. Phenix Ins. Co., 57 N.Y. Super. Ct. 199, 25 N.Y. St. Rep. 123, 6 N.Y.S. 3 (1889). Insanity was generally recognized as a defense to barratry, and it was sometimes the insurer who defended on these grounds. See Lawton v. Sun Mut. Ins. Co., 58 Mass. 500 (1848) (Shaw, C. J.) (owner's policy covered barratry so insurer defended by claiming the master was insane, but the court instead found he was intoxicated and willful when he committed the offending acts so the company was obliged to pay); Copeland v. New England Marine Ins. Co., 43 Mass. (2 Metcalf) 432 (1841) (Shaw, C.J.) (owner's policy did not cover barratry, so the insurer claimed that the master committed a willful wrong or, if found insane or otherwise incapacitated, that the ship was unseaworthy, but a majority of the court this defense rejected).

7. *Hays*, 6 N.Y.S., 3; aff'd, 127 N.Y. (82 Sickels) 656, 28 N.E. 254 (1891).

8. Hornblower, "Insanity and the Law of Negligence," 286–287. *Williams*, 143 N.Y. (98 Sickels), 454.

9. *Williams*, 143 N.Y., 451–452. In the event of such a finding, Earl emphasized that Hays might be found liable for the negligence of his first mate and crew. Indeed, he thought it "difficult to perceive how they could have failed to see that he was either incompetent to manage the vessel, or that he was willfully wrecking her" and flagged it as a question "worthy of careful consideration on retrial" (452).

10. Hornblower, "Insanity and the Law of Negligence," 291; Williams v. Hays, 2 A.D. 183, 73 N.Y. St. Rep. 382, 37 N.Y.S. 708 (1896), rev'd, 157 N.Y., 541, 548 52 N.E. 589, 591–592 (1899). Judge Haight suggested the fate of any argument based on the negligence of the first mate: "Possibly he might have put the captain in irons, and taken the command of the vessel, but mutiny at sea is criminal, and heavily punished. In order to justify such action, he must be satisfied of the derangement of his superior officer, and be able to command the assistance of the crew" (*Willliams,* 157 N.Y., 548–549. A dissenting judge found that the evidence conclusively established Hays's liability for the loss, either owing to his own negligence or that of his first mate (549).

11. Hornblower, "Insanity and the Law of Negligence," 293.

12. Ibid., 278, 288, 296.

13. Ibid., 278, 293–294, 297.

14. Jonathan Levy, *Freaks of Fortune: The Emerging World of Capitalism and Risk in America* (Cambridge, MA: Harvard University Press, 2012), 2; see also Toby L. Ditz, "Shipwrecked; or, Masculinity Imperiled: Mercantile Representations of Failure and Self in Eighteenth-Century Philadelphia," *Journal of American History* 81 (1994): 51–80. For other works sounding similar themes and linking them to the law of torts, see Sandra Macpherson, *Harms Way: Tragic Responsibility and the Novel Form* (Baltimore: Johns Hopkins University Press, 2010); Nan Goodman, *Shifting the Blame: Literature, Law, and the Theory of Accidents in Nineteenth-Century America* (Princeton: Princeton University Press, 1998).

15. Phenix Insurance Company of Brooklyn, N.Y. (graphic)(New York: F. B. Patterson, n.d.) [For advertisement, see the digital collection of Boston Athenaeum, reference URL is: http://catalog.bostonathenaeum.org/vwebv/holdingsInfo?bibId=420169.

16. On the pathogenic power of ideas, see Stephen Kern, *A Cultural History of Causality: Science, Murder, Novels, and Systems of Thought* (Princeton, NJ: Princeton University Press, 2004), 245–247.

17. Wai Chee Dimock, *Residues of Justice: Literature, Law, Philosophy* (Berkeley and Los Angeles, CA: University of California Press, 1996), 168 (quoting William Dean Howell's *The Minister's Charge* (1886)); see also Goodman, *Shifting the Blame*, chap. 4.

18. Morton J. Horwitz, *The Transformation of American Law, 1870–1960: The Crisis of Legal Orthodoxy* (New York: Oxford University Press, 1992), 16, 63, 68, 110, 131, 141, 181, 188–190; Thomas L. Haskell, *The Emergence of Professional Social Science: The American Social Science Association and the Nineteenth-Century Crisis of Authority* (Baltimore: Johns Hopkins University Press, 1977), 6, 41; John Fabian Witt, *The Accidental Republic: Crippled Workmen, Destitute Widows, and the Remaking of American Law* (Cambridge, MA: Harvard University Press, 2004), 2, 16–17, 144; Tom Baker and Jonathan Simon, eds., *Embracing Risk: The Changing Culture of Insurance and Responsibility* (Chicago: University of Chicago Press, 2002); Barbara Young Welke, *Recasting American Liberty: Gender, Race, Law, and the Railroad Revolution, 1865–1920* (Cambridge: Cambridge University Press, 2001); Michael Willrich, *City of Courts: Socializing Justice in Progressive Era Chicago* (Cambridge: Cambridge University Press, 2003); On the multiple meanings of "formalism" in late nineteenth-century American legal thought, see Thomas Grey, "Langdell's Orthodoxy," 46 *University of Pittsburgh Law Review* 45 (1983): 1–53; Grey, "Holmes and Legal Pragmatism," *Stanford Law Review* 41 (1989): 787–870.

19. Hilliard, *Law of Torts*, vo1. 1, iii–x.

20. Oliver Wendell Holmes, Jr., *The Common Law* (Boston: Little, Brown, and Co., 1881). For general discussions of these developments, see Witt, *The Accidental Republic*, 1–21, 43–70; G. Edward White, *Tort Law in America: An Intellectual History* (New York: Oxford University Press, 2003), 8–12; Patrick Kelley, "Infancy, Insanity, and Infirmity in the Law of Torts," *American Journal of Jurisprudence* 48 (2003): 179–252, 181–183. The notion that tort law in this era was shifting from a strict liability to a negligence standard been perpetuated by legal scholars and historians, particularly Morton J. Horwitz, who contends that this narrowing of the basis of liability operated to subsidize capitalist enterprises. Morton J. Horwitz, *The Transformation of American Law*, 1780-1860 (Cambridge, MA: Harvard University Press, 1977), 97–108; see also Charles O. Gregory, "Trespass to Negligence to Absolute Liability," *Virginia Law Review* 37 (1951): 359–397, 368, 382; but see Gary T. Schwartz, "Tort Law and the Economy in Nineteenth Century America: A Reinterpretation," *Yale Law Journal* 90 (1981); 1717–1775, 1727–1734; Peter Karsten, *Heart versus Head: Judge-Made Law in Nineteenth-Century America* (Chapel Hill: University of North Carolina Press, 1997), 8–15, 79–127.

21. Weaver v. Ward (1616) Hobart 134, 80 Eng. Rep. 284 (K. B.) (1616); Cross v. Andrews (1598) 78 Eng. Rep. 863, 40 Cro. Eliz. 622 (Q.B.) (1598); Stephen G. Gilles, "Inevitable Accident in Classical English Tort Law," *Emory Law Journal* 43 (1994): 575–646.

22. Brown v. Kendall, 60 Mass. (2 Cush.) 292, 296–298 (1850) (Shaw, C. J.); Shaw v. Boston & Worcester Railroad Corporation, 74 Mass. (8 Gray) 45, 66–68 (1857) (Shaw, C. J.); Harvey v. Dunlop, Hill & Den 193, 194–195 (N.Y. 1843) (citing and reinterpreting *Weaver* to require proof of "a neglect or want of due care"); Witt, *Accidental Republic*, 44–45; cf. Horwitz, *Transformation of American Law*, 1760-1860, 90–91. Francis Hilliard's treatise on tort law, summarized the doctrine thus: "Negligence is said to consist in the omitting to do something that a reasonable man would do, or the doing something that a reasonable man would not do; in either case, causing, unintentionally, mischief to a third party. A party who takes reasonable care, to guard against the accidents arising from ordinary causes, is not liable for accidents arising from extraordinary ones." Hilliard, *Law of Torts*, vol. 1, 124.

23. See, e.g., Vincent v. Stinehour, 7 Vt. 62, (1835), in which the court observed in dicta that one "deprived of all control over his will by idiocy, or permanent madness" was as exempt from civil liability as other wholly involuntary actors and that the liability of lunatics rested merely on "authority," not principle (65).

24. Brown v. Collins, 53 N.H. 442, 442, 450, 451 (1873).

25. "Hornblower, "Insanity and the Law of Negligence," 279.

26. Morse v. Crawford, 17 Vt. 499, 502 (1845); see also Behrens v. McKenzie, 23 Iowa 333 (1867) (following *Morse* in an action for damages on injunction bond where the defense of insanity was raised).

27. Cross v. Kent, 32 Md. 581 (1870); see also Ward v. Conatser, 63 Tenn. 64 (1874) (following *Cross* in action for damages resulting from shooting where the defense of insanity was raised); compare Morain v. Devlin, 132 Mass. 87 (1882) (imposing liability on an insane person because of his status as the owner of the property whose defective condition occasioned the injury, though both his person and property were under guardianship at the time).

28. McIntyre v. Sholty, 121 Ill. 660, 664–665 (1889); see also Feld v. Borodofski, 87 Miss. 727, 727 (1906) (following *McIntyre*, *Hays*, and *Morse* in holding lunacy to be no defense against civil liability for assault and battery because "the injury is the thing, regardless of intent, or malice, which is involved in intent"); Sheppard v. Wood, in 1 Lanc. Law Rev. 175 (1884) (jury charge acknowledging that there was "no case in the law reports of this State" on point and proceeding to invoke principles of fairness in denying insanity as a defense: "is it not equitable that the lunatic shall give up something of his estate to alleviate the misery that he has caused? I am sure every fair-minded man would answer in the affirmative").

29. Jewell v. Colby, 66 N.H. 399 24 A. 902 (1891).

30. See, e.g., Oliver Wendell Holmes's 1897 essay, "Privilege, Malice, and Intent," *Harvard Law Review* 8 (1894): 1–14, which Morton Horwitz reads as evidence of Holmes's loss of faith in the existence of "external standards" of liability grounded in custom, a marked change in the jurist's thought that Horwitz relates to the intensifying strife between labor and capital in the 1890s. Horwitz, *Transformation of American Law*, 1870-1960, chap. 4.

31. Compare Dickinson v. Barber, 9 Mass. 225 (1825), reserving judgment as to whether insanity constituted an excuse but admitting evidence of derangement to mitigate damages, with Bryant v. Jackson, 6 Humph. 199 (Tenn. 1845), admitting insanity as an excuse; and with Horner v. Marshall, 5 Munf. (Va.) 466

(1817), allowing *partial* insanity as an excuse where sufficiently connected to the slanderous words); and finally with Yeates v. Reed, 4 Blackf. 463 (Ind. 1838) (recognizing that partial insanity may be shown by way of excuse or to mitigate damages, depending on the circumstances).

32. See, e.g, Edwin A. Jaggard, *Hand-book on the Law of Torts*, (St. Paul, MN: West Publishing Co., 1895), 393, 448, 467, 518, which regards negligence as "a common battleground" between competing theories of liability for civil wrongs and observes "that the theory of personal culpability as the basis of liability in tort is gaining ground" (53–54).

33. Irvine v. Gibson, 11 Ky. 306, 316, 317, 318, 319, 321 (1904).

34. Isaac Ray, *A Treatise on the Medical Jurisprudence of Insanity* (Boston: Charles C. Little and James Brown, 1838), 238; Sedgwick, *Damages*, 455–456.

35. Lake Shore & M.S.R. Co. v. Pinchin, 112 Ind. 592, 13 N.E. 677, 679 (1887); Neal v. Gillett, 23 Conn. 437, 443 (1855). In announcing this individuated test, courts implicitly or explicitly deviated from the external standard famously announced in the English case of Vaughan v. Menlove (1837) 1312 E.R. 490, 3 Bing. N.C. (Eng.) 468, 475–476: "Instead, therefore, of saying that the liability for negligence should be coextensive with the judgment of each individual, which would be as variable as the length of the foot of each individual, we ought rather to adhere to the rule which requires in all cases a regard to caution such as a man of ordinary prudence would observe." A few state courts applied *Vaughan* or otherwise recognized the authority of the English rule: see, e.g., Tucker v. Henniker, 41 N.H. 317, 322 (1860); Hyde v. Town of Jamaica, 27 Vt. 443, 466 (1855). But the dissenting opinion in *Hyde*, penned by Judge Isaac Redfield, expressed the majority view in other jurisdictions: "Negligence, or prudence, is strictly a relative term, dependent upon the peculiar exigencies of one's position" (469–470).

36. See, e.g., Mich. Cent. R. Co. v. Hasseneyer, 48 Mich. 205, 209 (1882); O'Flaherty v. Union Ry. Co., 45 Mo. 70 (1869). This courtroom practice has been documented and analyzed by historians. Focusing on injured women, Welke, *Recasting American Liberty*, 81–124, finds a "pervasive, nagging sense" among judges, reflected in their instructions and opinions, "that women, by nature and experience, were more timid than men and less capable of understanding danger and exercising good judgment to avoid it or extricate themselves from it, and that men had an obligation to protect women that they did not owe to other men" (91). James D. Schmidt's *Industrial Violence and the Legal Origins of Child Labor* (New York: Cambridge University Press, 2010), 144–155, documents a growing tendency on the part of courts in the last decades of the nineteenth century to treat children as "'a class of persons of less discretion and judgment than adults'" in tort suits (154). On the shift from an economic to a more sentimental valuation of children in this period see Viviana A. Zelizer, *Pricing the Priceless Child: The Changing Social Value of Children* (New York: Basic Books, 1981).

37. Some courts made sweeping statements that begged the question of why these exceptional classes of persons ought to be treated any differently in the case of primary as opposed to contributory negligence. This remained true to the end of the century. See, e.g., Indianapolis &c. R. Co. v. Pitzer, 109 Ind. 190 (1886); Gulf C. & S.F. Ry. Co. v. McWhirter, 77 Tex. 366 (1890). For an

argument that infants and insane persons ought not to be subjected to a more stringent standard when charged with negligence as defendants, see Francis H. Bohlen, "Liability in Tort of Infants and Insane Persons," *Michigan Law Review* 23 (1924–1925): 9–37.

38. *Michigan Cent. R. Co.* 48 Mich., 211. See generally Thomas M. Cooley, *A Treatise on the Law of Torts, Or, the Wrongs Which Arise Independent of Contract,* 2nd ed. (Chicago: Callaghan & Co., 1888), 970. On the role of gender in shaping the decision in *Hasseneyer* and law of accidental injury more broadly, see Welke, *Recasting American Liberty,* and Barbara Young Welke, "Unreasonable Women: Gender and the Law of Accidental Injury, 1870–1920," *Law and Social Inquiry* 19 (1994): 369–403.

39. See, e.g., Village of Culbertson v. Holliday, 50 Neb. 229 (1897).

40. See, e.g., Robinson v. Cone, 22 Vt. 213 (1850). This remained the majority rule to the end of the century. See, e.g., Washington & G.R. R. Co. v. Gladmon, 82 U.S. 401 (1872); Sioux City & P.R. Co. v. Stout, 84 U.S. 657 (1873); Union Pac. Ry. Co. v. McDonald, 152 U.S. 262 (1894).

41. Compare *Gladmon,* 82 U.S., 401 (age), with *Robinson,* 33 Vt., 213 (capacity).

42. Hartfield v. Roper, 21 Wend. 615, 619–620 (N.Y. 1839). For other jurisdictions following *Hartfield,* see, e.g., Wright v. Malden M.R. Co., 86 Mass. (4 Allen) 283 (1862); Holly v. Boston Gas Light Co., 74 Mass. (8 Gray) 123 (1857); Leslie v. Lewiston, 62 Me. 468 (1873); Jefferson R.R. Co. v. Bowen, 40 Ind. 545 (1872).

43. *Robinson,* 33 Vt., 213; Boland v. Missouri R. Co., 36 Mo. 484, 490 (1865). Cooley, *Law of Torts,* 2nd ed. (1888), 818–823, lists cases in other jurisdictions likewise rejecting the doctrine of imputation.

44. Willetts v. Buffalo & R.R. Co., 14 Barb. 585, 587, 589, 592, 593 (N.Y. 1853).

45. Worthington v. Mencer, 96 Ala. 310, 315 (1892). This result is consistent with the story labor historians generally tell about the liability-limiting function of the contributory negligence doctrine in the context of personal injury litigation for workplace accident. See generally Witt, *Accidental Republic,* 50.

46. Baltimore & Potomac R. v. Cumberland, 176 U.S. 232, 238–239 (1900); see also Seattle Elec. Co. v. Hovden, 190 F. 7, 8–9 (9th cir. 1911).

47. Lorraine Daston, "British Responses to Psycho-Physiology, 1860–1900," *Isis* 69 (1979); 192–208; Martin J. Wiener, *Reconstructing the Criminal: Culture, Law and Policy in England,* 1830–1914 (Cambridge: Cambridge University Press, 1994); Constance M. McGovern, *Masters of Madness: Social Origins of the American Psychiatric Profession* (Hanover, NH: University Press of New England, 1985); Benjamin Reiss, *Theaters of Madness: Insane Asylums and Nineteenth-Century American Culture* (Chicago: University of Chicago Press, 2008); Charles E. Rosenberg, *The Trial of the Assassin Guiteau: Psychiatry and the Law in the Gilded Age* (Chicago: University of Chicago Press, 1968); Roger Smith, *Trial by Medicine: Insanity and Responsibility in Victorian Trials* (Edinburgh: Edinburgh University Press, 1981); Gerald N. Grob, *Mental Institutions in America: Social Policy to 1875* (New York: Free Press, 1973).

48. For an especially poignant case, see Abbott v. Abbott, 67 Me. 304 (1877). See generally Peter McCandless, "Liberty and Lunacy: The Victorians and Wrongful Confinement," in *Madhouses, Mad-Doctors and Madmen,* ed. Andrew Scull (London: Athlone Press, 1981), 339–362; McCandless, "Dangerous to

Themselves and to Others: The Victorian Debate over the Prevention of Wrongful Confinement," *Journal of British Studies* 23 (1983): 84–104.

49. Nancy Tomes, *A Generous Confidence: Thomas Story Kirkbride and the Art of Asylum-Keeping, 1840–1883* (New York: Cambridge University Press, 1984); Ellen Dwyer, *Homes for the Mad: Life inside Two Nineteenth-Century Asylums* (New Brunswick, NJ: Rutgers University Press, 1994); Lawrence B. Goodheart, *Mad Yankees: The Hartford Retreat for the Insane and Nineteenth-Century Psychiatry* (Amherst, MA: University of Massachusetts Press, 2003); Ian Dowbiggin, *Keeping America Sane: Psychiatry and Eugenics in the United States and Canada* (Ithaca, NY: Cornell University Press, 1997).

50. J. H. Balfour Browne, *The Medical Jurisprudence of Insanity*, (London: J & A Churchill / San Francisco: Sumner Whitney & Co., 1871), 23, 62, 184; Browne, *The Medical Jurisprudence of Insanity*, 2nd ed. (San Francisco: Summer Whitney & Co., 1875), 112, 123.

51. Shearman and Redfield, *Law of Negligence*, (1869), 63; Sedgwick, *Damages*, 455–456. Shearman and Redfield's treatise was among the authorities Earl cited in *Hays* even though it contained no case law on point; Earl's decision was cited by the jurists in a subsequent edition, noting the judge had quoted "with approval our old section 57, in which we argued this point." Shearman and Redfield, *A Treatise on the Law of Negligence*, 5th ed. (New York: Baker, Voorhis & Co., 1898), 192–193.

52. Timothy Brown, "The Liability of Persons of Unsound Mind and Infants for Torts in Civil Actions," *Southern Law Review*, n.s., 1 (1875): 346–353, 353; see also Edward P. Weeks, *The Doctrine of* Damnum Absque Injuria: *Considered in Its Relation to the Law of Torts* (San Francisco: Sumner Whitney, 1879), 29–31.

53. See Horwitz, *Transformation of American Law, 1870–1960,* 51, 54–59; compare Siegel, "Francis Wharton's Orthodoxy: God, Historical Jurisprudence, and Classical Legal Thought," *American Journal of Legal History* 46 (2004): 422–446; Siegel, "Joel Bishop's Orthodoxy," *Law and History Review* 13 (1995): 215–259; William M. Wiecek, *The Lost World of Classical Legal Thought: Law and Ideology in America, 1886–1937* (New York: Oxford University Press, 1998), 184–185; Grossman, "James Coolidge Carter and Mugwump Jurisprudence," *Law and History Review* 20, (2002): 577–629; Lewis A. Grossman, "Extending the Revisionist Project," *Law and History Review* 20, (2002): 639–641.

54. Wharton, *Law of Negligence*, 92, 824, 825; Wharton, *The Liability of Railway Companies for Remote Fires: Proximate and Remote Cause*, 2nd ed. (St. Louis: G.I. Jones and Co., 1878), 11, 17.

55. Wharton, *Law of Negligence*, 828, 829, 830n.2, 831, 842; Wharton, *Liability of Railway Companies*, 2, 3.

56. Wharton, *Law of Negligence*, 283–284.

57. Cooley, *Law of Torts* (1879), 98, 99, 100.

58. Ibid., 100–101

59. Thomas M. Cooley, *The Elements of Torts* (Chicago: Callaghan and Co., 1895). 27, 28; Cooley, *Law of Torts* (1879), 103.

60. Holmes, *Common Law*, 37, 49–50, 107. He developed this line of reasoning further in "Privilege, Malice, and Intent."

61. Holmes, *Common Law*, 50, 108.

62. Ibid., 109. This aspect of Holmes's formulationof the standard of negligence, as well as that of other judges and jurists, is explored in greater detail in Welke, "Unreasonable Women," which calls attention to what was and was not said about the standard of negligence as applied to women. For a critical account of the reasonable person standard that attends to Holmes's discussion of mental disability but focuses on contemporary legal doctrine, with the normative aim of clarifying what attributes ought to be taken as part of the standard's composition, see Mayo Moran, *Rethinking the Reasonable Person: An Egalitarian Reconstruction of the Objective Standard* (Oxford: Oxford University Press, 2003).

63. Holmes, *Common Law*, 109, 163.

64. Ibid., 50, 51, 96, 108, 109.

65. The leaders of the profession who formulated the negligence section of the American Law Institute's *Restatement* in 1934 still hedged on this question. The text originally included the following specific exemption: "Unless the actor is a child or insane person, the standard of conduct to which he must conform to avoid being negligent is that of a reasonable man under like circumstances." But in a "Caveat," this statement was partially retracted: "The Institute expresses no opinion as to whether insane persons are required to conform to the standard of behavior which society demands of sane persons for the protection of the interests of others." *Restatement of the Law of Torts: Negligence* (St. Paul, MN: American Law Institute, 1934), 283.

66. The interface between tort law and the insurance industry is illustrated well in two separate cases filed after an insane man burned down the house and barn he shared with his sister. He recovered on his fire insurance policy, but the insurer then successfully sued him after paying on a policy held by his sister. See Showalter v. Mutual Fire Ins. Co. of Chester County, 40 W.N.C. (1896); Showalter v. Mutual Fire Ins. Co. of Chester County, 17 Pa. C.C. 558 (1896).

67. Scheffer v. Railroad Company, 105 U.S. 249, 252 (1881); Welke, *Recasting American Liberty*, 186-88, 204-206.

68. Daniels v. New York, N.H. & H.R. Co., 183 Mass. 393, 398–399 (1903).

Conclusion

1. Benjamin Rush to John Montgomery, April 9, 1788, in Benjamin Rush, *Letters of Benjamin Rush*, ed. L. H. Butterfield (Princeton, NJ: Princeton University Press, 1951), vol. 1, 456; Benjamin Rush to John Adams, August 8, 1812, *Letters*, vol. 2, 1159; Benjamin Rush to Jeremy Belknap, May 6, 1788, *Letters*, vol. 1, 460–461. For an analysis of Rush's multiple uses of this phrase, see David Freeman Hawke, *Benjamin Rush, Revolutionary Gadfly* (Indianapolis: Bobbs-Merill, 1971), 247–262.

2. Benjamin Rush to John Adams, Nov. 4, 1812, in Rush, *Letters*, vol. 2, 1164.

3. Thomas Szasz, *The Manufacture of Madness: A Comparative Study of the Inquisition and the Mental Health Movement* (Syracuse: Syracuse University Press, 1997), 136–159; David Brion Davis, *The Problem of Slavery in the Age of Revolution, 1770–1823* (Ithaca, NY: Cornell University Press, 1975), 274.

4. Orlando Patterson, *Slavery and Social Death: A Comparative Study* (Cambridge, MA: Harvard University Press, 1982); Sander Gilman, *Difference and Pathology: Stereotypes of Sexuality, Race, and Madness* (Ithaca, NY: Cornell

University Press, 1985), 146; Andrew Scull, *The Most Solitary of Afflictions: Madness and Society in Britain, 1700–1900* (New Haven, CT: Yale University Press, 1993), 50.

5. [Benjamin Rush,] "On the Different Species of Mania," *Columbian Magazine* (December 1786): 182–187.

6. Ibid., 187.

7. Karen Halttunen, *Murder Most Foul: The Killer and the American Gothic Imagination* (Cambridge, MA: Harvard University Press, 1998), 6, 227–240; John Conolly, *An Inquiry Concerning the Indications of Insanity* (London: J. Taylor, 1830), vol. 1, 8, 59, 171; Joseph Chitty, *A Practical Treatise on Medical Jurisprudence*, 2nd Am. ed. (Philadelphia: Carey, Lea, and Blanchard, 1836), 353.

8. Here, I borrow a phrase from Uday S. Mehta, "Liberal Strategies of Exclusion," *Politics & Society* 18 (1990): 431.

9. This held true both before and after the Civil War. See Elizabeth B. Clark, "'The Sacred Rights of the Weak': Pain, Sympathy, and the Culture of Individual Rights in Antebellum America," *Journal of American History* 82 (1995): 463–493; Amy Dru Stanley, *From Bondage to Contract: Wage Labor, Marriage, and the Market in the Age of Slave Emancipation* (Cambridge: Cambridge University Press, 1998); Douglas C. Baynton, "Disability and the Justification of Inequality in American History," in *The New Disability History: American Perspectives*, ed. Paul K. Longmore and Lauri Umansky (New York: New York University Press, 2001), 33–57.

10. Ian Hacking, "Making Up People," in *Reconstructing Individualism: Autonomy, Individuality, and the Self in Western Thought*, ed. Thomas C. Heller, Morton Sosna, and David E. Wellbery (Stanford, CA: Stanford University Press, 1986), 222–236.

11. Baynton, "Disability and the Justification of Inequality," 35–36.

12. Charles E. Rosenberg, "The Tyranny of Diagnosis: Specific Entities and Individual Experience," *Milbank Quarterly* 80 (2002): 250; Ian Hacking, "Kinds of People: Moving Targets," *Proceedings of the British Academy* 151 (2007): 285–318. On the interfaces between folk psychology, medical knowledge, and legal doctrines, see Joel Eigen, *Witnessing Insanity: Madness and Mad-Doctors in the English Court* (New Haven, CT: Yale University Press, 1995).

13. J. F. Miller, "The Effects of Emancipation upon the Mental And Physical Health of the Negro of the South," *North Carolina Medical Journal* 38 (Nov. 20, 1896), 290. O. B. Frothingham, "The Real Case of 'Remonstrants' against Woman Suffrage," *The Arena* 2 (July 1890), 177; Cynthia Eagle Russett, *Sexual Science, The Victorian Construction of Womanhood* (Cambridge, MA: Harvard University Press, 1989); Gail Bederman, *Manliness & Civilization: A Cultural History of Gender and Race in the United States, 1880–1917* (Chicago: Chicago University Press, 1995).

14. Robert J. Richards, *Darwin and the Emergence of Evolutionary Theories of Mind and Behavior* (Chicago: Chicago University Press, 1987).

15. David Brion Davis, *The Problem of Slavery in the Age of Emancipation* (New York: Alfred A. Knopf, 2014), 40; Amos Dean, *Principles of Medical Jurisprudence Designed for the Professions of Law and Medicine* (Albany, NY: Gould, Banks and Gould, 1850), 486; Richard Rabinowitz, *The Spiritual Self in Everyday Life: The Transformation of Personal Religious Experience in Nineteenth-Century New England* (Boston: Northeastern University Press, 1989); Jon Butler, *Awash in a Sea*

of Faith: Christianizing the American People (Cambridge, MA: Harvard University Press, 1991); Jackson Lears, *Something for Nothing: Luck in America* (New York: Penguin Books, 2003), 82.

16. Robert B. Warden, *A Familiar Forensic View of Man and Law* (Columbus, OH: Follett, Foster, and Co., 1859), 205; Oliver Wendell Holmes, Jr., *The Common Law* (Boston: Little, Brown, and Co., 1881), 5; Morton J. Horwitz, *The Transformation of American Law, 1870–1960* (New York: Oxford University Press, 1992), 140; Oliver Wendell Holmes to Morris Cohen, July 21, 1920, "The Holmes-Cohen Correspondence," in *Portrait of a Philosopher: Morris R. Cohen in Life and Letters*, ed. Leonora Cohen Rosenfield (New York: Harcourt, Brace & World, 1962), 325.

17. Martin J. Wiener, *Reconstructing the Criminal* (New York: Cambridge University Press, 1990) 42–43. Originally published in London, 1874, Maudsley's work appeared in an American edition as well. See Henry Maudsley, *Responsibility in Mental Disease* (New York: D. Appleton & Co., 1898). Maudsley was a physician who served as an asylum superintendent, working in relatively small settings with a middle-class patient population, before being appointed coeditor of the *Journal* of *Mental Science* and professor of medical jurisprudence at University College London. For overviews of his life and work, see Andrew Scull, Charlotte MacKenzie, and Nicholas Hervey, *Masters of Bedlam*, (Princeton, NJ: Princeton University Press, 1996), chap. 8; Trevor Turner, "Henry Maudsley: Psychiatrist, Philosopher, and Entrepreneur," in *The Anatomy of Madness: Essays in the History of Psychiatry*, ed. William F. Bynum, Roy Porter, Michael Shepherd (London, Tavistock Publications, 1988), vol. 3, chap. 6. Maudsley's views on women have also been examined, largely as a result of his debate with Elizabeth Garrett Anderson over his notorious 1884 essay, "Sex in Mind and Education." The classic work is Elaine Showalter, *The Female Malady: Women, Madness, and English Culture, 1830–1980* (London: Virago, New York: Pantheon, 1986), chap. 4, "On the Borderland: Henry Maudsley and Psychiatric Darwinism," 101–120. See also Susan Hogan, "The Tyranny of the Maternal Body: Madness and Maternity," *Women's History Magazine* (Women's History Association) 54 (2006): 21–30.

18. Maudsley, *Responsibility*, 3–5 (quoting Esquirol).

19. Ibid., 3–4, 13–15.

20. Ibid., 5–6, 14, 21–22, 35–36.

21. Ibid., 25, 30.

22. Thomas L. Haskell, *The Emergence of Professional Social Science: The American Social Science Association and the Nineteenth-Century Crisis of Authority* (Baltimore: Johns Hopkins University Press, 1977), 1–23; Haskell, "Persons as Uncaused Causes: John Stuart Mill, The Spirit of Capitalism, and the 'Invention' of Formalism," in *The Culture of the Market: Historical Essays*, ed. Thomas L. Haskell and Richard F. Teichgraeber III (Cambridge: Cambridge University Press, 1993), 441–502, 502.

23. Charles E. Rosenberg, *The Trial of the Assassin Guiteau: Psychiatry and Law in the Gilded Age* (Chicago: University of Chicago Press, 1968), 67.

24. Haskell, "Persons as Uncaused Causes," 502.

25. For a philosophical exploration of this problem, see Thomas Nagel's *View from Nowhere* (New York: Oxford University Press, 1986), which describes the essence of the inquiry in striking terms: "We are in a sense trying to climb outside

of our own minds, an effort that some would regard as insane and that I regard as philosophically fundamental" (11).

26. William James to Oliver Wendell Holmes, January 3, 1868, in *The Letters of William James*, ed. Henry James (Boston: Atlantic Monthly Press, 1920), vol. 1, 124–27; John Weiss, ed., *The Origins of Modern Consciousness* (Detroit: Wayne State University Press, 1965); Haskell, *Professional Social Science*. On the genesis of the Metaphysical Club, see Louis Menand, *The Metaphysical Club: A Story of Ideas in America* (New York: Farrar, Straus, & Giroux, 2001); Bruce Kuklick, *The Rise of an American Philosophy: Cambridge, Massachusetts, 1860–1930* (New Haven: Yale University Press, 1979); G. Edward White, *Justice Oliver Wendell Holmes: Law and the Inner Self* (New York: Oxford University Press, 1993); Philip Wiener, *Evolution and the Founders of Pragmatism* (Cambridge, MA: Harvard University Press, 1949); Mark DeWolfe Howe, *Justice Oliver Wendell Holmes: The Proving Years*, vol. 2 (Cambridge, MA: Belknap Press, 1963); Paul Jerome Croce, *Science and Religion in the Era of William James: The Eclipse of Certainty, 1820–1880* (Chapel Hill: University of North Carolina Press, 1995).

27. *The Positive Philosophy of Auguste Comte*, ed. and trans. Harriet Martineau (New York: Calvin Blanchard, 1856); Menand, *Metaphysical Club*, chap. 9.

28. George Miller Beard, *American Nervousness, Its Causes and Consequences: A Supplement to Nervous Exhaustion (Neurasthenia)* (New York, 1881); William James, "Book Review," *Science*, 17 (1891): 234–235. Perry Miller, "Introduction," *American Thought: Civil War to World War I* (New York: Holt, Rinehart, & Winston (1965); Jan Goldstein, "Bringing the Psyche into Scientific Focus," in *The Cambridge History of Science*, ed. Theodore M. Porter and Dorothy Ross (New York: Cambridge University Press, 2003), vol. 7, 131–153; Haskell, *Professional Social Science*; Dorothy Ross, *Origins of Social Science* (Cambridge: Cambridge University Press, 1991); James Kloppenberg, *Uncertain Victory: Social Democracy and Progressivism in European and American Thought, 1870–1920* (New York: Oxford University Press, 1986); Barbara Sicherman, "The Quest for Mental Health in America, 1880–1917: (PhD diss., Columbia University, 1967); Charles E. Rosenberg, *No Other Gods: On Science and American Social Thought* (Baltimore: Johns Hopkins University Press, 1997), 98–108. On the social and psychic strains that characterized fin de siècle America, see John Higham, "The Reorientation of American Culture in the 1890s," *Origins of Modern Consciousness*, 25–48; Barbara Young Welke, *Recasting American Liberty: Gender, Race, Law, and the Railroad Revolution, 1865–1920* (Cambridge: Cambridge University Press, 2001); T. J. Jackson Lears, *No Place of Grace: Antimodernism and the Transformation of American Culture, 1880–1920* (Chicago: University of Chicago Press, 1981); Lears, *Rebirth of a Nation: The Making of Modern America, 1877–1920* (New York: HarperCollins, 2009).

29. Beard, "Who of Us Are Insane?" *Putnam's Magazine* 12 (1868): 513–527; Beard, "The Problems of Insanity" (1880) speech delivered before the New York Medico-Legal Society, March 3, 1880. George M. Beard, "A Reply to Criticisms on 'The Problems of Insanity'" (1880) Speech Delivered before the New York Medico-Legal Society, April 16, 1880 (location, if known). George M. Beard, "Recent Works on the Brain and Nerves," *North American Review* 131 (1882): 277–284; J. J. Elwell et al., "The Moral Responsibility of the Insane," *North American Review* 134 (1882): 1–39. Henry Maudsley, *The Physiology and Pathology of*

the Mind (New York: D. Appleton and Co., 1872), 26; Wiener, *Reconstructing the Criminal*, 170 (quoting Henry Sidgwick).

30. Beard, "The Problems of Insanity"; Beard, *American Nervousness*; S. Weir Mitchell, *Wear and Tear* (New York: Arno Press, 1897); Lorraine Daston, "British Responses to Psycho-Physiology, 1860–1900," *Isis* 69 (1979): 192–208; Wiener, *Reconstructing the Criminal*, chap. 4; Nathan G. Hale, *Freud and the Americans* (New York: Oxford University Press, 1971), 24–97; Tighe, "A Question of Responsibility," chap. 5. In this regard, Beard anticipated the work of Oxford forensic psychologist Edward W. Mitchell, whose *Self-Made Madness* (Aldershot: Ashgate, 2003), criticizes leading thinkers associated with the anti-psychiatry movement (including Szasz) and advances "the controversial notion that mental disorders (and possibly other 'illnesses') may be to varying extents the fault of the 'sufferer'," rendering him criminally responsible to the extent that he is culpable for his condition. His view recalls Wharton's arguments for diminished responsibility.

31. Menand, *Metaphysical Club*, 218–219. On the emergence of new academic divisions and professional norms in this period, see Bruce A. Kimball, *The "True Professional Ideal" in America* (Cambridge, MA: Blackwell, 1992); Kimball, *The Inception of Modern Professional Education* (Chapel Hill: University of North Carolina Press, 2009); Francesca Bordogna, *William James at the Boundaries: Philosophy, Science, and the Geography of Knowledge* (Chicago: University of Chicago Press, 2008); Joseph F. Kett, *Merit: The History of a Founding Ideal from the American Revolution to the Twentieth-First Century* (Ithaca: Cornell University Press, 2012); Haskell, *Professional Social Science*; Ross, *Origins of Social Science*; Christopher Tomlins, "Framing the Field of Law's Disciplinary Encounters," *Law & Society Review* 34 (2000): 911–972.

32. Menand, *Metaphysical Club*, 151, 216. See also Robert D. Richardson, *William James: In the Maelstrom of American Modernism* (New York: Houghton Mifflin, 2006) 218–219. On the emergence of new academic divisions and professional norms in this period, see Croce, *Science and Religion*; White, *Holmes*; Wiener, *Evolution*.

33. Peter Gibian, "Opening and Closing the Conversation: Style and Stance from Holmes Senior to Holmes Junior," in *The Legacy of Oliver Wendell Holmes, Jr.*, ed. Robert W. Gordon, *The Legacy of Oliver Wendell Holmes, Jr.* (Stanford: Stanford University Press, 1992), 187, 200; Menand, *Metaphysical Club*, 339–347; Croce, *Science and Religion*;

34. Croce, *Science and Religion*, 148 (quoting James); Oliver W. Holmes, "The Path of the Law," *Harvard Law Review* 10 (1897): 457–478; Menand, *Metaphysical Club*, 217, 226-232; Richardson, *William James*, 423.

35. Francis Wharton and Moreton Stillé, *A Treatise on Medical Jurisprudence* (Philadelphia: Kay and Brother, 1855), 2, 35-36n, 71; Mohr, *Doctors and the Law*, chap. 17.

36. [Oliver Wendell Holmes,] "Book Notices," *American Law Review* 1 (1867): 377; [Nicholas St. John Green,] "Book Notices," *American Law Review* 5 (1871): 704–709.

37. Mohr, *Doctors and the Law*, ch.15; Allen McLane Hamilton, "Introspective Insanity," *American Journal of Medical Sciences* 89 (1885): 130–137; Philip C. Knapp, "The Insanity of Doubt," *American Journal of Psychology* 3 (1890): 1–23; S. Weir Mitchell, "Address Before the Fiftieth Annual Meeting of the

American Medico-Psychological Association," *Proceedings of the American Medico-Psychological Association* (1894), vol. 1, 101–121; Thomas A. Green, *Freedom and Responsibility in American Legal Thought* (New York: Cambridge University Press, 2014), 21–124; Janet A. Tighe, "What's in a Name?: A Brief Foray into the History of Insanity in England and the United States," *Journal of the American Academy of Psychiatry and the Law* (2005): 255; William A. White, *The Principles of Mental Hygiene* (New York: Macmillan Company, 1917), 127.

38. Roscoe Pound, "The Role of the Will in Law," *Harvard Law Review* 68 (1954): 7; Jerome Frank, *Law and the Modern Mind* (New York: Brentano's, 1930), 19.

39. Davis, *Problem of Slavery in the Age of Emancipation*, 40. For an exemplary anthropological study along these lines, see Carol J. Greenhouse, Barbara Yngvesson, and David Engel's *Law and Community in Three American Towns* (Ithaca, NY: Cornell University Press, 1994).

40. Henry Adams, *The Education of Henry Adams*, ed. Henry Cabot Lodge (Boston, Houghton Mifflin Co., 1918), 434; Herman Melville, *Moby-Dick* (Boston: C. H. Simonds Company, 1892), 391.

Acknowledgments

IT IS DIFFICULT TO KNOW where to begin in thanking all the individuals and institutions that have made this book possible and even harder to put into words the many and varied ways my scholarship and my life have been enriched by their gifts.

I will start with my teachers. Judith Shklar ignited my interest in the history of ideas when I was an undergraduate at Harvard College, and she pointed me in the right direction when I was trying to make up my mind about whether to go to law school or graduate school. At Yale University, which provided an ideal laboratory for interdisciplinary work, David Brion Davis challenged me to take intellectual risks and provided invaluable criticisms as well as encouragement and inspiration along the way. Teaching by example in ways that continue to inform everything I do as a scholar, he enabled me to see and approach history as a moral inquiry, as a means of investigating some of the deepest problems of the human condition. I also owe an immeasurable debt to Robert Gordon, who introduced me to legal history and opened my intellectual horizons in innumerable ways. I am grateful for his penetrating insights, boundless generosity, and unstinting support over the years; they have made all the difference, evidence of which can be found on every page of this book. Jon Butler's mentorship has been equally decisive. I thank him for the wisdom and practical advice he has unfailingly dispensed at critical junctures, from my earliest years as a graduate student in New Haven to lunch last week in Minneapolis.

As this project evolved, many others contributed time, energy, and financial support. At Yale, my understanding of the craft of history was crucially shaped in seminars with Nancy Cott, John Demos, and Alan Trachtenberg, and my first foray into the history of psychiatry was masterfully guided by Mark Micale. Yale Law School proved an enormously stimulating environment within which to think about how to integrate law and history in scholarship and teaching, and for this I am especially indebted to Bruce Ackerman, Paul Kahn, Carol Rose, Reva Siegel, Akhil Amar, Paul Kahn, and John Langbein. My years in New Haven were also immeasurably enriched by fellow law and graduate students, especially April Lieberman, Linda Rottenberg, John Stauffer, and Wendy Weiser. At New York University School of Law I was welcomed into a wonderful community of legal historians, one forged and sustained by William Nelson and funded by the Samuel I. Golieb Fellowship program, under the auspices of which I came to know a group of scholars who remain to this day valued interlocutors. Lauren Benton, Richard Bernstein, Barry Friedman, Daniel Hulsebosch, and Rick Pildes deserve special mention along with Bill for their careful and critical reading of my work, to say nothing of what I have learned from their scholarship. I also had the privilege of serving as a law clerk to Judge Kimba M. Wood, who taught me more about the stakes of litigation and what it means to do justice than she knows.

The circle of generous readers has widened considerably in the years since I entered the academy, to my great benefit. Among many who have commented on, argued with, or listened to various portions and drafts of this manuscript, thanks are particularly due to Brian Bix, John Carson, David Chang, Cornelia Dayton, Tracey Deutsch, Ariela Dubler, Joel Eigen, Phoebe Ellsworth, Mary Lou Fellows, Risa Goluboff, Sarah (Sally) Barringer Gordon, Michael Grossberg, Philip Hamburger, Jill Hasday, Claire Hill, Karen Ho, Martha Jones, Laura Kalman, Heidi Kitrosser, Nicola Lacey, Sophia Lee, Ray Madoff, Deborah Malamud, Sandra Marshall, Serena Mayeri, John Mikhail, Jennifer Mnookin, Kevin Murphy, Tomiko Brown-Nagin, Richard Primus, Charles Rosenberg, Richard Ross, Austin Sarat, Daniel Schwarcz, Rebecca Scott, Sarah Seo, Tobin Siebers, Christopher Tomlins, Martha Umphrey, and John Witt.

Two residential fellowships provided me with invaluable time, space, and intellectual camaraderie at pivotal moments in the research and writing processes. The Radcliffe Institute for Advanced Study at Harvard University was an extraordinarily stimulating environment within which to map out the contours of this book and test the main lines of argument. I thank Drew Gilpin Faust, who was dean of the Radcliffe Institute at the time, and Judith Vichniac, director of the Fellowship Program, as well as my fellow fellows, especially Amy Bach, John Comaroff, Jane Gaines, Jacquelyn Dowd Hall, Cindi Katz, Mae Ngai, Katherine Park, and Lucy

Salyer. No less consequential was the opportunity to spend a year as a fellow at Princeton's Program in Law and Public Policy, helmed by the incomparable Kim Lane Scheppele, during which time I completed an initial draft of the book manuscript, thanks in no small part to the comments, critiques, and encouragement of Peter Brooks, John Darley, Paul Frymer, Bernadette Meyler, Ralf Michaels, Rebecca Rix, and Daniel Rodgers. Hendrik (Dirk) Hartog was part of the story there as well, but this was neither the first nor the last time he was to play a significant role in the development of this project. Along with Thomas A. Green, about whom I could write volumes without fully capturing what he means to me as a colleague and friend, Dirk read multiple versions of this manuscript from start to finish. Both shared their own research at many points in the process and supplied me with all sorts of good ideas and sage advice. Also indispensable in transforming a large and unwieldy manuscript into a book of reasonable proportions were Antony Duff, Bob Gordon, Ariela Gross, and Barbara Young Welke, who all gave generously of their time to read and provide incisive comments on the work in its entirety. And when it came time to prepare the final version of the manuscript, I was grateful to be able to draw upon the editorial acumen and critical insights of Grey Osterud, who also served as an immensely helpful sounding board and source of encouragement. It is no exaggeration to say that this book would never have been finished without her critical engagement with its structure, argument, and prose.

At Harvard University Press, I have had the good fortune of working with Michael Aronson, who has been an enthusiastic supporter of the project every step of the way and also extraordinarily patient. I am greatly indebted to him for his many efforts on my behalf, and to his assistant, Kathleen Drummy, for carefully and expertly seeing the book through to publication. Thanks are owed to Marianna Vertullo for her superb copyediting of the manuscript and to Derek Gottlieb for his assistance in preparing the index. I also benefited greatly from the two anonymous referees for the Press, whose reports helped to shape my revisions.

This project has depended heavily on library resources and archival collections all over the country. I acknowledge with gratitude the research assistance from numerous archivists, librarians, and clerks of court, including the Harvard Law School Library, the Francis A. Countway Library of Medicine at Harvard University, the University of Michigan Law Library, the University of Minnesota Law Library, the Lillian Goldman Library at Yale Law School, the Harvey Cushing and John Hay Whitney Medical Library at Yale University, the Seeley Mudd Library at

Princeton University, and the Library of the New York Bar Association. Special thanks are due to Joan Howland, Suzanne Thorpe, Mike Hannon, Vicente Garces, and David Zopfi-Jordan of the University of Minnesota Law Library for responding with superhuman dispatch to my endless queries and providing essential editorial assistance in preparing this manuscript for publication. Margaret Leary of the University of Michigan Law Library likewise deserves thanks for leaving no stone unturned whenever I pitched a difficult research question her way. For research and editorial assistance, I was also lucky to be able to draw upon the talents of Michael DePrince, Emily Wessels, and Nate Holdren while they were still students at the University of Minnesota. Nate deserves special thanks for offering insights beyond the editorial. At a critical juncture, the enormously talented Jenny Chan provided the inspiration for the book cover.

The opportunity to present this work in a variety of venues has been enormously rewarding, and doing so has improved this book in many ways. I benefited greatly from the feedback provided by participants in workshops, colloquia, and conferences, including those held at Amherst College, Boston University, Boston College, Brooklyn Law School, Cardozo Law School, Columbia, Cornell, Harvard, NYU, Princeton, Stanford, UCLA, USC, Illinois, Michigan, Minnesota, Pennsylvania, Virginia, and Yale, as well as the annual meetings of the American Society for Legal History, the American Historical Association, and the Law and Society Association.

Portions of Chapters 1 and 2 are reprinted with permission from "'The Mind of the Moral Agent': Scottish Common Sense and the Problem of Responsibility in Nineteenth-Century American Law," *Law and History Review* 26, no. 1 (Spring 2008): 99–159; copyright © 2008 by the Board of Trustees of the University of Illinois. Portions of Chapters 3 and 4 are reprinted with permission from "The Deviance of the Will: Policing the Bounds of Testamentary Freedom in Nineteenth-Century America," *Harvard Law Review* 119, no. 4 (February 2006): 959–1034, copyright © 2006 The Harvard Law Review Association. Additional portions of Chapter 4 are reprinted with permission from "A Mania for Accumulation: The Plea of Moral Insanity in Gilded Age Will Contests," in *Making Legal History*, ed. Daniel Hulsebosch and Richard B. Bernstein (New York: New York University Press, 2013), 181–234, copyright © 2013 by New York University. Portions of Chapter 5 are reprinted with permission from "'Death by His Own Hand': Accounting for Suicide in Nineteenth-Century Life Insurance Litigation," in *Subjects of Responsibility: Framing Personhood in Modern Bureaucracies*, ed. Andrew Parker, Martha Umphrey, and Austin Sarat (New York: Fordham University Press, 2011), 98–144, copyright © 2011 Fordham University Press. Portions of Chapters 1–7 and the introduction to Part II are reprinted with permission from "The Default Legal Person," *UCLA Law Review* 54, no. 1: 1135–1265, copyright © 2006 by the Regents of the University of California; all rights reserved. I thank the editors and staff of each of these publications for editorial assistance and the publishers for allowing me to reprint the material here.

This project has received generous support from a number of other individuals and institutions that I am pleased to recognize here: Dean David Wippman and the University of Minnesota Law School; the Andrew W. Mellon Fellowship for Junior Faculty from the American Council of Learned Societies; the William W. Cook Endowment Fund of Michigan Law School; the Pew Charitable Trusts' Program in Religious History; the Andrew W. Mellon Fellowship from the Center for the Study of New England History at the Massachusetts Historical Society; the American Historical Association's Littleton-Griswold Research Fund; the John F. Enders Fund at Yale University; and Yale Law School's Olin Foundation, Legal History, and Coker Teaching Fellowships.

I owe the greatest debt of all to my family. From as early as I can remember, my grandmothers, Hannah Blumenthal and Reba Frankel, were there to cheer me on, and I only wish I could share this book with them. Through thick and thin, I have always been able to count on my brother and sister, Jacob and Debra, and I also thank my sister-in-law, Susanne Goldstein, and my brother-in-law, Stephen White, both for tolerating a lot of stories about my historical characters and for drawing my head out of the past. And I am likewise grateful for the endless amusement supplied by my nieces, Lydia and Hannah, and my favorite nephew, Sam. As for my parents, no words can adequately convey how much I appreciate the love and support they have given me every step of the way. Surely one of the best parts of finishing this book is being able to dedicate it to them.

Index